The Expedition of Hernando de Soto West of the Mississippi, 1541–1543

# The Expedition of Hernando de Soto West of the Mississippi, 1541–1543

PROCEEDINGS OF THE
DE SOTO SYMPOSIA
1988 AND 1990

EDITED BY

Gloria A. Young and Michael P. Hoffman

THE UNIVERSITY OF ARKANSAS PRESS • FAYETTEVILLE 1993

Manufactured in the United States of America

03 02 01 00 99 5 4 3 2 1
First paperback printing 1999

*This book was designed by Ellen Beeler using the Minion typeface.*

The paper used in this publication meets the minimum requirements of the American National Standard for Permanence of Paper for Printed Library Materials Z39.48-1984. ♾

*Library of Congress Cataloging-in-Publication Data*

The Expedition of Hernando de Soto west of the Mississippi, 1541–1543: proceedings of the de Soto symposia, 1988 and 1990/edited by Gloria A. Young and Michael P. Hoffman.
p. cm.
Includes bibliographical references and index.
ISBN 1-55728-270-6 (cloth)
ISBN 1-55728-580-2 (paper)
1. Soto, Hernando de, ca. 1500–1542—Congresses. 2. Arkansas—Discovery and exploration—Spanish—Congresses. 3. Arkansas—History—Congresses. 4. Texas—Discovery and exploration—Spanish—Congresses. 5. Texas—History—To 1846—Congresses. I. Young, Gloria A. II. Hoffman, Michael P.
E125.S7E95 1993
970.01'6'092—dc20 92-28555
CIP

# Contents

# Preface

In 1988, in anticipation of the 450th anniversary of the A.D. 1541 *entrada* (Spanish for entrance) of the explorer Hernando de Soto and his Spanish and Portuguese followers into the lands west of the Mississippi River which make up present-day Arkansas and Texas, The University Museum of the University of Arkansas, Fayetteville, sponsored a symposium to assess the state of knowledge among anthropologists and historians about this historical event. The symposium was organized by the editors of this volume by contacting known scholars and soliciting their suggestions. From the onset of the project, scholars from all across the United States in the fields of archeology, history, ethnohistory, physical anthropology, linguistics, and folklore helped to mold the nature of that symposium, a subsequent symposium, and this book.

The October 1988 symposium, entitled "The De Soto Era in Arkansas," was held as part of the Museum's programming in connection with the exhibit "Crossroads of the Past," a survey of Arkansas's prehistory. Papers at the one-day symposium were given by Jeffery Brain, Richard Weinstein, James Atkinson, Samuel Dickinson, Charles Hudson, Dan Morse, Robert Rankin, Michael Hoffman, Phyllis Morse, George Sabo III, and Jerald T. Milanich. Discussants were Bob Lancaster of the *Arkansas Times* magazine and Marvin Jeter of the Arkansas Archeological Survey. Besides exploring the feasibility of several routes the de Soto expedition might have taken (including the one postulated by the U.S. De Soto Commission in 1939 and one proposed by Charles Hudson in 1985), the papers addressed the experiences of the expedition in Arkansas, the identity of the native people who met the expedition, and the impact of this meeting on the two cultures—European and Indian. During the symposium, proposed routes of the expedition were traced from the southeastern United States to the Mississippi River and the question of where the river might have been crossed by the expedition was addressed. The route was then postulated through the eastern part of Arkansas, perhaps one-half of the entire route of the expedition west of the Mississippi River. The presence or absence of the Quapaw Indians in the Mississippi River valley was questioned. It was an intense day of presentation, discussion, and controversy.

In retrospect, the symposium can be seen as one of the major factors stimulating research throughout the subsequent years in the de Soto era west of the Mississippi. The papers given by Robert Rankin, Michael Hoffman, George Sabo, and J. T. Milanich at that symposium and modifications of the papers by Dan Morse, Charles Hudson, and Phyllis Morse are included in this volume. Other participants published their papers elsewhere.

Sparked by the 1988 symposium, research began to be carried out on the rest of the route of the expedition before the explorers left the area in 1543. In order to make the results of new research known and to probe deeper into some of the mysteries of the era, a second symposium was planned. It developed into a three-day event including a workshop for schoolteachers and an evening lecture for the public. Held in March 1990, the teachers' workshop included presentations by Gloria A. Young, Charles Hudson, W. Fredrick Limp, Michael P. Hoffman, Ann Early, Richard A. Young, and Charles Ewen. The symposium papers were given by Frank Schambach, Nancy Kenmotsu, David Dye, W. Fredrick Limp, David Henige, George Lankford, Samuel D. Dickinson, Wallace Chafe, Timothy Perttula, Barbara Burnett, and Katherine Murray. In addition to these presentations three round table discussions were held, the participants of which included, besides the presenters of papers, the following scholars: James Corbin, Leslie (Skip) Stewart-Abernathy, Paul Hoffman, Tom Greer, Clark Larsen, Helen Tanner, and Marvin T. Smith. This three-day enterprise explored the route of the expedition west into the lands of the Caddoan Indians in southwestern Arkansas and Texas, including a computerized analysis of the various possibilities, and expanded the discussion and controversy on the use of historical written narratives from the expedition in connection with (and versus) archeology to establish proposed routes. There was more discussion of the sixteenth-century Europeans themselves, from the viewpoints of law and folklore, and some reassessing of the possible impact of diseases carried by the expedition on the native populations of the era. Papers given by Frank Schambach, Nancy Kenmotsu, David Dye, David Henige, George Lankford, Wallace Chafe, Timothy Perttula, and Barbara Burnett and Katherine Murray at the second symposium and modifications of the presentations by Gloria A. Young and Ann Early are included in this volume.

For the complete list of participants and their affiliations and the symposia schedules, see Appendix 2. Besides those named above, numerous other scholars have served as consultants, some of whom were present and some of whom were unable to participate in the two events. We gratefully acknowledge their role in helping to plan and shape this project. They include Charles Robert McGimsey III, David Sloan, Jerome Rose, Walter Brown, Hester Davis, and Elliott West of the University of Arkansas, as well as Ann Ramenofsky, Joseph Sanchez, James Bruseth, Hiram Gregory, Dee Ann Story, Kathleen Gilmore, Patricia Galloway, Kathleen Byrd, Henry Dobyns, John House, and Michael Gannon who are historians and archeologists with an interest in and knowledge of the early historical era of the southeastern and south central areas of the United States. Three graduate students at the University of Arkansas provided invaluable aid in planning and carrying out the symposia and in preparing this volume for publication. Thanks are extended to Don Warden and David Saunders (anthropology) and David Riggs (history).

The University Museum also gratefully acknowledges the Arkansas Endowment for the Humanities and the National Endowment for the Humanities for partial financial support of both symposia, the teachers' workshop, and this publication.

# Introduction

Gloria A. Young and Michael P. Hoffman

The crossing of the Mississippi River by the de Soto expedition in 1541 technically began the historic period for the trans-Mississippi South, the first time Europeans wrote down descriptions of the land and the native civilizations of this region. For the Spaniards, the time spent west of the Mississippi was the bitter end of an ambitious attempt to establish a rich colonial empire on mainland North America like those empires that had been planted in Central and South America. For native societies, the arrival of the Spaniards meant the first encounter with a profoundly different culture that brought new customs, technology, animals, plants, and diseases into their midst. It set in motion a chain of events that had brought dramatic changes in the form and distribution of native cultures of present-day Arkansas and Texas by 1673, when the next Europeans, the French, arrived in the area. In the Mississippi Alluvial Plain, for example, the culturally rich, densely populated polities, governed by hierarchical chieftainships, that once existed were gone by the time the French arrived, leaving only lofty flat-topped earthen mounds as evidence of their town sites.

During the time of change between the mid-1500s and late 1600s, no Europeans are known to have been in Arkansas or in northeast Texas to leave written records, although the region probably was influenced by a European presence both to the east, along the Atlantic and Gulf of Mexico coasts, and to the west in the American Southwest. The story of this era, sometimes called by archeologists the "Dark Ages" (1540–1673), is revealed only through the archeological record. The descriptions of native lifeways left by members of the de Soto expedition are essential to understanding the archeological record.

## THE EXPEDITION NARRATIVES

The surviving chronicles of the de Soto expedition give us the only written record of native life in the 1500s, for better or worse. They also provide a valuable account of the configuration, mission, and daily activities of a sixteenth-century Spanish expeditionary force.

## The *Relaçam verdadeira* by the Fidalgo of Elvas

The first published account was written by an unknown Portuguese nobleman, the Fidalgo (Gentleman) of Elvas (a town in Portugal), who accompanied the expedition. It was entitled *Relaçam verdadeira dos trabalhos que o gournador dõ Fernao de Souto e certos fidalgos portugueses passarom eno desubrimeto da Frolida* [Florida], a "true relation" of the trek through the region called by the Spaniards "La Florida," which extended from the Atlantic coast to Texas. The *Relaçam* was published in Evora, Portugal, on February 10, 1557 (Bourne 1904, 1:223). Inference has been drawn from the wording of the narrative that it may have been written by one Alvaro Fernandez (Lewis 1907; Swanton 1939), who lived in Mexico until 1544 (Avellaneda 1990:27–28). If he was the author of the account, he may have compiled it in Mexico, based on his own memories and conversations with other expedition members. T.H. Lewis (1907:130) stated:

> His narrative was written after his return from the expedition, and is evidently not based upon a diary, or even field notes, but seemingly was drawn entirely from memory. His descriptions are somewhat vague, the localities sometimes indefinite, the distances sometimes confused, and there are some palpable errors. The lengthy addresses of the caciques [Indian leaders] belong to romance rather than history; at least, they are open to grave suspicion that they were manufactured for the occasion. Nevertheless, when the narrative is considered as a whole, it is decidedly the best full account that has survived.

Elvas mentioned himself only once in the narrative, in relation to some relatives of his who were killed at Aminoya. Elvas' account was not reprinted in Portuguese until 1844, when it was published by the Royal Academy at Lisbon, and reissued in 1875.

In 1609, however, Richard Hakluyt had translated the *Relaçam* to English, publishing it in *Virginia richly valued by the Description of the Mainland of Florida,* and then reprinted it under the title *The worthye and famous Historie of the Travailles, Discovery, and Conquest of Terra Florida* in 1611. The latter, edited by William Rye (1851), was later published by the Hakluyt Society. Subsequent republications of the 1609 translation were made in 1809–12 and 1884–90, in new editions of the Hakluyt series, and it was also reprinted at Washington by Peter Force in 1846 and at Philadelphia by B. F. French in 1850 (Swanton 1939:4).

The first French translation was by Citri de la Guette and appeared in Paris in 1685 under the title *Histoire de la conqueste de la Floride.* A year later, in 1686, an apparently exact translation from this edition to English was published in London; the anonymous English translator was perhaps ignorant of Haklyut's 1609 and 1611 publications.

The first American translation of the *Relaçam* was by Buckingham Smith and appeared in New York in 1866, published by the Bradford Club (reprinted by Palmetto Books, Gainesville, Florida, in 1968). Edward Gaylord Bourne (1904, reprinted in 1922 and 1973) included the Buckingham Smith translation in his *Narratives of the Career of Hernando de Soto in the Conquest of Florida,* as did T. H. Lewis in *Spanish Explorers in the Southern United States* (Lewis 1907, reprinted by Texas State Historical Association and the University of Texas, 1984). This was followed, in 1933, by a translation by James A.

Robertson (1933). Thus, the Fidalgo of Elvas' narrative has been a readily available chronicle of the expedition for several hundred years.

## The Report by Luýs de Biedma

The discovery of two additional chronicles in the mid-nineteenth century confirmed the accuracy and authenticity of the Elvas narrative. The first account, by Luýs Hernández de Biedma, had been presented to the King of Spain and the Council of the Indes in 1544 and deposited in the Spanish archives soon afterward. It is the only chronicle that survived to the present in its original form. Biedma was the king's factor, or agent, one of three royal officials to accompany the expedition. He apparently kept a daily record and wrote his report from the diary after the expedition had reached Mexico. His perspective was as an observer representing the king's interests and is brief, generally lacking details concerning the events it reports. It does, however, furnish some information not found in other sources, such as the only clue to the direction pursued by the expedition under Moscoso, after de Soto had died, upon leaving the native polity (chieftainship) of Guachoya.

Biedma's narrative was first published in London by Buckingham Smith (1857) in his *Colección de varios Documentos para la Historia de la Florida,* then in Spain in 1865 among the "Documentos Ineditos." It was republished in Spain in 1865 and 1971.

Before any edition in Spanish was published, however, the Biedma narrative was translated into French by Henri Ternaux-Compans and printed in 1841, somewhat abridged and adapted, in his narratives of voyages. An English translation from the French appeared in America in 1850 and England in 1851 as appendices to the Hakluyt 1611 *Relaçam* reissues (Swanton 1939:6). Buckingham Smith translated Biedma's report directly from the Spanish version and published it with the Elvas account in 1866 and Edward Gaylord Bourne included the Smith translation of Biedma in his 1904 publication, also with Elvas.

## The Account by Rodrigo Ranjel

What is apparently a day-to-day account of the expedition was written by de Soto's private secretary, Rodrigo Ranjel. This account survived only in an edited version that was incorporated by Gonzalo Fernández de Oviedo y Valdes, cronista (the Spanish king's chronicler) of the Indies, in his *Historia General y Natural de las Indias.* The first volume of his history incorporated a vast range of information gathered from officials, soldiers, and commoners and appeared in 1535. The second volume, in which the Ranjel narrative appeared as Book 17, Chapters 21–28, was probably written between 1544, when Ranjel returned to the island of Santo Domingo where Oviedo worked, and 1546, when Oviedo left for Spain. The first part of the second volume of the *Historia* was published in Seville in 1557; the rest remained in manuscript until published in complete form in Madrid in 1851 (Bourne 1904, 2:48, Swanton 1939:7). The earliest English translation of Ranjel's journal was by Bourne (1904). In the form in which it has been handed down, Ranjel's narrative is incomplete, ending on November 2, 1543, with the expedition camped at Autiamque.

### Garcilaso de la Vega's *La Florida del Ynca*

What has often been called a "secondhand" narrative is *La Florida del Ynca* written by Garcilaso de la Vega, also called El Inca. Obtaining information about the de Soto expedition from three survivors: Gonzalo Silvestre, Alonso de Carmona, and Juan Coles, he wrote it in Peru probably between 1587 and 1591. *La Florida del Ynca* was first published in Lisbon in 1605 and then in Madrid, edited by Andres Gonzalez Barcia Carballido y Zuniga (under the pseudonym Gabriel Daza de Carderias), in 1723. In 1670, a much abbreviated translation to French by Pierre Richelet was published (reissued in 1709, 1711, 1731, and 1737). Barnard Shipp translated it from the French into English in 1881. The most modern translation is by John Grier Varner and Jeanette Varner (Garcilaso 1951). For a discussion of Garcilaso de la Vega's work, see Henige (this volume) and Sabo (this volume).

Most of the authors in the present volume use translations of the narratives by Buckingham Smith, Robertson, and the Varners.

## EARLY MAPS

Many people have speculated on where the de Soto expedition traveled. Some light on the history of these speculations can be shed by looking at the early maps. A map called the "de Soto" map (illustration 3) made by Alonzo de Santa Cruz, chief cartographer of the *Casa de Contracion* in Seville around 1544, incorporated information from the expedition (Boston 1939). While not showing a route, it indicated some of the provinces encountered by the expedition: Quizquiz, Casqui, and Pacaha. A map made in 1670, but not published until 1785 was probably the first depiction of the route. The de L'Isle map of 1718 is the most famous early map of the de Soto route (Boston 1939). De L'Isle, the great French cartographer, produced state-of-the-art maps, but the source of this information about the de Soto expedition is unknown.

The next map that treated the de Soto route was the Ross map, printed in 1775, but based on a 1765 survey. The survey covered the entire Mississippi River, and at a place identified as Osier Point the map carried the notation "Here Fernand DeSoto first discovered the Mississippi in 1541." His information may have been from the de L'Isle map, since it is known that he had French maps with him. Also, on the Ross map, "Old Guachoya" was a place name at the mouth of the Red River. In 1796, Tardjia's map showed the "Ancient village of the Arkansas" at the mouth of the Arkansas River with the notation "Hernando De Soto discovered the Mississippi here for the first time" (Brain 1988a).

## EARLY RECONSTRUCTIONS OF THE ROUTE OF THE EXPEDITION

In the early nineteenth century, Americans began to speculate about the actual route the expedition might have taken. Thomas Nuttall (1821) analyzed the de Soto expedition narratives and hypothesized a route which crossed the Mississippi somewhere near Memphis and went north into Southeast Missouri, then turned south and ended on the Ouachita River. An 1829 map by McCullough showed a route which was "inside-out" compared to Nuttall's route. The Spanish army was traced, after crossing the Mississippi River in the vicinity of present-day Commerce, Mississippi, to a location of Casqui due west on the Red River, to Pacaha up the Red River, to Caligua down the Red River, west to Autiamque, thence north to the Arkansas River. Monet, in 1848, traced a route first up and then down the Arkansas River, as did Schoolcraft in 1857, Brevort in 1865, and T. H. Lewis in 1907 (Brain 1988a).

## THE 1939 DE SOTO COMMISSION

In the 1930s, approaching the 400th anniversary of the de Soto expedition, Congress authorized a commission to study the narratives, maps, and any other evidence to establish a route on which historical markers could be erected to commemorate the events described in the chronicles. The evidence in historical sources was combined with geographic information and the archeological evidence as it was known at the time, and the Commission mapped out a route, often referred to as the Swanton route in honor of the Commission chairman, John R. Swanton. As early as 1932, Swanton had begun producing a reconstruction of the de Soto expedition route. The route he proposed at a conference in Birmingham, Alabama, that year showed the expedition traveling from a point near either Pontotoc or Tupelo, Mississippi, where it spent the winter of 1540-41 among the Chickasaw, down the Yocona River, across Yazoo Basin to Sunflower Landing (see illustration 5) in southern Coahoma County, Mississippi (Weinstein 1985). Basically, it was this route that was accepted by the 1939 De Soto Commission as the official determination. Several markers were erected along the route.

The Commission relied heavily on a geographic match between present-day terrain and the narrative descriptions of travel. The archeological evidence available in the 1930s indicated where native societies had been found, not archeological sites which were contemporary with the de Soto expedition or those which had been abandoned hundreds of years before the Spanish arrived. The very idea that Indians had lived in North America for thousands of years, since the last ice age, was still new, and chronologies were inexact. Methods for establishing the antiquity of archeological sites were still primitive. Neither radiocarbon dating nor other physical tests useful for establishing the chronological age of prehistoric campfires, mounds, ruined houses, or artifacts were available.

## CONTROVERSY OVER THE ROUTE

The Commission's determination of the route stood unchallenged until 1951, when Phillips, Ford, and Griffin (1951:347–91) applied then current archeological information to "repropose" a Mississippi River crossing at Commerce Landing (see illustration 5) like that on McCullough's 1820 map. On the basis of archeological evidence, they felt that a northerly route was more logical than a crossing at Sunflower Landing (see also Morse 1981; Morse and Morse 1983). Their hypothesized route took the expedition from a winter 1541 camp at Chicasa (the governmental seat of the ancestors of the modern Chickasaw) to a point near New Albany in Union County, Mississippi, where de Soto attacked an Alibamu stockade, then across the Yazoo Basin to either Council Bend or Walnut Bend in Tunica County, Mississippi (Weinstein 1985).

Swanton replied to Phillips, Ford, and Griffin, offering several points he felt could be challenged. Their route, he contended, placed the native provinces too close to one another. He felt that they misidentified the Arkansas River as the "river of Anilco," defending his identification of the "river of Anilco" as the Ouachita River.

Swanton's theory of the place of crossing the Mississippi River became known as the Sunflower Landing theory; Phillips, Ford, and Griffin's route became known as the Commerce Landing theory. A third theory, called the "Memphis Hypothesis," had been the favorite of nineteenth-century historians. It led the expedition north from their winter base among the Chickasaws to around the Fourth Chickasaw Bluff near Memphis, Tennessee, where they crossed the river (Brain, Toth, and Rodriguez-Buckingham 1974:244; Weinstein 1985:3).

By the 1970s, Jeffrey Brain and his associates felt that neither the Sunflower Landing nor Commerce Landing points had exactly the right fit, but they favored the Sunflower Landing vicinity. They proposed a crossing at Friar's Point, a few miles north of Sunflower Landing. In basic agreement with the Commission's route down either the Yocona or Little Tallahatchie rivers and then across the Yazoo Basin, the Friar's Point theory brought the expedition to a crossing near Clarksdale, Mississippi (Brain, Toth, and Rodriguez-Buckingham 1974; Brain 1984). Richard Weinstein (1985), after excavating an archeological site at Sunflower Crossing, agreed with parts of the "southern route" versions proposed by the Commission and by Brain, Toth, and Rodriguez-Buckingham. The route proposed by Phillips, Ford, and Griffin began to be referred to as the "northern" route. Several of the chapters which follow address this controversy over the point at which the Mississippi River was crossed.

## FINDING THE "FIT" BETWEEN ARCHEOLOGY, NARRATIVES, AND MAPS

Between the 1970s and 1990s, archeologists in the southeast and south central United States felt that it was becoming increasingly evident that some of the places the Commission identified as native provinces named in the chronicles did not match the growing understanding of the prehistory of the regions. For this reason, archeologists have been particularly active in restudying the de Soto route through the Southeast. The results of this revisioning have been coming in for the last several years (for a discussion of the restudy and his role in it, see Hudson this volume). Archeologists believe their understanding of what the cultural landscape was like in the 1500s, gained over the last half century, is of crucial importance in hypothesizing the route the de Soto expedition traveled.

## ABOUT THIS BOOK

The chapters which follow constitute a multidisciplinary restudy being carried out during the 450th anniversary year of the route of the de Soto expedition and the effects of the encounter between the expedition and sixteenth-century Native Americans west of the Mississippi. Most of the authors presented their works as papers at either a 1988 or a 1990 symposium, both held on the University of Arkansas, Fayetteville, campus, sponsored by the University Museum, and funded, in part, by the Arkansas Endowment for the Humanities and the National Endowment for the Humanities.

In the first chapter of this volume, Jerald T. Milanich provides an overview of the historical context and goals of the de Soto expedition. He also critically examines the sources of information about the expedition and its route. Milanich's work was presented as an evening lecture at the 1988 symposium. He presents the prevailing view of that time that the de Soto expedition introduced Old World diseases among native populations, a point which is contested in a later chapter (Burnett and Murray), but has remained an unresolved problem during the intervening years between the symposium and the publication of this volume.

Next, Dan F. Morse, in a revised version of his contribution to the 1988 symposium, explains the computer-generated map of Protohistoric sites in Arkansas. The Protohistoric era covers a time span of approximately A.D. 1400–1650 in northeast Arkansas and 1500–1700 in southwest Arkansas. At the beginning of the era, the Mississippi River valley of eastern Arkansas, along with the Arkansas River valley, was inhabited by large native populations in towns which make up what archeologists call the Mississippian culture area. Southwest Arkansas and east Texas were inhabited by the ancestors of the historic Caddo tribes and are referred to as Caddoan (this term also refers to speakers of Caddo languages). Since the location and nature of Protohistoric populations in Arkansas is critical to a determination of the route of the de Soto expedition, the map was developed specifically to help in researching the question of the route. Equally important are the vacant or uninhabited regions, which were noted in the Spanish accounts.

A series of chapters reconstructing the route of the expedition west of the Mississippi River begins with David H. Dye's contribution, hypothesizing a route across the Mississippi River and across the alluvial plain. Dye's work is a meticulous and comprehensive effort to link the narrative accounts with geography and archeological knowledge in this limited area. His reconstruction is in substantial agreement with those of Charles Hudson and the Morses.

In the next chapter, Phyllis A. Morse expands the data used for confirming this route by asserting that the Parkin archeological site in eastern Arkansas is the location of the capital of Casqui, one of the polities (a city-state type chieftainship) visited by the de Soto expedition. As evidence, she includes the archeological prominence of the site and artifacts found there.

Ann M. Early picks up the trail of the expedition as it enters the uplands of the Ouachita Mountains to the west of the Mississippi alluvial plain. Following the route first proposed by Charles Hudson in 1985, she tracks the route up the Arkansas River. She explains a major cultural boundary which archeology indicates existed at one point up the river between the Arkansas River valley and the Ouachita Mountains, pointing out that this boundary coincides with the descriptions in the expedition narratives. Early argues against the 1939 De Soto Commission theory that the expedition wintered in the Ouachita Mountains along the Ouachita River, citing the fact that the archeological record indicates no major cultural changes occurring in post–de Soto Caddoan archeological phases in the Ouachita Mountains.

Intrigued by the assertion of Charles Hudson and his associates that, after the death of de Soto in 1542, the expedition wandered into the Caddoan area of southwestern Arkansas and eastern Texas, Frank E. Schambach tested the archeological accuracy of the theory. First published in 1989 and presented at the 1990 symposium, Schambach's detailed examination of the archeological evidence has not been questioned. According to Schambach, Hudson's route through southwestern Arkansas fits the archeology better than the De Soto Commission route along the Ouachita River and into northern Louisiana.

Next, Nancy A. K. Kenmotsu, of the Texas Historical Commission, in collaboration with James E. Bruseth and James E. Corbin, concentrates on the route the expedition may have traveled in present-day east Texas. In this chapter, the authors attempt to correlate the scanty description in the expedition chronicles with geography, historical descriptions and trails, and archeological evidence. Two major alternative routes in Texas, called the Trammel's Trace route and the Blackland Prairie route, are examined. In this paper, presented at the 1990 symposium, the Blackland Prairie route was felt to have a better "fit" archeologically and historically.

Following the pursuit of theoretical routes of the expedition throughout the trans-Mississippi west from an archeological point of view, Michael P. Hoffman expanded the scope of the discussion, for the 1988 symposium, to include the ethnic identities of the native groups encountered. According to his interpretation, based on the Hudson-Morse route, most of northeastern and east-central Arkansas was inhabited by Tunican speakers at the time of the de Soto entrada. The Quapaw tribe was either not encountered by the expedition or was not yet in the area.

In the next chapter, Charles M. Hudson discusses the course of de Soto scholarship since 1985 when he boldly postulated the expedition route west of the Mississippi and challenged all researchers in the area to improve its "fit." His chapter is a modification of his paper for the 1988 symposium, based on further research and advice by Arkansas and Texas archeologists. The location of the sixteenth-century polity of Tula is moved significantly from the Ouachita Mountains to the Fort Smith area on the Arkansas River in this modification, and Naguatex is moved to the Spirit Lake locality. He differs from Kenmotsu, Bruseth, and Corbin in the reconstruction of the route through East Texas.

The next chapter, by David Henige, is a cautionary tale reminding both the reader and the other researchers represented in this volume how imperfect are the data from which understandings of the past are drawn. Henige disagrees fundamentally with Charles Hudson and his colleagues on many issues and humorously lambastes the usefulness of the de Soto narratives, archeology, and the logic used in interpreting the data. (Appendix I contains a reply to Henige written by Hudson and colleagues.)

Although framed in a less dogmatic way, the next contribution, by George Lankford, demonstrates through textual analysis that the Garcilaso de la Vega narrative contains traditional legends which survived in the minds of the survivors of the expedition. His findings, while adding to the scholarly consensus that the Garcilaso document is not reliable for reconstructing the day-to-day travel of the expedition, nevertheless suggest that in acting as an oral historian, Garcilaso produced a valuable collection of folklore which presents to modern readers the only way in which detailed accounts of the historic events were actually preserved by the sixteenth-century adventurers.

A different sort of critical textual analysis is the approach used by George Sabo in the next chapter to elicit from the written narratives the differing Spanish and Indian perceptions of their encounters. He isolates five Native-American cultural themes which affected Spanish thought, as evidenced in the narratives.

In the next chapter, linguist Robert L. Rankin analyzes Indian place names and personal names mentioned in the narratives—meager clues which may reveal the bases of linguistic and ethnic affiliation of the Native Americans contacted by the expedition. He concludes, significantly, that no Quapaw names or words are recorded in the chronicles, but that Tunican speakers were probably present in both northeastern and east central Arkansas.

Place and personal names identified by Swanton as Caddoan are next discussed by Wallace Chafe, a linguist who specializes in the Caddo language family. Of interest is his conclusion that the name "Tula" is not a Caddoan word, since Caddoan languages do not incorporate an "l" sound. Since archeological and historical data indicate the inhabitants of Tula were Caddoan, he attributes the name to a non-Caddoan interpreter. This emphasizes the effect interpreters may have had on the information available today.

With the next chapter, the volume turns away from questions of the route of the expedition and the identity of the native groups encountered, and offers two chapters which focus on the impact on the native populations in the localities said to be visited by the expedition according to the routes hypothesized. Barbara Burnett and Kathy Murray, basing their findings on epidemiological understandings and bioarcheological data, find no evidence that epidemic disease brought by the de Soto expedition caused the collapse of Native-American polities in the sixteenth century. They look for explanations other than European-introduced disease to account for a sixteenth-century depopulation of Protohistoric northeastern Arkansas, and see no evidence of stress by disease among Caddoan groups.

In the final chapter, Timothy K. Perttula, on the other hand, following the perspective of Anne F. Ramenofsky (1987), explores the probability of European-derived diseases causing an early massive depopulation among Caddoan groups. Careful readers will have to assess the strengths and logic of the two contrasting interpretations.

Throughout the volume, the editors have standardized some terms. We use bison rather than buffalo for the North American bovine *Bison bison,* and maize rather than corn for *Zea maize,* the "Indian corn." Distances are reckoned in miles or kilometers depending on the individual preferences of the authors.

# The Hernando de Soto Expedition and Spain's Effort to Colonize North America

Jerald T. Milanich

To those of us living in the United States Hernando de Soto is perhaps the most famous Spanish conquistador. We have counties, towns, automobiles, caverns, schools, bridges, and even shopping malls named for him. But the average American knows very little about the de Soto expedition and its relevance to our own past. Our view of the history of our country is a very Anglo-centric one that begins with the Pilgrims and Plymouth Rock. Few people realize that more than a century before the Mayflower set sail from England for the United States, Spanish sailors and settlers were attempting to establish a foothold on the coasts of eastern North America.

Not only has the role of Spain in the European colonization of the United States escaped public consciousness, but the long history of the native peoples who resided here prior to the coming of the Europeans has been largely ignored also. This volume seeks to help remedy these shortcomings and bring to the public some understanding of de Soto's incredible journey and the native peoples he encountered.

## PRELUDE TO EXPEDITION

The Spanish empire's attempts to explore and colonize the Southeast were a part of the spread of empire from the nascent settlements on Hispaniola and nearby Caribbean Islands that began in the late fifteenth and early sixteenth centuries. On his initial voyage in 1492, Christopher Columbus had attempted to leave a settlement, named La Navidad, on the north coast of Hispaniola (now Haiti). Returning to La Navidad on his second voyage, he found the settlement had been destroyed. Columbus then sailed further east along the island's north coast and established a second town, La Isabela. More settlements quickly followed as Spanish sailors and explorers sailed throughout the Caribbean and then to the mainlands of Central and South America, claiming lands and their wealth for Spain.

The Spanish empire also looked northward. Perhaps word of lands in that direction first came from Spanish slavers that illegally (without royal sanction) raided native groups living along the Florida coasts. Or perhaps Indians captured or encountered in the Bahamas or the Caribbean knew of northerly lands. If the 1502 Cantino map depicts the Florida peninsula, as some historians and geographers have suggested, it is certain evidence that Spanish sailors had reached the southeastern United States coast by that time, a decade earlier than the first official Spanish expedition (see Cumming, Skelton, and Quinn 1972:56–57).

## EARLY EXPEDITIONS

That first official Spanish exploratory voyage was led by Juan Ponce de León, the ex-governor of the island colony of San Juan (today Puerto Rico) (see T. F. Davis 1935; R. S. Weddle 1985:38–54). The Spanish crown had given Ponce a three-year *asiento,* or charter, to explore and settle Bimini, an island thought to be north of the Lucayos (Bahama Islands). Such charters were common and typically spelled out the responsibilities and rights of the conquistadors vis-à-vis their respective sovereigns as well as stating what benefits each would receive if the search for new lands was successful (e.g., shares of booty from the colony). Future Spanish conquistadors to La Florida, including de Soto, would have similar royal charters.

Ponce set sail on March 3, 1513, (or 1512, the year is disputed) on a northerly heading out of Puerto Rico that took him along the Atlantic side of the Bahama Islands. He rounded Great Abaco Island and then turned more northwesterly, a course that brought him to the east coast of Florida. His arrival coincided with the Feast of Flowers (Easter Holy Week), leading him to name the new land La Florida, literally "The Flowers."

Ponce then turned southward, sailing down the Atlantic coast of peninsular Florida past Cape Canaveral and what is now Miami before rounding the Florida Keys and traveling up the Gulf coast to Charlotte Harbor, which was named for him. The Bahia de Juan Ponce appears on sixteenth-century maps (Harrisse 1892), as well as in the Chaves *derrotero,* a navigation rutter compiled in the 1530s by the royal mapmaker at the behest of the Spanish crown (Castañeda, Cuesta, and Hernández 1983:366).

Antonio de Herrera's history of Juan Ponce's expedition records the first documented Spanish encounter with the La Florida natives (T. F. Davis 1935). Ponce and his men met native peoples along Florida's Atlantic coast as they sailed southward. On the lower Gulf coast they entered the territory of the Calusa Indians, a nonagricultural people who lived in the Charlotte Harbor-Fort Myers coastal region (Goggin and Sturtevant 1964; Marquardt 1987, 1988; Widmer 1988). On his return to San Juan, Ponce encountered the Chequescha (Tequesta) who lived in the vicinity of modern Biscayne Bay and Miami.

In 1521, Juan Ponce returned to La Florida, probably again to the Calusa in the greater Charlotte Harbor area, to attempt a settlement. The colony failed when the Spaniards were driven off by the native inhabitants of the region (T. F. Davis 1935).

Following Juan Ponce's first voyage, other Spaniards sought to take advantage of his discoveries, leading to additional voyages of exploration along the coasts of La

Florida. Pre-1520 voyages included that of Diego Miruelo, who possibly reached Apalachee Bay (at the northern end of the Florida peninsula on the Gulf side) in 1516; Francisco Hernández de Cordova to the southwest Florida coast in 1517; and Alonzo Alvarez de Pineda who sailed the entire Gulf coast in 1519 and provided the first map of the coastline of the Gulf of Mexico (R. S. Weddle 1985:55–65, 95–108). No information about Florida natives is provided by these exploratory voyages, although the sketch map from Alvarez de Pineda's voyage does show Charlotte Harbor and Tampa Bay. All of these early contacts with the Florida aborigines were unsustained and of a very limited nature, although slaving probably took place, and the spread of European diseases to native peoples may have occurred.

Voyages to explore the Atlantic coast of La Florida also were initiated. In 1521 Pedro de Quexo and Francisco Gordillo, on a slaving expedition, sailed into the Santee River and encountered a native group or town called Chicora. That voyage would give rise to Peter Martyr's written description of a fabled land "abounding in timber, vines, native olive trees, Indians, pearls, and, . . . perhaps gold and silver" that quickly spread through Europe in the first half of the sixteenth century (P. E. Hoffman 1984:419). The Chicora legend would lure Spaniards and Frenchmen to the southeastern Atlantic coast in search of fabled wealth.

The first colonization attempt to the Atlantic coast took place in 1526, led by Lucas Vásquez de Ayllón, who had been the backer of Francisco Gordillo (P. E. Hoffman 1984:423n. 13). Ayllon's royal charter required him to colonize Chicora and establish forts and settlements. But the attempt to establish San Miguel de Gualdape, a colony of six hundred persons on the Georgia coast, was a failure, lasting only three months.

These early Spanish efforts to explore and colonize La Florida were centered on the coasts, locales reached by sea. The first overland expedition was in 1528. Led by Panfilo de Narváez, an army of four hundred men and forty horses landed on the Gulf coast near Tampa (R. S. Weddle 1985:185–207). Narváez was to explore La Florida from the Florida peninsula around the Gulf of Mexico to northern Mexico (to the Rio de las Palmas, probably Rio Soto la Marina between the Rio Grande and the Panuco; see Weddle 1985:104-05). The account of Alvar Núñez de Cabeza de Vaca, a survivor of the ill-fated expedition, provides a surprisingly detailed firsthand description of his experiences, although he wrote it nearly a decade after the fact (Bandelier 1904).

Apparently the Narváez expedition landed south of Tampa Bay and then moved northward, intersecting the harbor. After reconnoitering the eastern portion of the bay and encountering various native groups, the expedition proceeded northward, probably hugging the coast as the explorers made their way toward the territory of the Apalachee Indians in northwest Florida.

The expedition met few aborigines until it reached Apalachee, where Narváez and his men stayed for twenty-five days before departing and traveling nine days to reach the native village of Aute on the Gulf coast, probably near the mouth of the St. Marks River (Mitchem 1989). In Aute, illness struck the army. Attempts to travel farther westward through the marshy coastal region further thwarted the Spaniards, who instead chose to build several boats and make their way to New Spain (Mexico) by water.

The attempt failed, and most of the soldiers were either swept out into the Gulf never to be seen again or washed ashore where they were taken captive by native peoples. Five survived, including Cabeza de Vaca, who was held captive in Texas for nearly eight years before he and four other survivors escaped and made their way westward into the Southwest United States or northern Mexico where they were found by Spanish slavers. Their tales of wealthy native towns on the northern Rio Grande River later led to the 1539 Fray Marcos de Niza and the 1540–42 Francisco Vásquez de Coronado expeditions into that region (Cordell 1989:25).

Following his ordeal, Cabeza de Vaca, one of the survivors, arrived in Sevilla at the Spanish court in 1538. There he led people "to understand that it [La Florida] was the richest country in the world" (Elvas in Bourne 1904, 1:6). Hernando de Soto, in Sevilla at that time, tried to enlist Cabeza de Vaca in his planned expedition to La Florida but failed. The stories told the crown by Cabeza de Vaca apparently did convince others to join de Soto, however. Some of them, including relatives of Cabeza de Vaca, even sold their properties in Spain to finance their participation (Bourne 1904, 1:6–9).

## Hernando de Soto, Conquistador

De Soto's expedition would be the most ambitious of the Spanish attempts to explore the interior of La Florida. De Soto was born about 1500 in Jerez de los Caballeros in the area of Spain called Extremadura, which produced many of the Spanish New World conquistadors, including Vasco Núñez de Balboa, Hernán Cortes, and Francisco Pizarro (tourist brochures today refer to Extremadura as "Land of the Conquistadors"). Like many of the Spanish aristocracy, de Soto's ancestors had distinquished themselves fighting the Moors during the *reconquista.* Military successes had embellished the family's coat-of-arms and resulted in many family members being knighted (for biographical information on de Soto, see Albornoz 1986; B. Smith 1866:xv–xxxii; Swanton 1939:65–74).

Little is known about de Soto's early years in Spain, and it is uncertain exactly when he came to the New World. The best evidence suggests that he sailed in 1514 in the entourage of the newly named governor of the Castilla del Oro (modern Panama), Pedrarias Dávila (Elvas in Bourne 1904, 1:3-4). Also accompanying the governor was Francisco Vásquez de Coronado, who later would explore the Southwest United States.

By 1520 at the age of twenty, de Soto was a captain who had already participated in military actions against the Panamanian Indians. As a portion of his share of booty, he received the right to use a number of Indians as laborers, providing him a source of revenue. His partner in many ventures was Hernán Ponce de León; another associate was Francisco Pizarro.

Throughout the 1520s, de Soto participated in military exploits in Panama and Nicaragua, some against rival Spaniards. By late 1531 when he left Panama, de Soto had amassed great wealth from slave trading and from gold taken from the Indians. With his wealth he was able to build ships and otherwise expand his activities, including maintaining a cadre of military aides, infantry, and cavalry. By standards of the day, he was a successful conquistador.

But de Soto was to garner even greater wealth. From 1531 through 1535, he accompanied Pizarro and other Spaniards in the conquest and looting of the Inca civilization in Peru. De Soto played an important part in the military engagements, experience that would later serve him in La Florida. Following the execution by the Spanish of the captive Inca leader Atahualpa and the occupation of Cuzco, de Soto helped to distribute the stolen wealth to the conquistadors. He departed Peru in late 1535, sailing on to Spain in early 1536. With him were men who would later accompany him on the Florida expedition.

Back in Spain, de Soto used his wealth to hire a number of servants and secure other trappings that befitted someone of his station. He was presented at court and, with his entourage of military aides who had accompanied him to Spain, must have created quite a stir. While in Spain he married Isabel de Bobadilla, the daughter of the Castillo de Oro governor with whom de Soto had first traveled to the New World.

De Soto next attempted to persuade the crown to grant him the right to New World lands which he could govern (and exploit). He asked either for lands in Ecuador and Colombia (north of Pizarro's holdings) or, failing that, Guatemala. Though these requests were denied, he was able to successfully negotiate an agreement to conquer and govern La Florida. The royal charter (*asiento*) given to de Soto by Carlos V is dated April 20, 1537 (Swanton 1939:75–79).

De Soto's charter was much the same as the contracts awarded by the crown to other New World Spanish adventurers (see Lyon 1976:220–23, for a comparison of de Soto's contract with those of Ayllón and Narváez). The charter required de Soto to conquer, pacify, and settle two hundred leagues of La Florida's coast (taking with him five hundred men and supplies for eighteen months), and he was to build three stone forts, using his own funds (evidently using his share of the booty taken from the Inca empire). In return he was to receive titles, lands, and a share of the colony's profits.

## DE SOTO'S CHARTER

A translation of de Soto's royal charter (originally published as an appendix in the 1866 edition of the Elvas and Biedma narratives translated by Buckingham Smith) follows. It is a relatively noncomplex but comprehensive legal document that spells out de Soto's rights and duties and, in considerable detail, the sovereign rights of the crown, especially the division of booty that might be found in La Florida.

CONCESSION MADE BY THE KING OF SPAIN TO HERNANDO DE SOTO
OF THE GOVERNMENT OF CUBA AND CONQUEST OF FLORIDA,
WITH THE TITLE OF ADELANTADO

The King

Inasmuch as you, Captain Hernando de Soto set forth that you have served us in the conquest, pacification, and settlement of the Provinces of Nicaragua and Peru, and of other parts of our Indias [Spain's New World lands]; and that now, to serve us further, and to continue to enlarge our patrimony and the royal crown, you desire to return to those our Indias, to conquer and settle the Province of Rio de las Palmas to Florida, the government whereof was bestowed on Panfilo de Narváez, and the Provinces of Tierra-Nueva, the discovery and government of which was conferred on Lucas Vásquez de Ayllón; and that for the purpose you will take from these, our kingdoms and our said Indias, five hundred men with the necessary arms, horses, munitions, and military stores; and that you will go hence, from these our kingdoms, to make the said conquest and settlement within a year first following, to be reckoned from the day of the date of these articles of authorization; and that when you shall leave the Island of Cuba to go upon that enterprise, you will take the necessary subsistence for all that people during eighteen months—rather over that under than time—entirely at your own cost and charges, without our being obliged, or the kings who shall come after us, to pay you, nor satisfy the expenses incurred therefore, other than such as you in these articles may be authorized to make; and you pray that I bestow on you the conquest of these lands and provinces, and with it the government of the said Island of Cuba, that you may from there the better control and provide all the principal and important material for the conquest and settlement, whereupon I have ordered to be made with you the terms and contract following:

First, I give you, the said Captain Hernando de Soto, power and authority, for us and in our name, and in that of the royal crown of Castilla, to conquer, pacify, and populate the lands that there are from the Province of the Rio de las Palmas to Florida. the government of which was bestowed on Panfilo de Narváez; and further, the Provinces of the said Tierra-Nueva, the government thereof was in like manner conferred on the said Licentiate Ayllón.

Also, purposing to comply in this with the service of God our Lord, and to do you honour, we engage to confer on you the dignity of Governor and Captain-General of two hundred leagues of coast, such as you shall designate, of what you discover, so that within four years, to be reckoned from the time you arrive in any part of the lands and provinces before mentioned, you shall choose and declare whence you would have the two hundred leagues begin; that from where you designate they shall be measured along the coast, for all the days of your life, with the annual salary of fifteen thousand ducats, and five hundred ducats gratuity, in all two thousand, when you shall receive from the day you set sail in the Port of San Lucar [the port for Sevilla], to go upon your voyage, to be paid to you from the duties and profits appertaining in those said lands and provinces which you so offer to conquer and colonize; and in that time should there be neither duties nor profits, we shall not be obliged to order that you be paid anything.

Also, we will confer on you the title of Adelantado over the said two hundred leagues which you shall thus select and make known for your government in the said lands and provinces you so discover and colonize, and will likewise bestow on you the office of High-Constable [*Alguazile mayor*] over those territories in perpetuity.

Also, we give permission, the judgment of our officers of said province being in accord, that you build there as many as three stone fortresses in the harbors and places most proper for them, they appearing to you and to our said officers to be necessary for the protection and pacification of that country; and we confer on you the Lieutenancy of them, and on one heir for life, or successor whom you shall name, with the annual salary to each of the fortresses of one hundred thousand maravedis, which you shall enjoy from the time they be severally built and finished and enclosed, in the opinion of our said officers; to be done at your own cost, without our being obliged, or any of the kings who shall come after us, to pay you what you may expend on those fortresses.

Again, inasmuch as you have petitioned us to bestow on you some portion of the land and vassals in said province you would conquer and populate, considering that you have served us, and the expenditure you will meet from this time in making said conquest and pacification, we receive the petitions favourably: hence we promise to bestow on you, and by these presents we do, twelve leagues of land in square in the said two hundred leagues you shall designate to hold in government in the said territories and provinces before declared, which we command our officers of the said province to assign, after you shall have designated the said two hundred leagues, to include no sea-port, nor the principal town, and that with the jurisdiction and title we shall confer at the time we give you the deeds.

Again, as has been said, you have petitioned us, that for the better governing and providing of all the principal and important matters for the conquest and settlement of said territories and provinces, I should order that there be given to you with them the government of the said Island of Cuba, which, to that end, we deem well, and is our pleasure, for the time it shall be our will, that you hold the government of said island; and for thus much we will order to be given you our provision by which you will be obliged to have a Chief-Justice, who shall be a lawyer, to whom we shall require you to pay yearly on that Island the salary of two hundred pesos of gold; and we give to you five hundred ducats annual gratuity for the government of said Island, while you hold the same, to be paid from the duties and profits we may have from the province you have thus to conquer, pacify, and hold in government; and if there be none there, we will not be obliged to pay you that, nor any other thing more than the two hundred pesos of the said Chief-Justice.

Also, we give you liberty and right that you from these our kingdoms and lordships, or from the Kingdom of Portugal, or Islands of Cabo Verde, of Guinea, do and may pass, or whosoever may exercise your power, to the said Island of Cuba fifty negro slaves, not less than one-third of them to be female, free of the import duties that of right may belong to us at said island, upon paying the license of two ducats on each to Diego de la Haya, which sum by our order he is charged to collect.

Again, also we promise that upon your arrival in that country of your government, which you have thus to conquer and settle, we give liberty and right to whomsoever shall have your power, that you may take thither from these our said kingdoms, or from Portugal, or the Islands of Cabo Verde, another fifty negro slaves, the third part of them females, free from all duties.

Also, we concede to those who shall go to settle in that country within six years first following, to be reckoned forward from the day of the date of these presents, that of the gold which may be taken from the mines shall be paid us the tenth, and the said six years being ended, shall pay us the ninth, and thus annually declining to the fifth part; but from the gold and other things that may be got by barter, or is spoil got by incursions, or in any other manner, shall be paid us thereupon one-fifth of all.

Also we give, free of import duty, to the inhabitants of that country for the said six years, and as much longer as shall be our will, all they may take for the furnishing and provision of their houses, the same not being to sell; and whatsoever they or any other, merchants or traffickers, sell, shall go free of duty for two years, and not longer.

Likewise, we promise that for the term of ten years, and until we command otherwise, we will not impose on the inhabitants of those countries any excise duty, or any other tribute whatsoever.

Likewise, we grant that to said inhabitants may be given through you the lots and grounds proper to their conditions, as has been done, and is doing, in the Island of

Española; and we also give you license, in our name, during the time of your government, that you take the bestowal of the Indians of that land, observing therein the instructions and provisions that will be given to you.

Again, we bestow on the hospital that may be built in that country, to assist the relief of the poor who may go thither, the charity of one hundred thousand maravedis from the fines imposed by the tribunal of that country.

Again, also, according to your petition and consent, and of the settlers of that country, we promise to give to its hospital, and by these presents we do give, the duties of *escobilla* and *relabes,* existing in the foundries that may there be made; and as respects that, we will order our provision to be issued to you in form.

Also, likewise we will order, and by the present command and defend, that from these our kingdoms do not pass into said country, nor go, any one of the persons prohibited from going into those parts, under the penalties contained in the laws and ordinances of our letters, upon which subject this by us and by the Catholic Kings are given, nor any counsellors nor attorneys to exercise their callings.

The which, all that is said, and each thing and part thereof, we concede to you, conditioned that you, the said Don Hernando de Soto, be held and obliged to go from these our realms in person to make the conquest within one year next following, to be reckoned from the day of the date of this charter.

Again, on condition that when you go out of these our said kingdoms, and arrive in said country, you will carry and have with you the officers of our exchequer, who may by us be named; and likewise also the persons, religious and ecclesiastical, who shall be appointed by us for the instruction of the natives of that Province in our Holy Catholic Faith, to whom you are to give and pay the passage, stores, and the other necessary subsistence for them, according to their condition, all at your cost, receiving nothing from them during the said entire voyage; with which matter we gravely charge you, that you do and comply with, as a thing for the service of God and our own, and any thing otherwise we shall deem contrary to our service.

Again, whensoever, according to right and the laws of our kingdoms, the people and captains of our armaments take prisoner any prince or lord of the countries where, by our command, they make war, the ransom of such lord or cacique belongs to us, with all the other things movable found or belonging to him; but considering the great toils and perils that our subjects undergo in the conquest of the Indias, as some recompense, and to favour them, we make known and command, that if in your said conquest and government any cacique or principal lord be captured or seized, all the treasures, gold, silver, stones, and pearls that may be got from him by way of redemption, or in any other manner whatsoever, we award you the seventh part thereof, and the remainder shall be divided among the conquerers, first taking out our fifth; and in case the said cacique or lord should be slain in battle, or afterward by course of justice, or in any other manner whatsoever, in such case, of the treasurers and goods aforesaid obtained of him justly we have the half, which, before any thing else, our officers shall take, after having first reserved our fifth.

Again, since our said officers of said Provinces might have some doubt in making the collection of our duties, especially on gold and silver, stones and pearls, as well those that may be found in sepulchers, and other places where they may be hidden, as those got by ransom and incursion, or other way, our pleasure and will is, that, until some change, the following order be observed.

First, we order that of the gold and silver, stones and pearls that may be won in battle, or on entering towns, or by barter with the Indians, should and must be paid us one-fifth of all.

Likewise, that all the gold and silver, stones, pearls, and other things that may be found and taken, as well in the graves, sepulchers, *ocues,* or temples of the Indians, as in other places where they were accustomed to offer sacrifices to their idols, or in other concealed religious precincts, or buried in house, or patrimonial soil, or in the ground, or in some other public place, whether belonging to the community or an individual, be his state or dignity what it may, of the whole, and of all other, of the character that may be and is sound, whether finding it by accident or discovering it by search, shall pay us the half, without diminution of any sort, the other half remaining to the person who has found or made the discovery; and should any person or persons have gold, silver, stones, or pearls, taken or found, as well in the said graves, sepulchers, *ocues,* or Indian temples, as in the other places where they were accustomed to offer sacrifices, or other concealed religious places, or interred as before said, and do not make it known, that they may receive, in conformity with this chapter, what may belong to them, they have forfeited all the gold and silver, stones and pearls, besides the half of their goods, to our tribunal and exchequer.

And we, having informed of the evils and disorders which occur in making discoverings and new settlements, for the redress thereof, and that we may be enabled to give you license to make them, with the accord of the members of our Council and of our consultation, a general provision of chapters is ordained and dispatched, respecting what you will have to observe in the said settlement and conquest, and we command it here to be incorporated in tenor as follows:

[As Buckingham Smith (1866:272) noted, this "general provision" was an ordinance, first incorporated in the royal charter of Francisco de Montejo granting him the conquest of Yucatan; Montejo's charter was dated December 7, 1526. The contents of this ordinance, which were not included in the copy of de Soto's charter that Smith translated, but which are known from other charters, are discussed below, following the closing section of de Soto's asiento.]

* * *

Hence, by these presents, you, the said Captain Hernando de Soto, doing as aforesaid at your cost, according to and in the manner before contained, observing and complying with the said provision here incorporated, and all the other instructions we shall henceforth command you to obey, and to give with regard to that country, and for the good treatment and conversion to our Holy Catholic Faith of the natives of it, we promise and declare that to you will be kept these terms, and whatever therein is contained, in and through all; and you doing otherwise, and not complying therewith, we shall not be obliged to keep with you and comply with the aforesaid, nor any matter of it; on the contrary, we will order that you be punished, and proceed against you as against one who keeps not nor complies with, but acts counter to, the commands of his natural king and lord. In confirmation whereof we order that the present be given, signed by my name, and witnessed by my undersigned Secretary. Done at the town of Valladolid, the twentieth day of the month of April, of the year one thousand five hundred and thirty seven.

I The King.

De Soto's charter followed a set form, one developed by the crown based on the outcomes of other New World expeditions. Likewise the ordinance referred to above was originally drawn up by the crown in consultation with various Spanish governmental and church officials. The ordinance, which evolved as a part of Spain's New World policy, set forth the ideology and basis of conquest and the role of church and state vis-á-vis the native inhabitants of the New World. The purpose of conquest was to bring the native peoples to the true faith and establish their allegiance to the Spanish crown. Indians were free people who were to be afforded the protection of the crown and the church and could not be used as laborers against their will (Chamberlain 1948:22–23).

The ordinance required that at least two members of the clergy accompany each expedition. These clergymen were further commanded to try to convert the natives to Christianity and to report to the crown any violations of the rights of the native peoples. A further requirement was that each expedition read a lengthy statement, the *requerimiento,* to the natives, outlining the desire of the Spanish monarchy that the natives pledge allegiance to the crown and accept Catholicism. The *requerimiento* made known to the Indians that they and their lands now belonged to the Spanish crown. It was to be read three times by the leader of the Spanish expedition or a representative (using an interpreter, if needed) and explained to the Indians so that they understood its meaning. The event was to be witnessed by a member of the clergy and duly recorded.

On the one hand it is easy to visualize the ceremony and pomp that accompanied the mandatory reading of the *requerimiento* when de Soto or another conquistador encountered a new native society. It is also easy to visualize the result. The *requerimiento* was a complex document that incorporated Catholic ideology along with legal and political complexities all based on European models. It is highly unlikely that it was immediately understood by New World peoples whose ideology and political organization was based on very different concepts.

The failure of a native person to obey the *requerimiento* meant disaster for that individual, since such failure meant that the Spaniards could use force to enslave the individual. In essence, the *requerimiento* offered the Spanish expeditions, such as that of de Soto, a legal excuse to wage war against the people of La Florida as necessary to further the Spanish empire in the New World. Excerpts of the *requerimiento* in use when de Soto first came to the New World in 1514 illustrate the complex nature of this document and the threat it implied (from Chamberlain 1948:24–25):

> On behalf of the king . . . and the queen . . . , subjugators of barbarous peoples, we, their servants, notify and make known to you as best we are able, that God, Our Lord, living and eternal, created the heavens and the earth, and a man and a woman, of whom you and we and all other people of the world were, and are, the descendants. . . . Because of the great numbers of people who have come from the union of these two in the five thousand years which have run their course since the world was created, it became necessary that some should go in one direction and that others should go in another. Thus they became divided into many kingdoms and many provinces, since they could not all remain or sustain themselves in one place.

Of all these people God, Our Lord, chose one, who was called Saint Peter, to be the lord and the one who was to be superior to all the other people of the world, whom all should obey. He was to be the head of the entire human race, wherever men might exist . . . . God gave him the world for his kingdom and jurisdiction. . . . God also permitted him to be and establish himself in any other part of the world to judge and govern all peoples, whether Christian, Moors, Jew, gentiles, or those of any other sects and beliefs that there might be. He was called the Pope. . . .

One of the past Popes who succeeded Saint Peter . . . , as Lord of the Earth gave these islands and mainlands of the Ocean Sea [the Atlantic Ocean] to the said King and Queen and to their successors . . . , with everything that there is in them, as is set forth in certain documents which were drawn up regarding this donation in the manner described, which you may see if you so desire.

In consequence, Their Highnesses are Kings and Lords of these islands and mainland by virtue of said donation. Certain other isles and almost all [the native peoples] to whom this summons has been read have accepted Their Highnesses as such Kings and Lords, and have served, and serve, them as their subjects as they should, and must, do, with good will and without offering any resistance. . . . You are constrained and obliged to do the same as they.

Consequently, as we best may, we beseech and demand that you understand fully this that we have said to you and ponder it, so that you may understand and deliberate upon it for a just and fair period and that you accept the Church and Superior Organization of the whole world and recognize the Supreme Pontiff, called the Pope, and that in his name, you acknowledge the King and Queen . . . , as the lords and superior authorities of these islands and mainlands by virtue of the said donation. . . .

If you do not do this, however, or resort maliciously to delay, we warn you that, with the aid of God, we will enter your land against you with force and will make war in every place and by every means we can and are able, and we will then subject you to the yoke and authority of the Church and Their Highnesses. We will take you and your wives and children and make them slaves, and as such we will sell them, and will dispose of you and them as Their Highnesses order. And we will take your property and will do to you all the harm and evil we can, as is done to vassals who will not obey their lord or who do not wish to accept him, or who resist and defy him. We avow that the deaths and harm which you will receive thereby will be your own blame, and not that of Their Highnesses, nor ours, nor of the gentlemen who come with us. . . .

## THE DE SOTO EXPEDITION

Buttressed by this ideology—which made them representatives of God, the pope, and their sovereign—and armed with weapons from another world, de Soto and his army sailed to the New World from Spain in April 1538 (Elvas in Bourne 1904, 1:11). After a stop in the Canary Islands, de Soto's fleet arrived in Santiago, Cuba. He sent a portion of his expedition on to Havana via ships while he and 150 of his men went overland on horseback. Forty days later, they too arrived in Havana (Elvas in Bourne 1904, 1:18, 20).

In Havana, de Soto, who had been given the governorship of Cuba, took control of the colony and began to finalize plans for his La Florida expedition. On May 18, 1539, he and his army departed for the mainland "to conquer and settle and reduce to peaceful life those provinces which his Majesty has bestowed upon him . . ." (Ranjel in Bourne 1904, 2:50–51). The La Florida expedition had begun.

One week later, May 25, de Soto's fleet sighted the western coast of Florida and dropped anchor near the mouth of the harbor they had sought, most likely Tampa Bay (Milanich 1989). Over the next few days they made their way into the harbor and unloaded about 500 people (including two women, tailors, shoemakers, a stocking-maker, a notary, a farrier, a trumpeter, servants, priests, cavalry, and infantry), 220 horses, a drove of pigs, and supplies. The exact number of people who accompanied de Soto is uncertain. Biedma (in Bourne 1904, 2:3) says 620 men, while Ranjel (in Bourne 1904, 2:52) says 570 men plus 130 sailors totalling "fully 700."

After establishing a camp and reconnoitering the adjacent territory for six weeks, de Soto, about 500 Spaniards, and perhaps hundreds of captive native bearers marched north, leaving behind a portion of the army and supplies at their base camp (see illustration 1). During the late summer of 1539, the expedition moved northward and then west across northern Florida, reaching Anhaica, the major Apalachee town, in the early fall. The exact location of Anhaica, where the expedition wintered, has been established and portions of the site excavated (the site is in modern Tallahassee; see Ewen 1988, 1989a; also see Milanich and Hudson 1993).

In spring 1540, de Soto and his army broke camp and headed in a northeasterly direction across Georgia toward the Carolinas and the mythical land of Chicora, which was never found. They then turned north, crossing the Appalachian Mountains into Tennessee. It is likely that the discovery of native wealth in the highlands of Peru and Mexico influenced de Soto to seek the mountains. Across the Appalachians the army traced the Tennessee River Valley southwesterly through the native chiefdom of Coosa, reaching well into central Alabama. Farther south in Mobila, a town in the chiefdom of Tuscaluza, a major battle against native peoples was fought. Afterwards the army turned northwest, across Alabama into Mississippi, where another major battle was fought and where they again wintered (1540–41).

Their route brought the Spaniards to the Mississippi River, which they floated across on rafts. The march to the river, reached in May 1541, had taken nearly two years. De Soto's third year was spent in Arkansas, marching from one native village to another, searching for mineral wealth that did not exist, before returning to the Mississippi River where de Soto, sick with a fever, died on June 20, 1542.

Luís de Moscoso took over the leadership of the army, and the Spaniards attempted to cross Texas to reach New Spain (Mexico). But after traveling hundreds of miles, they realized it was futile to continue. They had left the region of the densely populated native farming societies with their stored food supplies that had sustained the army along its march from Florida. In Texas the native groups, probably hunter-gatherers, had no such surpluses to be seized, forcing the army to trace its way back to the Mississippi, which they reached in December 1542. The first six months of the next year were spent constructing boats in which the Spaniards could travel downriver to the Gulf of Mexico and then to New Spain. Twenty days after setting out, in late June 1543, they reached the Gulf. Two and a half months later, the 311 survivors reached a

Spanish settlement on the River of Panuco (near present-day Tampico, Mexico), ending their incredible odyssey.

## SPANISH EXPLORATION AND SETTLEMENTS AFTER DE SOTO

The de Soto expedition was not the only Spanish army to penetrate the interior of North America in the 1540s. In February 1540, Francisco Vásquez de Coronado and an army of 230 soldiers, 800 Indian bearers, and livestock set out from Compostela in northwestern Mexico to establish settlements in the Southwest United States. Two years earlier a much smaller expedition, led by Father Marcos de Niza, had traveled northward into New Mexico, returning with stories of great wealth.

Coronado, like de Soto, would travel great distances, probably crossing the Arkansas River and reaching as far as central Kansas. But on his two-and-a-half-year trek, Coronado, like de Soto in the southeastern United States, failed to establish any settlements.

Thirty years had passed since Juan Ponce de León's first voyage and the crown still did not have a single colony in La Florida, despite the expenditure of a great deal of resources. For the next decade and a half, La Florida would largely be ignored while Spanish efforts in the New World were focused elsewhere.

But the strategic importance of La Florida could not be ignored forever. Spain's shipping lanes along the Gulf of Mexico coast needed protection (R. S. Weddle 1985:253–55), and missions to administer to the native peoples of the Southeast were sought (P. E. Hoffman 1984:429). The crown also desired an overland road leading from the Atlantic coast of La Florida to New Spain. With one end in South Carolina at Santa Elena (see illustration 1), a point on the coast, the road would extend westerly to the Gulf coast near modern Pensacola and on to Mexico. A communication route from Mexico to Santa Elena on the Atlantic would negate the need to sail the storm-prone and dangerous coasts of La Florida. Goods could be transported to the Atlantic coast overland and then loaded on ships for the voyage to Spain. Still another objective was to thwart growing French interest in the southeastern Atlantic coastal region.

These goals could be accomplished with the establishment of settlements on the Gulf (at Pensacola Bay on the northwest Florida coast) and on the Atlantic (at Santa Elena) coasts (P. E. Hoffman 1984:428–29). Still another settlement was sought inland in Coosa, the large and rich aboriginal chiefdom described in glowing terms by de Soto's army.

Funded by the viceroy of New Spain and led by Tristán de Luna y Arellano, an expedition was organized to accomplish these aims. Thirteen ships and fifteen hundred people (including Mexican Indians and men who had marched with de Soto twenty years earlier) set sail from Mexico for the Gulf coast of La Florida in the summer of 1559. The colonists first landed at Mobile Bay before locating Ochuse (at Pensacola Bay), which was their objective (Hudson, et al. 1989; Priestley 1928). De Luna sent men into the adjacent interior countryside to locate native settlements that could provide food, but few were found. A hurricane struck and sank several ships which had not yet been unloaded, destroying supplies and creating a desperate situation. To feed the colonists de Luna sent most of them well into the interior to a large native town, Nanipacana, where there was food (Hudson, et al. 1989:126–29). A contingent of men was then sent farther inland to locate Coosa, which they found greatly changed from two decades earlier when de Soto had been there.

It became obvious that de Luna's colony was failing. Colonists rebelled and some returned to New Spain. The end came in March, 1561, when Angel de Villafañe arrived with orders to move the colony to the Atlantic coast, to Santa Elena. But that effort also failed when Villafañe lost three of his four ships in storms and apparently never reached Santa Elena (P. E. Hoffman 1984:430–31).

It would be four years before Pedro Menéndez de Avilés would finally establish a Spanish colony in La Florida. Menéndez ousted short-lived French settlements on the Atlantic coast and placed towns at St. Augustine in northeast Florida and Santa Elena in South Carolina. He also ordered garrisons, some with Jesuit missions, to be located along the Gulf and Atlantic coasts of La Florida (Lyon 1988). These would protect the shipping routes and aid shipwrecked Spanish sailors, as well as make allies of the coastal natives.

Menéndez realized that coastal settlements alone would not sustain the new colony. Wealth—land and labor for ranches, pearls, minerals, etc.—could only be found in the interior, in places like Cofitacheque (in South Carolina) and Coosa, native polities visited by de Soto. To establish inland forts and missions and to (finally) establish the route from Santa Elena to northern Mexico, Menéndez in 1566–68 sent two expeditions northward from Santa Elena. Both were led by Juan Pardo (DePratter, Hudson, and Smith 1983; Hudson 1990). On the second and longer of the two, Pardo and his men reached as far as just south of Nashville, Tennessee. The forts and missions established by Pardo were as short-lived as the coastal garrisons and missions. Santa Elena itself was abandoned in 1587 and Spain was left with only the coastal town of St. Augustine.

After the failure of the Jesuit missions in the early 1570s, Pedro Menéndez arranged for the Franciscan order to serve his colony. In 1587 missionary efforts began in earnest and *doctrinas,* missions with resident priests who taught Catholic doctrine to the native villagers, were established around St. Augustine and up the Georgia coast.

After 1606 Franciscans founded *doctrinas* in interior northern Florida. Gradually the inland mission chain moved westward, by 1633 missions reaching the Apalachee Indians in northwest Florida. Over time, more than 130 doctrinas and *visitas* with churches would be built (Hann 1990).

The mission system lasted for more than a century, but it was a century of dwindling native populations as disease took its toll. Spain's hold on her colony continued to weaken as other European powers, especially the English in the north and the French in the west, began to establish a presence on the Atlantic and Gulf coasts. Much of the mission system itself was destroyed in 1702–04 by English raiders from the Carolina colony. Soon Spain's La Florida colony was restricted largely to a geographical area roughly equal to modern Florida. In 1821 the colony became a part of the United States of America, ending Spanish control.

# RECONSTRUCTING THE ROUTE OF DE SOTO'S ARMY

How can we trace the route of the Hernando de Soto expedition through the southeastern United States, from Florida to Arkansas and beyond? How do we know, for instance, that the expedition landed at Tampa Bay and not somewhere in southwest Florida as some scholars have claimed (Schell 1966; Wilkinson 1954; L. W. Williams 1986, 1989)? How can we show which archeological sites in Arkansas correlate with those actually visited by de Soto and his army? Where did the army cross the Mississippi River? Which native groups were directly impacted by the expedition?

The answers to these questions are derived from interdisciplinary research that incorporates documentary/historical research, cartographic/geographical interpretations, and archeological investigations. Data gathered from these various sources are cross-checked, cross-referenced, and correlated to produce a reconstruction of the route. That reconstruction is continually tested and refined as more information becomes available.

## Narratives and Documents

The best-known and most often referenced documentary sources are three firsthand narratives of the expedition written by participants. All three are available in English, although all the translations could be improved. The first is by an unknown Portuguese knight from the town of Elvas who participated in the expedition (Bourne 1904, 1; Robertson 1933). The second is what appears to be an official account of the expedition, written by Luÿs Hernández de Biedma, who was perhaps the crown's representative (See Relaçam verdadeira; Robertson 1933; Lewis 1907; Bourne 1904, 2; B. Smith 1866).

The third firsthand account is by de Soto's personal secretary on the expedition, Rodrigo Ranjel (Bourne 1904, 2). The original manuscript of his relation or diary, which has almost daily entries, has been lost, but a copy of it was preserved in a work by the Spanish historian Gonzalo Fernández de Oviedo y Valdez. Oviedo's five-volume *Historia General y Natural de las Indias* (Swanton 1939:4–11, for a discussion of the various translations and editions of the three de Soto expedition narratives).

A fragment from a fourth firsthand account, also written by a survivor of the expedition, has been found by historian Eugene Lyon in the Archivo General de Indias in Sevilla (Lyon 1982). The fragment, by Father Sebastian de Cañete, contains rich description of aboriginal life in the chiefdom of Cofitachequi (in interior South Carolina), but is of little use in interpreting the route.

A secondhand account of the expedition authored by Garcilaso de la Vega (nicknamed the Inca because his mother was a native woman from Peru) also exists (Garcilaso 1951). It is based on interviews with survivors and other sources of information. Approximately one-quarter of the manuscript was completed by 1587, and it was not until 1599 that it was completed, more than a half century after the expedition took place. Consequently, much of the information in the account is jumbled or exaggerated (for a critique, see Henige 1986a).

In addition to these accounts, there are also documents and letters relating to the de Soto entrada, its preparation, and its aftermath. Several of these have been published in the appendix to the Biedma and Elvas narratives published in 1866 and translated by Buckingham Smith. They include a letter sent from Havana to the Spanish crown written by Juan Gaytan, Juan de Añasco, and Luís Fernández and dated May 18, 1539; a letter from de Soto to the King of Spain, written at Tampa Bay (Espíritu Santo) on July 9, 1539; the Memorial of Alonso Vásquez, which contains testimony of several individuals who participated in the entrada, including Ana Mendez, a woman; and the *asiento,* or contract, between the crown and de Soto, dated April 20, 1537. Other documents are as yet unpublished; some of these (this list was provided by Eugene Lyon) are: a 3720-page *Justicia* covering the period 1540–45 and containing a lengthy lawsuit filed by Isabela de Bobadilla (de Soto's widow) against Hernan Ponce de León, former partner of de Soto in Peru and Nicaragua; and voluminous documents recounting the controversies among de Soto's heirs and Francisco Vásquez de Coronado, Hernán Cortes, and the viceroy of Mexico; and de Soto's *Residencia,* the investigation carried out in 1554 (after his death) to determine whether or not he had fulfilled his responsibilities as outlined in his *asiento.* These materials, however, do not contain new information relative to the route in Florida (see Robertson 1933:397–428, for a discussion of these and other sources and documents).

Still other pre- and post-de Soto entrada documents are available and provide evidence on the landing. For instance, the pre-de Soto *Espejo* by Chaves describes Bahía Honda, where de Soto's fleet went ashore on the Gulf coast, leaving little doubt that it is Tampa Bay (Castañeda, Cuesta, and Hernández 1983). And bits and pieces about the expedition and especially the survivors are found in Ignacio Avellaneda's *Los Sobrevivientes de la Florida: The Survivors of the de Soto Expedition* (1990).

Documents recounting the explorations by the French and the Spanish in the southeast in the 1560s and documents from the period of the Spanish missions also provide excellent clues to the locations of some of the Indian villages mentioned in the de Soto narratives.

These historical materials, especially the narratives of the Gentleman of Elvas, Biedma, and Ranjel, provide descriptions of natural and cultural features along the route which must then be located on modern maps. For instance, if the accounts say the expedition stopped at an Indian village by a lake, then crossed a very large swamp, bridged a swift river, and came to another Indian village, we must find on our maps a lake, swamp, and river in the proper sequence and in the correct relative location along the route.

## Maps

Another line of evidence used in reconstructing the expedition's route is the use of old maps that show trails and paths that existed prior to modern roads. From the narratives themselves, it is certain that de Soto and his army usually traveled along Indian trails. Many of those same trails continued to be used into the eighteenth and nineteenth centuries, when the first accurate maps of much of the interior of the Southeast were compiled (and many of these same trails have become our modern highways and railroad beds). By using early maps in conjunction with modern maps and aerial photographs on which old trails sometimes can be seen, we can locate those trails along which de Soto's army might have traveled, looking, for example, for a trail that goes by a lake and then crosses a swamp and river, as described in the narratives.

## Archeological Evidence

Using these documentary and cartographic sources of information we can generate a hypothesized reconstruction of the route. The problem then becomes a matter of proving that the reconstruction is the correct one. The best proof would seem to be physical evidence gathered through archeological investigations. If our interpretation of the lake, swamp, river, and trail is correct, then we should be able to find the archeological sites corresponding to the Indian villages mentioned in the narratives. The correct sites would have been occupied in the early sixteenth century, and they should contain at least some artifacts that could have been left by the de Soto expedition, things such as the European glass beads mentioned in the narratives (e.g., Brain 1975; Deagan 1987; Fairbanks 1968; Mitchem 1989, 1989a; M. T. Smith 1987; Smith and Good 1982).

Fortunately, most southeastern states maintain a file of all known archeological sites. And archeological research in the Southeast has been ongoing since the nineteenth century, and much information has been gathered and is available in published sources, museum collections, and archives. Site files and reports and artifact collections from earlier archeological investigations are used to help locate known sites that fit the reconstructed route. Descriptions of the geographical setting and appearance of each site should also correlate with the appropriate description of the Indian town given in the de Soto narratives (e.g., a moated and palisaded town next to a river).

Another way to find predicted sites is to look for them. Archeologists across the Southeast have expended a great deal of effort looking for the Indian villages that are predicted by reconstructions of the route. When such sites are found they must be tested using archeological techniques to determine if they are of the proper period and if they contain artifacts that can be associated with the de Soto expedition.

Because the southeastern United States has a long history of Spanish exploration and settlement (from 1513 into the nineteenth century), the finding of Spanish artifacts alone is not good evidence for the presence of de Soto. We must be able to show that the artifacts date from the 1530s or earlier and are not items salvaged from Spanish ships or given out by seventeenth-century Spanish missionaries. Using information gathered from elsewhere in the Southeast, the Caribbean, Central and South America, and from Spanish museums and other sources, we now have a list of early sixteenth-century Spanish artifacts that we feel strongly are items brought by de Soto. It is when these artifacts are found in archeological sites that are on or near our predicted route that we have the best evidence for de Soto's route. In Florida, such artifacts have been found around Tampa Bay and at several sites along the route, including the village of Anhaica. Some of the same beads and other European artifacts from those sites have been found at presumed de Soto contact sites elsewhere in the Southeast.

This research is demonstrating that it is possible to trace the route of the

Hernando de Soto expedition 450 years after those Spanish explorers first traveled through La Florida. The physical evidence presented by archeological sites and artifacts is allowing modern researchers to provide perspectives on the expedition not previously available.

## DE SOTO'S LEGACY

In terms of its charter, the de Soto expedition was a failure. It can be argued that it accomplished none of its objectives. The best available evidence also indicates that the expedition had a severe negative impact on the native peoples encountered. Thousands of Indians were killed as a result of battles and maltreatment. Even more, perhaps tens or even hundreds of thousands were infected with Old World diseases and succumbed. Gradually archeologists are gathering evidence that points toward a massive demographic catastrophe across the Southeast following de Soto. The resulting impact on native lifestyles was tremendous. Cultural changes occurred rapidly as the survivors adjusted to the new conditions.

Why, then, should we study the de Soto expedition? The answer is simple. The story of that expedition is also the story of the native peoples of the Southeast. Once we can confidently trace the route and have located the various native villages visited (and impacted) by de Soto and his army, we can apply the ethnohistorical information in the narratives to known archeological complexes and sites.

The de Soto narratives contain the only known firsthand accounts of native peoples in the interior of the Southeast as those peoples were on the eve of European contact. These data provide scholars with a way to bridge the gap between archeological evidence and ethnohistorical reality. Such research allows us not only to put names on archeological remains, but also to gain information on such things as intervillage political ties, the geographical extent of political hegemony, and political hierarchies. Interpretations of the de Soto expedition narratives will help us to relate the story of the southeastern Native Americans as they were and to trace the rapid cultural and social changes that occurred in specific societies in the centuries following contact. Perhaps that is de Soto's most important legacy.

# Archeology and the Population of Arkansas in 1541–1543

Dan F. Morse

## INTRODUCTION

The location and nature of the population in present-day Arkansas during the Protohistoric period (A.D. 1500–1650) is critical to a determination of the route of the de Soto expedition. A computer-generated map of Protohistoric sites has been developed specifically to aid research into the route of the expedition in Arkansas (illustration 6).

By January 1, 1990, the Arkansas Archeological Survey had entered all of its recorded 22,000 sites into a computer file known as AMASDA (Automated Management of Archeological Site Data in Arkansas). In this system, the major attributes of a recorded site are filed by encoding the ways they are recorded on a site sheet (Hilliard and Riggs 1986). The site file is not perfect by any means. Site sheets are filled out by a variety of individuals (avocational and professional archeologists) with varying backgrounds and expertise. A single page format was used until 1979, when it was replaced by the present multiple page form. Most sites were recorded when first discovered and the forms represent single visits, not always made at the best time to make observations on a site (uncultivated, while raining, etc.). Not until the 1980s did a revisit form begin to be used consistently for sites.

In 1987, an update of the AMASDA system was begun by the appropriate archeologists of the Archeological Survey and University of Arkansas Museum. The pilot program was a review of sites thought to have been occupied about the time of the de Soto Expedition into Arkansas. This review was primarily prompted by the observation that the de Soto accounts stated very explicitly that de Soto went to large habitations because he was dependent on Indians to provide food as well as intelligence. The accounts also pinpointed "deserts" or uninhabited areas where the lack of processed food was of much concern to the Spanish army exploring a potentially hostile and unknown region. Until some control was gained over where the Indians lived in 1541–43, discussion of the different de Soto route hypotheses was in limbo.

A second reason for this site review was the availability of GRASS (Geographical Resources Analysis Support System), a method to produce distribution maps with a computer (Westervelt 1988; Arkansas Archeological Survey 1989; Farley, Limp, and

Lockhart 1990). GRASS is "a geographical information system (GIS) . . . [which is] Grid . . . based . . . [and] . . . is capable of data digitizing . . ." (Westervelt 1988:2). In other words, a base map can be created and site locations mapped according to their Universal Transverse Mercator grid coordinates, superimposed on that map. What had to be done was (1) review each site, (2) select those which probably dated about 1541–43, (3) enter that information into AMASDA, (4) interdigitate those data into the GRASS system, (5) choose a base map, and (6) finally put it all together and print it.

Fortunately, the computer steps could be done by experts in the Arkansas Archeological Survey Coordinating Office. Jerry Hilliard, registrar, agreed to encode the data to AMASDA, and Jami Lockhart, GIS specialist, agreed to produce the map under the supervision of Fred Limp, assistant director in 1987. The following archeologists accepted responsibility for reviewing sites in different regions of the state: Dan F. Morse (NE), George Sabo (NW), Michael Hoffman (upper Arkansas River), Martha Rolingson (central Arkansas River and SE), John House (lower Arkansas River and SE), Marvin Jeter (SE), Ann Early (Ouachita Mountains), and Frank Schambach (SW).

## SITE REVIEW PROCESS

It took two years to review the site files and to select 350 sites thought to have been inhabited about 1541–43. As a result, the data base is thought to be about as good as it is possible to make it. In addition, almost 150 person-years of accumulated Arkansas archeological experience are represented by the personnel who reviewed the site files. This situation is almost unique in professional archeology and underscores the dedication to research experienced in Arkansas.

Another advantage in Arkansas is that numerous intensive pedestrian surveys have been accomplished, many by (or supervised under) the aforementioned archeologists. In addition, each of these archeologists has worked extensively in one to several other regions in the eastern United States and is not easily misled by "odd" artifacts or concepts. This situation is not necessarily unique to Arkansas, but does constitute a definite advantage in identifying late prehistoric/initial historic period sites.

The first step in the review process was for Hilliard to provide a printout of sites identified in the past as dating to about 1541–43. In this initial printout, sites were identified in the files as "Contact Period," "Early Historic," "Protohistoric," and as specific late prehistoric cultural names such as "Caddo IV," "Late Caddo," "Late Mississippian," and "Nodena phase" (illustration 7). We decided to use the term "Protohistoric" to indicate a period dating between around A.D. 1400 and 1650. This period was easily recognized over all of Arkansas (see following section), and the population concentrations for this general period were thought to be representative of 1541–43. In some cases, this assumption could be checked by the presence of European artifacts known to date from about the mid-sixteenth to early seventeenth centuries.

The initial printouts were found to include several erroneous identifications. Of a total of thirty-one sites checked in northeast Arkansas, twenty were discovered to be invalid identifications. In both northeast and southwest Arkansas, intensive contract surveys were found to have involved more invalid than valid identifications. Even a fluted point site and sites with small nondiagnostic lithic scatters were labeled "early contact." In the Ozarks of northwest Arkansas, the "early contact" label was applied to twentieth-century garbage found in a rock shelter. The classic "early contact" site, however, was 3VB6 (Indian Rock House in Van Buren Co. in the Ozarks) which exhibited a bronze plaque stating that "De Soto camped here in 1542." Each site identified as potentially "early contact" was reviewed and the erroneous identifications corrected.

The next step was to identify probable sites dating to the Protohistoric period, then reviewing those critically. Identification was done simply by going through the original site files and the collections. Each Archeological Survey station has its own collections and most of the extant collections were made by the archeologist at each station. The Museum collections were checked by Michael Hoffman and Phyllis Clancy (1985) for the upper portion of the Arkansas River Valley, since no station archeologist stationed there until 1989 had accumulated significant data on the local archeology. This has now been corrected, and this very important region is being sufficiently surveyed to help clear up the Protohistoric picture there.

## PROTOHISTORIC CRITERIA

### Northeast Arkansas

The three primary artifact types used to identify sites dating circa 1400–1650 in northeast Arkansas are: (1) Nodena points, (2) Parkin Punctated pottery, and (3) Barton Incised pottery. A variety of other artifact types characteristic of the Nodena and Parkin phases are also unique to this period, but are very rare in comparison to the three outlined above, and a complete list is necessary only to reaffirm the Protohistoric identification (P. A. Morse 1981; D. F. Morse 1989; Morse and Morse 1983, chapter 12). Other phases include Old Town, Kent, Belle Meade, Greenbrier, and Little Red River. The contrast between adjacent sites which date respectively to the Middle and Late Mississippian periods is very striking. Middle Period sites contain large percentages of Mississippi Plain pottery and points are invariably Scallorn in type. One afternoon, I was able to demonstrate the differences to an avocational archeologist by simply going with him to two large sites about a quarter mile apart where he wanted to collect surface material. We identified one site as Parkin phase before we took five steps and reaffirmed that identification in the next five paces, and so on. The other site was positively identified as Middle Period only after two hours of intensive searching. That avocational archeologist quickly became a very valuable site surveyor for us.

End scrapers occur on many but not all sites. Our rule of thumb is that end scrapers are associated with Nodena points after about 1500 to 1550. There is some verification of this inference. Sites with early Nodena style points ("Banks variety") usually do not contain end scrapers. Sites with early European artifacts contain abundant end scrapers. Those latter sites also contain ceramics thought to date later than 1500. Most northeast Arkansas late sites are thought to be ancestral to the Quapaw while the westernmost sites, those located along the White River, may be ancestral to the Tunica.

## Northwest Arkansas

The Neosho phase (also known as the Neosho focus) forms the basis for the identification of Protohistoric sites in northwest Arkansas (George Sabo, personal communication). Two radiocarbon dates from the Jug Hill site in Oklahoma indicate the temporal range is approximately 1400–1600 (Rohrbaugh 1984:270; Wyckoff 1964). Neosho may be ancestral to the historic Osage, and sites extend from Oklahoma into Missouri and Arkansas.

Diagnostic artifacts include: end scrapers, bison bone tools, triangular arrow points of the Shetley and Fresno types, and Woodward Plain "*Neosho variety*" and Neosho Punctate pottery. European artifacts have been found at Jug Hill (Wyckoff 1964) and at 3CW93 near Fort Smith (Sabo, personal communication). I think these European artifacts date fairly late, circa seventeenth century.

## Upper Arkansas River

Sites along the Arkansas River were identified by Michael P. Hoffman (personal communication) and Phyllis Clancy (1985) as Protohistoric on the basis of donated museum collections from the Arkansas River valley above Little Rock. This presents a problem because kitchen debris is not represented in the donated collections. Diagnostic artifacts include Nodena points, painted pottery, and pottery representative of the Carden Bottoms phase (Clancy 1985; M. P. Hoffman 1986). There are some resemblances to the Menard Complex (formerly called "Quapaw phase"; see below). The time period is estimated to be around 1400 to 1650.

## Middle Arkansas River

The main criterion used to identify Protohistoric sites in central Arkansas is the presence of one or more Nodena points (Martha Rolingson, personal communication). Menard Complex ceramics were also useful for identification (John House, personal communication). A major published site is Kinkead-Mainard (M. P. Hoffman 1977). Diagnostic pottery includes Wallace Incised, Old Town Red, Keno Trailed, Barton Incised, Parkin Punctated, "Teapot"-shape, "helmet"-bowl shape, and the "hour-glass" bottleneck shape. European artifacts (beads made of glass, brass, and bronze) have been found in association with these artifacts at the Goldsmith-Oliver site, suggesting a terminal date around 1600–50 for the complex (M. T. Smith 1989a, Leader 1989, Jeter, Cande, and Mintz 1990).

## Southeast Arkansas

The southeastern quarter of the state may be the location of as many as a dozen Protohistoric phases or geographical clusters of Protohistoric sites, all of which may not be contemporaneous with one another (John House, personal communications). Three of these are actually mostly in northeast Arkansas (including the Kent and Old Town phases) and two are mainly located in central Arkansas.

The major grouping is known as the "Menard Complex." Three to four very tentative phases are proposed (by John House and others), but for now "Menard Complex" is sufficient to describe the Protohistoric remains on the lower Arkansas River below Little Rock. Together with sites farther upstream and with sites on the White River, the "Menard Complex" (formerly "Quapaw phase") may actually be ancestral to Tunica rather than to Quapaw Indians. Nodena points constitute the main artifact used to identify sites, and pottery diagnostics already mentioned for central Arkansas reinforce those identifications.

The identification of the Tillar and Hog Lake complexes or phases of the southeast Arkansas "Delta" interior is also dependent on shell-tempered ceramics (dating after 1400), particularly Winterville Incised, Barton Incised, Parkin Punctated, and Leland Incised, plus some resemblances to Menard Complex ceramics. Arrow points are very rare, but resemble the Jordan type of northeast Louisiana, stemmed with barbed shoulders. The Wilmot phase, along Bayou Bartholomew near the Louisiana state line, has been defined by Rolingson (1976:117). Shell-tempered ceramics are characteristic; Winterville Incised and Parkin Punctated are prominent. The phase seems to represent a single dispersed population around a ceremonial center. The dating of this phase would seem to be from around 1400 or 1500 to 1650.

The Caney Bayou phase was described for the Felsenthal region of the Ouachita Valley by Rolingson and Schambach (1981). It is represented by a predominance of shell-tempered ceramics including Winterville Incised. Nodena points occur but are not definitely associated with this phase (Hemmings 1982a). They may be representative of intrusive hunting camps. The guess date for this phase is 1500–1700.

## Ouachita Mountains

The mountainous region between the Coastal Plain and the upper Arkansas River is relatively unknown. Some of this lack of data is due to an absence of late Caddo remains in parts of this region, but in other areas Caddo IV ceramics do exist (Ann Early, personal communication). There are six possible complexes or site clusters which date between 1500 and 1700 (Ann Early, personal communication).

## Southwest Arkansas

The sites chosen by Schambach are of the Caddo IV culture period, and date to around 1500–1700. The two phases are Texarkana, located north of the town (E. M. Davis 1970; Schambach and Rackerby 1982) and Belcher, located south of Fulton, mainly in Louisiana (Webb 1959, Schambach 1982). The pottery assemblage outlined by Schambach and Rackerby (1982:9) for Caddo IV in the Great Bend region is the basis for identification.

### Protohistoric Population

The beauty of this approach is that phase or complex territories do not have to be guessed at in a map. Sites are selected and reviewed without regard to location, then the computer defines population clusters by plotting the sites. To make the site map more meaningful, we defined types of sites as follows. There are sites ranging up to twenty-eight acres in size. We arbitrarily differentiated between "larger" and "smaller" sites by choosing one acre as the criterion of size. This helps us to get a feel for population since most Caddoan, Felsenthal region, and interior southeast Arkansas sites are small and are representative of a dispersed settlement system. Most Mississippian sites in the rest of the state, on the other hand, are large and are representative of major nucleated populations, probably mostly distributed in fortified town sites.

Probable mid sixteenth-century Spanish artifacts have been found at a few sites. These sites are represented on the map by large circles. This is an important distinction, since the presence of Spanish artifacts could indicate the occurrence of direct contact.

Many sites in northeast Arkansas are known only by the presence of Nodena points. Most have produced one or two points. A very few have produced many points. Two and possibly three distinct hunting areas have now been discovered, represented by a single large hunting site (base?) and several single occurrence sites (camps?) located nearby (Morse 1986a). This observation is important because Biedma (Bourne 1904, 2:29–30) described hunters in an area uninhabited by Protohistoric villages. Not all of these sites have been plotted to date because they are still being recognized through a general review process. We did not know twenty-five years ago that Nodena points were diagnostic of the 1400–1650 time period, and those points collected are not yet segregated from other arrow points in our collections.

## SUMMARY

The Arkansas Archeological Survey has the computer know-how and equipment to produce a distribution map of Protohistoric archeological sites. In addition, its personnel have the detailed knowledge necessary to identify late sites after twenty-five years of intensive research in the archeology of the state from 9,500 B.C. to the present.

The site files and collections had to be reviewed since the twenty-five years of accumulated data have not yet been fully incorporated into the computerized site files. This review took two full years by many individuals working simultaneously.

No single artifactual criterion could be used to identify Protohistoric sites. The state of Arkansas is a political region including various major ecological zones, including mountains, delta, coastal plain and wide alluvial valleys, and varied Protohistoric cultures.

The computer definition of "Protohistoric" is a compromise. We only know at best seven locations which have produced probable sixteenth-century Spanish artifacts. This is an insufficient sample to give us meaningful data on the sixteenth-century population in Arkansas. We defined the Protohistoric in its broadest possible meaning, about 1400–1500 to about 1650–1700. In eastern Arkansas the date is 1400–1650 while in southwestern Arkansas the date is 1500–1700. The reasons for this approach are to provide (1) an ample sample of sites and (2) an easily recognized minimal time period which encompasses the 1541–43 required time period. If the population of 1400–1650 was distributed in distinct geographical clusters, then this is probably indicative of a stable population in most of these cases which can be interpreted as representative of the period 1541–43.

The results are spectacular. We now have the basis for connecting prehistoric populations with known Indian tribes of the eighteenth century. We also have a basis for accurately determining the route of de Soto, the first European to directly impact upon the natives of Arkansas. Phyllis A. Morse (this volume) has specifically used the map to plot the route in northeast Arkansas. Other chapters in this volume used this map to help the respective authors investigate the route of de Soto.

I wish to particularly thank Marvin Jeter for many helpful suggestions and his editing proficiency. The present paper is a result of three years of work by many individuals who are referenced in the appropriate places in the manuscript.

# Reconstruction of the de Soto Expedition Route in Arkansas: The Mississippi Alluvial Plain

David H. Dye

> It is unsafe to regard any point [along the de Soto route] as established unless it can stand on its own merits by close agreement with existing topographical and archaeological conditions. Only such points can be used as anchors for a certain distance forward and backward along the route. (Phillips, Ford, and Griffin 1951:383)

A great deal of ink has been spilled concerning the route of the Hernando de Soto entrada generally, and the point at which the expedition crossed the Mississippi River on June 18, 1541, specifically. The first careful consideration of the route and the Mississippi River crossing was made in 1718 by the French cartographer Guillaume de l'Isle, who based his map on Elvas (Swanton 1939:12–13). Over the years archeologists and historians have attempted to define the route throughout the Southeast, but much of the discussion has been little more than idle speculation until the archeological chronology was strengthened through the application of relative dating (seriation) in the 1940s and chronometric (radiocarbon) dating after 1950. During the early years, prior to a consideration of temporal placement of archeological sites, the usual procedure was:

> to establish the approximate location of events and places described in the narratives by a combination of dead reckoning and topographical study; then having established such locations, to look for archaeological sites on the ground tallying with them, without regard to the all-important question as to *when* such sites were being occupied. (Phillips, Ford, and Griffin 1951:361)

Phillips, Ford, and Griffin's (1951:364) Lower Mississippi Survey provided for the first time data which could: "provide a rough working hypothesis in terms of a tentative ceramic scale that will eliminate some of the uncertainty that has resulted from the indiscriminate use of archaeological data by De Soto scholars in the past."

Their relative chronology, based primarily on ceramic seriation, provided the means to establish an archeological sequence which in broad outline is still in use today. Phillips, Ford, and Griffin's primary interest in the de Soto route was the hope that the 1541 date line would contribute to the archeological chronology (Phillips, Ford, and Griffin 1951:362).

Phillips, in taking exception to the route proposed by the U.S. De Soto Expedition Commission Report (Swanton 1939), pointed out that Swanton and his co-workers had been "obliged to work almost without benefit of archaelogy" (Phillips, Ford, and Griffin 1951:361). Phillips, Ford, and Griffin's extensive archeological survey from southeastern Missouri to southeastern Arkansas reported in 1951 provided archeological data which had not been available during the 1930s when Swanton was preparing the commission report. Phillips, Ford, and Griffin (1951:361–62) succinctly summarized a basic flaw of the Swanton report: "Little attention has been paid to the archaeological character of the sites or the materials found on them. Obviously, it is not sufficient that a given site occurs in a place that satisfies documentary requirements, it must also have existed at the proper time." Phillips, Ford, and Griffin (1951:362) hoped to "set up an hypothetical 1541 period in terms of archeology—within limits that will at least eliminate a large number of sites from consideration—and test this working hypothesis against the narratives and the De Soto Commission's interpretation of them."

## THE COMMERCE LANDING CROSSING

In locating the route, Phillips, Ford, and Griffin followed Theodore H. Lewis' (1902) topographic interpretation which he based primarily on Ranjel (Oviedo y Valdés 1851–55). Lewis (1900, 1901, 1901a) had earlier published the first English translation of Ranjel, albeit abridged, and he used it to reconstruct the de Soto route (Swanton 1939:7). Lewis was later supported by Dunbar Rowland (1927, 1927a) and Charles A. Barton (1927). Phillips, Ford, and Griffin (1951:385) noted that Lewis' theory that the de Soto expedition crossed the Mississippi River at Tunica or Commerce Landing and the subsequent route through the Mississippi Valley "makes a good deal of sense both topographically and archaeologically." Thus, both Lewis (1902:455) and Phillips, Ford, and Griffin (1951:391) placed the entrada on the Mississippi River at Commerce Landing (Council or Walnut Bend), which they identified as the 1541 Province of Quizquiz. Upon crossing the river, the expedition traveled to the vicinity of the mouth of the Tyronza River (Lewis 1902:457; Phillips, Ford, and Griffin 1951:387) to the "capital" of the Casqui polity. Lewis (1902:457) placed Pacaha in the vicinity of Osceola, Arkansas, while Phillips, Ford, and Griffin (1951:387) set Pacaha twenty kilometers south of Osceola near Wilson, Arkansas. Lewis (1902:457) located the polity of Quiguate "on the west side of the St. Francis river, in the northern part of Lee County or the southern part of St. Francis County." Phillips, Ford, and Griffin (1951:388) believed Lewis' location of Quiguate was the "essential weakness" of his theory, but nevertheless accepted it for lack of a better archeological and topographical configuration. Lewis (1902:457-458) and Phillips (1951:388) agreed the River of Coligua mentioned in the narratives was the White River (Phillips, Ford, and Griffin 1951:388).

Dan F. Morse and Phyllis A. Morse (1983:308–13) followed the Lewis-Phillips route, but added significant archeological and topographic details. They placed the expedition at specific archeological sites along the route and correlated 1541 native polities with archeological phases. Charles Hudson (1985), with help from local archeologists, adopted much of the Lewis-Phillips-Morse route with several changes. He moved the 1541 province of Quizquiz north from Commerce Landing to the Lake Cormorant area, placed Pacaha between Pecan Point and Wapanocca Lake (Bradley Ridge), identified Quiguate with the Kent archeological phase and the town of Grant, and associated the polity of Coligua with the Greenbrier archeological phase. Hudson was the first scholar since Lewis to tie the Mississippi Valley portion of the route to an overall route scenario. Morse and Morse (1990) have since reiterated the basic theme of Hudson's model.

## THE MEMPHIS CROSSING, FRIARS POINT CROSSING, AND SUNFLOWER LANDING CROSSING

Alternative views to the Commerce Landing crossing site have been proposed. Memphis, Tennessee, as the point of crossing was a favorite among nineteenth-century historians (See Brain 1985:xxxiv–xxxv; Malone 1922; Swanton 1939:12–46; 234–38; Young 1927), beginning with Thomas Nuttall (1821:248) in the early portion of the century, but it currently lacks endorsement from archeologists and ethnohistorians and is no longer considered a viable candidate as a crossing locale. The Friars Point Crossing (Atkinson 1987; Brain, Toth, and Rodriguez-Buckingham 1974; Brain 1978, 1984, 1985, 1985a) and the Sunflower Landing crossing (Swanton 1939, Weinstein 1985) have received serious attention in recent years based on archeological and physiographic grounds.

## THE NORFOLK LANDING CROSSING

In this paper I take a detailed look at specific physiographic landmarks noted by the Spanish chroniclers during de Soto's May 8 to September 10, 1541, 312-kilometer trek across the Mississippi Alluvial Plain and place them on the contemporary landscape (illustration 8) based on a detailed geomorphic reconstruction of the sixteenth-century terrain. Emphasis is placed on identifying geomorphic features mentioned in the ethnohistorical texts and evaluating the viability of the Norfolk Landing crossing, rather than attempting to identify a specific crossing point relative to other hypothetical crossing scenarios. Information concerning the regional alluvial physiography (Fisk 1944; Saucier 1964, 1974, 1981) provides data which is used in conjunction with ethnohistorical documentation (Elvas, Biedma, and Ranjel in Bourne 1904; Garcilaso 1951) and archeological knowledge (Morse and Morse 1983:305–15; Phillips 1970; Phillips, Ford, and Griffin 1951:348–91) to pinpoint geomorphic features in the Mississippi Alluvial Plain recorded by the de Soto expedition participants.

## NARRATIVES OF THE EXPEDITION IN THIS STUDY

Primary emphasis has been placed on the eyewitness accounts of Luýs Hernández de Biedma, the king's factor or accountant, and of Rodrigo Ranjel, de Soto's private secretary. Both individuals apparently kept diaries during the entrada.

The Biedma account has been considered an unreliable source for specific information about the entrada or the terrain over which it passed (Anderson 1990a:97), while Ranjel's account is considered the most reliable (Bourne 1904, 1:xvi; Hudson, Smith, and DePratter 1984; Swanton 1932:571).

A third account, by an anonymous expedition member from Elvas, is noteworthy for its abundance of detail about the expedition, the landscape over which the Spaniards traveled, and the native people they encountered. The Elvas account has been used in this study to provide additional detail to the Ranjel account, but the use of the Elvas account does not change the basic scenario presented by Ranjel.

A fourth account written by Garcilaso de la Vega (1951) between approximately 1587 and 1591 is the least reliable with regard to place and time (Henige 1986a; Hudson 1987a:1; Hudson, Smith, and DePratter 1984:655; Swanton 1932:571). Born in 1537, Garcilaso did not accompany the expedition. Much of his information came from Gonzalo Silvestre, a survivor of the expedition, with additional information from two other expedition members, Alonso de Carmona and Juan Coles (Swanton 1939:5–6). Garcilaso has been used sparingly in this study.

## THE STUDY AREA

The Mississippi Alluvial Plain (Omernik 1987) in the Memphis vicinity (illustration 9) is bounded on the east by loess uplands and on the west by the Ozark Plateaus. West of the Mississippi River, within the plain, Crowley's Ridge, a low, narrow, erosional remnant, divides the floodplain into two entrenched valleys, the Eastern and Western Lowlands. Topographic and fluvial features further subdivide the plain into basins and lowlands on the eastern (Yazoo Basin) and western (St. Francis Basin) sides of the Mississippi River (illustration 10).

In order to provide detailed areal measurements of sunk lands, natural levees, backswamps, and meander lakes,[1] and to measure linear distances accurately, a base map was constructed using fifteen minute topographic quadrangles for the study area.[2] Soil associations, indicating natural levee and backswamp soils, were drafted from U.S.G.S county soil surveys. Meander lakes were taken from geological maps (Kolb, et al. 1968; Saucier 1964; F. Smith and Saucier 1971). Sixteenth-century Mississippi River channel reconstructions are based on Fisk's (1944:Plate 22) Mississippi River Channel 15.[3] The various maps were registered, the data superimposed, and a detailed, cumulative map subsequently compiled (illustration 8).

## RECONSTRUCTION OF THE ROUTE

According to the route proposed in this study, the Hernando de Soto entrada entered the Mississippi Alluvial Plain near present-day Walls, Mississippi, on May 8, 1541. They had reached the area after traveling northwest across northern Mississippi from their winter encampment among the Chickasaw near Columbus, Mississippi (Hudson, Smith, and DePratter 1990:196–97). This route, originally proposed by Perino (1966: 140–41), has more recently been supported by Hudson and others (Hudson 1985:3; Hudson, DePratter, and Smith 1989:88, Hudson, Smith, and DePratter 1990:200–01; Morse and Morse 1990:201; G. P. Smith 1990:167).

The expedition wintered among the Chickasaw in 1540–41. The winter encampment has not been located, but is believed to be in the Tibbee Creek area (Atkinson 1987; Hudson, DePratter, and Smith 1989:88, Hudson, Smith, and DePratter 1990:194–96). After recovering from a Chickasaw dawn attack on March 4, 1541 (Elvas in Bourne 1904, 1:103–06; Ranjel in Bourne 1904, 2:133–34; Biedma in Bourne 1904, 2:22–23), and an aborted Chickasaw raid on March 15 (Ranjel in Bourne 1904, 2:135), the Spanish expedition moved a short distance northwestward on April 26 to the adjacent province of Alibamo in their search for food so they might prepare for travel through an unpopulated land. The Spaniards spent the night in a small Alibamo town.

On April 28 they arrived at an Alibamo fortification, which was located by a scouting party of fifteen horsemen and forty footmen led by the expedition *contador* or accountant, Captain Juan de Añasco on April 26 (Elvas in Bourne 1904, 1:108). De Soto and members of the expedition attacked the fortification and eventually captured it. Neither the town nor the fortification has been located, but the upper tributaries of Tibbee Creek, especially lower Line Creek in the vicinity of the Lyon's Bluff site (22OK1) (Hudson, Smith, and DePratter 1990:196) or Chuquatonchee Creek and Houlka Creek (Atkinson 1987:67–68) have been suggested as the sixteenth-century Alibamo locale.

When de Soto left the Alibamo territory he made preparations to head directly for the Mississippi River, even though he was told it required crossing "a deserted country and by a rough way" for twelve days (Ranjel in Bourne 1904, 2:137). De Soto was apprised by Chickasaw prisoners of the "region in advance" upon leaving the Chickasaw polity (Elvas in Bourne 1904, 1:108). The prisoners may have informed de Soto of the Mississippi Valley's extant human populations and resources and may have guided the expedition there. The Spaniards typically had access, usually through force, to native geographic knowledge and local guides to lead the expedition to populous areas for clothing, food, labor, and services.

De Soto knew from experience in Central and South America that silver, gold, and precious gems would be found in mountainous areas and that native wealth would be controlled by powerful and centralized political formations. That de Soto had such a scenario in mind is borne out by his determined efforts to head for the largest polity in the Central Mississippi Valley, Pacaha,[5] within close proximity of mountains (Ozark Plateaus). The journey to Pacaha, in fact, required the expedition to take a forty-kilometer detour around a swamp bordering the Mississippi.

On April 30, the entrada began an eight-and-one-half-day trek across northern Mississippi from the Alibamo fortification toward the Mississippi River. They passed through a buffer zone or unpopulated "wilderness," described as pondy or swampy, but fordable on horseback; some basins or lakes were negotiated by swimming (Elvas in Bourne 1904, 1:110–11). Two centuries later, on February 20, 1740, Captain Pierre-Joseph Céloron de Blainville, leading an army of 201 Frenchmen and 395 Indians against the Chickasaw, portrayed the northern Mississippi uplands in a strikingly similar manner to Elvas' description: "We camped after having marched constantly through very rough country, cut up by rivers, streams and swamps all covered very thickly with cane" (Chaussegros de Léry 1923:160).[6]

## The Province of Quizquiz

After negotiating the northern Mississippi uplands, through the Yalobusha, Yocona, and Tallahatchie headwaters, the expedition, most likely the vanguard, encountered the first Quizquiz[7] town on May 8, 1541. Quizquiz, a vassal polity of the upriver Pacaha chiefdom (Biedma in Bourne 1904, 2:25), is believed to be the archeological Walls phase (Hudson 1985:3; Hudson, Smith, and DePratter 1990:202–03; Perino 1966:140–41; G. P. Smith 1990:134–40).

Six towns located on the twenty-four-square-kilometer Walls and four-square-kilometer Norfolk Meanders, and their sixty-six square kilometers of associated natural levees, form the core archeological expression of this fifteenth- and sixteenth-century polity (Brown 1926:288–320; Phillips 1970:936–38; Phillips, Ford, and Griffin 1951:243–53). Additional northern and southern outlying towns and hamlets are included in the current definition of the Walls archeological phase (G. P. Smith 1990:134–40). The Walls phase locality is bounded on the north and west by the Mississippi River, the east by loess bluffs (Fourth Chickasaw Bluff), and the south by an extensive rimswamp (Coldwater Lowland). These physiographic constraints demarcate the Walls phase as a tight cluster of sites on the Mississippi's eastern side (Phillips 1970:936).

The first town encountered by the expedition, within two leagues[8] (9.6 kilometers) of the Mississippi (Biedma in Bourne 1904, 2:25), was attacked by surprise at midday on the May 8 (Ranjel in Bourne 1904, 2:137). All of the people were seized, including some 300 women, among whom was the chief's mother. The men were not captured, as they were working in the horticultural fields away from the village, probably preparing the gardens for planting. Much clothing was appropriated, especially items made of animal skins and woven shawls, but little maize was found. De Soto released his captives and returned their goods for fear of reprisals. However, he requested their canoes in order to cross the Mississippi, which he had not seen, but knew was in the immediate vicinity. The Spaniards first heard of Quizquiz's vassalage to Pacaha at this first Quizquiz town (Biedma in Bourne 1904, 2:25).

The next day "many Indians came, with bows and arrows," but stopped at the distance of a crossbow shot[9] near a river bank. Six "chiefs" (elite individuals) approached the Spanish camp and presented skin clothing and shawls and then returned to the others who awaited them near the shore. The elite individuals and their followers left without an altercation, but did not provide the requested canoes.

The chroniclers clearly identified the physiographic position of this town. It was on a body of water with access to the Mississippi River, which was located nearby. The maize fields must have been located west of the town. Presumably this was in the opposite direction of the Spanish approach, which would have been from the east. Also, the town may have been relatively small because only a small amount of maize was found there. The town does not appear to have been the seat of political power, as the chief and additional elites, perhaps his retinue, had come from another town to this Quizquiz town.

The Irby site (22DS516), believed to be this first Quizquiz town, is located on a natural levee west of Johnson Creek and south of the Walls Meander and is a modest (5.4 hectare) site on the eastern periphery of the Walls archeological settlement. Johnson Creek drains the adjacent uplands, cuts through a twenty-eight-meter loess bluff, and flows into the Walls Meander. The Spanish expedition could have descended the bluff by way of Johnson Creek Valley. By staying south of the creek it would not have been necessary to cross it. Native guides (Chickasaw or Alibamo) would have taken the expedition directly to the town, approaching it from the southeast. The town, which does not seem to have been fortified, may not have been heavily defended because it faced a two-hundred-kilometer buffer zone between the Alibamo, Chakchiuma, and Chickasaw to the east.

The Walls phase political center appears to have been the Walls site (22DS500), located north of the Walls Meander from Irby, some 9.6 kilometers to the northwest. Walls may have been the residence of the elites and "nobles" who accompanied their ruling elites to Irby, waiting on the north side of the Walls Meander. Accordingly, the Irby farmlands would have been located on the broad natural levee west of Johnson Creek and the loess bluff.

Upon leaving the first Quizquiz town, apparently on May 9, the expedition traveled a league (4.8 kilometers), presumably along the meander's natural levee, with the meander lake to the north and the backswamp to the south. At the second town they found an abundance of maize (Ranjel in Bourne 1904, 2:137). This town may be the Lake Cormorant site (22DS501) (Phillips, Ford, and Griffin 1951:248–53), a 3.0 hectare habitation positioned where a Walls Meander overflow channel (Lake Cormorant Bayou) drains south into the 176 square kilometer Coldwater Lowland.

They then moved another league (4.8 kilometers) to the third town, which was also amply provisioned (Ranjel in Bourne 1904, 2:137). They saw the Mississippi River for the first time half a league from this village (Elvas in Bourne 1904, 1:112). While at this town, de Soto went to assess the river and to locate a suitable encampment. He found an area containing a quantity of sizeable timber for building barges and a plain suitable for locating a good camp.

The Woodlyn site (22DS517), a 2.5-hectare town on the Norfolk Meander, may have been this third town where a temporary camp was established for approximately two weeks while the entrada scavenged nearby towns for food, building supplies, and clothing. The sixteenth-century Mississippi River channel would have been 1.1 kilometers southwest of Woodlyn. The Woodlyn location would have been attractive from a strategic point of view. The site lay between two large lakes (Walls and Norfolk Meanders) and could be easily defended. Access to both lakes would have provided the Spaniards with food from other lakeside towns. De Soto may have ordered crews to establish the encampment before moving there.

On May 21, they set out from this town (Woodlyn) to a plain or savannah, between the river and a small village, a fourth town mentioned by Ranjel (Bourne 1904, 2:137). The encampment, a crossbow shot (273 meters) from the river, was established to construct four barges, each capable of carrying 60 to 70 people and 5 to 6 horses (Biedman in Bourne 1904, 2:26). Food from towns previously visited was brought to the encampment.

The encampment may have been near the Norfolk site (22DS513), a small town on the Norfolk Meander 1.3 kilometers east of the sixteenth-century Mississippi. Norfolk site was destroyed in the 1970s, but in 1940 Phillip Philips described it as a "small village."[10] If Norfolk site was the small town mentioned by Ranjel, then the entrada moved 1.6 kilometers southwest from Woodlyn and immediately southwest of the Norfolk site.

References to plains or savannahs in the Mississippi Alluvial Plain in many instances may indicate natural levees with tall grass prairies or old field successional vegetation. The Walls area physiography would have dictated the Spaniards' placement of the encampment south of the Norfolk site because of the Norfolk Meander to the north, the Mississippi River to the west, the Coldwater Lowland to the south, and the Walls Meander to the east (illustration 11).

During the expedition's stay at the Norfolk Landing encampment, native armed forces set out across the Mississippi River each day from the Mississippi's western bank. Warriors of the Pacaha chiefdom of the Aquixo polity, located west of the Mississippi River, monitored the expedition's progress each afternoon from the vantage of a flotilla of 200 to 250 large war canoes (Biedma in Bourne 1904, 2:26; Elvas in Bourne 1904, 1:112–13; Ranjel in Bourne 1904, 2:137–38).

Timber for the barges could have been obtained in the Norfolk Landing area. Cypress trees could have been cut from the swamp at the western end of the Norfolk Meander immediately to the north. Oaks and other hardwoods could be taken from the cut bank two to three kilometers to the south.

## Crossing the Mississippi River

The barges were completed on June 17, twenty-seven days after moving from Woodlyn. The Spaniards began crossing the Mississippi the next day (Ranjel in Bourne 1904, 2:138), three hours before dawn (Elvas in Bourne 1904, 1:114) or approximately 1:50 A.M. All made the crossing by two hours after sunrise or 6:45 A.M. A waning crescent moon rose at 12:30 A.M. and may have provided sufficient light by 1:50 A.M. for the expedition to begin crossing under cover of darkness. The crossing took approximately five hours and could have been made in two trips.

In the first crossing, commanded by Captain Juan de Guzman, four horsemen went in each of the three barges; accompanied by some of the crossbowmen "of foot," and men without horses, the "infantry." Presumably, the barges were tied together as oarsmen in the fourth barge paddled the expedition to the other side (Elvas in Bourne 1904, 1:115).

Guzman took the barges upriver along the eastern riverbank a quarter of a league (1.4 kilometers) upriver before crossing in order to land opposite the camp. To determine how far the barges would have to be taken upriver required knowledge of the river currents perhaps obtained from the Quizquiz. Before landing, at twice the distance of a stone's throw (seventy-five to one hundred meters), the horsemen rode out from the barges to an open area of hard and even ground. To leave the barges on horseback required landing near a shallow shelf adjacent to a point bar in shallow water extending out into the Mississippi; they could not have scaled a Mississippi River concave bank, nor could they have paddled along the riverbank on a bend, because of the swift current. The evidence suggests they were in a reach between bends (illustration 12).

The distance across the river at the crossing site was estimated as half a league (2.8 kilometers) (Elvas in Bourne 1904, 1:115). The Mississippi River at Norfolk Landing in 1981 was 2.5 kilometers wide, suggesting that the Spanish estimate is reasonably close to the modern channel configuration in the Norfolk Landing vicinity, although the river has moved 300 meters to the west.

To avoid being swept toward the concave bank (east) downriver, the lead barge would have had to be paddled rapidly to overcome the prevailing current, which would have crossed the river diagonally from the upriver concave (west) bank. That is, the thread of maximum surface velocity in the reach would have been the middle of the river as it migrated from the upriver concave bank to the downriver concave bank (Kniffen 1968:46; Russell 1967:9). Once the maximum current was overcome, the barges could have been paddled with less difficulty because the currents would have been weaker. Counter currents might have been helpful.

Many trees and much timber are reported to have been brought downriver (Elvas in Bourne 1904, 1:115), perhaps indicating the river was at flood stage (Phillips, Ford, and Griffin 1951:353). Flood stage at Memphis in 1990 was 10.2 meters; between 1944 and 1986 the mean high river was 8.1 meters, 2.1 meters below flood stage, casting doubt that the river was flooding at the time the de Soto expedition crossed. Bank erosion and sloughing could have accounted for the timber floating downriver.

During their stay at both the temporary camp (Woodlyn) and the encampment (near Norfolk), de Soto and his "officers" may have studied the prevailing currents and discussed various options with local elites who would have known the crossing locales and the characteristics and locations of various currents. In fact, de Soto could have observed and employed the river crossing route and procedures used by the Aquixo on their trips across the Mississippi. The encampment may have been located near a canoe landing as indicated by the Aquixo beaching their war canoes when the encampment was constructed.

## The Province of Aquixo

The expedition's activities for the remainder of June 18 remain unclear, but it would have been unusual had de Soto not sent expeditionary forces scouting the immediate area for clothing, food, and local informants. A punitive raid by the vanguard or expeditionary force at a nearby town would have been especially crucial in subduing the local population considering de Soto's firsthand knowledge of the Aquixos' capacity and ability to draft a sizable armed population capable of sophisticated military maneuvers. Aquixo not only had the military capability, but may have had close political ties with Pacaha. The main body of the expedition may have regrouped and rested on the eighteenth; if they worked until sunset (7:16 P.M.) the day before with crossing preparations and began crossing three hours before sunup (1:50 A.M.), they may have had little rest the night prior to the crossing.

On the nineteenth (Ranjel in Bourne 1904, 2:138), they set out toward a town near the river and 1.5 leagues (8.4 kilometers) upriver (north) from the crossing (Elvas in Bourne 1904, 1:116). The main force would have arrived mid-morning at this first Aquixo town, which may have been discovered and assaulted on the eighteenth by a scouting party, perhaps explaining the village's abandonment. The town had access to the Mississippi via a waterway, as the barges used in the crossing were taken by water to the town to be dismantled (Elvas in Bourne 1904, 1:116–17, Ranjel in Bourne 1904, 2:138).

The task force taking the barges by water to the Aquixo town were attacked by some Aquixo who hid among the river bank ravines. The Spaniards were forced to stay close to the river bank because of the swift current. Eroded steep banks, creating ravines, created a concave bank north of the Norfolk Landing crossing place on the west bank. Three-and-a-half kilometers upstream from the crossing at Norfolk Landing, a concave bank is found on the western side of the river. The Aquixo who attacked the men transporting the barges upstream may have been from the Rhodes site (3CT3), a 9.6-hectare habitation 6.4 kilometers north of this bend.

Pouncey (3CT34), a 5.8-hectare Horseshoe Lake phase archeological site on a natural levee with a meander lake (Patoka) nearby and 12.8 kilometers northwest of the Norfolk Landing crossing, fits the physiographic requirements for the town visited on June 19. The site has two large pyramidal mounds with smaller house mounds arranged around a plaza (Phillips, Ford, and Griffin 1951:386). The thirty-four-square-kilometer Patoka Meander is east of a twenty-seven-square-kilometer natural levee. Six Horseshoe Lake phase archeological sites are located on the Patoka Meander's natural levee (G. P. Smith 1990:157–59). The expedition would have been forced to travel west and then north around the lake because of the lake's proximity and connection to the Mississippi River.

The Spaniards captured fifteen of thirty Aquixo who approached "over a plain" to spy on the expedition (Elvas in Bourne 1904, 1:116). From them de Soto learned the neighboring polity, Casqui, was three days' travel, presumably to the west (Elvas in Bourne 1904, 1:107). Mention of the plain confirms the location of a natural levee west and immediately upriver from the crossing.

The Spaniards dismantled the barges on June 20 in this town (Pouncey) to salvage the metal spikes used in their construction (Elvas in Bourne 1904, 1:116–17). The expedition may have spent the night here, although Elvas (Bourne 1904, 1:122) stated they spent one night, which would have been the night of June 19. However, Ranjel (Bourne 1904, 2:138) noted they arrived on June 19 and did not leave until June 21.

On June 21 they departed the town (Pouncey) and "went in quest of a province called Pacaha . . . where the Indians said there was gold" (Elvas in Bourne 1904, 1:117).

The Spaniards had heard of Pacaha while at Quizquiz (Biedma in Bourne 1904, 2:25) and may have become aware of it from Alibamo captives even earlier during their residency among the Chickasaw. The Spaniards were told that Pacaha was a "lord of wide repute and highly thought of in that country" (Ranjel in Bourne 1904, 2:139) and "famed throughout all the land" (Biedma in Bourne 1904, 2:25). During the twenty-first, the entrada passed several large Aquixo villages "beautifully situated"; possibly the archeological sites of Edmondson (3CT33) (1.8 hectares) and Turner (3CT32) (0.06 hectares) to the expedition's north. The "beautiful situation" of the Aquixo towns almost certainly alludes to their location on the elevated and productive Patoka Meander natural levee (Phillips, Ford, and Griffin 1951:376).

The Spaniards then came to a small river over which they built a bridge (Elvas in Bourne 1904, 1:117). The river may have been Fifteen Mile Bayou (Lewis 1902:456), a Mississippi River bypass or diversion channel and a major eastern drainage for a large swamp to the north and west. The night of the twenty-first may have been spent at the Young site (3CT10), a town approximately 6 hectares in size, located east of Fifteen Mile Bayou, to prepare for crossing the large swamp immediately to the west.

On June 22 they crossed the river (perhaps Fifteen Mile Bayou) and descended into a swamp, "the worst tract for swamps and water that they had found in all Florida" (Ranjel in Bourne 1904, 2:138). Elvas (Bourne 1904, 1:117) records the experience as walking through "water, in places coming to the knees; in others, as high as the waist" until sunset. If the Spaniards came out of the swamp at sunset, presumably they spent the night in the swamp's immediate vicinity.

The swamp crossed by the expedition is identified here as a 274-square-kilometer backswamp located at West Memphis. The swamp was created by alluvial drowning as a result of Mississippi meander belt aggradation to the east and St. Francis and Mississippi River meander belt aggradation to the west. Phillips, Ford, and Griffin (1951:386) note that any route between the Mississippi River and the St. Francis River "would have involved the Spaniards in the backswamp lying between the present Mississippi meander belt and the older St. Francis segment of the Mississippi meander belt."

If the Spanish traveled through the swamp for ten hours at 0.8 kilometers per hour, about half the normal expedition speed, then the point at which they crossed would have been approximately 8.4 kilometers wide. According to modern geological maps (Saucier 1964), the shortest path across the swamp is 8.4 kilometers in the vicinity of the Young site. This swamp served as an important natural boundary separating neighboring Mississippian polities: the Wapanocca District of the Nodena phase (the polity of Pacaha) to the north, the Horseshoe Lake phase (the polity of Aquixo) to the south, the Parkin phase (the polity of Casqui) to the west, and the Walls phase (the polity of Quizquiz) to the east (illustration 13).

## The Province of Casqui

De Soto did not proceed directly to Pacaha according to this route scenario because he was forced to circumvent this large swamp. Instead, the expedition traveled forty kilometers out of its way. Of course, the detour may have been made to enlist Casqui's aid in thwarting a potential conflict with Pacaha; de Soto knew of their enmity (Biedma in

Bourne 1904, 2:26; Elvas in Bourne 1904, 1:121; Ranjel in Bourne 1904, 2:139) and would have taken advantage of native power struggles as he had done many times in the past. On the other hand, de Soto could not have gauged how well Casqui would have received him. All in all, de Soto probably would have taken a direct route if the opportunity had been available.

The higher ground encountered by the expedition on June 23 appears to have been the natural levee west of the swamp (Saucier 1964). Vegetation for the higher ground mentioned in the accounts, common persimmon (*Diospyros virginiana*), pecan (*Carya illinoensis*), and red mulberry (*Morus rubra*), seen growing in the horticultural fields (Elvas in Bourne 1904, 1:117–18), supports a natural levee interpretation. These three species are constituents of Mississippi Alluvial Plain bottomland hardwood forests such as the sugarberry-ash-pecan forest occupying lands flooding less than 10 percent of the time (Arkansas Department of Planning 1974:176; Braun 1950:163, 295; Fowells 1965:121–22, 168–69; Pell 1983:21; Putnam and Bull 1932:23, 28, 73; Shelford 1963:100).

Part of the day of June 23 may have been spent drying clothing and supplies which became wet while crossing the swamp. However, by midday they arrived at the first Casqui towns. They took two towns by surprise, as had been the case at Quizquiz, capturing many men and women and much clothing, blankets, and skins. They probably traveled no more than three leagues (16.8 kilometers) from the swamp to these towns. Unfortunately, the towns have not been identified archeologically. The second town was half a league (2.8 kilometers) from the first (Elvas in Bourne 1904, 1:117), presumably to the west. The entrada apparently spent the night in the vicinity of the two towns, although no specific town is mentioned as a bivouac.

These Casqui towns were small and the land higher, drier, and more level than any they had seen since crossing the Mississippi (Elvas in Bourne 1904, 1:117). This statement characterizes the natural levee topography (Phillips, Ford, and Griffin 1951:378) in the east central area of the Parkin archeological phase; the relative elevation west of the swamp is approximately two meters higher than the swamp's eastern side: The natural levee elevation east of the swamp is approximately sixty-three meters above mean sea level, the swamp sixty meters amsl, and the area west of the swamp sixty-five meters amsl. A mosaic of natural levees could be followed to the St. Francis River from the swamp's western side.

On June 24, the entrada traveled to the main Casqui town. Elvas (Bourne 1904, 1:118) noted they continued to pass through horticultural fields, among which were many great towns, located close together; from any single town, one could see two or three others. But Ranjel (Bourne 1904, 2:138) wrote that the villages were small, and Garcilaso (Garcilaso 1951, 2:431) stated the villages contained fifteen to forty houses each. These towns have not been identified.

The expedition made camp on a plain near a grove of trees approximately a quarter of a league (1.4 kilometers) from the main town (Biedma in Bourne 1904, 2:27, Elvas in Bourne 1904, 1:120). Biedma (Bourne 1904, 2:27) stated they camped on the plain for two days, but Elvas (Bourne 1904, 1:118) contended they traveled on June 23 and 24. In fact, they may have traveled short distances across the plain because of the extreme heat and humidity, typical for late June in eastern Arkansas. One chronicler commented on the excessive heat on June 24 (Elvas in Bourne 1904, 1:120).

On June 25 they entered the Casqui polity capital, believed to be the Parkin site (3CS29), a 6.9-hectare occupation and civic-ceremonial center site of the Parkin archeological phase (Lewis 1902:457; P. Morse 1981, 1990:120–27; Morse and Morse 1983:290–95; 1990:202; Phillips, Ford, and Griffin 1951:387). The site, located on the St. Francis River near the confluence of the Tyronza River, has a large pyramidal mound and plaza surrounded by a ditch and palisade on three sides with the St. Francis River on the west. Sixteenth-century European artifacts have been found at the Parkin site (P. Morse 1981:69–72, 1990:125): a chevron bead (H. A. Davis 1966:11) and a Clarksdale bell (Klinger 1977:figure 19). Additional European bells have been reported from Parkin (Morse and Morse 1990:208) (illustration 15).

## The Province of Pacaha

The expedition set out toward Pacaha, located on the Mississippi River and upriver from the crossing, on the morning of June 26, passing several Casqui villages, possibly the archeological sites of Smithdale (3CS108) (0.4 hectares) and McKnight (3CT39), a small (about 0.2 hectare) site on the south side of the Tyronza River. They stayed overnight in one of the towns, perhaps at the McKnight site. On June 27 they returned to the Mississippi in search of Pacaha. Unless the expedition had been traveling parallel to the great river, their return to the Mississippi would have taken them in a generally eastward direction.

The Casqui told de Soto that Pacaha was one-day's travel from Casqui, but it is not known if they were referring to the polity center or border. The distance from the Casqui administrative center (Parkin) to the Pacaha administrative center (Bradley) is thirty-eight kilometers. The distance from the Casqui center (Parkin) to the Pacaha border (Blackfish Bayou) is eleven kilometers. Also, it is not clear whether the informants are referring to native daily travel rates by foot, approximately forty-eight kilometers (Morse and Morse 1990:209; Stubbs 1982:43) or the expedition's average daily speed of about twenty to twenty-four kilometers, roughly half the native pace (DePratter, Hudson, and Smith 1985:110; Hudson, et al. 1985:723).

On June 27 they passed in sight of two towns to the north, possibly at Glover (3CT37), a 3-hectare site, and Berry (3CT47), a 0.5-hectare site, 0.8 and 1.7 kilometers north of the hypothesized route respectively, and they came to a lake (Elvas in Bourne 1904, 1:121) or swamp (Ranjel in Bourne 1904, 2:139) on the Casqui/Pacaha polity boundary half a crossbow shot across (about 135 meters). The lake, connected to the Mississippi, would have been the Gibson Meander's upper or northern arm. Gibson Meander fits the Spanish location and flows into the Mississippi by way of Blackfish Bayou and Fifteen Mile Bayou. A bridge was built over the lake, presumably by a joint Casqui and Spanish work force.

An overland route from Parkin site (Casqui) to the southern Nodena phase sites, hypothesized to be the Pacaha polity (D. Morse 1990:73–74), may be taken by following the Wapanocca natural levee between Big Creek to the north and the swamp at West Memphis to the south. Also, a water route is known to have existed between Casqui and Pacaha; the chief of Casqui sent his warriors in dugout canoes from Casqui to the

Mississippi River in search of the chief of Pacaha (Elvas in Bourne 1904, 1:124–25). This water route between Casqui and Pacaha would have been: St. Francis River-Tyronza River-Big Creek-Wapanocca Lake-Mississippi River. Big Creek is the outflow channel for Wapanocca Lake.

On June 28 the expedition entered the Pacaha chiefdom along the Wapanocca natural levee and approached the main town, possibly late in the day, as they did not enter it. On June 29 they went into the civic-ceremonial center, a large fortified town, located on a plain, next to a large lake (Elvas in Bourne 1904, 1:123). A ditch almost encircled the town, and a canal connected the lake with the Mississippi River (Elvas in Bourne 1904, 1:123; Garcilaso 1951:436).

The Bradley site (3CT7), a 9.5-hectare occupation identified as the main Pacaha town (D. Morse 1990:79–80; Morse and Morse 1990:202), matches the Spanish description of Pacaha with its size, location on a large natural levee, a sizable stockaded community or series of towns, its position on the Wapanocca Meander, and access to the Mississippi River; Bradley was within two kilometers of the sixteenth-century Mississippi River and would have had access to it by way of Wapanocca Bayou.

A late sixteenth-century and possible early seventeenth-century component is evident for the Bradley area; European artifacts, including two blue glass beads, dating to the late sixteenth century were recovered from Bradley site by Clarence B. Moore (1911:431.) A sixteenth-century musket ball, from either a military arquebus or a small cannon, has been found at Site 3CT43, an 11-hectare site located 0.8 kilometers west of Bradley. Additional sites located in the immediate area include sites 3CT40 (1.6 hectares) and 3CT245 (2.8 hectares). These sites, 3CT7, 3CT40, 3CT43, and 3CT245, may represent the series of stockaded towns reported by the chroniclers (Morse and Morse 1990:208). The total habitation area for the Bradley community may have been as large as 25 hectares, representing the largest population encountered by the expedition in the Mississippi Alluvial Plain, confirming the Spanish descriptions of political and military power for the Pacaha polity.

De Soto spent a month at Pacaha. While there, he dispatched reconnoitering expeditions to the north (Biedma in Bourne 1904, 2:29; Ranjel in Bourne 1904, 2:140) to obtain information concerning the land and its people. Two reconnoitering expeditions which were sent out from Pacaha during de Soto's occupation of the polity were described by the chroniclers (Phillips, Ford, and Griffin 1951:380; Morse and Morse 1990:203).

Two Galicians, Pedro Moreno (Swanton 1939:362), who may have been in charge of this expedition as he was commander of the harquebusiers, and Diego de Silvera (Avellaneda 1990:52–53), traveled northeast toward some mountains with several Pacahas and two traders to investigate rumors of salt and a yellow metal. They took pearls, chamois skins, and beans to trade. Eleven days later, they returned with six loads of salt, a load of copper, and news that the lands they saw were "sterile and poorly populated" (Garcilaso 1951:449–50).

The Moreno-Silvera expedition apparently visited the Nodena phase, Pemiscot Bayou cluster site of Campbell (23PM5), an eight-hectare site located about ninety-five kilometers north of Bradley (Chapman and Anderson 1955, D. Morse 1990:81–82; Morse and Morse 1983:312, 1990:203; Price and Price 1990). The nearest source of copper and salt is found 160 kilometers north of Campbell site in the Ste. François Mountains (Morse and Morse 1990:203). The area between Pemiscot Bayou and the Ste. François Mountains was uninhabited during the sixteenth century based on available archeological information. Sixteenth-century brass bells and at least twenty-four chevron beads have been reported from the Campbell site (Morse and Morse 1990:203). In all likelihood these historic artifacts represent items traded by Moreno and Silvera.

Another expedition, composed of thirty horsemen and fifty footmen, explored for eight days to the northwest, traveling to the province of Caluça[12] (or Caluç), characterized by wide plains producing a plant so profuse and tall the horses could not break through and large, pondy swamps lacking trees. The inhabitants subsisted by hunting, fishing, and gathering (Biedma in Bourne 1904, 2:29–30; Elvas in Bourne 1904, 1:128–29). One of the camps was depicted as a "collection of huts, covered with rush sewed together" (Biedma in Bourne 1904, 2:29).

The open swamps described by Luýs Hernández de Biedma, the king's official agent who apparently accompanied and may have led the expedition, seem to characterize the St. Francis Sunk Lands of the St. Francis and Little River drainages. Over 90 percent of the sunk land area in the late 1840s was shallow to deep swamp creating open lakes (Saucier 1970:337), such as Big Lake (41 square kilometers), the Hatchie Coon Sunk Lands (150 square kilometers), Lake Nicormy (23 square kilometers), Lake St. Francis (98 square kilometers), and Tyronza Lake (8 square kilometers) (Fuller 1912:Plate 1; Transeau 1935:Figure 1). The sunk lands originated from alluvial drowning due to rapid natural levee formation along Little River's Left Hand Chute (Saucier 1970:339), rather than post–sixteenth-century seismic activity (Fuller 1912).

The plains and associated tall vegetation mentioned in the Biedma and Elvas narratives may refer to the 260-square-kilometer Big Lake Highland-Grand Prairie[13] running between Big Lake, Lake Nicormy, and Lake Tyronza to the east and the Hatchie Coon Sunk Lands and St. Francis Lake to the west. However, the expedition may have passed through the sunk lands and continued west to the Western Lowlands (House 1975:161; Morse and Morse 1983:298–300, 1990:203; Perino 1966:69). According to this view, they may have visited the Gibson site (3LW509), a 9.1-hectare, late Middle-period Mississippian ceremonial center in the Western Lowland which became a hunting camp by the sixteenth century (D. F. Morse 1986a:91–92; Morse and Morse 1990:203). Biedma did not mention crossing Crowley's Ridge; if the Biedma expedition visited the Western Lowlands and traveled across the sunk lands rather than parallel to them, it would have been a difficult journey. A less arduous route would have been to travel between the lakes and move north along the prairie corridor into Dunklin County, Missouri. The main difficulty in this route would have been the challenge of traveling through the prairie.

Grand Prairie is 100 kilometers long and 3.5 kilometers wide. Bluestem or tall grass prairies, once common on the loess plains east and west of Crowley's Ridge (Pell 1983:21), also flourished on the Mississippi Alluvial Plain terraces and ridges east of Crowley's Ridge. Big Bluestem, an important constituent of the tall grass prairie,[14] gave travelers difficulty in more recent times (Baber 1942:39) as it did for Biedma's party.

The northeastern Arkansas and southeastern Missouri tall grass prairies of the sixteenth through the eighteenth centuries were maintained through Native-American use of fire (Cottier and Waselkov 1977:28–31).

The Caluça adaptation resembles Midwestern village horticulturalists who abandoned their winter villages to conduct short, communal summer hunts on the tall grass prairies (D. F. Morse 1986a:93; Phillips, Ford, and Griffin 1951:359). The late seventeenth-century Illinois-speaking Michigamea (Bauxar 1978:595–96; Callender 1978:674) and perhaps the Chepoussa (Bauxar 1978:595–96) went on communal summer hunts on the Central Mississippi Valley prairies. Illinois summer hunting camps, consisting of temporary reed-covered structures, were built on prairie edges at sites providing coolness and defense against surprise attacks (Callender 1978:675; Liette 1934:308). Late seventeenth-century Osage village horticulturalists in northwestern Arkansas and southeastern Missouri also employed a temporary hunting camp structure covered with bark, skins, or reed or rush mats for summer hunts on the prairies (Chapman 1959:31-32). The use of temporary reed-covered structures, as witnessed by Biedma, may have been a component of some Central Mississippi Valley horticulturalists who incorporated summer communal hunts on the prairies as part of their subsistence-settlement strategy.

Upon hearing gold was not to be found to the north, the main expedition left Pacaha on July 29 and spent the night in a Casqui village, perhaps the same one in which they stayed during their approach to Pacaha (possibly McKnight site). On July 30 the entrada returned to the main Casqui town (Parkin site) for the night.

On August 1, they left the main Casqui town and turned south, arriving at a Casqui town located on the Casqui River (St. Francis). This town may have been the Rose site (3CS27), a 2.9-hectare occupation on the St. Francis' eastern side (P. A. Morse 1981:49–50; Phillips, Ford, and Griffin 1951:284–90). A protohistoric occupation is evident at Rose Mound based on the presence of snubnose scrapers and a non-repoussé copper eagle (S. Williams 1980:107). The next day Casqui ordered his people to ferry the expedition across the river, perhaps at a ford near Rose Mound.

## The Province of Quiguate

Once across the river they encountered a burned village, perhaps indicating they had arrived at a different polity. This site may be Big Eddy (3SF9), a 2.2-hectare protohistoric site (P. A. Morse 1981:50–51). Two human head effigies, Protohistoric markers, are reported from this site (P. A. Morse 1990:131). The St. Francis appears to be the border between the Casqui province (Parkin phase) to the east and north and the Quiguate province (Kent phase) to the west and south, although the archeological configuration places the southern terminus of the Casqui (Parkin phase) at Big Eddy (P. A. Morse 1981:48) or further south at Castille Landing (3SF12) (Phillips 1970:Figure 447).

On August 3, they slept in another burned village, possibly the Clay Hill site (3LE11, 3.6 hectares). A Clarksdale Bell (House 1987:50–51; Williams 1980:Figure 2c) and a possible arquebus support (Hathcock 1983:158) have been found at Clay Hill (Morse and Morse 1990:209).

On August 4, they came to the chief's town in the Quiguate polity; the largest town they encountered in La Florida (Biedma in Bourne 1904, 2:31; Elvas in Bourne 1904, 1:130). This town may be the 6-hectare Grant site (3LE15) (Hudson 1985:4). Some 180 meters from the town of Quiguate was a river (presumably the St. Francis) too large for the horses to cross. Grant site is located near Mossy Lake Bayou, an old St. Francis River channel to the north. The Spaniards noted Quiguate resembled Casqui and Pacaha, a level and fertile land with rich river margins (natural levees) on which the Indians made extensive fields (Elvas in Bourne 1904, 1:132).

Both Clay Hill and Grant sites contain early protohistoric markers. A non-repoussé copper eagle,[15] Nodena points, snubnosed end scrapers, and bundle burials have been found at the Clay Hill site (Morse and Morse 1983:313; House 1987:51). Grant site is the only other Kent phase site, besides Clay Hill, to contain Nodena arrow points and snubnose scrapers (House 1987:51).[16]

The Quiguate informed de Soto of large towns to the south, or downriver, whose caciques governed wide territories with numerous people; a possible reference to other Kent phase towns or the Old Town phase. They added that mountains would be found by traveling to the northwest.

## The Province of Coligua

On August 26, lead by a Quiguate guide, the expedition moved northwest toward the mountains in search of the polity of Coligua. Crowley's Ridge is not mentioned and could have been avoided by passing through the Marianna Gap (Phillips, Ford, and Griffin 1951:388). They then crossed an immense, pathless and uninhabited region for seven days, passing through four swamps in as many days before arriving at Coligua (Ranjel in Bourne 1904, 2:146). The swamps compare favorably with the present-day locations of the L'Anguille River, Bayou de View, Cache River, and Village Creek basins (Hudson 1985:6; Lewis 1902:457; Morse and Morse 1983:313; Phillips, Ford, and Griffin 1951:388). In addition, braided stream surfaces throughout eastern Arkansas, particularly the Western Lowland, were devoid of permanent settlements after approximately 1350 or 1400 (House 1975:160–61; Morse and Morse 1983:280, 1990:198–99; Price and Price 1990:59; Price, Price, and Harris 1976:50; S. Williams 1983, 1990).

On September 4, the entrada came to Coligua, located at the foot of a mountain between some ridges along the gorge of a river (Biedma in Bourne 1904, 1:133–34; Ranjel in Bourne 1904, 2:146–47). This location places the expedition at the Ozark Plateaus where the White River enters the Western Lowland in the vicinity of the Greenbrier archeological phase (Akridge 1986:4; Morse and Morse 1983:299–300; 1990:204). The main Coligua town visited by the expedition may have been the 5.6-hectare Greenbrier phase Magness site (3IN8). The distance from the Grant site to the Magness site is 116 kilometers. The expedition could have made the trip in four days by traveling 29 kilometers per day, a distance well within its capabilities when moving from one populated area to another through buffer zones (Elvas in Bourne 1904, 1:85–86).

## Calpista, Palisema, and Guachoya

Upon leaving Coligua on September 5, the Spaniards passed some mountains (Ranjel in Bourne 1904, 2:147), suggesting they skirted the eastern margin of the Springfield Plateau and the Boston Mountains of the Ozark Plateaus. South of the Greenbrier phase, the Ozark Escarpment rises 90 to 150 meters above the Western Lowland, presenting a striking view.

Two days after leaving Coligua they encountered a salt spring at the town of Calpista. This salt spring would have been one located north of Liberty Valley in White County approximately two-days' travel south of the Magness site (Akridge 1986:5). The expedition's average daily travel rate, about twenty to twenty-four kilometers (Hudson, et al. 1985), accords well with the forty-five-kilometer distance from Coligua (Magness site) to the salt spring near Liberty Valley (Calpista site).

From Calpista they headed southwest along the Ozark-Western Lowland border on the Little Red River, arriving at Palisema on September 8. On September 9 they camped in the open. On the tenth they camped at a "water," perhaps Cypress Bayou (Hudson 1985:6). At this point they appear to have headed directly west along Cypress Bayou by a route between two ridges rising sixty meters above the valley floor. The east-west corridor is six kilometers wide and fifty kilometers long with less than thirty meters difference in elevation from one end to the other. The Cypress Bayou corridor is an economical means of traveling from the Mississippi Valley to the Arkansas Valley. The Cypress Bayou corridor may have been used at an earlier time by individuals traveling from the Arkansas Valley to northeastern Arkansas.

Upon entering the corridor the expedition left the Mississippi Alluvial Plain and continued west approximately twenty-two kilometers to the Cayas polity (perhaps Carden's/Gallas Rock Bottom locality) in the Arkansas Valley. The Spanish expedition did not re-enter the Mississippi Alluvial Plain until April 17, 1542, when it arrived at Guachoya on the Mississippi River where Hernando de Soto died on May 21.

# SUMMARY

The de Soto expedition traveled approximately 312 kilometers through the Mississippi Alluvial Plain between May 8 and September 10, 1541. During their entrada, the Spaniards encountered and noted numerous physiographic landmarks, including natural levees, backswamps, rivers, meander lakes, sunk lands, tall grass prairies, and floodplain forests. In this study I have attempted to locate the de Soto route through the Mississippi floodplain on a day-by-day basis by augmenting the Spanish eyewitness accounts with modern physiographic and archeological data. Sixteenth-century geomorphic features, in many instances, are evident in the modern landscape despite claims of the Mississippi's widespread destructive meandering. In the study area, for example, the Mississippi has remained within a maximum 10-kilometer corridor during the past 450 years.

By comparing the written accounts of the expedition's course through the Mississippi Alluvial Plain with environmental reconstructions of the sixteenth-century landscape, anchoring points along the route may be evaluated as degrees of conformity with archeological, historic, and environmental data. As new interpretations and data come to bear on the de Soto route, the itinerary of route segments may be recalibrated to provide a "best fit" model for the overall route configuration, thus allowing for the strengthening or discarding of competing anchoring points within the framework of a hypothetical model based on testable hypotheses. Environmental reconstruction, augmented with archeological and ethnohistorical models and data sets, will continue to serve as an important methodological tool for studies concerned with the de Soto route. It is hoped that future research will support or reject this model and in one way or the other will lead to a more detailed understanding of the dynamic interaction between the cultural and geomorphic forces which played a role in the decisions which determined the Hernando de Soto expedition route through the Mississippi Valley.

## ACKNOWLEDGMENTS

I wish to extend my thanks to the Arkansas Archeological Survey, in particular Jerry Hilliard and Pamela Beasley, for information concerning the sizes of many of the sites mentioned in this paper. Jack Roberts contributed helpful information concerning the size of the Young site. The Lower Mississippi Survey, Peabody Museum, Harvard University graciously provided access to site records for several sites mentioned here.

The Memphis State University Interlibrary Loan Department, under Deborah Brackstone's cheerful and competent guidance, was particularly instrumental in my efforts to obtain documents used in this paper.

The Memphis District, U.S. Army Corps of Engineers, Roger Saucier, Waterways Experiment Station, and Ronald C. Brister, Memphis Museums, Inc., graciously loaned copies of the geological maps used in building a cartographic model of the sixteenth-century landscape.

Thanks are extended to Jim Atkinson, Natchez Trace Parkway, for providing a copy of the *Gaspard-Joseph Chaussegros de Léry* journal.

Thanks are also expressed to George Brown of the Memphis Museums, Inc. for contributing the solar and lunar information for June 17 and 18, 1541.

I wish to thank the numerous graduate and undergraduate students who, during the last five years, traced and compiled topographic, geological, and pedagogical maps used for the final composite model upon which this research is based. Without their efforts and numb fingers this study would not have been possible.

# Notes

1. **Natural levees,** associated with most meandering rivers, result from the deposition of sands and coarse silts in narrow zones along the rivers during times of flooding when the load of the river is held in suspension. Natural levees are usually best developed on the outside of river bends as a low sloping wedgelike ridge of sediments, often over a mile in average width and 15 to 25 feet above the general level of the floodbasin, tapering into the adjacent lowlands. Because of their increased height above the surrounding floodplain, proximity to either an active river or abandoned meander, and easily tilled and fertile soils, natural levees were prime habitation sites for Native-American farming communities. **Backswamps,** also known as flood basins, accumulate as a result of the load carried by the flooding of meandering rivers such as the Mississippi. Unlike natural levees, backswamps constitute long-continued accretion of fine silts and clays which remain in suspension until they are deposited in quiet waters impounded in low-lying areas adjacent to the natural levees and other elevated topographic features within the floodplain. **Meander lakes,** often called oxbow or cut-off lakes, result from the shifting of the Mississippi River channel laterally across the landscape through erosion of the riverbank and deposition of sediments. The resulting meandering of the river brings about the narrowing of the neck of land between the meanders. As the river scours out the concave bank the neck width becomes increasingly narrow. Often during floodstage the river erodes through the neck, cutting off the meander and thus forming a lake from the meander. Meander lakes were attractive locales for Native-American settlements because of the great numbers of plants and animals associated with them. They were also an important part of the transportation system. **Rim swamps,** a type of backswamp or floodbasin, are created through the accumulation of fine sediments near floodplain walls such as Crowley's Ridge or the loess bluffs. The aggrading Mississippi River builds up sediments which impound the adjacent, now low-lying area thus creating a rim around the swamp. **Sunklands** in part may be a result of seismic activity, but much of the Mississippi Valley sunklands have resulted from the buildup or aggradation of the Mississippi River which results in adjacent areas becoming backswamps. Sunklands in eastern Arkansas are extensive, often characterized by large open bodies of water ringed with extensive cypress and gum forests (Fisk 1944; Saucier 1964).

2. All areal measurements were recorded with Planim (ver. 2.0), an Autocad planimeter emulation program used in conjunction with Autocad Rel. 10. Linear measurements were taken with a Peco swivel handle map measurer.

3. Four Mississippi River channel locations (17–20) have been accurately charted to 1765 (Fisk 1944). However, there is less certainty concerning Channel 15's integrity (Saucier 1981:15). Channel 15 has been employed in sixteenth-century Mississippi River channel reconstructions for the Commerce/Walls crossing by Phillips (Phillips, Ford, and Griffin 1951:305, 368) and Smith (1990:161).

4. All dates are from the pre-Gregorian calendar used by the Spanish in the mid-sixteenth century.

5. Pacaha is believed to be the Quapaw name for themselves (Lewis 1902:457; Morse and Morse 1990:208; D. F. Morse 1990b:96–97; and Rankin this volume). See M. P. Hoffman (1986, 1990) and Rankin (this volume) for an alternative interpretation.

6. *Nous campâmes aprés avoir presque toujours marché dans de mauvais pays de cotteaux entrecoupés de rivières, ruisseaux, et moulins, le tout rempli de cannes très épaisses.*

7. Quizquiz has been interpreted by Halbert (Lewis 1902:455) as the Choctaw "Koi ish kish,"

(mountain lion's [*Felis concolor*] anus). However, it could be Chickasaw "koi" (mountain lion) "ishto" (to be great) (Humes and Humes 1973:148). One suspects the name derives from a Muskogean speaker among the Spanish such as one of the Alibamo or Chickasaw captives/guides. Their pronunciation may have reminded the Spanish of the Incan general, Quizquiz, against whom de Soto fought in northern Peru in late 1533 (Lockhart 1972:196). The word "ish kish" among modern Choctaws is not used in a derogatory (scatological) manner, but merely refers to a part of the body. If Halbert is correct, "koi ishkish" may have referred to this particular polity in a symbolic, perhaps nonderagotory manner. In the spirit of bold speculation, Quizquiz might just as easily have been derived from the Choctaw "kuchichi," to cast out (Byington 1915:240).

8. The traditional *legua común* or "common league" equals 5.572±0.02 kilometers (Chardon 1980:302; Hudson, Smith, and DePratter 1984:66) or 3.455 miles. Garcilaso de la Vega (1951:329) stated that the *legua común* was used by the expedition. Blake (1988) and Swanton (1939:104), on the other hand, argue for the use of the legua legal (4.19 kilometers or 2.63 miles).

Garcilaso de la Vega (1951:329) noted that the expedition generally averaged 4.5 leagues (25.1 kilometers) per day. Elvas (Bourne 1904, 1:85–86) stated that the "amount of travel usually performed was five or six leagues a day, passing through settled country; and when through desert, all the haste possible was made, to avoid the want of maize." His statement suggests a rate of 27.9–33.4 kilometers per day through settled or populated areas.

9. A crossbow shot was a distance of about 300 yards or 273 meters (Hudson 1990:38; Swanton 1939:108).

10. Phillips visited Norfolk on November 6, 1940, and noted it was a "Small village site on natural ridge, Site occupies crest of a small oval ridge tending N*S" (Site survey form for Norfolk (13-P-7), Lower Mississippi Survey, Peabody Museum, Harvard University).

11. The Voyager program (ver. 1.2) was used to compute sunset (7:16 P.M.) for the evening of June 17, 1541, and moonrise (12:31 A.M.) and sunrise (4:48 A.M.) for the morning of June 18. On June 18 a waning crescent moon, three days past one quarter, rose in the morning sky at 12:31 A.M. The moon was low on the eastern horizon (20 degrees) when the sun rose.

12. Caluça may be a Muskogean term for black water, "oka loosa" (Halbert in Lewis 1902:453; Morse and Morse 1990:203; Swanton 1939:60, 229). The Caluça of northeastern Arkansas and southeastern Missouri should not be mistaken for another province called Caluça located near the Chicaça who "gave the Christians guides and interpreters to go to Caluça, a place of much repute among the Indians. Caluça is a province of more than ninety villages not subject to any one, with a savage population, very warlike and much dreaded, and the soil is fertile in that section" (Ranjel in Bourne 1904, 2:132).

The similarity in polity names might be reconciled if the Caluça had horticultural villages east of the Mississippi and summer hunting grounds on the opposite side to the north. The Chickasaw and Choctaw both hunted west of the Mississippi in the eighteenth and early nineteenth centuries. If the Caluça were located in the Mississippi Alluvial Valley in western Tennessee, some 250 kilometers northwest of the Chicaça (in the Columbus, Mississippi, area), a stronger case might be made for their hunting across the river. A late prehistoric occupation for the area is evident (G. P. Smith 1990:153), but it does not appear to be sizable.

13. The Grand Prairie (Big Lake Highlands) of Mississippi County, Arkansas, and Dunklin County, Missouri, should not be confused with the Grand Prairie in Prairie County, Arkansas.

14. Dominants of the bluestem prairie include big bluestem (*Andropogon gerardi*), little bluestem (*Andropogon scoparius*), switchgrass (*Panicum virgatum*), and Indian grass (Sorghastrum utans) (Küchler 1964:74).

15. The non-repoussé copper "eagle" is said to have been found in the same burial which contained the Clarksdale bell (House 1987:51).

16. Based on information which became available after this chapter was in press, two additional sites, Soudan and Noel Carnes, should be added to Grant and Clay Hill (House 1991:94). Starkley may be a fifth Kent phase site to contain Nodena arrow points and snubnosed end scrapers.

# The Parkin Archeological Site and Its Role in Determining the Route of the de Soto Expedition

Phyllis A. Morse

## INTRODUCTION: WHERE WAS THE PROVINCE OF CASQUI?

The route of de Soto into Arkansas has long been controversial. In the *Final Report of The United States De Soto Expedition Commission,* Swanton (1939:250) discussed the location of the town and province of Casqui, claiming that the "River of Casqui" could only be the White River. The St. Francis River bottoms were thought to be the swamp between Casqui and Pacaha, with the town of Pacaha itself located at the mouth of the St. Francis. The Casqui capital, then, was located "southwest of Barton, and between Lexa and La Grange" on a modern map (Swanton 1939:249). All these interpretations were based on his choice of Sunflower Landing as the major crossing point of the Mississippi River. However, Swanton did note in his foreword that:

> . . . we may expect new light to be thrown upon the problem . . . mainly, we believe, as the nascent State archeological surveys expand and begin to reconstruct the aboriginal history of the southwest. This is one major result to be expected from the pursuit of archeology in this territory. (Swanton 1939:2)

In a very careful review of archeological knowledge acquired between 1939 and 1950, Phillips, Ford, and Griffin (1951:347–91) examined the Swanton route most critically. They found the Swanton route "somewhat unsatisfactory." In reference to the location of Casqui, the Lower Mississippi Survey found no village sites at all where Swanton placed the province of Casqui. The documentary evidence Swanton cited was also seen as very contradictory. Phillips, Ford, and Griffin presented a new hypothesis for the de Soto route in Arkansas and proposed Commerce Landing as a suitable area for crossing the Mississippi. They described the area of the confluence of the St. Francis and Tyronza rivers as an immensely rich archeological development, with "St. Francis type" sites being abundant. In fact, they proposed one of two archeological sites, Parkin or Neeley's Ferry, as the location of the Casqui capital. The Commerce Landing theory seemed to fit both the archeology and geography much better than the Swanton route.

Swanton was not pleased with these conclusions. In his 1952 review he stated that the river identifications were critical to his route and ". . . if the Ouachita was the River of Anilco then the identification of the others are beyond doubt" (Swanton 1952:159). He further stated that he had "*proved*" this point. Swanton obviously did not like to be questioned.

In 1972, Brain, Toth, and Rodriguez-Buckingham won the Goggin Award for their paper "Ethnohistorical Archaeology and the De Soto Entrada into the Lower Mississippi Valley" (Brain, Toth, and Rodriguez-Buckingham 1974). In this paper, they discussed the merits of the various proposed crossing points of the Mississippi River by the de Soto expedition. They concluded that Friar's Point, which is near the Swanton crossing point, was the most suitable location when evidence from such disciplines as ethnohistory, geology and archeology was combined. They argued that both the Parkin and Nodena phases did not seem to exist as late as 1541 when viewing certain diagnostic pottery types as time markers. They placed Casqui near the Starkey site and Pacaha in the southern end of Crittenden County, with the Belle Meade site being the capital.

Phyllis A. Morse (1981:65–69) briefly discussed this review of the de Soto route in the report on Parkin, a mound site in Cross County. At that time, the aforementioned diagnostic pottery types were listed and proof that they did indeed occur on both Parkin and Nodena phase sites was presented. The presence of sixteenth-century European artifacts at Parkin was also discussed. Further discussion of the de Soto question was published by Morse and Morse in 1983.

Charles Hudson (1985) began his study of the de Soto route west of the Mississippi in 1984. He was careful to involve other interested scholars while determining the most logical path by visiting all possible locations on the ground using the de Soto accounts and topographical maps. A National Historic Trail prepared for the National Park Service (Hudson 1990a) reviewed the entire length of the de Soto Trail. Hudson agreed that Parkin was probably Casqui. For the first time, the more northern route proposed by Morse and Morse (1983) was logically connected both on the west and the east.

In his introduction to the reissue of the *Final Report of the United States De Soto Expedition Commission*, Brain (1985) discussed evidence on the route of de Soto since the Swanton publication. In reference to the province of Casqui, Brain (1985:xxxviii) still placed it in the southern part of the St. Francis Basin, corresponding to the Kent phase. He then equated the province of Pacaha with the Walls phase. Brain did acknowledge the publication of our alternative route (P. A. Morse 1981; Morse and Morse 1983:305–13) with Parkin interpreted as Casqui. He mentioned that "Parkin and some other related sites probably were occupied at the time of De Soto" (Brain 1985:xxxix). He also discussed the sixteenth-century artifacts found at Parkin. However, Brain also commented that "contemporaneity alone . . . is not adequate grounds for establishing a visitation by the entrada" and that this segment of the route remains "moot."

Further discussion of the archeological evidence pinpointing Parkin as Casqui has been published (P. A. Morse 1990:118–34). The carbon-14 dates available from Parkin phase sites range from A.D. 1350 ± 90 to 1580 ± 70 (Morse and Morse 1983:295). A more detailed study of the diagnostic pottery types present during this time period showed that a majority of these types not only occur at both Parkin and Nodena phase sites, but also are actually named for sites in these phases.

By 1990, a map of known Protohistoric sites in Arkansas was produced (illustration 6) and all route possibilities could be tested (see Dan Morse this volume). The present volume is a result of a vigorous re-examination of Swanton's original conclusions. None of the previous attempts had available the Arkansas Archeological Survey's map of Protohistoric sites.

The Parkin site is certainly central to our detailed reconstruction of the route in northeast Arkansas. If Parkin, or a site nearby, is not the capital of Casqui, then the reconstructed route has lost its anchor. In this chapter, I will examine the route critically, using the anchor of Parkin.

## THE PARKIN SITE

The Arkansas Legislature commissioned the Arkansas Archeological Survey in 1978 to produce an archeological study of the Parkin site (illustration 14) as part of a master plan in developing Parkin as a state park (P. A. Morse 1981). A conscious choice was made at that time not simply to do some preliminary archeological testing at Parkin, but to study the Parkin site in the context of its relationship to other sites in the area which were determined to date to the same time period. As these other sites in the Parkin phase were identified, measured, and sampled, several new lines of investigation were explored. The relationship of the sites to one another in terms of size, nearness of critical resources, and strategic locations revealed that Parkin was both the largest site in the area and was placed to control traffic on two rivers. This alone would make it a viable candidate as the residential town of a paramount chief, such as the chief of Casqui, who was described in the de Soto narratives

The conclusion that Parkin was the capital of Casqui, visited by de Soto in 1541, came about in part from this study of site location, partly from the presence of artifacts definitely dating to the de Soto timeline at the site, and partly from reading the four accounts of the de Soto expedition. These accounts (Bourne 1904; Garcilaso 1951) provide some information such as topographical features, days of travel, and descriptions of towns which could be dovetailed into recently recovered archeological data.

The Parkin site, 3CS29, is a large Mississippian town located inside the limits of the city of Parkin, Cross County, Arkansas (P. A. Morse 1981). The site area inside the "moats" measures approximately 6.9 hectares or 17.1 acres in size. It is situated on the east bank of the St. Francis River. Still observable features include a 6.5-meter-high flat-topped temple mound on the western edge of the site, a 1.5-meter-high apron or extension on the southern end of the temple mound, a central plaza area, and a wide ditch circling the site defining the northern, eastern, and southern perimeters. Six smaller house mounds were mapped in 1940 (Phillips, Ford, and Griffin 1951:331). The site rises above the surrounding flood plain 2.5 meters and more. Test excavations by the University of Arkansas uncovered burials, rows of post holes, and an oval structure (H. A. Davis 1966; Klinger 1977). One test showed complex stratigraphy, with as many as 15 building stages present on the mound apron.

A surface survey of other sites thought to belong to the Parkin phase showed that at least 21 sites in the St. Francis/Tyronza River area date to the 1400–1650 time period. These sites ranged in size from 0.2 hectares to 6.9 hectares in size (0.6 acres to 17.1 acres). Eighteen of these sites were upriver from Parkin. Five sites still had large pyramidal mounds. Parkin was by far the largest site. Four others ranged from 2.7 hectares to 3.7 hectares in size. Ten sites were 1.5 hectares to 2.4 hectares. Six were 0.2 hectares to 0.8 hectares in extent. The Parkin site is probably in the geographical center of the Parkin phase (P. A. Morse 1981:58). The next larger sites are located approximately 8 kilometers apart from Parkin and from one another. The 2-hectare size villages are spaced between these, about every 4 kilometers. All of these sites were probably fortified. No single family farmstead locations were identified as Parkin phase sites.

A study was made of the types of soil available in a 1-kilometer circle around each Parkin phase site (P. A. Morse 1981:73–88). It was assumed that Mississippian farmers would place their habitations near large areas of soil favorable for agriculture. In most cases, the larger sites were located near larger areas of Class I soils, those most agriculturally productive. Parkin itself was the exception. It was assumed that the large number of people living within the boundaries of the Parkin site were partly being fed by tribute from the rest of the population. This is normal behavior in chiefdom societies. It was probably more important for Parkin to be located near the conjunction of two rivers—the Tyronza and St. Francis—to control canoe traffic on these rivers than to be near a large area of prime farm land.

Intensive surface survey of a 1-kilometer area around the Parkin site produced 148 separate artifact locations. Not one of these was a Late Mississippian or Protohistoric farmstead. Further surface surveys, from Parkin to Smithdale, some 3.8 kilometers away, still showed no farmsteads. The practice of spacing family farmsteads in agricultural fields around larger villages was considered to be the norm for Mississippian societies. The lack of such farmsteads in the Parkin phase was most unusual. Accounting for this lack of farmsteads led to one of the most interesting conclusions of the Parkin project. Inhabitants of the Parkin phase had to remain in fortified villages for protection. The threat of raiding or warfare made security more important than agricultural efficiency. This type of warlike behavior is described often in the de Soto narratives.

## Spanish Artifacts found at Parkin

A small brass bell was found in an excavation at Parkin (H. A. Davis 1966:11) (illustration 15). The bell was made of sheet brass and had a shell bead as a replacement clapper. It is a style known as the Clarksdale bell (Brain 1975). Clarksdale bells were made in two halves and then joined by a crimped and soldered seam. Two large holes in the base are joined by a single cut. The bell was found in a child's burial and was accompanied by four pottery vessels. It is now at the Museum of the Red River in Idabel, Oklahoma. Clarksdale bells have also been found at the Carden Bottoms site near Russellville, Arkansas, and at 3LE11 in Lee county, Arkansas (Morse and Morse 1990:209). Several others are reported to have been found at the Campbell site in southeast Missouri. All these sites are along the projected Morse-Hudson de Soto route or that of a side expedition.

A glass chevron-style bead was found by a University of Arkansas field school participant on the surface of the Parkin site (Klinger 1977:Fig. 19). The bead is approximately eight millimeters round and contains seven layers of glass: blue, white, red, white, green, white, and green. Both the green color and the seven layers date this bead to the sixteenth century (M. T. Smith 1977:15). Faceted chevron beads are found at several sites dating to the de Soto time period including the Martin site in Tallahassee, Florida (Ewen 1990:86), and Buck Island, Weeki Watchee, Ruth Smith, and Tatham Mound sites, Florida (Mitchem 1990:54–56).

## CASQUI

"Casqui" refers both to the polity observed by the Spaniards and to the principal chief of that polity. The province of Casqui was first seen by the Spanish from a "summit of some high hills, where they beheld a town of four hundred houses, situated beside a river larger than the Guadalquivir at Cordoba" (Garcilaso 1951:430; this description is thought to be exaggerated). They noted numerous fields of maize and fruit trees. After resting there because of the great quantity of food, they went seven leagues up the river to the town where the Casqui chief resided. All the land was observed to be fertile and inhabited. The Casqui chief offered de Soto his own home, which was on one side of the town on a high mound. There were also ten or twelve other large structures for the chief's wives and servants. De Soto chose to stay in an orchard outside the town.

One of the most dramatic events of the entire expedition took place during this stay at Casqui. The chief asked de Soto to make it rain, as their crops needed water. De Soto arranged a religious ceremony, in which a great cross was made and placed on top of a tall mound overlooking the river. A religious procession possibly involving over a thousand people was held. Fifteen to twenty thousand people may have observed the ceremony across the river. At midnight it began to rain.

Casqui offered to accompany de Soto in attacking the province of Pacaha, furnishing both warriors and servants. For many centuries the Casqui and Pacaha provinces had been at war, and Casqui did not dare go beyond his boundaries (Garcilaso 1951:435). So the Casqui chief took advantage of the Spaniards' presence to avenge old injuries. They followed a river upward toward Pacaha, spending the night in one Casqui village while passing by others. A great swamp separated Casqui and Pacaha. Perhaps as many as five thousand warriors and three thousand bearers were provided for de Soto. The Casqui army was composed of a vanguard, a battalion, and a rear guard. This army succeeded in sacking the main town of Pacaha, in particular, desecrating the bodies of the ancestors of the Pacaha chief which were in a temple. They also removed the heads of slain Casqui which were decorating the temple entrance and freed various Casqui captives.

The Casqui provided canoes for an attack on the island retreat of Pacaha. The Pacaha defended themselves bravely, and threatened the Casqui "Remember well what you are doing . . . for when these strangers have departed, then we shall see what manner of men you are in battle" (Garcilaso 1951:442). The Casqui fled, leaving the

Spaniards unprotected. De Soto arranged a truce and later forced the Casqui and Pacaha chiefs to reconcile. When de Soto gave a feast, it was decided that the young Pacaha chief would sit at his right hand, as his ancestors were more noble than those of the Casqui chief. What happened in the long-term power struggle between these two chiefdoms after the Spaniards departed will probably never be known.

## DE SOTO IN NORTHEAST ARKANSAS

### THE CROSSING

The expedition crossed the Mississippi River on July 1 and arrived at the capital of Casqui on St. John's Day, Friday, July 6, 1541, having occupied the province of Aquixo July 2 and 3 before marching toward Casqui. It took one day or slightly under one day to reach the River of Casqui crossing, "the worst tract for swamps and water that they had found in all Florida," and two days or slightly less to march upriver to the capital.

The estimated distance per day for the expedition was thought to be around twelve to fifteen miles per day, particularly through habitated areas and with swine being herded (Swanton 1939:104–05). The distance from where de Soto arrived at the River of the Casqui to the Casqui capital should be around twenty-four to thirty miles. The distance from that point across a major swamp to the western extent of the province of Aquixo should be about twelve to fifteen miles. The crossing occurred around the southeast corner of Horseshoe Bend about six miles south of Memphis. This is about twenty miles due east of the St. Francis River, but the expedition probably traveled north and west to just opposite the southern border of Memphis where it roughly followed present Route 50 west toward Widener, Arkansas, for a distance of about ten miles as the crow flies (3CS5 is the westernmost *known* site in the Belle Meade phase). Fifteen Mile Bayou and a large number of swamps left over by the meanderings of the Mississippi and St. Francis rivers over much of the Holocene era separate the western border of the Belle Meade phase and the southern extent of the Parkin phase.

Unfortunately the area south of Parkin has not been systematically surveyed and Parkin phase sites south of Parkin are underrepresented in the sample. The swampy region between the two rivers was not detailed on the nineteenth-century maps; there were no roads or fields indicated. Geologically, it is difficult to tell which St. Francis River existed during the sixteenth century and which specific areas are locations of post–sixteenth century redeposition. Until there is a systematic survey in this region we cannot be sure of the identification of specific sites.

### THE RIVER AND PROVINCE OF CASQUI

The Spaniards first came to an area of high hills and looked down on a Casqui town, according to Garcilaso (Garcilaso 1951:430). Crowley's Ridge is a prominent geological formation near the St. Francis River and has been postulated as the "high hills." However, Crowley's Ridge is on the west side of the St. Francis River, and there is no evidence that the Spaniards crossed over. The "high hills" probably were natural levees which are characteristic here. Garcilaso also mentions "high hills" near Pacaha (Garcilaso 1951:436).

About 19 miles due north of this area where the expedition may have reached the St. Francis River is the Parkin site. The actual traveled distance would have been longer since the expedition would have not been able to travel as the crow flies. An estimate of around 20 to 30 miles would not be unreasonable.

The River of Casqui was described as a tributary to the Mississippi which was larger than the size of the Guadalquivir at Cordoba. In 1986, Jeff Mitchem measured the length of an old Roman bridge which spanned a wide spot of the Guadalquivir River at Cordoba as approximately 750 feet or 227 meters. At the Big Eddy site, 3SF9, on the edge of Crowley's Ridge, the St. Francis River approaches this width in the spring.

The Parkin phase sites north of Parkin are along both the St. Francis and Tyronza rivers. The expedition most probably went up the Tyronza toward Pacaha. The known extent of the Parkin phase extends about a single day's march up the Tyronza (14½ miles). The size of the province of Casqui as indicated in the de Soto accounts equates well with the known extent of the Parkin phase south of Parkin on the St. Francis and north of Parkin on the Tyronza. Parkin itself is located where these two rivers join. The Parkin phase does extend about another 20 miles north of Parkin on the St. Francis River, but it appears that the northernmost sites had been abandoned by the time of de Soto.

## The Province of Pacaha

The capital of Pacaha was located a day's march from the edge of the province of Casqui, near where there was a lake or swamp which drained into the Mississippi River. The expedition had to wait until a bridge had been built. Big Creek actually connects the Tyronza River with Wapanocca Lake which drains via Wapanocca Bayou into the Mississippi River. It is also possible to make a case for Gibson Bayou or Brougham Lake to "drain" or at least connect with Mississippi River drainage.

The description of the capital of Pacaha is most interesting. It was a fortified town surrounded by a ditch connected to the Mississippi River by a canal. Elvas (Bourne 1904, 1:123–24) added that a "great lake" was part of the ditch system and that the ditch did not completely surround the town. In addition, there were other towns half a league to a league away. Site 3CT7 fits the description, particularly that of Elvas. The Indians had widened that part of Wapanocca Bayou which flows by the site into a lake. Sites 3CT43 and 3CT40 are one- and two-and-one-half miles away (D. F. Morse 1989). One rather curious account is that given by Elvas (Bourne 1904, 1:124–25) describing the Casqui bringing canoes upriver from Casqui to Pacaha. Since Casqui was located on a distant tributary of the Mississippi, this doesn't make much sense. However, if the canoes were brought up the Tyronza to Big Creek and then into Wapanocca Lake, this mystery is solved.

Two known trips were made out of Pacaha. One, led by Biedma, went northwest for 8 days, or a distance of perhaps 96–120 miles. The only people seen were hunters in a "province" called Caluç or Caluça (which is "black water" in Chickasaw and

Choctaw). Site 3LW509 is located 25 miles from 3CT7 as the crow flies so an estimate of 96–120 miles is not unreasonable given the crooked path which would have been taken when walking and riding across northeast Arkansas. Site 3LW509 is located along the side of the Black River and represents an abandoned Middle Period Mississippian center utilized by Protohistoric hunters at about the time of de Soto with both Nodena points *and* end scrapers as common artifacts (D. F. Morse 1986a). Other Protohistoric remains in this region consist of one or two Nodena points at prehistoric sites. No sites with Protohistoric pottery have been recorded. The only Protohistoric activity in this region was hunting.

The second trip was made by Pedro Moreno and Hernando de Silvera with some Indian traders to the north. After eleven days they returned with copper and salt. The land was "poorly populated." Copper and salt are available in and near the Ste. François Mountains 160 miles or more to the north. However, a prominent Protohistoric site, 23PM5, is located about 60 miles up Interstate 55 from the Bradley site, 3CT7. This site has produced a significant quantity of mid sixteenth-century artifacts which suggests it was a major trading site. In addition, 23PM5 and 3CT7 are the only two sites known in northeast Arkansas to have produced significant early seventeenth-century artifacts. It should have taken a small party only about two to three days to go to 23PM5 and the same to return. They may have spent five days looking around or the number of days may have been just a typical Garcilaso exaggeration.

## The Province of Quiguate

From Casqui the expedition went downriver to Quiguate. It took two days to reach the capital of Casqui and almost three days more to reach the capital of Quiguate. The river was "heavily populated" beyond where they stopped. This is the area of the Kent phase on the St. Francis River. The Kent phase is being reconstructed by John House of the Arkansas Archeological Survey. An incongruity consists in the expedition reference to the "largest town in Florida." Only by inferring the "town" was two or three archeological sites located adjacent to each other (a situation which exists in this region) can this be reconciled with reality. The "towns" of 3CS29, 3CT7, and 3CT43 are the largest recorded sites in northeast Arkansas. The total acreage of the entire known Kent phase is smaller than that of 3CT7, 3CT40, 3CT43, and 3CT245 (located near each other on Bradley Ridge) combined. Mid sixteenth-century artifacts have been found in association with Kent phase deposits, but the Kent phase ranks third in size, behind Parkin and Nodena, but greater than the fourth-ranked Belle Meade phase.

## The Trip to Coligua

From Quiguate, the expedition traveled northwest to Coligua. The trip took 7 to 8 days, for a distance of about 84 to 120 miles. Distance from the Kent phase to 3IN8 (a prominent Greenbrier phase site) is about 80 miles, as the crow flies. This region was uninhabited by Protohistoric peoples (as described in the account), and there were major backswamps associated with major north-south streams. These swamps probably equate with the "four swamps" crossed by the expedition: the L'Anguille, Bayou de

View, Cache River, and perhaps Village Creek. They crossed the River of Coligua twice. The White River here makes a 90-degree turn and would have to be crossed twice. The Greenbrier phase is situated within a prominent valley of the Ozarks as described in the accounts. The population was sparse, and bison were hunted upriver as mentioned in the accounts. The White River is similar to the Caya of Estremadura.

After Coligua, the expedition probably moved down the Ozark escarpment toward but not all the way to present-day Little Rock, Arkansas. A "Mountain" was passed. While the escarpment is highest at this point, we hesitate to call it a mountain. Salt was found, probably near the mouth of Little Red River where it occurs and near where a very small polity existed in the Protohistoric which retreated up a narrow valley when its occupants were pursued by cavalry. This is the final known archeological polity in northeast Arkansas; amazingly *all* seem to have been directly visited by the de Soto expedition.

## CONCLUSIONS

As Phillips, Ford, and Griffin (1951:383–84) so aptly articulated:

> We have shown how crucial for the (De Soto) Commission's reconstruction is the location of Casqui. The crossing of the Mississippi . . . , the location of Pacaha . . . , the identification of the River of Casqui . . . , and the location of Quiguate . . . all depend on reasoning forward and backward, from an assumed location of Casqui.

One of the more satisfactory results of the statewide research team, put together by the Arkansas Archeological Survey twenty-four years ago, has been the following of the route of Hernando de Soto and his entourage. Enough precise information about local chronologies had to be gathered to even begin to make sense out of the vast amount of data once called merely "Mississippian." The sophisticated computerized site files and mapping programs had to be in place to produce the map of sixteenth-century sites in Arkansas (illustration 6). Tying in what happened in Arkansas with what was occurring outside the state borders took an even broader research effort, funded by the National Park Service (Hudson 1990a).

The geographical information derived from the Spanish accounts fits the interpretation of Parkin being Casqui quite neatly. The River of Casqui, which was an arm of the Great River, equates with the St. Francis River. The location of the capital of Casqui, going north up the river, fits Parkin. The description of the main Casqui town, with a high mound on the edge of the river corresponds nicely. Following the Tyronza River from its conjunction with the St. Francis River above the Parkin site back toward the Mississippi River and the Nodena phase also fits the description of the attack on Pacaha neatly. The varying swamps and the salt locality described by the chroniclers are still present in suitable places. The number of days of march match up well with the topography of the Parkin phase.

Even more conclusive is the archeological information. It is obviously important to know the dates of these sites. Regional chronologies, such as that developed for northeast Arkansas (Morse and Morse 1983) are a necessary first step. It was also important to know where societies were and were not present during the sixteenth century. The uninhabited area mentioned in the accounts matches the blank region on the map. Our route, using Parkin as the Casqui anchor, fits the more than 7,500 known sites in the Survey files for northeast Arkansas very well indeed. The presence of two sixteenth-century artifacts at Parkin is only one more bit of corroborative testimony. At the present time, the conclusion that Parkin indeed was the capital of Casqui is more certain than most archeological interpretations can be, viewing a limited amount of material evidence as best we can.

# Finding the Middle Passage: The Spanish Journey from the Swamplands to Caddo Country

Ann M. Early

## INTRODUCTION: INTO THE UPLANDS

The Spanish expedition led by Hernando de Soto crossed the Mississippi River in the spring of 1541. In the alluvial valley of eastern Arkansas, they encountered densely populated communities and extensive agricultural fields belonging to several distinct and highly organized chiefdoms. They became embroiled in the political rivalries between some of these societies and were duly impressed by the authority and political sophistication of the leaders of these "provinces." The Spaniards found abundant stores of food and other provisions they needed to replenish their depleted supplies, having lost much of their baggage, clothes, and food in pitched battles with native societies in present-day Alabama and Mississippi. But they found neither gold nor other goods that would mean wealth back in Spain, so they headed into the uplands.

After de Soto and his followers left the Mississippi Valley swamps, they embarked on what became the last phase of their quest for wealth and lands suitable for colonization, discoveries that would mean success to the increasingly disillusioned expedition. Instead of their long-sought objective, however, they reaped only minor and perhaps equivocal military success in encounters with native people in the provinces of Cayas and Tula, and the disappointment of discovering that searching further west was more likely to yield starvation than gold. Retreating southeast, they spent the winter where they could conscript enough food from native farming communities to sustain themselves. They began the year 1542 without any information that offered encouragement for their search and, after the death of de Soto early in that year, without the driving force that had brought them across the Southeast. The remainder of their expedition is primarily an account of their attempts, under the leadership of Luís de Moscoso, first to walk and then to sail back to their own world in New Spain and beyond.

## SPECULATIONS ABOUT THE EXPEDITION'S MOVEMENTS IN 1542

The story of this portion of the expedition's route recounted in the original documents is abbreviated, and, in parts, frustratingly contradictory. Descriptions of travel become perfunctory, and the latter portion of one document, the Rodrigo Ranjel narrative, is incomplete. At the same time, however, modern legends about the activities of the de Soto expedition in the uplands of Arkansas far overshadow either the documentary or archeological evidence of Spanish activities. Nineteenth- and early twentieth-century speculation about the Spaniards' route, and about the sites of Tanico and Tula in particular, culminated in the 1939 De Soto Commission decisions, dependent to a great extent on the interpretations of Col. John Fordyce of Hot Springs, establishing Hot Springs, Caddo Gap, and the Ouachita River Valley as the locations of this part of the expedition. Over the last half century, the commission route has become another layer of historical "proof." Not only is it viewed as the ultimate authority on the whereabouts of native communities and Spanish travels, but also it has inadvertently discouraged new considerations of either the original documents of the expedition or the growing body of archeological evidence about where and how native populations arranged themselves across the western Arkansas landscape. Questioning the accuracy of the 1939 de Soto route now becomes a challenge to several generations of popular legends that are woven into the early histories of places like Hot Springs. That these legends derive from the interests of modern residents to forge a local historic connection to the first European presence in the state, rather than from an abundance of documentary or archeological evidence, is a point often overlooked in reactions to the current re-evaluation of where the Spanish were in Arkansas.

## THE ROUTE PROPOSED BY CHARLES HUDSON

The restudy of the expedition route led by Charles Hudson, Chester DePratter and Marvin T. Smith (see Hudson, Smith, and DePratter 1984; Hudson, et al. 1985; Hudson, DePratter, and Smith 1989, Hudson 1990a) and taken up by numerous researchers across the Southeast, has stimulated a vigorous series of debates in scholarly circles. It has also instigated serious reassessments of the archeological evidence of sixteenth-century native settlement in the areas where the Spanish may have traveled, according to either the Swanton or Hudson versions of the route, and a new search for evidence of their presence.

In evaluating the Spaniards' activities west of the Mississippi River, Hudson (1985) proposed a route that was significantly different from that of Swanton. For eastern Arkansas, it drew from recent research on protohistoric societies by Dan and Phyllis Morse (1983), who were also interested in comparing the expedition route to the archeological sites and phases in northeast Arkansas. Over the last several years, Hudson's initially proposed route has been refined as he and several archeologists familiar with current archeological knowledge in Arkansas have reviewed the evidence, discussed problem areas and alternative routes, and used the results of the last fifty years of archeological research to test the "fit" between where we now believe sixteenth-century native societies lived and what the Spaniards described in their travels. As a result, the current consensus among archeologists in Arkansas is that the Hudson route for the de Soto expedition in Arkansas is far more internally consistent and compatible with current archeological knowledge than the Swanton route.

## THE PROVINCE OF CAYAS

The de Soto route from the Mississippi River to the province of Cayas proposed by Hudson and the archeologists has been discussed in detail elsewhere (Hudson 1985; Akridge 1986; Hudson, DePratter, and Smith 1989; Morse and Morse 1990; Dye, this volume). Their interpretation locates Cayas, which de Soto reached in late summer of 1541, in the Arkansas River valley in the Russellville or Carden Bottoms vicinity (see illustration 16). The army spent a month in this area, near the town of Tanico, foraging successfully in the native cornfields and fattening their horses. The Spaniards were impressed by the quality of the maize they found in Cayas, a testimony to the productivity of the soil. This is where the anonymous Gentleman of Elvas reported that there was a "very warm and brackish lake" that made the horses swell up when they drank after feeding in the cornfields, according to one translator (Bourne 1904, 1:136). The version of the Elvas narrative translated by Richard Hakluyt (Rye 1966:107) presented it as a very hot and brackish lake.

It is worth noting that this brief passage, along with a notation "Hot streams and the salt made from the sand" in an outline for one of the unfinished chapters in the diary of Rodrigo Ranjel (Bourne 1904, 2:150), constitutes the evidence for associating the de Soto expedition with Hot Springs National Park. The Ranjel notation is found at the end of his diary. If it records this item of information in proper chronological sequence, knowledge of hot streams took place after the death of de Soto, presumably at the time the survivors were traveling west in their attempt to reach New Spain by land. This brief notation does not indicate whether some of the Spaniards actually saw the natural phenomenon, or whether they merely heard about it. The "hot streams" and the warm or hot brackish lake, therefore, are likely to have been in two different places. I don't interpret this warm lake to have been hot springs, but instead to have been a shallow backswamp or oxbow pond that would have been noticeably warm at that time of year.

The Spaniards paused in Cayas to make salt. John Hann, Spanish colonial historian, translated this passage in the Elvas narrative as:

> Up to there [meaning Cayas] the Christians had lacked salt and there they made a great deal, which they carried on forward. The Indians carry it from there to other places to exchange for skins and cloaks. They gather it along the river, which it leaves on top of the sand when it goes down. And because they cannot gather it without taking more sand mixed with it, they throw it into some baskets that they have for this, wide of mouth and

narrow in the bottom. And they place it in the air above a frame and they throw water into it. And under it they place a vessel in which it falls . . . filtered and put on the fire to boil, diminishing, it provides the salt at the bottom of the pan." (Hann 1991:personal correspondence to J. Mitchem)

According to current evidence (Morse and Akridge 1988), Spanish saltmaking could have been possible along the west fork of Point Remove Creek within easy traveling distance of a proposed Russellville/Dardanelle location for Cayas (see illustration 16).

## THE PROVINCE OF TULA

From Tanico the Spanish made their famous foray to the province of Tula, reported to de Soto by the cacique or leader of Cayas as the largest neighboring population one-and-a-half days' travel away. Biedma (Bourne 1904, 2:32) wrote that by ascending the river and passing over some rough hills, they reached Tula. The Gentleman of Elvas (Bourne 1904, 1:137) reported that Tula lay south of Cayas.

Judging from the Spaniards' descriptions, the Tula inhabitants were culturally distinct from the people of Cayas. They spoke a different language and were described as traditional enemies. The cacique said he could not give de Soto a guide who could speak to them for the Spanish. According to Garcilaso de la Vega (1951:458), the Tula practiced head deformation and body tattooing as well, customs not found among prior groups.

De Soto, with some cavalry and infantry, made a sortie to Tula where they encountered fierce resistance. The Spaniards retreated, returned with the full army, and succeeded in taking possession of a town. The natives fought on foot and from their rooftops, and used spears and bows and arrows in combat. After the Spanish had assumed control of the community, the cacique and his entourage met de Soto with a ritualized display of weeping and gifts of cow (*sic*) skins. These were undoubtedly bison hides, some with the hair still on them, and not skins from feral or domesticated cattle. Public weeping was part of a formal greeting practice that was also described by later European explorers among the Caddo, not simply anguish at the capture of the town. The Indians reported, according to Elvas (Bourne 1904, 1:140), that "nearby to the northward are many cattle," and a thinly populated area with little maize.

## THE PROVINCES OF QUIPANA AND AUTIAMQUE

De Soto learned that there were "great towns" to the southeast, principally in a province called Autiamque, eighty leagues and ten days away and near a "great water" (Bourne 1904, 1:141). Leaving Tula, the Spaniards marched five days over mountains to the province of Quipana, with a town "among ridges." Neither Quipana nor Tula were densely populated communities like those found in eastern Arkansas, but rather they were composed of dwellings scattered over a wide area. Most distressing to the

Spaniards, there were no central storehouses with harvest surplus to be seized, facilities that de Soto had counted on previously to feed his army and its slaves and animals.

At Quipana, captured natives told the Spaniards that Autiamque was another six days distant, and that there was another populous province, Chaguate, eight days' travel to the south.

Ranjel (Bourne 1904, 2:149) reported that Quipana was "between ridges of mountains near a river: and from there they went for the night to a place where they could cross over . . . ," entering a plain the next day, and reaching Autiamque (or Utiamque as spelled by Ranjel) two days later where the Spaniards spent the winter of 1541–42 (Morse and Morse 1990:205). Elvas did not mention the descent to a plain, nor any other topographic feature between Quipana and Autiamque.

## SIXTEENTH-CENTURY ARCHEOLOGICAL EVIDENCE

The sketchy descriptions, inconsistencies, and general lack of detail for this stretch of the trek leave the precise route still uncertain. We can, though, postulate a route and a probable identity of the people of Tula. De Soto crossed a linguistic and cultural border between Tanico and Tula. The people of Tula, who lived in dispersed settlements, spoke a language new to the Spaniards and their native intermediaries, practiced head deformation and tattooing, wept during important greeting ceremonies, and had access to bison, were located west or southwest of Russellville. They must have been a Caddoan population because the settlement pattern, practices of body decoration, and greeting are all consistent with historic accounts of Caddo cultural practices.

Who were the Tula? There are no good ethnohistoric descriptions of indigenous native populations in the interior highlands of the northern Ouachita Mountains and adjacent Arkansas River Valley prior to the arrival of Cherokee migrants in the nineteenth century. Archeological evidence of the probable sixteenth-century residents of the region, however, does exist even though it is still incomplete. The archeological entity that fits this description is the Fort Coffee phase, best described in the Arkansas River valley upstream from modern Fort Smith near Spiro, Oklahoma. Dating to the 1400s and 1500s at least, this phase is marked by dispersed agricultural settlements whose inhabitants occasionally hunted bison. Their culture, as reflected in settlement patterns, material culture assemblage, and burial practices, shows relationships to Caddoan groups in the Ouachita and Red River valleys and to societies on the eastern edge of the plains (J. Brown, Bell, and Wycoff 1978; Rohrbaugh 1982, 1984; Sabo, et al. 1988).

The Fort Coffee phase was defined primarily on the basis of pottery vessels and other artifacts found during the excavation of several archeological sites in the vicinity of Spiro, Oklahoma, in the 1930s, and on the results of excavation at several small prehistoric residential sites in the same general area in the 1960s. Charles Rohrbaugh (1982, 1984) described the phase most recently when he examined the Works Progress Administration collections of the 1930s for his dissertation research. In examining the age of the Fort Coffee phase, Rohrbaugh (1984:268–70, Table 12.1) summarized radiocarbon dates from many sites. These indicate that the phase existed from perhaps as early as the late 1300s up to around 1600, with several dates falling within and after the 1540s. There is little doubt that the Fort Coffee phase was at least partly contemporary with the arrival of de Soto's army in western Arkansas.

The known archeological entity in the vicinity of Russellville and Dardanelle is the Carden Bottoms phase which was first defined as the Carden Bottoms Complex (M. P. Hoffman 1977:5). It is primarily based on the collection of pottery vessels and other artifacts dug from graves in the region in the early twentieth century (M. P. Hoffman 1977a, 1983; Clancy 1985; Sabo et al. 1988:118–19).

These artifacts are stylistically similar to collections found downstream in the Arkansas River valley in the vicinity of Little Rock and below. Unfortunately, no domestic sites of Carden Bottom phase people have yet been studied in detail. Although a few European artifacts from the Carden Bottoms area were picked up in or near the places where the native pottery was found, the exact age of the Carden Bottoms phase is still unverified. Some Caddoan pottery vessels (similar to those made in the Ouachita Valley in the southern Ouachita Mountains) found in Carden Bottoms collections suggest by their shape and design that the Carden Bottoms phase is roughly contemporary with the Fort Coffee phase.

## THE CULTURAL BOUNDARY BETWEEN MISSISSIPPIAN AND CADDOAN

Archeological evidence for a cultural boundary between the Fort Coffee and Carden Bottoms phases also exists. Very few artifacts from either the Carden Bottoms phase (Clancey 1985) or the Fort Coffee phase indicate interaction between these two polities during this time. When the Carden Bottoms artifact assemblage of whole pottery vessels is compared with both Spiro and Fort Coffee phase ceramics from upstream, there are strikingly few shared technological and decorative attributes (see illustration 17). Carden Bottoms utilitarian vessels are typically shell-tempered, globular, round-bottom jars. Spiro and Fort Coffee phase utilitarian ware includes primarily flat base shell tempered jars that are an outgrowth of preceding grog and grit-tempered Fourche Maline wares indigenous to the highlands and the upper Arkansas River region. Red slipped and painted decorations are characteristic of Carden Bottom bowls and bottles, but painting was not a part of the Fort Coffee ceramic decorative tradition.

Other elements of material culture, such as the styles of stone arrow points, also differ between these two areas. The indigenous traditions are not only different, but there is little evidence of trade in these material items between the two phases even though they lie close to each other along the same waterway. Key Caddoan vessel types that do occur at Carden Bottoms have counterparts in the Middle Ouachita drainage, however, and are good chronological indicators suggesting that the Spiro vicinity and Carden Bottoms assemblages are at least partly contemporary.

## THE FORT COFFEE PHASE IN ARKANSAS

Thus, for the Arkansas River valley between Russellville and the mouth of the Canadian River in eastern Oklahoma, there exists a material record of artifacts that reflects a hostile relationship between Tula and Tanico as described by the Spanish. There is no such archeological boundary in the Ouachita River basin between Hot Springs and Caddo Gap, the locations picked for Tanico and Tula by the 1939 Swanton report.

How far the Fort Coffee phase was distributed down the Arkansas River, or into the northern Ouachita Mountains is uncertain because we have so little archeological data from the interior highlands between the Arkansas and Ouachita rivers. However, artifact collections from this region housed in the Arkansas Archeological Survey laboratory at Arkansas Tech University and whole pottery vessels from this region in the Lemley Collection at the Gilcrease Institute in Tulsa, Oklahoma, both indicate that the Fourche LaFave, Petit Jean, and Poteau River valleys (see illustration 4) were inhabited by Fort Coffee and/or Fort Coffee-related populations, rather than by Carden Bottoms phase people. The southern boundary of the Fort Coffee phase is probably the watershed divide between the Ouachita and Fourche rivers, with Buckville phase (Early 1981, 1988) populations to the south. Fort Coffee ceramics from the Norman Site (Early 1990b) and the Standridge Site (Early 1988) in the upper Caddo River valley were important evidence of the southern extension of this phase.

The political center of Caddoan settlement in the northern Ouachita Mountains may have been the upper Fourche LaFave River valley near Bluffton (see illustration 16). A Caddoan site, as yet unassigned to any phases, with two pyramidal mounds, the largest mounds in the Ouachita Mountains in Arkansas, is located here. Typically, a surface survey indicates that this is not a nucleated, or compact, village site, but a "mound center" where few people lived, used by a farmstead-based dispersed population scattered along the river valley. According to Hudson's reconstruction of the route, this site may be the politico/religious core of the province of Tula. He places the Spanish-Tula encounter in this vicinity.

In comparison, prehistoric Caddoan populations in the upper Ouachita River valley were sufficiently dense to support a mound center, but a much smaller one, at the Adair site which is now under Lake Ouachita (Early 1982). A still smaller and less complex mound site, the Standridge Site, in the Caddo River drainage at Caddo Gap, indicates an even smaller and more dispersed population in this valley at the location proposed by Swanton for Tula (Early 1988).

## THE SPANISH-TULA ENCOUNTER

I consider the Fort Coffee, or Fort Coffee-related, phase in this region to be the remains of the Tula, but I am not certain of placing the Spanish-Tula encounter in the Bluffton vicinity, and I offer an alternative hypothesis for testing. The relative distances, or travel-times, between Tula, Quipana, Autiamque, and Chaguate, allowing for discrepancies among the various chronicles, indicate that Quipana was roughly half-way between Tula and Autiamque, that Chaguate was farther from Quipana than was Autiamque, and that it took five days to go from Tula to Quipana.

The geometry of distance and direction among these polities (plus additional information about archeological settlement patterns and prehistoric saltmaking activities) suggests that the populous Chaguate was in the Middle Ouachita River valley between Malvern and Arkadelphia, and Quipana was in the upper Ouachita River valley. The Bluffton vicinity may be the location of Tula, but I suggest that an equally good, or better, fit would be upstream from Carden Bottoms in the neighborhood of Ozark, Arkansas, in the Arkansas River valley. Constrictions in the Arkansas River floodplain near both Ozark and Clarksville are compatible with the topography described between Tanico and Tula, and the distance from this Tula location to Quipana is more satisfying to me. Furthermore, either of these options fits the current evidence better than the 1939 proposed route.

European artifacts from this time period in this area are virtually nonexistent, with only a single metal Clarksdale bell, an artifact associated with sixteenth-century Spanish explorers, attributed to the Carden Bottoms vicinity at present (Clancy 1985). Protohistoric settlement (1500–1700) in the vicinity of the town of Ozark, Fort Coffee Phase or otherwise, is still poorly documented. This is at least in part because farmstead-sized sites that would be the remains of a single household or family settlement, typical of the Fort Coffee phase upstream of Fort Smith, are very small. Little material evidence of the existence of these sites, such as broken and discarded pottery and stone tools, is visible on the surface of the ground. Because of their small size and the lack of mounds and/or dense midden deposits that would make them easily visible to searchers, these sites are certainly severely under-represented in the current data base.

If Quipana was in the upper Ouachita River region, de Soto and his men would have traveled down the Ouachita and crossed over (as the Ranjel chronicle indicates) a narrow watershed divide near Mountain Valley into the headwaters of the Saline River basin. They then followed this stream down to the Benton vicinity, and then went east from there to the Arkansas River.

## THE SPRING OF 1542: INTO CADDO COUNTRY

In the spring of 1542, after de Soto's death, the expedition tried to go west and south to New Spain. Soon after leaving their winter camp in the Arkansas River Valley, they stopped at Chaguate where they made salt. As Schambach (1989, this volume) and others have pointed out, this "province" was almost certainly in the Middle Ouachita Region, which is the section of valley between where the Ouachita River leaves the mountains near Rockport and its junction with the Little Missouri River below Arkadelphia. Salt is available as brine in streams and seeps in several places in this portion of the valley, and a dense late prehistoric and protohistoric Caddoan population resided here (Early 1982, 1991; I. Williams and Early 1990). This location is compatible with the directions to Chaguate given to the Spanish the autumn before at Quipana, even though the distance may seem too short at first. The airline distance for our placement of the route from Quipana to Chaguate is not as great as the straight-line distance from Quipana to Autiamque, but as they say in the hills today, "you can't get there from here." Foot travel would have been either at right angles to the east-west trending novaculite ridges of this core area of the Ouachita Mountains, or would have been downstream along the Ouachita River, which flows first east and then south before exiting the mountains and flowing southwest to Arkadelphia (see illustration 16).

Recent research at the Hardman Site (3CL418) has led to a better understanding of the sequence of prehistoric Caddoan occupation of the Middle Ouachita Region before and after the de Soto expedition (I. Williams and Early 1990). The Hardman site is part of the protohistoric native saltmaking community along Saline Bayou and is situated across the bayou from the Bayou Sel Site (3CL27), which Schambach (1989 this volume) has identified as the probable location of the Spaniards' 1542 saltmaking activities. Three archeological phases are now identified. The Mid-Ouachita phase, once the only phase identified in this region, is now estimated to have extended from around 1400 to 1500. It was followed by the Social Hill phase from around 1500 to 1650, representing the de Soto-era population in this portion of the Ouachita Valley. A final resident regional population is marked by the Deceiper phase from around 1650 to 1700.

The number and distribution of Social Hill phase and Deceiper phase Caddoan sites known in the Middle Ouachita Region indicates that Caddoan communities continued to exist there without any cataclysmic population decline or social disruption through the Deceiper phase. Deceiper phase sites are not as numerous as preceding Social Hill phase sites, and may reflect a slightly diminished population as a result of Spanish contact. The pattern of life as reflected in the location and distribution of Deceiper phase sites shows few significant differences from preceding occupations.

The viability of a Caddoan community in this valley after the de Soto expedition in Arkansas offers indirect support for Hudson's reconstruction, and contradicts the expected impact from a sustained encounter that would have been a result of the route proposed by Swanton. The encounter between natives and Europeans at Chaguate was brief, because the latter paused only long enough in their trek to replenish supplies and make a little salt. It was not marked by the extensive violence, social disruption, and food seizures that occurred in many other communities that were unwilling hosts to the Spanish army for longer periods of time. As Schambach (this volume) points out, historic Caddo communities did not have centralized food warehouses, and this lack made Spanish efforts to provision the army difficult wherever they went in Caddo Country.

If the new de Soto route is correct, the Spaniards would have passed quickly through the Ouachita River valley on their walk west, and then briefly again on the return retreat to their last winter (1542–43) in the Mississippi Valley. By contrast, the 1939 de Soto Commission report concluded that the Spanish army wintered in the Ouachita valley in 1541–42 after the encounter at Tula, which they located at Caddo Gap. Had this been so, Spanish-Indian interaction in the Middle Ouachita Region during several months of foraging expeditions would have been far more sustained. This would have been a necessity, because we understand now that downstream on the Ouachita River, below Camden, late prehistoric people were thinly distributed across a landscape that they exploited primarily by collecting wild foods (Schambach 1990a:122–23). There are no large late prehistoric farming populations in this portion of the valley in far southern Arkansas, and therefore no maize surpluses for the Spaniards to have seized to feed themselves that winter. If the expedition camped on the Ouachita that winter instead of along the Arkansas as the new route indicates, the Spaniards would have stripped the farmers of the Middle Ouachita River valley of their stored crops, bringing natives and Europeans into repeated, violent contact and leaving behind economically devastated communities.

There is no indication that this level of regional disruption occurred in the Social Hill or Deceiper phases in the Middle Ouachita region. Instead, bioarcheological analysis of the human remains from the last, Deceiper phase, occupation at the Hardman site (Burnett 1990a) indicates a higher general level of nutritional adequacy and lower incidence of serious disease for these last indigenous native inhabitants of the valley than for their immediate ancestors.

There is, however, some biological and archeological evidence which suggests, perhaps, a short disruptive period after 1500. One Social Hill/Deceiper phase site, 3CL195, about twenty-two kilometers from Hardman, had a population that showed virtually none of the normal disease and degenerative disorder patterns found in other pre-Columbian populations. One individual from this site is believed to have survived a case of smallpox (Burnett 1990a:11–91). Another contemporary site, 3CL196, fifteen kilometers from 3CL195 and seven kilometers from the Hardman site, dug by amateur archeologists in the 1930s, yielded an unusually large number of burial features suggesting an episode of social disruption and/or disease occurring shortly before the valley was abandoned about 1700. Whether these disruptions were the result of the de Soto expedition, or some other episode of social disruption, remains to be determined.

After a brief rest, the Spanish army left Chaguate heading west. When they realized they would not find sufficient supplies to continue their overland trek through the non-agricultural native societies in present-day Texas, they retraced their steps through Caddo country to the Mississippi River. It would be more than one hundred years before Europeans returned to this portion of Arkansas.

# The End of the Trail: Reconstruction of the Route of Hernando de Soto's Army through Southwest Arkansas and East Texas

Frank F. Schambach

## INTRODUCTION

The first phase of de Soto scholarship began with the work of the French cartographer Guillaume de l'Isle in 1718 (Swanton 1939:12) and culminated with the publication in 1939 of the *Final Report of the United States De Soto Expedition Commission* by the great ethnohistorian, John R. Swanton. We are now in the midst of a second phase of de Soto scholarship, stimulated mainly by another leading ethnohistorian of the Southeast, Charles Hudson of the University of Georgia, and based on the wealth of archeological data, including recent discoveries of de Soto sites and de Soto artifacts (for example, Ewen 1988) that have accumulated since the De Soto Commission report. It is, of course, no reflection on the work of Swanton and his many collaborators to say that these new data, particularly radiocarbon dates—undreamed of in 1939—have given modern scholars a new and superior perspective on the de Soto expedition route.

The subject of this essay is the extreme western end of the invasion route, the bitter end of the expedition, when for almost six months after the death of de Soto the dwindling remnants of the Spanish army wandered through southwest Arkansas and east Texas with no goals other than to stay alive and to somehow get to Mexico. For various reasons this is the least-known part of the entire route. While there has always been some semblance of a consensus on the general path of the army from Tampa Bay to the Mississippi (and it is improving in the light of recent work), things began to unravel when we came to the Arkansas segment of the route. And when we come to the place that marks the beginning of the end of the expedition, the town of Guachoya where de Soto died (probably somewhere in southeast Arkansas), what little remaining consensus there was evaporated and the proposed routes went off in completely different directions (Swanton 1939:Map 2; Hudson 1985). Did the Spaniards go south after de Soto died, down the Ouachita River, and then west across north Louisiana to the Red

River Valley and east Texas, as Swanton thought? Or did they go overland across southwest Arkansas to the Red River Valley, as Hudson thought? Were the "salt boilers of Chaguate" Tunica people in northcentral Louisiana (Swanton 1939:273) or Caddo people in southwest Arkansas (Hudson 1985:9)?

Poor documentation was the main reason for the confusion. The Ranjel narrative, the best and most detailed of all the de Soto documents on the day-to-day movements of the army, is missing for this part of the route. It ends on Wednesday, November 2, 1541, when the Spaniards reached Autiamque, probably near present Little Rock (Swanton 1939:331; Hudson 1985:7). To make matters worse, the movements of the army probably became more erratic once it lost its leader. It was now a hungry, exhausted army, its military superiority waning as its few remaining precious horses were wounded or killed in battle after battle with the Indians. Although it was moving generally southwest, the direction of its day-to-day marches was determined mainly by the availability, real or alleged, of Indian maize and salt. Near the end, as one of the chroniclers, Biedma, reported: "We were obliged to go where the Indians directed us" (Bourne 1904, 2:36).

There were also some problems peculiar to the interpretation of this part of the route. When the Spaniards marched from Guachoya to Chaguate, they left the Mississippi valley, the western edge of the homeland of the great Mississippian societies that dominated the Southeast in the sixteenth century, and crossed into another country, the Caddo area of the Trans-Mississippi South (Schambach and Early 1982; Jelks 1988:493). The Caddo area, besides being all but completely unknown archeologically at the time of the de Soto Commission report, was different in many ways, some of them quite basic, from anything the Spaniards, or the scholars who translated and interpreted the narratives, were familiar with. This has led to various ambiguities in the narratives and perhaps to some errors in the translations and the interpretations. Also, when the Spaniards entered the Caddo area, they were marching off the map as far as most archeologists and ethnohistorians were concerned. Their main interest has been the Mississippian societies, societies so complex and spectacular they make Caddo culture, spectacular enough in its own right, look drab by comparison. What in the Caddo area could compare with the Lady of Cofitachequi, carried in state on a white litter to meet the Spaniards, or with the town of Talomico with its five hundred houses and its lofty and spacious temple with chests full of pearls and furs (Hudson 1976:110–11)? So, interest in this segment of the route has been minimal. The De Soto Commission report devoted less than ten pages to it, and Jeffrey Brain seems to have voiced the scholarly consensus with the remark that "About this abortive overland attempt very little can be said" (Brain 1985:xlv). He was right in many respects, but we can still add something to what has been said, and even that needs clarification.

The stimulus for this essay came entirely from Charles Hudson. Prior to receiving a letter from him in July 1988, I had little interest in the de Soto expedition because none of the more plausible of the reconstructed routes traversed my primary research area in southwest Arkansas. Swanton's early reconstruction had the Spaniards crossing the Red River in northwest Louisiana, north of Shreveport, and Hudson's original reconstruction (1985) had them skirting my area on the north, following a route from

Arkadelphia west to Oklahoma, then turning south and crossing the Red River into Texas (Swanton 1939:348b, Map 10; Hudson 1985:Figure 1). But when Hudson proposed a new version of his route that had the Spaniards cutting right through my research area from the northwest to the southwest, I was obliged to check it against the archeology. I found that this route could be modified to fit the local archeology very well, without—I think—putting undue strain on the documentary evidence; but the latter must be left to the ethnohistorians to decide (illustration 18).

I am particularly impressed with the correspondence between the five Indian provinces the Spaniards traversed (from Chaguate to Naguatex) and the five archeological regions or subregions we have identified in southwest Arkansas (Schambach and Early 1982:Figure sw1). Thus, Chaguate would be in the Middle Ouachita region; Aguacay would be in the Little Missouri region; Pato would be in the Little River region; Amaye would be the western (Texarkana phase) subdivision of the Great Bend region; and Naguatex would be the southern (Belcher phase) subdivision of the Great Bend region (illustration 19).

Hudson told me that ethnohistorians had not had similar success along other parts of the route in matching the Indian "provinces" or polities described in the narratives with sixteenth-century archeological phases. One reason for our apparent success in southwest Arkansas is the extraordinary variability of Caddo pottery compared to Mississippian pottery. This has enabled us to identify many small, highly distinct regional ceramic traditions with considerable time depth, many of which can be linked with important Caddo polities of the historic period such as the Kadohadacho, the Nasoni, the Cahinno, and the Hasinai (Schambach 1982:18; C. H. Webb 1959; Hodges and Hodges 1944; Swanton 1942). In this respect, the culture history of the Caddo area is substantially different from the culture history of most of the country the Spaniards traversed east of the Caddo area. There, assuming it was ever in the cards, the development of small distinct regional cultures like those in the Caddo area was stifled by the development and spread of Mississippian culture, beginning around A.D. 900, so that during most of their travels in the Southeast the Spaniards encountered only Mississippians. In the Caddo area, where there was no Mississippian intrusion and Mississippian influence was superficial, culture history followed a course toward balkanization, rather than homogenization, from at least A.D. 1000 on.

My discussion of Hudson's route is based on varying levels of expertise. For the Arkansas segment I am on home ground and, for whatever it is worth, I can bring to bear more than twenty years of field experience with the sites and the countryside of southwest Arkansas. For the Texas segment I claim no special knowledge. Other than sheer curiosity, my only justification for trying to follow the trail of the Spaniards into Texas is my conviction that unless the Texas segment can be shown to fit the archeology and ethnohistory reasonably well, there must be something wrong with my reconstruction of the Arkansas segment.

Now let us proceed to a comparison of the 1985 Hudson route with the archeology and with the narratives of Elvas and Biedma, the only two (of the four) chroniclers of the expedition who cover this segment of the route. My main source for these narratives is the Robertson translation in Quinn 1979, volume 2. Occasionally, where there are discrepancies that seem to be instructive, I also refer to the Hakluyt translation (Rye 1851).

## THE SPANIARDS ENTER THE CADDO AREA

On June 20, 1542, de Soto's army entered the Caddo area from the east and arrived in a province called Chaguate. The Spaniards had already passed through the northernmost Caddo provinces of Tula, Quipana, and Quitamaya in the Ouachita Mountains the previous fall, on their way to the Mississippian town of Autiamque on the Arkansas River south of Little Rock, where they spent a cold and snowy winter (Hudson 1985:7; Quinn 1979, 2:134–42; Early this volume). The army was now led by Luís de Moscoso, because de Soto had died, at forty-two, of a raging fever on May 21. By this time the army had lost about half of its fighting men and most of its horses. But it still numbered at least three hundred Spaniards, perhaps as many as five hundred "Indians of service" (men, women, and children, many of them in chains), about forty horses, at least seven hundred hogs, and a pack of wardogs trained to attack and kill Indians[1] (Swanton 1939:87–92; Quinn 1979, 2:149–50). The army we must picture entering Chaguate on that June day, and wending its way across southwest Arkansas for the next 59 days before moving into east Texas, was a "great caravan, soldiers and scouts in the lead, Indian bearers carrying the goods of the expedition, but the bulk of the men with their female slaves walking slowly behind, and a long trail of hogs winding slowly behind them" (Quinn 1979, 2:90).

## CADDO SETTLEMENT PATTERNS

The cultural landscape the Spaniards were about to enter as they marched west toward Chaguate and the northeastern border of the Caddo area was different from the one they were leaving behind. In the Caddo area they would no longer find large compact towns with dozens or even hundreds of houses like Talomico, or like Quiguate (possibly the Grant site in Lee County), which had so many houses de Soto was able to quarter his whole army in half of them and burn the rest (Hudson 1985:4; Quinn 1979, 2:132–33). In the Caddo area, populations were smaller and settlements consisted of small farmsteads and other types of compounds dispersed over the countryside for miles around the mounds or mound groups that were the ceremonial centers for these communities. These centers did not have large resident populations, just a few priests or caretakers.

We have good documentary evidence for this type of settlement pattern in the form of the so-called Teran "map" (illustration 20), actually a marvelously detailed drawing of a complete Caddo settlement somewhere near present Texarkana in 1691–92, one hundred and fifty years after the Spaniards passed through the Red River Valley. The archeological data indicate this settlement pattern developed in the eleventh century (M. M. Wedel 1978; Schambach 1982:6–9). The settlement in the Teran drawing consists of twenty-five clusters of buildings, of which twenty-three appear to be farmsteads, dispersed along both sides of the Red River and around two oxbow lakes, over a distance of no less than 2.5 miles and possibly 6 miles or more. At the western edge is a compound containing a platform mound with a building on top and a brush-covered arbor close to the base of the mound, but no other structures. The documentary data pertaining to the Teran expedition are very clear on the point that the compound of the "caddi," as the Caddo called him, or the cacique,[2] as the Spaniards would have called him, was about a mile and a half east of the mound, near the center of the settlement. His compound (identified on the map by a cross and the notation "Caddi") is similar to the others, but it is in a much larger clearing, and, very significantly, it is the only one without a storage bin. This would prove to be a problem for the Spaniards who were to find that, unlike Mississippian chiefs, the caddices of the Caddo did not collect food in central granaries for the purpose of redistributing it to the population later on. From historic accounts, it is known that Caddo farmers kept their own maize in their own granaries; it was they who fed the caddices, and not vice versa (Griffith 1954:62–65).

To the Spaniards this meant they could not plunder the corn of a whole province or town by finding the town or the house of the *caddi*; they had to get it the hard way, by going from farmstead to farmstead. To us, trying to interpret the narratives and reconstruct the invasion route, all this information on Caddo settlement patterns means, for one thing, that we should not assume the Spaniards moved through the Caddo area by going from ceremonial center to ceremonial center. They did not. As important as ceremonial centers were to the Caddo, they were of no interest to the Spaniards because they were not places where either maize or political leaders were to be found. It also means the remains of the "towns" of the Caddo caddices the Spaniards visited through the Caddo area will be all but unrecognizable archeologically (certainly not without extensive and careful excavation). These "towns" were no more than small compounds with a house or two or three, and a brush arbor or two. They were, as far as we know, indistinguishable from ordinary farmsteads except, of course, for the lack of storage bins, a diagnostic trait that could hardly be more useless archeologically. We might suppose the word "town" would have meant a group of dwellings larger than this, and the Spaniards certainly used it that way in Mississippian country. But in the Caddo area they seemed to have used it for these very small compounds as well. For example, in both the Robertson translation and the Hakluyt translation, a group of "four or five" houses in the "miserable" Caddo province of Nisohone in east Texas is described as a "town" (Quinn 1979, 2:145; Rye 1851:135).

To return, for a moment, to the problem of recognizing the towns of the caddices archeologically, it does appear that at certain sites away from ceremonial centers (the centers always have flat-topped mounds), certain Caddo personages, perhaps they were caddices, perhaps not, were buried in low dome-shaped mounds constructed over the burned remains of houses. So the sites of some of the "towns" of the caddices which the Spaniards visited may be marked by unobtrusive dome-shaped mounds, probably no more than three feet high.

## THE PROVINCE OF CHAGUATE, BETWEEN MALVERN AND ARKADELPHIA

Now, let us pick up the trail of the Spaniards as they entered the Caddo province of Chaguate. Hudson (1985:9)placed Chaguate on the Ouachita River between Malvern and Arkadelphia. This is the heart of the Middle Ouachita archeological region (Schambach and Early 1982:12). In this province the Spaniards "passed through a small town where there was a lake where the Indians made salt. The Christians made some on a day they rested there from some briny water which rose near the town in pools like springs" (Quinn 1979, 2:143). Hudson, with advice from Ann Early, has identified this place as the Bayou Sel site (3CL27) on Saline Bayou. I agree.

Briny water rising in pools like springs is a good description of the salt springs at Bayou Sel. There is more than one cluster of salt springs in this part of the Ouachita Valley,[3] but if we assume the Spaniards would have headed for the most productive and most heavily used salines (if for no other reason than there were probably good trails leading to them), then Bayou Sel would have been the site. The earliest European salt works in Arkansas were established here, in large part because the salt springs were extremely productive. In 1965 and again in 1969, I excavated small areas of the Bayou Sel site and found excellent stratigraphy with pottery indicating heavy occupation throughout the sixteenth century, during the Mid-Ouachita phase (Schambach and Early 1982).

The Spaniards stayed six days in Chaguate. There they learned of a province called Aguacay "three days journey to the west" so they set out to find it.[4] A three days' journey to the west, say forty or forty-five miles, would have taken them into the heart of the Little Missouri region (Schambach and Early 1982:11–12). This region was heavily occupied throughout the Caddo period, and population was probably at its peak during the sixteenth century. There are at least twenty ceremonial centers, each with from one to eleven mounds, distributed in a forty-mile-wide band along the general route that the Spaniards must have taken from Arkadelphia toward Texarkana and the Red River Valley. Many of them were in use during the sixteenth century, so the Spanish were probably always within about twenty miles of an active temple mound, whether they knew it or not, and they must have seen farmsteads and other types of compounds everywhere.

## FROM CHAGUATE TO AGUACAY, PROBABLY NEAR NASHVILLE

When the Spaniards arrived in Aguacay on Wednesday, July 4, the Indians were expecting them, for they were met by fifteen people carrying presents of skins, fish, and roasted venison. But when they reached the "town of the cacique of Aguacay," it was empty (Quinn 1979, 2:143). Probably, as we have seen, this "town" was not much different from all the other farmsteads in this province. The Spaniards stayed there "for some time"—about eleven days according to my calculations—during which they "made several inroads in which many Indians, both men and women, were captured" (Quinn 1979, 2:143), to be added to the forlorn train of bearers and slaves that accompanied the army. Evidently many people were living in farmsteads scattered around the countryside. There was also much maize in the granaries at these farmsteads, enough to feed the army for eleven days. The Spaniards observed that "There a considerable quantity of salt was made from the sand which they gathered in a vein of earth like slate" (Quinn 1979, 2:143). This salt source need not have been—and probably was not—at the town of the cacique, because Elvas' narrative gives the impression it was a place the Spaniards discovered on one of the "inroads" or forays they made while they were there. The term used in the Hakluyt translation is "roades" (Rye 1851:131), literally an armed foray on horseback in hostile territory. Foraging for the maize stored at Caddo farmsteads scattered over the countryside was probably the main reason for these "roades."

The site of the town of the cacique of Aguacay is probably somewhere around Nashville, Arkansas. This locality is forty-three to forty-five miles west of Arkadelphia, and, equally important, it is also an easy one-day march northeast of a major salt site (3SV69), which was, I believe, the Spaniards' next stop. A three-day march of forty-three to forty-five miles does not seem too long for this segment of the route. The Spaniards were fresh from a six-day stay in Chaguate. They also had the advantage of the long summer days of late June and early July, but perhaps without the debilitating heat and humidity of southwest Arkansas in mid-July and August. Later, on July 23, they did complain about the "great heat" when they reached the province of Naguatex in the Red River Valley (Quinn 1979, 2:144). The narratives hint they were on a trail of some sort, because the welcoming party sent out by the cacique of Aguacay apparently knew exactly where to wait for them. I suspect they were following a very good trail that led from Arkadelphia (and probably from all points north to Cahokia in Illinois) to the Red River Valley.

Assuming we could find it, the site of this "town" might just possibly be identifiable through careful archeological investigation, since the army spent so many days there. But I do not know how we would ever recognize it to begin with. At most, it might be marked by an inconspicuous low dome-shaped mound covering a house floor and perhaps some graves.

The place where the Spaniards saw salt being extracted from sand must have been somewhere along the Little Missouri in Pike County. According to the State Geologist's Office, the reference to salt-laden sand being collected from a "vein of earth like slate," is a plausible description of a salt spring in a fissure in the slate bedrock that is quite common in southern Pike County. There are at least two saltmaking sites (3PI18 and 3PI20) in this area. There are no salt sources south of the Little Missouri in Hempstead County (N. F. Williams 1959:75), so this place could not have been any closer to Nashville (and to my proposed location for the town of the cacique of Aguacay) than somewhere along the north side of the Little Missouri River in Pike County.

## SOUTHWEST FROM AGUACAY, TOWARD THE RED RIVER VALLEY

Upon leaving their bivouac at the town of the cacique of Aguacay, the Spaniards apparently turned southwest, because Biedma wrote: "After leaving this place, the Indians told us we should see no more settlements unless we went down in the southwest-and-by-south direction where we should find larger towns and food; that in the course we asked about, there were some large sandy wastes, without any people or subsistence whatsoever" (Quinn 1979, 2:185–86). This statement is a little puzzling because while it is generally true, it is not strictly true. Had the Spaniards gone far enough west, they would have come to sandy wastes eventually, but only after about two hundred miles. First they would have passed through the extensive territory of the McCurtain phase Caddo population along the Red River and its northern tributaries in western Arkansas and southeastern Oklahoma (see illustration 3). And while "large towns" and food were to be found to the south, these "towns" were, of course, Caddo-style dispersed settlements. On the whole it sounds as if the Spaniards were having trouble communicating through their Indian translators, a major problem for them ever since the death of their own translator, Juan Ortiz, in March (Quinn 1979, 2:137). Less likely, but just possibly, this may have been an attempt by the people of Aguacay to divert the Spanish army away from the McCurtain phase people. The archeology of these two regions is similar, and these groups may have been allies.

The best account of where the Spaniards went when they left their bivouac site comes from the narrative of Elvas (Quinn 1979, 2:143): "On the day the governor left Aguacay, he went to sleep near a small town subject to the lord of that province. The camp was pitched quite near to a salt marsh and on that evening some salt was made there." This is a good clue because the locations of all the productive salt springs in southwest Arkansas have been known since the 1830s, due to their great importance in the frontier economy (Littlefield 1973).

If the Spaniards went south-southwest from Nashville and found a salt marsh, they must have gone to site 3SV69 on the west side of the Saline River about twelve miles from Nashville.[5] This is the one site between Arkadelphia and Fulton that actually fits a description in the narratives; the extensive Indian and European salt works there are on low ridges surrounding a small salt marsh. This marsh is a unique feature for southwest Arkansas salt sites. At all the other major salt sites I have examined, such as Bayou Sel at Arkadelphia, the Holman Springs site (3SV29), and the Old Bell Estate (3SV39), both near De Queen, and the Cerro Gordo site (3SV38) south of De Queen on the Oklahoma border, the saline springs rise out of deeply incised stream beds. My sherd collections indicate that site 3SV69 was occupied throughout the sixteenth century, and, judging from the size of the middens, it was much used. This means there were trails leading to it. Since the Spaniards made some salt there in the evening, it is likely they went there specifically to get salt. Considering their maize diet, the heat, and their strenuous activity day after day, their physiological requirements for salt must have been very high. Mayan peasants on a similar diet require up to thirty grams per day while working their fields (Andrews 1983:8–10). This suggests the army must have required, at the least, about two pounds a day to keep moving, not to mention the requirements of the "Indians of service."

From 3SV69 it is about twenty-five miles downriver to the confluence of the Little River and the Red River near Fulton. Possibly the Spaniards went that way but travel in the Saline River and Little River bottoms in July would have been difficult. I suspect they moved south-southwest on a good overland trail that led from 3SV69 to the vicinity of Texarkana. In 1710, Benard de la Harpe sent men twenty-five to thirty miles north-northeast from his trading post near Texarkana to get salt (M. M. Wedel 1978; see also Swanton 1942:139–40). It looks as if they were making a beeline for 3SV69, which suggests there was a trail. Also, John Mitchell's 1755 "Map of the British and French Dominions of North America" (M. M. Wedel 1981:Figure 18) shows a place called "Salt House" on the Saline River, which is probably site 3SV69. This map also shows some Caddo towns on the Red River west of Fulton but little else in that area, creating the impression that in the eighteenth century, at least, this site was a salt source for the Red River Caddo.

Another reason for suspecting that the Spaniards traveled south-southwest from 3SV69 is they traveled through at least one and possibly two cultural provinces (Pato? and Amaye) before they got to Naguatex (Quinn 1979, 2:143). A route southeast from the 3SV69, perhaps simply following the Saline River and then the Little River southeast to Fulton, would have taken them directly into the province of Naguatex, i.e., the Belcher phase (see illustration 3) territory from Fulton south to Shreveport (illustration 18). They would have missed Amaye entirely, and probably Pato as well.

Their first overnight camp south of 3SV69 was "between two ridges in a forest of open trees" (Quinn 1979, 2:143). This would have been somewhere around Ben Lomond and Paraloma (illustration 16). I do not have a specific place in mind, but the countryside in that area lends itself to this description.

"The next day," the narrative continues, the Spaniards "reached a small town called Pato" (Quinn 1979, 2:143). Assuming they were traveling south-southwest, they would have crossed the Little River near White Cliffs, where it was probably easy to ford. It may be more than coincidence that there is a group of six small house mounds at White Cliffs (M. P. Hoffman 1971:371–455). This site (3LR12) is mainly early Caddo (A.D. 1000 to 1200), but occupation continued through the sixteenth century. Pato could have been there or nearby. The sixteenth-century archeology of the Little River drainage has yet to be worked out, but it is possible there was a distinct polity here, one that was more closely related to the McCurtain phase of Oklahoma (see illustration 3) than to the polities of the Little Missouri region or the Great Bend region of Arkansas. That could account for the ambiguity in the narratives over the cultural affinities of Pato.

## THE SPANIARDS REACH THE RED RIVER VALLEY AND APPROACH THE GREAT PROVINCE OF NAGUATEX

Still following the salt trail, the Spaniards would have entered the Red River valley due north of Texarkana, in the vicinity of Ogden. There they found "the first settlement of a province called Amaye" (Quinn 1979, 2:143).[6] The Ogden-Texarkana area is near the eastern boundary of the territory of the sixteenth-century Texarkana phase (E. M. Davis 1970:50–51). An Indian the Spaniards captured in Amaye told them "it was a day and a half journey to Naguatex, all of which lay through an inhabited region" (Quinn 1979, 2:143). From Ogden it is thirty to thirty-two miles east along the north side of the Red River to Fulton and then south to the vicinity of Garland City, the area that, as we shall see, I consider the very heart of the province of Naguatex. Thirty-two miles sounds like a reasonable day and a half trip for Indians following good trails through settled country in the Red River valley. The phrase "all of which lay through an inhabited region" is an excellent description of what the Red River valley must have looked like in 1542, with Caddo farmsteads everywhere.

Turning east, now, and traveling along the north side of the Red River from Ogden, the Spaniards came to a "brook in a luxuriant grove between Amaye and Naguatex" where they made camp at midday on Saturday, July 20 (Quinn 1979, 2:143; Swanton 1939:332. Swanton claims the correct date was July 22). The archeological boundary between Texarkana phase territory and Belcher phase territory is generally thought to be somewhere not far east of Texarkana. A half-day's travel, about seven miles, sounds right. Camping along a brook also sounds right. In the Red River valley, the Spaniards had to camp along brooks because it would have been impossible to water their livestock in the Red River. Because its precipitous twenty-five-foot banks cave constantly, they would have had trouble finding trails leading down them. In most places a man cannot climb them because they overhang. The brook would have been Bois D'Arc Bayou, a tributary of Hudson Creek, which is a tributary of Little River. Bois D'Arc Bayou runs more or less parallel to Red River for about six miles east from Temple. It is about a mile and a half north of the Red River and it was occupied in prehistoric times. We have recorded eleven sites along it, although we are not sure any of them are from the sixteenth century.[7]

On the same day the Spaniards made camp in the grove between Amaye and Naguatex, the cacique of Naguatex, who had obviously been keeping track of their movements, launched a well-organized attack, evidently with the intention of stopping them at his northwestern border. Although the Spaniards did not credit it as such, this attack seems to have included a feint designed to separate the cavalry from the rest of the Spanish army, and it almost succeeded: ". . . many Indians came in two bands from two directions. As soon as they saw they had been perceived, uttering loud cries they rushed upon the Christians with great fury, each band in its own part. But on seeing the resistance they met with from the Christians, they turned and fled, and in their flight many of them lost their lives. While most of the horse were going in pursuit of them, quite forgetful of the camp, two other bands of Indians who had been concealed, attacked them" (Quinn 1979, 2:143).

In this battle many Caddo men were killed (or so the Spaniards claim; we have not heard the Caddo side), and many Spaniards and horses were wounded, but none seriously. Afterwards, the one Indian taken alive told the Spaniards the attack was a joint effort of the caciques of Naguatex, Amaye, and Hacanac and that the cacique of Naguatex "came as captain and head of all" (Quinn 1979:144).

We have already identified the province of Amaye as the archeologically defined Texarkana phase, and this in turn has been linked with the protohistoric Little River phase and the historic Nasoni tribe (S. Williams 1964; M. P. Hoffman 1971; M. M. Wedel 1978; Schambach 1982:10). According to Swanton (1942:31), the word Amaye resembles the Caddo word for "male human being." This has a ring of truth to it. Around the world the same scene was acted out again and again as the European invaders encountered native peoples. The Europeans demanded to know "who are you?" and the natives replied "we are human beings, men, people."

There are no clues in the narratives to the location or the archeological identity of the province called Hacanac. According to Swanton (1942:8) "Hacanac . . . may be identical with Lacane." This is not too helpful since the Lacane were a small group living well southwest of the Great Bend region, probably in the Cypress Creek drainage, or so I will argue presently. Most probably the Hacanac were a group living west or southwest of the Texarkana phase people of Amaye, either in the Red River valley, or somewhere between the Red River and the Sulphur River in east Texas. That would put them within the probable sphere of influence of the cacique of Naguatex, and close enough to get men to the battlefield on a few days' notice.

## THE LOCATION AND ARCHEOLOGICAL IDENTITY OF NAGUATEX

We can be much more positive about the province, or polity, of Naguatex, whose cacique was a sophisticated strategist and also a man with enough political power to permit him to organize a joint defense against the Spaniards using the warriors and leadership of three polities, with himself "as captain and head of all." If the Spaniards were where I think they were (on the north side of the Red River somewhere along Bois d'Arc Bayou between Temple and Fulton), then the province of Naguatex, whose western border they were threatening, had to be the archeologically delimited Belcher phase territory which extends along both sides of the Red River from the vicinity of Fulton south to Shreveport, Louisiana (Schambach 1982:9). The Belcher site (C. H. Webb 1959), about fifteen miles north of Shreveport, is the southernmost Belcher phase ceremonial center. Although the Spaniards evidently penetrated the western border of Naguatex somewhere slightly west of Fulton, the archeology tells us that the population center of this province had to be in the vicinity of Garland City, about twenty miles south of Fulton, within the area I call the Spirit Lake locality (Schambach 1982:93–94).

The Spirit Lake locality takes in the Red River valley from about ten miles north of present Garland City to about fifteen miles south of it. Known or suspected Belcher phase mounds or mound groups occur from the Moore site west of Fulton to the Belcher site north of Shreveport, but Caddo specialists (e.g., C. H. Webb 1959:203) agree that the cultural and ceremonial center for the Belcher phase, and also, I suggest, for the sixteenth-century "province" of Naguatex, was within the Spirit Lake locality. The key sites are the Battle Place (3LA1), the site of the largest Caddo mound, a two-platform mound, 592 feet long, 157 feet wide, and 33 feet high (Moore 1912:566), and other sites with smaller mounds, including the Foster site (3LA27), the McClure site (3MI29), the Friday site (3LA28), and the Egypt site (3LA23). Throughout this locality there were farmsteads, as depicted in the Teran drawing, but probably in greater numbers than anywhere else in the Caddo area, each with two or three houses, a storage bin, and a brush arbor (Schambach and Miller 1984:168-169).

The Cedar Grove site (3LA97) is the only farmstead site of this period that has been excavated to any extent, but many others have been identified (Schambach 1982:7–9; Hemmings 1982:55–89; Trubowitz 1984:83–96; Schambach and Miller 1984:168–69). In the Cedar Grove site report, I presented evidence supporting my hypothesis that these farmsteads and all of the mounds, large and small, were part of a single great Caddo settlement (I call it the Spirit Lake complex), which coalesced early in the Belcher phase (about A.D. 1400) if not before, and persisted down through the succeeding protohistoric-to-historic period Chakanina phase (Schambach and Miller 1984:168–69). It was certainly in place and thriving through the sixteenth century. The ruins of the last surviving compounds in this settlement were observed and unequivocally identified in 1806 by members of the Freeman-Custis expedition as the last village of the Kadohadacho, abandoned between 1788 and 1790 (Freeman and Custis 1806). Thus it seems clear, from both the archeological evidence and the historical evidence, that the people of the province of Naguatex were the Kadohadacho.[8]

Swanton's (1942:5–6) comments on the meaning and derivation of the term Kadohadacho are of interest here: "Just as the Hainai were sometimes regarded as the Hasinai tribe par excellence, so in the confederacy on Red River were the Kadohadacho eminent above all the rest. The name is derived from Kadi, or rather Kaadi, Ka'edi, meaning 'chief,' and Kadohadacho signified 'real chiefs.' Strictly, it was applied to one of a group of four bands."

We can be sure this "band" was a much more complex social group than that term would suggest today. It was certainly a lineage, and the term "chief," which is surely a loose translation, probably indicates it was a paramount lineage. Judging from a remark by Swanton (1942:10) ". . .the Nasoni formed one town of the Kadohadacho, which sometimes bears the name." The Nasoni, whom I have identified as the people of the province of Amaye, were still subordinate to the Kadohadacho in the eighteenth century, just as they were to the cacique of the province of Naguatex in the sixteenth century. The longevity and stability of this relationship suggests that Swanton's four "bands" were actually a system of ranked lineages with the Kadohadacho, or the "real chiefs" of the European observers, at the top.

The interpretation of the term "Naguatex" presents some problems. It is generally considered a place name, so it does not contravene my identification of the people of Naguatex as the Kadohadacho. Gregory (1980:359) has commented on the Caddo practice, confusing to ethnohistorians, of using place names and ascribed names interchangeably with socially specific designators, such as "Kadohadacho." Thus, Natchitoches means "Paw-Paw Place," and Yatasi simply means "those other people." This phenomenon is not limited to the Caddo area. Anthropologists and ethnohistorians have encountered similar confusions and ambiguities throughout the world. Nonetheless, the generally accepted interpretation of the term Naguatex, which is Swanton's interpretation, is certainly inaccurate and probably an incorrect translation. He considered the Spaniards' "Naguatex" a dialect form of Namidish, a term he says ". . . is a plain Caddo term meaning 'Place of salt' (Swanton 1942:139) or 'People of the place of salt'" (Swanton 1939:274). Namidish was also the name of a "tribe" living (in the seventeenth century) "about six miles west of the Neches River in the northeastern part of the present Houston Co., Texas" (Swanton 1939:274). As Swanton admits, this is a very long distance from the Red River valley in southwest Arkansas and northwest Louisiana, but he thought the Namidish originally lived in the Red River valley, not far north of Shreveport, where the Spaniards encountered them in 1542 as the "Naguatex." He also thought that at some point after the Spanish invasion, but before 1687, the Kadohadacho moved south from the Great Bend of the Red River near Fulton and pushed the Naguatex into the Neches River valley where they came to be known in the late seventeenth century as the Namidish. This was a reasonable argument in 1939 when nothing was known of Caddo archeology. Now, however, we can say with certainty that no such move ever occurred. If it had, the archeological evidence would be unmistakable. Red River valley pottery would be conspicuous and easily identified in the Hasinai country of east Texas, which, on good archeological evidence, was a completely different ceramic province in the sixteenth century.

The major weak point in Swanton's argument is his supposition that "Naguatex" was a variant of "Namidish." Even if "Naguatex" and "Namidish" are close enough to be considered cognates (something for the linguists to decide), the similarity may be accidental, a basic problem in historical linguistics. Also, Swanton was comparing an unverifiable and possibly significantly inaccurate sixteenth-century Spanish transliteration of a name heard in the country of the Kadohadacho confederacy in the Red River valley with an equally problematical French transliteration by Henri Joutel of a name heard over a century later (in 1685) in the distinctly different dialect area of the Hasinai confederacy in east Texas. Finally, there is no salt in the Red River valley in southwest Arkansas and northwest Louisiana where Swanton supposed the "Namidish" were living in the sixteenth century, and where they presumably acquired their name. The closest salt sources to the north were, as we have seen, in the Little Missouri region, probably in the territory of Aquacay. To the south the closest sources were in the hill country of central and northcentral Louisiana (Brown 1980:Figure 2). Indeed, Swanton's (1939:273–74) version of the invasion route, in which he brought the Spaniards across northern Louisiana to enter the Red River valley from the east, just north of Shreveport, was based on the location of these north Louisiana salt sites. At this point, the most reasonable solution to this problem is the one offered to me by Hiram Gregory, namely, that Swanton's interpretation of "Naguatex" is wrong. Some ethnohistorians, Gregory included, think Naguatex probably meant something like "place of the red earth." That would certainly be a better name for the Kadohadacho country in the Red River valley.

## THE SPANIARDS ENTER NAGUATEX

After driving off the Indians on July 20 (or July 22), the Spaniards spent one more night at their camp on the north side of the Red River between Temple and Fulton. "The next day they reached the village of Naguatex,"[9] the center of the territory of the Kahodahacho, the old, powerful, paramount lineage of the Red River Caddo whose cacique had come "as captain and head of all" to do battle with them. When the Spaniards entered the "village" of Naguatex they marched directly for the "town" of the cacique, as was their habit. This town was on the west side of the Red River, and the Spaniards were on the east side. When they arrived opposite it, they did not dare cross because of their wounded men and horses, because they did not know where the fords were, and because Moscoso "saw many Indians on the other side waiting for him, so posted as to forbid his passage" (Quinn 1979, 2:144). Therefore he "made up his mind to rest for a few days. Because of the great heat he made camp near the village, a quarter of a league from the river, in an open forest of luxuriant and lofty trees near a brook" (Quinn 1979, 2:144). A "quarter league" would be between .65 and .85 miles, depending on whether the Spaniards were using the *legua legal* (2.63 miles) or the *legua comun* (3.45 miles) (Blake 1988:2). Field Bayou parallels the Red River meander belt throughout the Spirit Lake locality from about 10 miles north of Garland City to about 15 miles south. In many places it is within ¾ mile of the meander belt. Moscoso's camp, where the Spaniards spent 20 days (Swanton 1939:322), must be along Field Bayou somewhere between the Foster site and the Battle Mound.

What was it like, this province or village of Naguatex, which Swanton (1942:32) pronounced "the most fertile and populous of all the provinces through which the army passed" on the leg of the expedition that Moscoso captained? According to the Robertson translation, the "village of Naguatex . . . was very extensive" (Quinn 1979, 2:144). I do not think this was a reference to its size alone, meaning that Naguatex was simply big in the style of a large compact Mississippian village, because, as we know, there were no such settlements in the Great Bend region, or anywhere else in the Caddo area. Instead, it must have meant that Naguatex was a large dispersed village similar to the Caddo village shown on the Teran drawing. Here I prefer the Hakluyt translation (Rye 1851:132). It reads: "The next day he came to the habitation of Naguatex, which was very scattering." "Very scattering" is a much better description of a Caddo village, and I suspect is closer to the original meaning.

Apparently, the chroniclers of the expedition (and their translators) had difficulty finding the right words to describe the unfamiliar Caddo settlement pattern, so they resorted to some nuances that are rather instructive. Twice in describing the province of Naguatex they used the words "village" (Robertson) or "habitation" (Hakluyt) to describe the whole settlement, and then they used the word "town" in a way that indicates they were referring to the individual farmsteads and other kinds of compounds that constituted a Caddo village. The Robertson translation says, ". . . they reached the village of Naguatex" and then "asked where the town of the cacique was . . ." Similarly, the Hakluyt translation (Rye 1851:132) reads, ". . . the day he came to the habitation of Naguatex, which was very scattering, he inquired where the caciques' chiefe towne was." A bit further on in the narratives there is still another example of this usage. After the Spaniards had been in Naguatex for some days, they crossed the Red River where they "found a village without any people" whereupon Moscoso lodged in an open field and sent "two captains, each in a different direction to burn the towns" (Quinn 1979, 2:145). Since we know the Spaniards would use the term "town" for a group of four or five houses, it seems reasonable to conclude they were using it here to describe the farmsteads of Naguatex. And perhaps the compounds of the village of Naguatex in 1542 were a little larger than they were in the Nasoni settlement of 1691, shown by Teran (illustration 20), after European diseases had killed many people. William S. Soule photographed "Long Hat's Camp," (illustration 21) a traditional farmstead in central Oklahoma, built by Caddo refugees from the Great Bend region of the Red River valley in 1868 and 1872. These photographs show seven structures: four houses (although one has collapsed); a bark-roofed drying rack about the same size as the houses; a ramada; and a large thatch-roofed storage bin or granary on stilts.

When they are interpreted in this way, the narratives give us an oblique but recognizable description of Naguatex that is comparable to the one we have already developed on the basis of other historical evidence and on archeological evidence (Schambach 1982:7 and 120–21; Schambach and Miller 1984:168–69). This "village" or "habitation" extended for quite a distance along both sides of the Red River. It contained dozens of farmsteads, each with one to several houses, storage bins, bark-covered drying racks, and ramadas. While the narratives add nothing new to our knowledge of the physical aspects of this village, they show it was a prosperous, socially sophisticated community, with resources well beyond what the Spaniards were able to steal or destroy, and with leadership that was probably more than a match for Moscoso, whether he knew it or not. The granaries of Naguatex must have contained hundreds of bushels of corn, even in July at the very end of the horticultural year when the new late summer crops of flint corn had yet to be harvested, although the sweet corn had probably already matured and been consumed (Griffith 1954:110). There was enough to feed the entire army, which still numbered about three hundred Spaniards, five hundred "Indians of service," and at least thirty horses (the latter were so essential to the military effectiveness of the Spaniards that they, too, were probably receiving daily rations of maize). The abundance of maize was probably the main reason the Spaniards lingered in Naguatex. When they finally left, the supply was still not exhausted for "they burned many provisions and captured many Indians" (Quinn 1979, 2:145). Undoubtedly those Indians were added to the train of bearers and forced to help carry still more maize for the journey west. Yet, despite all the plundering, when the Spaniards came back through Naguatex in October, after their misadventures in present-day Texas, they found "The towns which they had burned . . . had now been rebuilt and the houses full of maize" (Quinn 1979, 2:147).

We can infer from the narratives that the cacique of Naguatex was at least the equal of the Grand Xenisi, the supreme civil and religious authority of the historic Hasinai of East Texas (Griffith 1954:59–60), and probably comparable in status and power to the Great Sun of the Natchez tribe (Le Page du Pratz 1774:351–56). Three days after the Spaniards entered his territory, when this man finally deigned to appear before Moscoso, he came in a regal manner. First "he sent many Indians ahead, among whom were some of the principal men" who "reported he was coming and immediately returned." He himself "came two hours later well attended by his men. They all came after his manner, one ahead of the other in double file, leaving a lane in the middle through which the cacique came. They reached the place where the governor was, all weeping after the manner of Tula . . ." (Quinn 1979, 2:144).[10]

After the Spaniards forced his western border and took up residence in the center of his territory, the cacique of Naguatex had the authority (and the wisdom) to resist quietly and effectively by spiriting most of the population away to the other side of the river, and perhaps many supplies as well. Although the Spaniards stayed there for over three weeks, they seem to have had almost no contact with the Indians, other than the formal visit described above. Even after the Spaniards finally crossed the Red River they found, to their chagrin, "a village without any people" (Quinn 1979, 2:145).

Where was the "town" or compound of the cacique of Naguatex? I doubt that we will ever relocate it, but we must at least examine an apparent discrepancy between the narratives and the archeology with respect to its general location. The narratives clearly place it on the west side of the river, but all of the major mound sites are on the east side, a fact that might suggest the Spirit Lake complex could not be Naguatex. I do not think this is a real problem. For one thing, as we saw earlier, in Caddo settlements (if we can generalize from the Teran drawing), the compound of the cacique, or Caddi, was not at a platform (or "temple") mound site; it could be at least a mile away from any platform mound. There is also the possibility that he did not actually live on the west side of the river. He may well have done what any good general would do and moved his headquarters to some convenient farmstead on the opposite side of the river from the invading army. Obviously, he knew the Spaniards were coming and he had plenty of time to make preparations, including establishing a picket line along the west bank to keep them at bay.

Although I dislike arguments based on negative evidence, we must also consider the possibility that his town was on the west bank, but the site has been washed away, like many others. The Red River is extremely destructive, and the Caddo practice of placing their mounds and farmsteads within the active meander belt (Pearson 1982:Figure 2-7 and 2-8) has led to the loss of many sites. We cannot find 23 of the 49 mounds C. B. Moore reported at 31 sites in 1912, and we know that many of them, like the big Friday mound group, were washed away (Schambach 1982:11). Except for a mound on the west bank just north of Garland City that disappeared before Moore's time, all but two of the missing mounds were on the east bank. So we cannot invoke one of them as our missing site. The exception, and it could be the site of the "town" of the cacique, if one believes in miracles, is C. B. Moore's (1912:575–81) McClure site. McClure is the right period, late Belcher phase, but when Moore saw it, it was not very impressive. It was a midden area with two small plowed-down burial mounds. I suspect these covered the remains of burned houses, something Moore would not have noticed with his "trial hole" excavation technique. One was only 1.3 feet high and the other was 3.5 feet high. The burials were not spectacularly rich in pots and other offerings. If anything, they are on the poor side compared to some burials of this phase, like those at the Foster site. Assuming the river had not cut away some platform mounds at the McClure site before Moore recorded it, it was not a ceremonial center. It probably was the home of a person of rank, although it does not look like the home of the paramount chief that the Spaniards described. But, maybe it was the burial mounds rather than grave goods that signified high status. At the very least, the McClure site is an example of a compound of some person of high status who was living on the west side of the river in the sixteenth century. It is also the one excavated example of the large number of farmsteads and, apparently, other kinds of compounds that stood on the west side of the river (as well as the east side) in the Spirit Lake locality (Schambach 1982:94–95). We have not been able to relocate the McClure site. Probably it, too, has been cut away by the Red River since Moore explored it.

## THE SPANIARDS LEAVE NAGUATEX

After about twenty-eight days of marauding and resting in the province of Naguatex, the Spaniards crossed the Red River and moved west, probably up the Sulphur River valley, for reasons I will give shortly. Here the question is why did they suddenly go west, quickly leaving the Red River valley and all of its food in favor of the "miserable" hill country they were to find in east Texas? Why didn't they stay in the Red River Valley and go south where they might have supposed they would continue to find settlements with lots of maize? Clearly they were not just wandering, for the cacique of Naguatex "on beholding the damage that his land was receiving, sent six of his principal men and three Indians with them as guides who knew the language of the region ahead where the governor was about to go" (Quinn 1979, 2:145).

## THE GREAT RAFT

Apparently the Spaniards knew, or the cacique of Naguatex knew, that the Red River, and virtually all of the valley as well, was blocked by the Great Raft beginning somewhere around Shreveport, Louisiana. This "raft" was an ancient 140-mile-long log jam, a nearly solid dam of logs and silt, covered with vegetation—even large trees—that plugged the Red River from near the mouth of Loggy Bayou in Louisiana almost all the way north to the Arkansas line. The raft raised the river level as much as 15 feet on the upstream side and created vast swamps and lakes across the valley (Bowman 1911:534–38). Between 1868 and 1872, when the raft was at its maximum northern extent, the entire valley south of the mouth of the Sulphur River at Spring Bank, Arkansas, was blocked by a "raft lake" called Posten Lake on the east, by another raft lake called Black Lake on the west, while the clogged river channel itself blocked the middle. Posten Lake was deep enough that steamboats used it to bypass the clogged channel of the river between Coushatta and Spring Bank (Bowman 1911:214–19). In 1719, it took La Harpe three months to drag his pirogues and flatboats from the mouth of the Red River to the mouth of the Sulphur River (M. M. Wedel 1978:2). His problems in coming up the river with boats were not the same as the problems the Spaniards would have had marching south in the valley, but this does indicate the Red River valley south of the Arkansas line would not have struck the Spaniards as an attractive route.

The raft was in place by A.D. 1500, according to geologists (Lenzer 1980:56–57), and probably much earlier. We do not know how far north the upstream end was in 1542. The comparatively light late Caddo occupation of the Red River valley south of Shreveport (which seems to indicate the abandonment of much territory since the early Caddo period of A.D. 1000 to A.D. 1300) suggests that by 1542 the raft was close enough to Shreveport, if not already above it, that much of the valley between Shreveport and the mouth of the Sulphur River was probably covered by raft lakes. Perhaps that is why the population center for the Red River Caddo was in the Spirit Lake locality from the fifteenth century on, not farther south.

Two clues in the narratives suggest the raft was significantly affecting the river level in the Spirit Lake locality in 1542. One is the difficulty the Spaniards had fording the river. Clearly they were wary of it, and when they asked the Indians they were told it was only fordable "at times in certain places" (Quinn 1979, 2:144). In July and August it should have been easy to ford just about anywhere, particularly when "it had not rained for a month" (Quinn 1979, 2:144). These days under those conditions, it is hard to find water deep enough to float a small outboard motor boat in that stretch of the river, and one is apt to spend as much time walking and towing the boat as riding in it. Only if we factor in the possibility the raft had raised the river level by five to ten feet do we get a river that would have slowed the Spaniards down, veterans that they were of many crossings of major rivers in the Southeast.

The other clue is the mysterious rise that came on August 12 when Moscoso had finally decided to leave Naguatex. He left his camp, probably on Field Bayou, ". . . but on reaching the river could not cross, as it had swollen greatly. This appeared a wonderful phenomenon to him because of the season there and because it had not rained for more than a month. The Indians declared that it swelled often in that way without it having rained anywhere in the land . . ." (Quinn 1979, 2:144–45). As Swanton (1939:275), and others, have pointed out this is pretty good evidence the river of Naguatex was, in fact, the Red River because it frequently rises in response to rains far to the west in Texas and Oklahoma. However, nothing short of cataclysmic rains out west would cause it to be "swollen greatly" in August, although it does sometime rise moderately in summer. But with the raft in place not far south, even a moderate midsummer rise would cause considerable ponding.

The narratives do not give the direction that Spaniards took when they left Naguatex on or about August 19. We know they wanted to go southwest since their goal was to march overland to Mexico. We also know the cacique of Naguatex wanted them out of his territory as soon as possible since he sent them six of his "principal men" and three guides to lead them away. So we can assume they were led out of Naguatex by the first available route. Perhaps there were overland trails leading west out of Naguatex; if so, we have no clues as to where they were. Overland travel in that direction might have been difficult because in 1542 the broad western side of the Red River valley was probably heavily forested and very boggy much of the year, as it is now even without the elevated river levels caused by the Great Raft. To judge from recent very intensive survey work by Claude McCrocklin in that area (large portions of which have only recently been cleared for the first time), it was not occupied by the Caddo, who clearly preferred the extensive prairies and better-drained soils closer to the river. Thus, I suspect their Caddo guides led the Spaniards down the Red River, along long-established trails, as far as the Sulphur River, and then northwest up the Sulphur River valley (illustration 4). Early in the eighteenth century, the Sulphur

River valley was an important route to the upper arm of the Great Bend of the Red River at Texarkana and probably to all other points west and southwest as well. When La Harpe ascended the Sulphur River in 1719, he was guided by Natchitoches Indians, who knew it was a shortcut to the "upper Nasone" settlement west of Texarkana (M. M. Wedel 1978:2–3).

## THE SPANIARDS ENTER EAST TEXAS

After "marching for three days," the Spaniards "reached a town of four or five houses, belonging to the cacique of that miserable province, called Nisohone. It was a poorly populated region and had little maize" (Quinn 1979, 2:145). Three days' travel by this route would have taken them just beyond the present Texas state line but probably not quite to the site of the Texarkana Reservoir dam, forty to forty-five miles from Garland City. An important consideration relative to the location of Nisohone is that the narratives emphasize that the country became "miserable," from the Spaniard's point of view, soon after they left Naguatex. That is exactly what happens when one leaves the Red River valley and travels up the Sulphur River into east Texas. Compared to the Red River valley with its abundant farmsteads, the lightly occupied hill country would have seemed miserable to an army looking for maize, particularly in the great heat and humidity of mid-August.

The archeology of this part of the Sulphur River valley was described in a report by Jelks (1961) on salvage excavations he did prior to construction of the Texarkana Reservoir. He found two small sites, Knights Bluff and Sherwin, a short distance west of the dam. Both had long time spans, but show some sixteenth-century occupation. The Spaniards probably did not get quite that far by the end of the third day, but I suspect there are other sites of this period closer to the Texas line. Jelks thought the artifact assemblages from the Knights Bluff and Sherwin sites were more like the Texarkana phase assemblages (of Amaye) than the Belcher phase assemblages (of Naguatex), so it makes sense that the Spaniards considered Nisohone a different province from Naguatex. Swanton (1942:32) considered Nisohone a Caddo name and suggested it referred to the Nasoni. This also makes sense, because early in the eighteenth century there were Nasoni who were known as the "Upper Nasoni" in the Red River valley near Texarkana, and others known as "the Lower Nasoni," on the Sabine River.

Two days out of Nisohone, the Spaniards were provoked because the guides from Naguatex "if they had to go toward the west, guided them toward the east, and sometimes they went through dense forests, wandering off the road" (Quinn 1979, 2:145). Perhaps the guides were deliberately trying to lead the Spaniards into the wilderness. Possibly, but less likely, they themselves were lost. But why did they try to go east? Almost certainly the Spaniards were pressuring them to find a province with maize, and, in chains and justifiably fearing for their lives, the Indians might have lost their nerve and made a desperate attempt to turn back to the province of Amaye in the Red River valley where they knew there was maize.

## THE SPANIARDS HEAD SOUTHWEST TOWARD THE HASINAI COUNTRY

After hanging these guides, the Spaniards coerced a woman from Nisohone to guide them back to the "road." This road was probably the "trace" mentioned by Mildred Wedel (1978:3) that in 1719 led north from the Hasinai Caddo country of the Neches and Angelina Rivers to the Texarkana phase settlements along Red River. If so, the Spaniards would have been heading southwest, directly for the Hasinai settlements. "Two days later" they "reached another wretched land called Lacane" (Quinn 1979, 2:145). Lacane was probably in the Cypress Creek drainage. There they ". . . captured an Indian who said that the land of Nondacao was a very populous region and the houses scattered about from one another . . . and that there was an abundance of maize" (Quinn 1979, 2:145).

The "very populous" land of Nondacao with its scattered houses and its abundant maize must have been within the territory of the Western Caddo, the Hasinai, who were living on the upper tributaries of the Angelina and Neches Rivers in 1690 (Swanton 1939:348) and probably were there in 1542. Nondacao looks like a Hasinai name. Except for the Hasinai themselves, the name of every group in the Hasinai confederacy beings with N (Nabedache, Nacogdoche, Nasoni, Neche, Nacono, Nechaui, Nacao, and Nadaco). Early in the seventeenth century, the northeastern-most Hasinai group (probably the first group the Spaniards would have encountered) were the Nadaco. Nadaco seems very close to Nondacao. Swanton (1939:276; 1942:43) considered them one and the same, but in keeping with his reconstruction of the invasion route, he arbitrarily located them in western Louisiana in 1542 (Swanton 1939:348, Map 9) and then conjectured that they moved to the upper Angelina country in Texas sometime between 1542 and 1690.

After dealing almost exclusively with obscure and forgotten names over the entire southwest Arkansas portion of the route, it is surprising to find a plausible correspondence between a name in the de Soto narratives and a name in the later literature. The reason for this is that as we trace the Spaniards from Naguatex in the Red River valley southwest to the Hasinai country of east Texas, we move from an unusually shallow historic time zone in southwest Arkansas to a moderately deep one in Texas, the northern limits of the latter being the extent of the late seventeenth-century Spanish exploration and missionizing out of Mexico and slightly later French activities out of Natchitoches, Louisiana.

We might suppose the Spaniards marched straight to Nondacao, plundered its granaries for maize, and killed, maimed, or captured everyone they could get their hands on, since that was their *modus operandi.* Perhaps they did, but the narratives do not say so. Strangely, there is no mention of maize, by now an obsession with the wandering, starving army, and there is no indication they actually entered Nondacao. Instead they seem to have been met somewhere along the trail by the cacique of Nondacao and his Indians ". . . who came weeping like those of Naguatex. . . ." The cacique made Moscoso "a gift of a great quantity of fish." Then "he took his leave of him and gave him a guide to the province of Soacatino" (Quinn 1979, 2:145). The gift of fish is revealing because Griffith (1954:113) tells us fish were an important supplementary food for the Hasinai, "especially in summer" when the streams would begin to dry up, trapping fish in pools. The Hasinai would camp at these pools and catch all the fish they could eat on the spot plus enough to "return home with quantities of cooked fish."

After this encounter, the Spaniards, now led by their new Nondacao guide, set out in an unspecified direction to find the province called Soacatino that the Indians told them about. Seven days later, after first leading the Spaniards into a hostile province called Aays, and then trying to lose them in the wilderness, this guide admitted under torture that the cacique of Nondacao had ordered him to lead the Spaniards to the province of Aays, because the people there "were his enemies." In other words, the cacique of Nondacao seems to have deliberately deflected the Spaniards away from the Hasinai heartland, which was probably just to the southwest of where he met them with his gift of fish. Perhaps this entire episode was a well-planned ruse by the Hasinai Caddo.[11] In the late seventeenth century, the Hasinai Caddo and the Red River Caddo visited back and forth constantly, often in large groups, to exchange gifts, trade, and socialize (Griffith 1954:133). Unless we deny the Caddo theocracies of the sixteenth century the slightest capacity for planning and concerted action, we must consider the possibility that the whole Hasinai confederacy knew the Spaniards were coming, and what to expect from them, and had planned accordingly. Even the gift of fish may have been a deliberate choice. Did the Hasinai realize a gift of maize would draw the Spaniards straight to their settlements, but that by offering fish they might be able to mollify them and still send them off in another direction?

## FROM NONDACAO TO SOACATINO

From Nondacao on, the descriptions of the route are so vague there is little to work with. Most of the time, we do not even know in which direction the Spaniards were going. The best clues are several more correspondences between names of tribal groups identified in this region in the late seventeenth century and names used in the de Soto narratives. But the less evidence there is, the easier it is to invent hypotheses, so I have produced (almost out of thin air) the following reconstruction of where the Spaniards went after they relieved the people of Nondacao of their fish.

Although the narratives leave no doubt that the cacique of Nondacao sent the Spaniards into enemy territory, which way did he send them? It is not likely he could have tricked them into going northwest, since they were under a compulsion to move south or southwest where they hoped to find Mexico, or at least other Christians. More likely, he sent them south or southeast, his only other option, thereby deflecting them from the Hasinai country to the southwest of him, so Aays must have been southeast of Nondacao. In the late seventeenth century, people called variously the Hais, or the Eyeish, or the Eyish, or the Haish, whom Swanton (1942:32) identified as the Aays, were living to the southeast of the Nadaco in the area between the Sabine River and the confluence of the Angelina River with the Neches River (Swanton 1939:348, Map 9).

The Hais were not friends of the Hasinai, who considered their shamans the source of various deadly diseases (Griffith 1954:88). This kind of belief suggests a well-established enmity.

The people of Aays gave the Spaniards a hostile reception (further evidence the cacique of Nondacao knew what he was doing): ". . . as soon as they perceived that they had entered their lands, the country was aroused. As soon as fifty or a hundred had gathered together, they would go out on the road to fight. While some were fighting others came and attacked them on the other side, and when some pursued, the Indians pursued them" (Quinn 1979, 2:145). This skirmishing lasted most of the day, and "some horses and Christians were wounded." The Spaniards claimed, "Great damage was done the Indians," but by this time they may well have developed a "body count" mentality. After they reached the village of the Aays, five days from Nondacao, the Nondacao guide was able to lead the Spaniards—who now "feared lest they get lost in some unpeopled region . . . off the road"—for two more days by telling them "that the Indians of Soacatino had seen other Christians". (More evidence that the Caddo knew enough about the Spaniards to tell them what they wanted to hear.) After being tortured, the Nondacao guide, a nameless hero of the Hasinai Caddo people, was "thrown to the dogs" (Quinn 1979, 2:145).

When the Spaniards finally reached Soacatino, after enlisting a new guide and traveling one more day, they found it "a very poor land" where "there was great lack of maize" (Quinn 1979, 2:145). Swanton believed Soacatino was a Caddo name, but he gave no reason for that statement. He also wrote it "is not certainly identifiable in late Caddo history," and I am skeptical of the Caddoan connection. If the Soacatino were Caddo, they certainly were not living like Caddos. They seem to have been hunter-gatherers, growing little or no maize. A 1718 map by Guillaume de Lisle (M. M. Wedel 1981:Figure 9) shows a group called the Kanoatinos located a little north of the latitude of Natchitoches and west of a river called "Rivera des Cenis," which translates "river of the Hasinai." Because of the way the map is truncated on the south, I am not sure which river this is, but it looks like the Neches. This would put the Kanoatino of 1718 west or slightly southwest of where the Hais were about fifty years later. Assuming the Spaniards really did contact the Hais, and assuming the Hais and the Kanoatinos did not move very far between the mid-sixteenth century and late seventeenth or early eighteenth century, the Kanoatinos may have been the Soacatinos or a related group.

## FROM SOACATINO TO GUASCO, THE SPANIARDS RE-ENTER THE HASINAI COUNTRY FROM THE SOUTHWEST

Upon leaving the province of Soacatino, traveling "southward" initially, the Spaniards "marched 20 days through a very poorly populated region where they endured great need and suffering" (Quinn 1979, 2:145). This was forested (scrub oak?) country, and the Indians were not growing much maize, for we are told that "the little maize the Indians had they hid in the forests and buried it." At the end of this long, miserable journey, the Spaniards arrived at "a province called Guasco" (Quinn 1979, 2:145). There they suddenly found enough maize to load their horses and their Indian bearers and to supply a reconnaissance party for a ten-day trip to the west.

They also found a village called Naguiscoca. According to Swanton (1939:54; 1942:32) this is a Hasinai name (in fact, it looks as if it could be a poor transliteration of Nacogdoches). So is Nacacahoz, the name of the "domain" they reached two days from Naguiscoca, to the west apparently. This province of Guasco with its abundant maize and its Hasinai names could not have been twenty days south or southwest of Aays and Soacatino. Twenty days' travel in that direction would have taken the Spaniards to Atakapan country somewhere between the Trinity River and the Brazos River in central Texas. That far southwest there was no abundance of maize nor any Caddo polities. Therefore, they must have gone south for only part of their twenty-day journey. Then, lost and searching for maize and other Christians, they must have circled north and then northeast back to the Hasinai country,[12] which was Guasco, the very country the cacique of Nondacao had steered them away from a month earlier.

One clue that this actually happened is Biedma's report that when the Spaniards left the forested country with little maize, "the Indians guided us eastward" (Quinn 1979:186). Swanton (1939:262) thought it unlikely they were going east because the Indians of Soacatino were also said to be guiding them to "where there were other Christians" (Quinn 1979:186), and he did not think that would have been to the east. It did not occur to him that the "Christians like us" the Indians of Soacatino had heard of might have been month-old reports of sightings of these Spaniards, themselves, when they were approaching Nondacao from the northeast. This did occur to Biedma, who thought the Indians' claim that they could take them to other Christians must have been false because ". . . they could have had no knowledge of any others than ourselves, although, as we made so many turns, it might be in some of them they had observed our passing" (Quinn 1979, 2:186).

## THE SPANIARDS RETURN TO THE MISSISSIPPI RIVER

Wherever and whatever it was, the province of Guasco was the end of the westward march of the Spanish army. They reconnoitered for ten days to the west,[13] but they found only poor land and, living in small huts, people whose language none of the guides could interpret. Then, Moscoso called a council "of the captains and principal persons . . . in order to plan what he should do . . ." and it was agreed to turn back to the Mississippi, although many of the Spaniards were reluctant to leave poor, poorer, in fact, than when they arrived in Florida (Quinn 1979, 2:46). The narratives are almost silent on the subject of the long return trip through Caddo country. We are told that on the way back (it was now early October 1542) "they found maize to eat with great difficulty for where they had already passed the land was devastated, and any maize which the Indians had, they had hidden. Only in Naguatex did they find the "towns" rebuilt and the houses full of maize, prompting Elvas to describe it as a region ". . . very well populated and well supplied with food . . ."[14] After pausing at Chaguate to try, unsuccessfully, to find Francisco de Guzman, the bastard son of a gentleman of Seville who had deserted the army on the way west to live with his Indian mistress, the Spaniards left the Caddo area, and there we part company with them (Quinn 1979, 2:147).

## THE DE SOTO COMMISSION ROUTE VERSUS THE SOUTHWEST ARKANSAS ROUTE

This route, which we have now traced from Chaguate to Guasco and back (the southwest Arkansas route), will stand or fall on its own merits. But, in closing, I wish to point out why I considered it superior to the official De Soto Commission route which took the Spaniards down the Ouachita River well into northeast Louisiana, then west overland to the Red River valley (Swanton 1939:348b, Map 10). As Jeffrey Brain (1985:xli) said in 1985, "this segment of the official route has not been seriously challenged."

The De Soto Commission report had the Spaniards spending the winter of 1541–42 in the Caddo area, rather than in the Lower Mississippi valley, at a large town called Autiamque in a province called Cayas. This town is placed somewhere in the Ouachita valley between Camden and Calion, which would put it either at the southern end of the Middle Ouachita region or the northern end of the Felsenthal region (Schambach and Early 1982:12–13). Camden is on the border between these two regions. The town of Autiamque was obviously the kingpin of this part of the de Soto Commission route, and, just as obviously, it could not have been in this part of the Ouachita valley. The sixteenth-century Caddo settlement pattern from Camden north—and we know it quite well from considerable site survey work in the last twenty-five years—is the normal Caddo pattern of dispersed farmsteads. There were no Mississippian style towns here. In fact, the population in the southern part of the Middle Ouachita region, from Arkadelphia to Camden, was markedly lighter than in either the Little Missouri region or the Great Bend region because this environment was marginal for the Caddo. Here the Ouachita valley was (and still is) rough, swampy, seasonally flooded, heavily forested ridge and swale terrain with abundant oxbow lakes in various stages of development. The late Caddo period sites, all small sites, large enough for two or three houses at most, are thinly dispersed throughout the woods, generally on the small natural levees that border the old Ouachita River oxbows. If there are fifty of these little sites between Camden and Arkadelphia, that would be a lot; I doubt if there are more than thirty. Some maize was being grown here (we have good samples from recent work at the Georgia Lake site, 3OU112), but this was marginal land for horticulture, as it certainly is today for agriculture, yet excellent for hunting, fishing, nutting, and shellfish collecting, as the middens at these small sites amply attest. This country could not by any stretch of the imagination have been the land described by Ranjel as a "plain, well peopled and of attractive appearance" (Quinn 1979, 2:183), or the "cultivated and well peopled" land of Biedma where de Soto set up winter quarters in a large village (evidently a Mississippian style town). Nor could it have been the place where food was so plentiful that the entire army lived for three months on a "great abundance of maize, beans, walnuts, dried plums," and rabbits, which the Indians showed them how to snare in their evidently extensive maize fields (Quinn 1979, 2:37). Neither the population, nor the fields that could produce such abundance, were present in this part of the Ouachita Valley. Autiamque had to be a Mississippian town in the Mississippi Valley. Even the reports of the severe winter weather, with a month of snow, do not sound right for the Camden area. Even allowing for the effects of the Little Ice age of 1430 to 1850, these conditions would have been much more likely farther north and east in the Lower Mississippi valley, closer to Little Rock, because southwest Arkansas is considerably warmer and enjoys considerably more frost free days in winter than that area.

Had the Spaniards tried to winter south of Camden, closer to Calion, which is in the Felsenthal region, they would have found conditions even worse, from their point of view, than what they would have experienced had they tried to winter in the Middle Ouachita region. This is a Lower Mississippi Valley region, both environmentally and culturally. In the sixteenth century it was most likely inhabited, probably quite thinly, by Koroan peoples, who, I am virtually certain, practiced no horticulture at all because this was (and still is) such wonderful country for hunting, fishing, and gathering, and just as poor for horticulture. For the Spaniards this would have been a wasteland. The Koroans, who were not tied to farmsteads and granaries, could have avoided them and provided them with no food. Had the Spaniards tried to winter around Calion, or around Camden, they would have perished within a month.

## Notes

1. At his death, de Soto's "share" of the hog herd was seven hundred head, and apparently he had kept control of most or all of them until then. He also owned "two men slaves, two women slaves, and three horses" (Rye 1851:127).

2. Cacique is a general term that the Spaniards used for all leaders they encountered in the Southeast. Some were probably chiefs, others may have been priests or petty kings. We cannot use the term chief for these Caddo personages. They were more like theocratic priests or kings, or even demigods in the style of the Natchez tribe. Rather than get into this problem here, which is not the place for it, I will stick to the the term "cacique" throughout.

3. N. F. Williams (1959:75) stated, "Salt in the form of brines occurs at many locations in Arkansas. In Hot Spring and Clark counties, the surface wells and ponds in the alluvial bottoms between the mouth of De Roche and L'Eau Frais creeks contain brines that were worked for salt during the Civil War. In about 1815 white settlers pre-empted brine sources in Saline County from the Indians, and these were operated until about 1840. Shallow brine wells also occur in a belt extending from Arkadelphia in Clark County to Ultima Thule, Sevier County. Salt springs are known in Clark, Conway, Crawford, Franklin, Sevier, and Van Buren Counties."

4. Actually, the paramount ceremonial center in the Little Missouri drainage is the Hineman site (3OU20), near the confluence of the Little Missouri River and the Ouachita River. Its main mound is the second largest in the Caddo area; only the mound at the Battle site is bigger. This site has never been excavated. Judging from sherd collections and artifacts in private collections, I know it was important in the sixteenth and seventeenth centuries. I don't know if it was the center for the Little Missouri polity, perhaps even Aguacay, or some Ouachita Valley polity, or maybe a polity combining parts of both regions. Since it was the practice of the Spaniards to head for important places, one must wonder why they did not go there.

5. There may have been one other European salt works in the vicinity of 3SV69, but it is poorly documented and we have not been able to find it. 3SV69 was evidently the best saline, since it was the locus of the most important European salt works in this area.

6. This location of Amaye was, of course, not my idea originally; nor was the location for Naguatex. In a letter of 29 August 1988, in which he listed several alternatives, Charles Hudson wrote: "Another possible location of Amaye was the Red River west of its junction with the Little River. That is, Moscoso may have come to the easternmost town of Amaye, with its location being, say, within 5 miles or so of present Fulton. This would place the domain of Naguatex from a point somewhat south of Fulton down the Red River for some unknown distance." My contribution is to demonstrate that this particular alternative is the best one, considering the archeology and the geography.

7. For the location of Texarkana phase and Belcher phase, see illustration 3.

8. There has never been any real doubt about the approximate location of Naguatex. In the De Soto Commission report, Swanton (1939:Map 10), with the advice of C. H. Webb, offered an essentially identical identification except that he had the Spaniards entering it near its southern limits and never getting to the center of the province, which was north of the Louisiana state line, because in his reconstruction the Spaniards came overland through north Louisiana to the Caddo country. Two wrongs would not make a right, but I think it is significant that these two otherwise widely divergent reconstructions are in agreement on the approximate location of Naguatex, although not on its ethnohistorical identification.

9. This means they forded the Little River soon after they left camp (in July this would not have been difficult), but this is not mentioned in the narratives. In their travels from Chaguate,

they also would have forded the Ouachita River (the salt sites are all on the east side of the Ouachita), the Little Missouri River, the Saline River (to get to 3SV69), and the upper part of the Little River as they traveled south to Amaye in this reconstruction. None of these crossings were mentioned either. Evidently crossing small rivers was not a noteworthy event. However, it is interesting that the "de Soto map" (Swanton 1939:Map 1), which some scholars consider a "fifth chronicle" of the expedition (Curren 1987:4), shows that the Spaniards crossed three rivers between Chaguate and Naguatex. These would most likely have been the Ouachita, the Little Missouri, and the Little River at Fulton. For the other two crossings, the Saline near 3SV69 and the upper part of the Little River, I suspect the water was too shallow to present much of an obstacle, particularly during a dry July.

10. This "weeping" should not be construed as a sign of submission or disorganization. It was probably a sign that Caddo social organization was intact and functioning with confidence. Since the Spaniards observed it at Tula, at Naguatex, and Nondacoa, it was obviously a widespread custom to weep ceremoniously when greeting visitors. Whether it was used for all visitors or just hostile visitors, we do not know. There is some interesting historical and linguistic evidence suggesting that this was an ancient custom. As Hemmings (1982:61) has noted, the place where the Battle Mound stands is called "Chickaninny Prairie" and nineteenth-century maps show a Chicanini or Chicanina Landing there. Hemmings also informs us that these names are versions of the Caddo word "Chaccanenah" or "Chakanina" (Hemmings 1982:61), which means "ground upon which tears have been shed" or "the place of crying" and that these names are attached to sacred hills in various versions of the Caddo origin myth. To me, the obvious implications of this are that Chaccanenah was a generic term for all ceremonial centers, which were basically meeting places for Caddo communities, and that it derives from the Caddo custom of greeting each other by weeping as they came together at these centers.

11. Biedma's account of this incident reads: "The cacique of Nondacao gave us an Indian purposely to put us somewhere whence we could never come out: the guide took us over a rough country and off the road" (Quinn 1979, 2:186).

12. Possibly as they traveled south they intersected the trail that was to become the Camino Real in the late seventeenth century, and they turned and followed it northeast to the Hasinai settlements.

13. It is interesting that once they arrived in Guasco, they reconnoitered only to the west, not to the south or southwest as they generally did, probably because they had just come up from the southwest.

14. In his account of the journey back east through Naguatex, Elvas compared the pottery of Naguatex to the pottery of two villages in his native Portugal: "pottery is made there of refined clay, which differs but little from that of Estremoz or Montemor . . ." (Quinn 1979, 2:147). This clue could lead to the positive identification of Naguatex, thus anchoring this key segment of Hudson's route. I think it is significant that the Spaniards had been traveling through Caddo country, presumably seeing Caddo pottery every day, from Chaguate at Arkadelphia, on the east side of the Caddo area, all the way to Nondacao and Naguiscoca, probably somewhere in the Hasinai country on the west side of the Caddo area, but only the pottery of Naguatex struck Elvas as looking like Portuguese pottery. This suggests that he was referring to pottery that was unique to Naguatex and also distinctive in some way that would have caught the attention of someone who did not have an archeologist's eye for subtle differences in form or decoration. To me, this suggests it was pottery vessels of some distinctive shape that caught his eye. And the reference to "refined clay" suggests it was something in the Caddo fine ware series (bowls and bottles) rather than the cooking pots and storage jars, which are of a coarser ware. The prime candidate here is the unique double-shouldered bowl type that C. H. Webb (1959:120–23) called

Belcher Engraved. All Caddo groups had bowls, but only the Belcher phase people of the Red River valley between Shreveport and Fulton had these double-shouldered bowls. I wouldn't be surprised if an odd specimen or two made its way into the Texarkana phase country (Amaye) west of Fulton, but they have never been found in the Little Missouri region or in the Hasinai country in east Texas. The Spaniards would have seen piles of these bowls at every farmstead in Naguatex. They probably ate from them. Not to leave even a possible red herring unturned, Caddo bowls have been called *cazuelas* in the literature for a long time (since Harrington's 1920 publication at least), suggesting that bowls are the form most likely to resemble pottery made in Portugal or Spain. Another possibility—not quite as good as Belcher bowls because of the ware requirement and also the possibly fishy Portuguese connection—is the large melon-shaped cooking pots and storage jars that C. H. Webb (1959:136–39) called Belcher Ridged. They are different in form and decoration from the utility vessels of all other Caddo provinces, and they are not found outside of the Great Bend region from Fulton south to Shreveport. Dr. Carmen McClendon at the Center for Latin American Studies at Moore College, University of Georgia, has pursued this lead with Charles Hudson.

# Moscoso and the Route in Texas: A Reconstruction

Nancy Adele Kenmotsu, James E. Bruseth, and James E. Corbin

## INTRODUCTION

The attempt to identify the route of de Soto's men through Texas is fraught with difficulties. The documentary and archeological evidence for their travels in the general east Texas area is at best minimal, and at worst non-existent. Yet, the identification of Moscoso's trajectory in the state would be of great value to archeological research. It has long been speculated that many Caddoan groups encountered by Moscoso in 1542 were identical to those recorded by Joutel, Teran, and Casanas in the late seventeenth century (Swanton 1942:7–10). If the locations of these groups in the mid-sixteenth century could be compared to their locations in 1690, our understanding of movement or displacement of native groups and their affiliation to each other would be vastly improved. It would also enhance our knowledge of the effects of this early entrada on native populations.

Given the importance of identifying Moscoso's route through Texas, we have utilized the meager data base to attempt to reconstruct the route of the 1542 trek. We first sought to fit the available archival and archeological data with modifications of the routes previously set forth by Schambach (this volume), and to a lesser extent Swanton (1985:348a–b). This reconstruction is called the "Trammell's Trace Route" after the name of a well-known, early nineteenth-century contraband trail. While this reconstruction fits some of the archeological and archival data with the information in the chronicles, other data are at odds with the chronicles. These problems forced us to seek an alternative route that would perhaps better reconcile the archeological and archival data with the historical narratives. Our alternative route, called the "Blackland Prairie Route," was inspired by discussions and correspondence with one of the authors (James E. Corbin), and by the route through Texas depicted in Hudson (1989a:26). Neither route is final nor definitive, and considerable field investigation would be required to verify their accuracy. However, they are presented as a starting point for future research. In both Trammell's Trace Route and the Blackland Prairie Route the final segment is the same and is based on the known route of the "Camino Real."[1]

Before proceeding to a discussion of the routes, the general evidence for the Moscoso presence in Texas is reviewed. The review includes information on the natural setting, the nature of the archeological record, the information available in the chronicles from the expedition, and the use of annotations on historic maps.

It should be noted that the chronicles of Elvas and Biedma are the primary sources for this report. Ranjel's chronicle for the portion of the route in Texas has been lost or destroyed, and while Garcilaso de la Vega's account has not been ignored, he has not been relied upon for primary documentation given the inherent problems with his work (cf. T. H. Lewis 1927:5; Swanton 1985:9–10). We have employed the Robertson (1933) translation of the Gentleman of Elvas, although the Buckingham Smith translation has also been of assistance (T. H. Lewis 1907). For Biedma we have used the well-known Bourne (1904) publication translated by Buckingham Smith, along with an early Spanish transcription of Biedma (1865) from the *Real Archivo de Indias*. It should be noted that place names follow Spanish spellings in the latter reference, including la Came for Lacane. Where Spanish place names are unavailable, Elvas (Robertson 1933) has been followed.

## THE NATURAL SETTING

Whether or not the route of the de Soto/Moscoso expedition in Texas can ever be delineated with any degree of accuracy, most scholars agree on two aspects of the route. First, there is consensus that the general area of the state entered by the Spaniards, along with their horses, dogs, hogs, and Indian slaves, was northeastern Texas (T. H. Lewis 1927; Swanton 1985; Hudson 1989a; Schambach this volume). This conclusion is based upon the fairly compelling archeological inference (detailed by others) that Moscoso's final route in Arkansas took the expedition roughly west through south central Arkansas and then south-southeast along the Red River and its tributary Little River, to the great bend of the Red in southwestern Arkansas (Hudson 1989a; Schambach this volume). The crossing of the Red River and Naguatex appear to be located somewhere in the great bend, and likely in the Spirit Lake locality as suggested by Schambach (this volume). Biedma (1865:438) strangely fails to mention Naguatex at all, but does state that from Aguacay to Nisione the travel was generally south or southwesterly. While no cardinal direction of travel is noted by Elvas (Robertson 1933:247), a detailed account of the province of Naguatex is given, and scholars agree it is on the Red River above the Great Raft. It is also clear that once they crossed the Red, the expedition would not have traveled east (back the way they had come), north (due to the general desire to reach Mexico), or due south (which would have required a recrossing of the final curve of the great bend). The favored direction of travel, then, would have been west or southwest from the great bend region, and into Texas somewhere either just above or just below the Sulphur River.

The second point of agreement concerns the data in the chronicles indicating environmental change in the area traversed by Moscoso. Once past the Red River, selection of a route through the state of Texas has differed from one scholar to another. However, they agree that the narratives imply that the river called Daycao, reached by the Spanish, was located beyond the heavily vegetated east Texas region. Biedma (1865:437) notes "they came across some poor peoples who did not have houses but rather some miserable huts" and lived off flesh and fish. Elvas is more specific, "the land beyond the river of Daycao . . . was the land which Cabeza de Vaca said in his relation he had traversed and was of Indians who wandered about like Arabs without having a settled abode anywhere, subsisting on prickly pears, the roots of plants, and the game they killed" (Robertson 1933:254).

A review of the general biogeography of northeastern Texas and adjacent regions shows two, and possibly three, zones present in the general area of Texas traversed by Moscoso (illustration 22). In general, as one moves from east to west across these zones, rainfall, vegetation, and topographic relief decrease. At the eastern extreme is the Oak-Hickory-Pine forest consisting of a gently rolling landscape dominated by a series of roughly east-southeast–trending river basins with numerous tributary streams (Kuchler 1964). The rivers tend to exhibit characteristics of mature fluvial systems with moderate gradients, meanders on their valley floors, and intersection by large tributaries (Collins and Bousman 1992). The zone is covered by various species of oak, hickory, and pine trees with a fairly lush understory vegetation. This eastern zone experiences relatively high rainfall amounts (thirty-six to forty-five inches per year) which contribute to its heavily vegetated character (Bomar 1983). White-tail deer, bear, small mammals, turkey, and other birds, turtles, and fish were common throughout the area and were exploited prehistorically (Story 1981:141).

West of this zone is the Post Oak Savannah (Kuchler 1964). It is represented by a narrow belt beginning in Oklahoma and running from northeast to southwest through Texas. Various species of oaks and hickories occur and form an open canopy surrounded by stands of grasses. The zone contains portions of the same river systems found in the eastern Oak-Hickory-Pine forest. Although topography is still gently rolling, the relief is less than to the east. It is important to note that the northern part of this zone along the Sulphur River has a pronounced eastward projection into the more heavily vegetated Oak-Hickory-Pine forest biogeographic zone. The projection is discussed further under the Blackland Prairie Route.

The third zone is a northeast to southwest zone of tall grass prairie, known in Texas as the Blackland Prairie. Topographic relief in this zone is substantially reduced from that encountered in more eastern zones, and the dominant vegetation is dense stands of medium-tall to tall grasses. The Blackland Prairie terminates on the west at the oak-juniper savannah of the Edwards Plateau, a major uplifted and dissected limestone plateau covered by grasses, and scattered oak and juniper trees (Kuchler 1964).

In sum, the portions of Texas crossed by Moscoso and his men began with the moist, heavily vegetated woodlands of east Texas, which contain rolling hills and numerous creeks and rivers. This area is essentially identical to, and a continuation of, the environment traversed in southwestern Arkansas. As they moved to the west and south, they would have encountered drier prairie regions with fewer streams and less topographic relief. The accounts of Biedma and Elvas indicate this trend from wetter to drier, as they note the "wretched" situation of the peoples beyond the River Daycao who subsisted on prickly pears and roots.

## THE ARCHEOLOGICAL EVIDENCE

Clarksdale bells, Nueva Cadiz beads, and other artifacts from the expedition have been recovered in several southeastern states. In Texas, however, there is virtually no artifactual record from the Moscoso expedition, except some potential finds in the Dallas area (Crook 1988). The authors have reviewed the collections of early historic contact material at the University of Texas at Austin for all counties in east Texas. The collections contain small quantities of glass beads, gun parts, knives, metal tinklers, other metal fragments, and occasional hawk bells. All date to the seventeenth and eighteenth centuries. Several Dallas County artifacts are perplexing. A halberd was found in Dallas County in the early 1950s (Harris 1951). Subsequently, the Dallas Archeological Society recovered a cache of pottery vessels, sherds, and a mano of volcanic material (basalt?) from the same farm (Hanna 1940). The University of Michigan identified the vessels as coming from the St. Francis River area in Arkansas (Crook 1988:109). A possible gauntlet dating to the sixteenth century was recovered from another Dallas County location (Crook 1988:109). Identification of the halberd was by the Department of Arms and Armature of the New York Metropolitan Museum, but was only based on an artist's sketch. While tantalizing, the artifacts merit re-identification with modern dating techniques, and this activity is underway.

The lack of authenticated artifacts dating to this time period is not altogether surprising. The chronicles made it clear that by this time the sole intent of Moscoso and his men was to reach Mexico as quickly as possible (Biedma 1865:437; Añasco 1939). Even Garcilaso gave Texas hasty treatment (Garcilaso 1951:509–21). Additionally, none of the documents mentioned trade or barter. They showed that the forces simply seized what they needed and moved on (Biedma 1865:438–39; Robertson 1933:241–54). It is likely that few European goods were left by the time the expedition crossed the Red River. After their trek through Texas, Biedma (in Bourne 1904, 2:39) notes that only swords and targets (small round shields) were left, and Elvas (Robertson 1933:298) commented on the native clothing worn when they arrived in Mexico. In the absence of authenticated artifacts dating to the time of Moscoso, then, the evidence that can be brought to bear on potential routes is secondary and indirect. It consists of generalized information from the chronicles of Elvas, Biedma, and Garcilaso, together with the archeological record from east Texas and adjacent areas.

The most important secondary line of evidence is present in the accounts themselves. These documents indicate that at least some of the provinces encountered by the Spaniards in Texas represented a continuation of the Caddoan peoples they had met in southwestern Arkansas. Indian guides were consistently acquired in each new territory or province entered. These guides were able to interpret the speech of the people of Nisione, Nandacao, la Came, and other Texas groups mentioned in the narratives (Biedma 1865:438; Robertson 1933:249–53). Too, the accounts generally suggested a similarity in customs between the province of Nandacao and the Caddo of southwestern Arkansas: "The cacique [of Nandacao] and his Indians came weeping like those of Naguatex, that being their custom in token of obedience" (Elvas in Robertson 1933:248). In addition, many of the place names (Nandacao, Nisione,

Nacacahoz, etc.) are Caddoan (Swanton 1942:8; Chafe this volume). Finally, the presence of sufficient quantities of maize at Nandacao and Guasco also suggests encounters with Caddoan groups. Maize was a staple of the Caddo and would have been abundant at their sites in August and September when visited by the expedition.

On the other hand, the evidence is not clear for some provinces, specifically the Hais, Xuacatino, and Nisione. Maize was not abundant in these provinces, and populations were apparently low at the latter two. Their associations with the Caddo are not clear, and different explanations for this discrepancy are offered in each of the alternative routes. Certainly any similarity in languages and customs had ended by the River Daycao. The people beyond the River Daycao spoke a language incomprehensible to the guides and maintained a "wandering" hunting and gathering lifestyle (Robertson 1933:254). This inability to find an interpreter became a major factor in the Spaniards' decision to return to the Mississippi. In summary, the groups east of the River Daycao had some aspects of commonality. At the very least, they had enough in common that their customs and language were recognizable to both the Spanish and their native guides. These eastern groups were quite unlike the people west of the river, both in language and in socio-political organization.

Some indirect evidence for potential routes of Moscoso is present in the archeological record. Considerable archeological investigation has been carried out in east Texas, and it is known that the region was occupied in the mid-sixteenth century by Caddoan peoples (Story 1981:149–52). In a review of the Caddoan area, Story (1981:149) states, "Although temporal control is poor, it is evident that from early to historic Caddo times there was a hierarchical settlement system." The complexity of this hierarchical system varied both through time and space. By the 1550s it appears that clear evidence of social stratification was present only in the northeastern extreme of Texas along the Red River (Story 1981:151). To the south, mounds may have continued to have been used for special purposes, but there are no known instances of mound construction in sites of this period in the Cypress Creek drainage (Thurmond 1981:451), or areas south of Cypress Creek (Gregory 1973:8; Story 1981:149; Story and Creel 1982:28).

Late Caddoan settlement patterns in east Texas have been intensively reviewed for the Cypress Creek drainage (Turner 1978:7; Thurmond 1981:453). Archeological investigation has been less intense outside the Cypress Creek drainage. There are, however, hints that the same settlement model pertains in the upper Neches (Woodall 1969) and Angelina rivers (Story and Creel 1982) as in Thurmond's (1981:446) Three River Basins Subgroup located in White Oak Bayou, Lake Fork Creek, and portions of Cypress Creek. In these areas the archeological record consists of a series of small, dispersed sites in the vicinity of a small cemetery and at least one larger site with limited evidence of status differentiation. It is important to note, however, the variable quality of the data base. Few absolute dates are available from late Caddoan sites, and there is a critical need for dates from reliable contexts.

Archeological data from the western, prairie-like portions of the area of concern indicate a different type of cultural adaptation. Synthesis of material from the upper Trinity by Prikryl (1987:177–83;1990) and Peter and McGregor (1988:367) indicates the northern part of the western margins of east Texas contain evidence of small, mobile groups whose subsistence practices included bison hunting. Data from the Richland Creek project on the middle Trinity indicate a low population density of small family groups who constructed temporary shelters (Bruseth, McGregor, and Martin 1987:246). The authors conclude that these groups maintained a centrally based settlement pattern dependant upon foraging certain wild food resources. Evidence from the middle Brazos River basin also demonstrates the presence of a relatively small population with a cultural tradition based on hunting and gathering (Story et al. 1990:658). Archeological sites in these drainages along the western edge of east Texas consist of small, ephemeral sites with stone tools, some pottery, hearths, subsurface storage pits, cemeteries, and post molds indicating structures.

It is clear that the archeological record demonstrates the presence of more than one cultural tradition in the area traveled by the Spanish. The first was a western extension of the sedentary, hierarchically organized Caddoan peoples. Status differentiation was present but not pronounced in late Caddoan groups in Texas. West of the Caddoan area, the socio-political nature of the archeological record is quite different. Here, the evidence suggests the presence of nomadic groups of hunters and gatherers.

## THE EVIDENCE FROM HISTORIC TRAILS

The first reconstruction set forth here is Trammell's Trace Route. This reconstruction depends to some extent upon evidence from historic trails, while the Blackland Prairie Route considers evidence from historic trails to a lesser extent. Therefore, this section presents details on historic trails in East Texas, and is used to better understand potential 1542 routes.

A number of scholars have noted the likelihood that de Soto's army traveled on pre-existing Indian trails (DePratter, Hudson, and Smith 1985:109; Schambach this volume). This was the case in Texas as well. First, the portion of the chronicles dealing with Texas occasionally referred to pre-existing trails. Biedma noted, "the guide took us over rough country, and off the road"; and later, "we returned by the same road we had taken" (Bourne 1904, 2:36-38). Second, the de Soto expedition passed through heavily vegetated regions which would have necessitated either cutting new trails or following pre-existing native trails. Interior North America was *terra incognita,* and Moscoso had no way to determine where one settlement was in relation to another. Hence, it seems unlikely that new routes would have been cut, except in rare instances. Instead, the expedition would have followed extant trails. Third, as Hudson (1987:14) notes, "Neither Pardo nor de Soto were stumbling blindly through the wilderness. They had Indians to guide them where they needed to go." Although there were instances in which guides deliberately misled them in Texas (Biedma 1865:438; Elvas in Robertson 1933:250–51), these instances were rare and not especially successful. Native groups experienced greater success in ridding themselves of the Spanish when they provided guides to remove the expedition from their homelands. For example, burned towns and the capture of local residents at Naguatex caused the cacique to provide the guides Moscoso demanded (Elvas in Robertson 1933:246–47). The quickest means of removing the Spanish threat would have been to guide them out of the local area using a known trail.

In addition to employing pre-existing trails in Texas, the evidence suggests that the trails chosen were well-used routes linking major settlements. The size of the army is one reason to conclude that the trails used were frequently traveled. An army as large as that of Moscoso's, with slaves, horses, dogs, and several hundred hogs, would have tended to remain on well-worn and marked paths for their passing. In addition to the need for trails linking settlements, Moscoso would have sought those trails that he had been told would lead from one major settlement to another. The expedition's earlier experiences from Florida to the Mississippi had shown that these types of trails existed, and that they usually resulted in an encounter with a settlement sufficiently large to provide enough food for the army. Although large towns like those found in the Mississippi valley would not be encountered in Texas, Moscoso could not have anticipated the reduced, scattered settlements of the western Caddo. He continued to hope that each new settlement described to them represented a large village. Finally, typical information in the chronicles on the groups encountered in Texas relates to the group's ability to provide sufficient maize for the army. Nisione, Nandacao, and la Came were described by Biedma (1865:438) as "each time more sterile and with less food." Similarly, Xuacatino was described as "poorly populated" with little maize (Robertson 1933:250). Although Guasco was visited three times, it too is given no descriptors other than its ability to provide sustenance to the army. Statements like these underscore the army's focus on major population centers with supplies of maize linked by a major overland trail system.

Under the assumption that pre-existing trails were traveled by Moscoso where available, some seventeenth- and eighteenth-century routes can be plotted with relative accuracy by piecing together several lines of evidence that rely heavily on historic maps. First, there exist some maps from these centuries. For example, in 1690, Governor Alonso de León and his party met Hasinai Caddo hunting in an area well south and west of their homeland along the Neches River (Bolton 1952:374, 409). These Caddo guided de León to their homes along an existing overland trail. The trail was mapped by Teran in 1691, and it has become known in Texas as the "Camino Real." While early maps like Teran's contain errors, they are also surprisingly detailed, and researchers can trace routes and place names through time using successive maps of the same area. Second, settlers in the eighteenth and early nineteenth centuries used existing trails, often building their houses adjacent to them. The Olifant house in Sabine County, constructed in 1828, was specifically built on the Camino Real, as was Bernard D'Ortolan's Rancho del Loco (41NA27, est. 1796), and Mission Dolores de los Ais (41SA25) in 1716 (Gilmore 1980:223). In addition, the Texas General Land Office has a series of early to mid-nineteenth-century maps of northeast Texas based on surveys of early land grants. These maps frequently note early towns, trails, and Indian villages (illustration 23). Their locations can be plotted on modern maps to provide a general trajectory of early trails.

Obviously a trajectory based on historic maps must be used with considerable caution. Floods, erosion, and other natural occurrences would have caused locational adjustments in the trail system. Too, population movements of prehistoric and historic settlements would cause certain trails to gain or lose popularity. Consequently, this type of research can provide only generalized routes. Specific routes must be verified by on-the-ground archeological survey and excavation such as at Mission Dolores where a portion of the Camino Real was identified from excavations (Corbin, Kalina, and Alex 1980:82). With these cautions in mind, several trails in northeast Texas, documented on early historic maps, have been employed to develop trajectories of Moscoso in Texas.

## TRAMMELL'S TRACE ROUTE

The Trammell's Trace Route is the more traditional of the two reconstructions of the Moscoso expedition in Texas. That is, this route is based upon the general notion that the groups encountered from Naguatex to Guasco were basically well inside the areas of the Caddoan tradition in east Texas. The route that it takes would necessitate that the groups encountered were primarily Caddoan. Difficulties with this interpretation will be pointed out in the discussion. It proceeds generally south by southwest as do the proposed routes of Swanton (1939:348a–b), Hudson (1985), Schambach (this volume), and also the "de Soto Map" (Martin and Martin 1982:12–13; illustration 3), although specifics of the present route differ from each of the other routes. Again it is noted that the final segment of the Trammell's Trace Route is the same as in the Blackland Prairie Route.

Several north-south trending trails are documented on historic maps from the east Texas region (illustration 23). Trammell's Trace was selected for the present study because it was known historically as a major north-south travel route in east Texas. Also, the portion of interest to this study begins relatively near the general vicinity where a southwestern trajectory into Texas from Naguatex would have crossed the Sulphur and Cypress drainages. Finally, it was chosen because several Caddoan provinces that are mentioned in the chronicles of Moscoso's journey (Robertson 1933; Biedma 1865; Bourne 1904) coincide with names of native groups that archival documents suggest were located along this route in the eighteenth century (Bolton 1908; Jones 1968).

The name Trammell's Trace refers to an early nineteenth-century trail from Nacogdoches to Fulton, Arkansas, on the Red River. Between 1804 and 1826, Nicholas Trammell was a transporter of stolen or contraband horses between these two locations, and the route was apparently named after him. In the absence of any firm evidence, it can only be guessed that the naming of these northward routes after Trammell was a result, not of his being the first to travel, mark, or cut them, but because he made considerable use of them (Clark and Ivey 1972:114).

The 1840 Harrison District map of the Texas General Land Office documents Trammell's Trace from Cypress Creek in Marion County south to near Mount Enterprise in Rusk County. Historic maps from Cass County (1848), Rusk County (1846), and early Spanish and Texas land grants also document portions of Trammell's Trace. Clusters of archeological sites that date between the sixteenth and eighteenth centuries are present at several intervals along this historic trail. Their presence suggests that the trace was in existence long before 1804 when Trammell made it famous.

No trails are recorded on Texas General Land Office maps for the portion of Trammell's Trace in southern Rusk and northern Nacogdoches counties. However, there are archeological sites with eighteenth-century and aboriginal artifacts present in this area. There are also several early historic sites present in this general area. If these sites were situated to take advantage of a known travel route, then they may represent the possible southern extension of Trammell's Trace. It should be noted that the data for this conclusion is very minimal and sketchy. No intensive surveys have been completed in southern Rusk or northern Nacagdoches counties other than those completed for Lake Nacogdoches (Prewitt, Clark, and Dibble 1972) and unreported fieldwork carried out by avocational archeologists Bill Young, along the East Fork of the Angelina River, and Tom and Janice Mayhew, in the Bayou Loco and Legg Creek areas. Considerable field investigation and analysis would be required to verify if other sites are present in this general area and if they represent a more probable trajectory of the portion of the trace from southern Rusk County to Nacogdoches.

Historic map documentation and archeological data north of Cypress Creek are minimal at best. Early district and county maps at the Texas General Land Office for these areas provide only the barest of topographic and ownership details. The R. W. Loomis Farm (41MR26) in Marion County was reported by the owner to contain pottery, arrowpoints, and an "old Indian trail" (Texas Archeological Research Laboratory 1934). The Cass County map of 1848 notes the location of a small segment of Trammell's Trace, and an 1840 Red River District map illustrates the location of the Epperson Crossing of the Sulphur River. Both of the latter, however, appear to be situated too far north and west to represent segments of the Moscoso route. A small cluster of archeological sites with eighteenth-century and aboriginal artifacts near present-day Atlanta, Texas, may, however, indicate the presence of a travel route that could have been used by Moscoso.

In summary, the nineteenth-century Trammell's Trace is a generally north-south route from Fulton, Arkansas, to Nacogdoches and possibly to the south. While the trace roughly parallels the reconstructed routes of Moscoso described by Schambach (this volume) and Hudson (1985), the present route differs from theirs. Specifically, the routes of those researchers follow a path generally west of the Trace, and are not based on historic trails. From Cypress Creek to mid-Rusk County, Trammell's Trace is known from historic maps. In this portion of the route, groupings of archeological sites from the sixteenth to eighteenth centuries are found, indicating the trail may have been in existence in earlier centuries. Both south and north of the known segment of the route are small clusters of sites which date from the sixteenth to eighteenth centuries and may suggest the general directions of those portions of the route. Given this background, Moscoso's trek along the Trammell's Trace Route is delineated (illustration 24) using the locations and events as given in the chronicles. Data from the narratives and linguistics will be given first, followed by the proposed location of the named places along the route.

## Nisione (Nissohone)

The cacique of Naguatex provided Moscoso with "six of his principal men and three Indians with them as guides who knew the language of the region ahead." The expedition then marched for three days to Nisione "that miserable province . . . poorly populated [with] little maize" (Robertson 1933:247). Biedma (1865:483) added little detail to this. He fails to mention Naguatex at all, and simply gives a general statement that travel from Aguacay to Nisione was southwest and south. Linguistic evidence (Chafe this volume) indicates that the name Nisione is Caddoan and equivalent to the eighteenth-century name Nasoni.

The statement by Elvas that the Spaniards were given guides who knew the language of the region ahead suggests that the language of Naguatex differed in some respects from the language of Nisioni, and Biedma suggests Nisione was roughly southwest of Naguatex. The guides also indicated Nisione was some fifty to sixty miles from Naguatex, using the estimate of Elvas (Robertson 1933:92) that travel in the wilderness was seventeen to twenty miles per day. Elvas gave no direction of travel, and Biedma's notation of southwest over such a long distance may not be trustworthy. On the other hand, if Biedma's statement does apply, then a southwesterly direction from Naguatex would have resulted in their eventual movement into the area of Trammell's Trace. While this is speculative, the area of the Hunt (41CS23), Clements (41CS25), and Atlanta State Park (41CS37) sites, located west of Atlanta, Texas, and situated some fifty miles southwest of Spirit Lake, Arkansas, represents a possible location of Nisione in 1542 (illustration 25). The former two sites are late Caddoan cemeteries excavated by A. T. Jackson in 1932. Seventeen burials, containing whole vessels including *Simms Engraved* and *Hodges Engraved*, ceramic pipes, arrowpoints, manos, green pigment, and pitted stones, were removed from the Hunt site (Jackson 1932). One burial also contained a small fragment of metal. At the larger Clements site, Jackson (1932a) removed twenty-two burials and also noted the presence of a rich midden associated with the cemetery (1932a). Several of the burials contained small quantities of eighteenth-century blue wound and drawn glass beads; others contained no European trade material. *Simms Engraved, Cass Applique, Clements Brushed, Hodges Engraved, Keno Trailed,* and *Foster Trailed-Incised* dominated the pottery vessels removed from the site. The Atlanta State Park site is another burial site located northwest of Atlanta, Texas. Numerous glass beads, an iron awl, brass bracelet, and other eighteenth-century historic and aboriginal grave goods were recovered (Texas Archeological Research Laboratory 1988). While none of these sites contain sixteenth-century European material, they are situated close together, contain substantial quantities of sixteenth- and seventeenth-century aboriginal materials, and have a sufficiently high number of burials to indicate occupation in the general vicinity extending back to the time of Moscoso.

## La Came (Lacane)

Leaving the Nisione after two days, the guides deliberately tried to mislead the army. Moscoso hanged the guides, and a Nisione woman guided them to la Came in two days. Part of the two days was used simply to search for the trail (Elvas in Robertson 1933:247). Confusion exists between Elvas and Biedma at this juncture, as the latter placed la Came after the town of Nandacao, saying it was the guide of the Nandacao who deliberately misled the expedition. This conflict in the accounts cannot be fully reconciled. In the absence of better information, Elvas is accepted since his is the most complete account for Texas. La Came is not a Caddoan word (Chafe this volume).

The crossing of Trammell's Trace on Cypress Creek is approximately thirty-five miles south southwest of the area postulated to be Nisione. This distance is in concert with the approximately two days spent to reach the la Came region. Just west of the general area is the location of Thurmond's Big Cypress Creek subcluster, dating to the mid-sixteenth century (Thurmond 1985, 1:1990). Given its distance from Nisione and the presence of archeological sites of this time period, this locale is put forth as the location of la Came. However, this fit of the information in the historical narratives with the archeology is tenuous. La Came is not a Caddoan word, and the narratives describe the province as "wretched," suggesting there was little available food. The Big Cypress Creek subcluster contains a number of sites (Thurmond 1985:446), suggesting a population sufficient to have supplied the army with adequate food supplies. In the absence of additional archival or archeological documentation, the data cannot be fully reconciled.

## NANDACAO

In la Came, Moscoso captured an Indian who described Nandacao as "a very populous region [with] houses scattered about as is customary in mountains . . . and with an abundance of maize" (Elvas in Robertson 1933:248). Elvas also described the ceremonial weeping greeting at Nandacao, which was the same as at Tula and Naguatex. Biedma (1865:438) mentioned Nandacao, but stated it was in a more sterile region with less food than previous settlements. No distances were given in either. Chafe (this volume) has identified Nandacao as a variant of the eighteenth-century Caddoan place name Nadaco.

The chronicles are not especially helpful about the location of Nandacao. Although there is a discrepancy between Elvas and Biedma, Elvas is again taken to be more correct. Certainly the weeping custom indicates affiliation with the Caddo from southwestern Arkansas, and the abundance of maize described by Elvas supports that conclusion. The mountains and scattered settlements mentioned in Elvas, however, could be found in several areas of east Texas. As discussed previously, the settlement pattern of the Caddo in east Texas is generally dispersed. Unfortunately, this only leaves us with the statement that the land was well populated. Without any distances, the location of Nandacao on Trammell's Trace is very tentative.

One possibility is the general vicinity of the Kinsloe Focus sites north and south of the Sabine River, which is close to the documented route of Trammell's Trace. Here, there are a number of known sixteenth- to eighteenth-century component sites. The sites in this vicinity are best known from cemeteries which typically yield substantial quantities of grave goods (B. Jones 1968; C. H. Webb et al. 1969). These include the

Susie Slade site (41HS13); the J. O. Brown site (41HS261); and the Henry Brown site (41HS262) in Harrison County 41RK77 (B. Jones 1968); the Williamson site (41RK3); and the Taylor site (41RK36) in Rusk County (Clark and Ivey 1972). Jones (1968:211) concluded that eighteenth-century sites in this general area represent the remains of the Nadaco, a historic Caddoan group mentioned by a priest in 1691 as located north of the area occupied by the Hasinai Caddo (Casanas in Swanton 1942:250). These sites, from which he defined the Kinsloe Focus, share traits with each other and with sites in the immediate vicinity which lack historic contact goods. He suggested that those other sites are ancestral (e.g., sixteenth century) to the Kinsloe Focus sites.

Certain pottery types, burial patterns, and an absence of complex ceremonial development are shared with both Titus and Frankston foci and provide for cultural continuity and possible origins from the Fulton Aspect for the Focus. Similar traits and certain pottery types shared with other historic foci and unassigned components including Glendora, Allen, Norteño, and the Hunt and Clements sites [mentioned above with the Nisioni], also indicate relations and contemporaneity (B. Jones 1968:213).

Although not definitive, the number of graves and grave goods suggests that the region was generally prosperous and had a substantial population. This hypothesized location of Nandacao is approximately thirty miles south by southwest of la Came, and on Trammell's Trace. Too, its name has been associated with a historic Caddoan group that one researcher (B. Jones 1968) has located in this general vicinity.

## Hais (Aays)

Although Hais is a Caddoan word, its etymology is not known (Chafe this volume). Elvas (in Robertson 1933:248) wrote that a guide to this province and the following, Xuacatino, was provided by the chief of Nandacao. He stated the distance as five days' march, and remarked that the Indians, who had not heard of Christians, fought them. Biedma's (1865:438) account is substantially different. He has no time frame for the distance from Nandacao, but noted that the guide from Nandacao deliberately misled them on this leg of the route. While agreeing with Elvas on the fierce nature of the group, Biedma wrote that the Hais lived in a province where "some cows [bison?] are accustomed to going at times." There are two translations of this passage. Smith's translation (Bourne 1904, 2:36–37) stated "where cattle are wont to herd." The 1865 version of Biedma uses the Spanish verb "acudir" meaning to respond or to go to. In the Trammell's Trace Route the latter has been chosen, as will be explained below. Upon seeing the Spaniards, the Indians called to each other "that they should kill the cows that were coming," apparently mistaking Spanish horses for *cows*. Garcilaso de la Vega has considerable information on a group he calls "Province of the Herdsmen," but it is difficult to discern fact from fiction. Like Biedma, he recounted a journey where they were misled. He also indicated that the herdsmen's province was located beyond "deserts, forest, and craggy lands" that they traversed for twenty-one days. He described the Hais' settlement as sterile and weak, with dispersed houses. "Province of the Herdsmen" was defined by Garcilaso as referring to the beef and cowhides present in the houses. Garcilaso noted that no cows "on the hoof" were seen and wrote that the province was "upwards of 30 leagues across" with mountain ranges just to the west (Garcilaso 1951:516).

It is believed that the term cow refers to bison. Certainly, Garcilaso's description of this group as herdsmen suggests this, and "vaca" in Biedma seems to clearly mean something other than deer, as he has consistently used "venado" for that species in previous passages. It is curious that Elvas made no mention of the bison. If Garcilaso's descriptions of the bison were all that we had, they could be dismissed. Garcilaso had Coronado's descriptions available by the time he wrote his book, and the inclusion of bison there could be based on Coronado's narratives. Biedma's mention of them indicates that they cannot be dismissed. However, it should be noted that a locale in east Texas will not accommodate bison. East Texas has pockets of clearings, but is too wooded for groups of bison to be accustomed to coming to forage. One possibility is that east Texas is simply not the location of the Hais. If, however, the Trammell's Trace reconstruction is to be selected, then the comment merits explanation. The only possible explanation is that the proper translation is that the bison were brought to this place by the Hais (perhaps to be butchered?). The explanation is relatively close to Garcilaso's description. Inspection of the handwritten document would be needed to determine the appropriateness of this translation.

All accounts suggest this was a quite distinctive group. Elvas stated that the Hais had not heard of Christians, and Biedma's description of their surprise and their mistaking horses for cows tend to support Elvas. Both suggest a fairly substantial population, and Garcilaso de la Vega tended to corroborate this in his flowery descriptions. No mention was made of a language change. If the guide was able to translate their cry to kill the cows, then it seems that at least the guide understood the language of the Hais. Biedma referred to an effort to mislead the Spanish, and Garcilaso de la Vega referred to a similar effort. Elvas was silent on this issue and refers to a five-day march. (The twenty-one days described by Garcilaso de la Vega are here discounted.) If Elvas' version is correct, then continued movement along the Trammell's Trace route would place the Hais near the Angelina/Cherokee County line—a location along the southern edge of the Caddoan area of east Texas which would have moved the army through an area with several known clusters of sites dating to the sixteenth to eighteenth centuries. Yet these clusters are not mentioned in the narratives. Hence, a southerly direction of travel along Trammell's Trace seems unlikely.

We suggest that the location of the Hais in this reconstruction would be San Augustine, which is their location in Swanton's (1939:276) route. San Augustine is located approximately eighty-five miles from the Trammell's Trace crossing of the Sabine River near the postulated location of Nandacao. A five-day march equates to a distance of eighty-five to one hundred miles (Robertson 1933:92). Additionally, the narratives imply the army was misled in a direction that took them away from Trammell's Trace. San Augustine is situated east of the known route of Trammell's Trace. Finally, it has been well documented that the Hais were located in the vicinity of modern San Augustine in the eighteenth century, and Mission Dolores de los Ais (Hais) was built in 1716 to convert them. Unfortunately, early Spanish documents do not clarify if the Hais were present in the San Augustine area in the mid-sixteenth century. Little archival or archeological work regarding the location and movement of historic Indian groups has been accomplished to date in Texas. Too, archeological excavations have concentrated on the site of the mission where it was rebuilt in 1722 (Corbin et al. 1990:10). Excavations at the original mission site would be needed to determine whether the Hais were present in the area prior to the eighteenth century. In the absence of better information, and since their eighteenth-century location corresponds with the distance from Nandacao, San Augustine is put forth as the location of the Hais met by Moscoso.

## Xuacatino (Soacatino)

According to Elvas (Robertson 1933:250) the Nandacao guide deliberately misled the army between Hais and Xuacatino for two days. A new guide then led them to Xuacatino in one day. Elvas also noted this was a poor land with little maize. Biedma too noted the lack of food, and commented that Xuacatino was located in close forests. Like Hais, Xuacatino is a Caddoan word, but its etymology is not fully understood (Chafe this volume).

We use archeology to suggest the location of Xuacatino. Although no directions of travel were noted in the narratives, it seems unlikely that the army would have moved northwest along the Camino Real. This would have quickly placed them in contact with the Nacacahoz (Nacogdochi), a province that was not visited by the expedition until several weeks later. It is also unlikely that they traveled east, since Guasco was the province visited after Xuacatino, and, for reasons that will be detailed later, Guasco appears to be situated on the western margins of the Caddoan area. Therefore, we suggest the location of Xuacatino is southwest of San Augustine near the confluence of Attoyac Bayou and the Angelina River. This locale is approximately one day's journey from the Hais' locale noted above. Too, the floodplain of the Angelina River is broad, flat, and heavily vegetated. Biedma's remark about close forests may refer to the heavy vegetation. Excavations conducted prior to the construction of Sam Rayburn Reservoir documented the presence of sixteenth- to eighteenth-century sites in this area, such as the Wylie Price site (41SA94). The Wylie Price site contained material from the eighteenth century in the form of a burial with three pottery vessels and a necklace of simple eighteenth-century blue beads along with material from the sixteenth century and earlier (Jelks 1965:80). While admittedly tentative, the general Sam Rayburn Reservoir area is hypothesized as the location of Xuacatino. It is pointed out, however, that the description of the area without much maize is a problem. Caddoan provinces should have contained sufficient maize at this time of year.

## Guasco

In both the Trammell's Trace and Blackland Prairie routes, Guasco is situated on the Camino Real, and the remaining segment of the army's journey in Texas is put forth as a single possibility for both reconstructions. As noted above, the Camino Real was first mapped in 1691 and appears on a number of early maps. From these maps the actual route and several deviations of it are fairly well known. The route runs roughly east-west and is situated along the southern portion of the Caddoan cultural tradition. Swanton's (1939:348b) reconstruction of Moscoso's route paralleled the Camino Real to the south. Along the known route of the Camino Real, there are three clusters of sixteenth- to eighteenth-century sites which may represent possible provinces visited by Moscoso. However, it is important to note the general paucity of intensive archeological surveys in the area. Other clusters may be present, but not yet identified.

After Xuacatino Elvas wrote of the army traveling for twenty days through a poorly populated land with little food. No directions were given other than when an unidentified Indian told Moscoso maize was to be found "southward" (Robertson 1933:250). He also noted that Guasco contained turquoise and cotton blankets brought from the west. In contrast, Biedma noted a turn to the east after leaving Xuacatino, and visits to a series of small, poor villages. No time frames were provided by Biedma. Guasco is Caddoan place name of unknown etymology (Chafe this volume).

This leg of the journey is a problem for the Trammell's Trace Route. Twenty days represents between three hundred and four hundred miles—a sizeable distance under any circumstances. If, as Biedma suggested, they traveled east after Xuacatino, they would have entered Louisiana, visited both Caddoan and non-Caddoan provinces, and re-encountered both the Red River and the Mississippi River. Since this is at odds with the narratives, an easterly direction of travel from Sam Rayburn Reservoir seems unlikely. A southerly direction of travel for twenty days also seems unlikely if the Trammell's Trace Route is chosen. Although wooded, this area is peripheral to the Caddoan area of east Texas, and local groups were small and semi-nomadic and would have had little maize. While this fits with the information in Elvas, its proximity to the Gulf of Mexico does not. At the River Daycao, Elvas remarked that they knew of no way to reach the sea other than to return to the Rio del Espiritu Santo. In Panuco another survivor wrote a letter to the king of Spain which confirms their general belief that they were never very close to the Gulf of Mexico (Añasco 1939:98). Any three hundred-mile journey to the south would clearly have placed them in contact with groups familiar with the nearby Gulf. Further, if they began from Sam Rayburn reservoir and went south, then finally reached Guasco (a locale of considerable maize and thus Caddoan), they would need to have eventually returned north. None of the accounts refers to a circuit back to the north. In sum, the twenty days represent a considerable difficulty for the Trammell's Trace Route.

In the Trammell's Trace Route, it is proposed that the next twenty days represent a summation of the remaining travel time prior to reaching the River Daycao, rather than representing the period spent between Xuacatino and Guasco. Under this scenario the Spaniards traveled in a circuit for the next twenty days, visiting Guasco, Naquiscoca, and Nacacahoz, returning to Guasco, and then marching to the River Daycao (Robertson 1933:250–51). The circuit was made because an Indian at Xuacatino had told Moscoso that Christians could be found to the south. They traveled in a poorly populated, forested region with little maize and eventually returned west again to Guasco, which had considerable quantities of maize. This is not a thoroughly satisfactory explanation of the twenty days, but provides a tentative means to correlate the twenty days with the Trammell's Trace Route.

Since there is no clear information about the distance or direction to Guasco, archeological and archival data are employed to suggest Guasco may be located west of Xuacatino in the vicinity of the Camino Real crossing of the Neches River near the confluence of San Pedro Creek and the Neches. The locale appears to have had sufficient populations to produce adequate quantities of maize for the army. The earliest Spanish documents record a large Hasinai village (three leagues long) along the San Pedro, and later documents, as well as the 1805 Juan Pedro Walker map, indicate that the road proceeded through the village along the floodplain of the San Pedro.[2] The 1805 map also indicates that the 1690 location of Mission San Francisco de los Tejas was at the west end of the village near the Camino Real crossing of the San Pedro. A cluster of sites containing historic artifacts occurs within the San Pedro Creek floodplain: 41HO6 (breechlock from a seventeenth-century Spanish *verso*), 41HO64 (six burials contain glass beads, a gunflint, and rifle cock), 41HO65 (early pipe fragment), and another unrecorded aboriginal site with glass beads. Other sites in the general vicinity (41CE293, with several aboriginal burials reported to have contained glass beads; 41CE20, containing drawn eighteenth-century beads; 41HO1, which contained glass beads, lead bullets, and gunparts) also contain historic trade materials. This cluster of sites, supported by the archival material, appears to represent a group of hamlets that date to the seventeenth and eighteenth centuries. Sixteenth century (Frankston phase) sites are fewer, but have been reported from this locale. Finally, Elvas' later statement that Guasco had cotton blankets and turquoise brought from the west, implying that other provinces encountered in the route did not have these goods, suggests that this is the location of Guasco. Far from conclusive, if Guasco is the only locale with these trade goods, it seems likely that this province was situated on the margins of the Caddoan area. The Camino Real crossing of the Neches River is the approximate southwestern boundary of the Caddoan tradition.

## Naquiscoca

The chronicles provide only limited information on Naquiscoca, simply stating that it was located south of Guasco. Under torture, the residents informed Moscoso that "Christians" had reached a town ahead (Nacacahoz) (Robertson 1933:251). No additional information on Naquiscoca was provided by Biedma or Garcilaso de la Vega. Chafe (this volume) states that the name is Caddoan.

If Guasco were at the crossing of the Neches, there are several historic maps (e.g., 1827 Stephen F. Austin's Map of Texas; 1805 Walker map; 1840 Nacogdoches District map; and 1857 Nacogdoches County map, all except the Walker map are at the Texas General Land Office) illustrating a lower road from there to Nacogdoches. The road ran slightly south of east, incorporating the earlier direction of Biedma and current direction of Elvas. Too, the road eventually passed through a cluster of sites that are situated on Bayou Loco and Legg Creek. The sites in the group include Deshazo 41NA13/27, Mayhew 41NA21, Iron Rock 41NA22, and Henry Mast 41NA60. All are aboriginal sites with eighteenth-century European goods. The DeShazo site locale also contains a structure and artifacts associated with the D'Ortolan's Rancho del Loco discussed above (Story 1982:9). The historic continuity of occupation along Bayou Loco and Legg Creek may be indicated by the presence of a number of Frankston phase sites (dating to the sixteenth century) that are situated near the eighteenth-century sites (Story and Creel 1982:33) as well as the presence of Caddoan names for several tributary streams (e.g., Nacasote and Nadusto) of Bayou Loco which cross the boundaries of the Santos-Coy land grant (1832) on the middle reaches of Bayou Loco. It is here hypothesized that this area, located about twenty-five miles east of the Neches River, is the location of Naquiscoca.

## Nacacahoz

The only information about this province is that it was situated two days from Naquiscoca (Robertson 1933:251), and that it was east of Guasco (Biedma 1865:439). The name Nacacahoz was a Caddoan word which may mean Nacuduchz (place of cold), and is the same as the later Caddoan word Nacogdoches (Chafe this volume).

This effort locates Nacacahoz within or near the modern city of Nacogdoches. Mission Nuestra Senora de Guadalupe was formally established in the area in 1716 within the main village of the Nacogadochi, one of the nine Hasinai Caddo. Although the exact site of the mission has yet to be identified, it has been well documented in archival records, and was located near or on the east-west Camino Real. Too, the name Nacacahoz represents a variant of the Caddoan word for Nacogdoches (Chafe this volume), corroborating the placement of Nacacahoz. One aboriginal site (41NA113) recorded within the city contained a burial with glass trade beads and sixteenth- to eighteenth-century pottery (Corbin 1986:25). There also have been recorded a number of sixteenth-century aboriginal sites within the boundaries of Nacogdoches as well as north and south of the city (Corbin 1986:25). Nonetheless, it should be noted that it would have taken only one day rather than two from Naquiscoca to reach this plotting of Nacacahoz. Without additional information it is not possible to reconcile the archeological and archival data with the distance.

## River Daycao

From Nacacahoz the Spaniards returned west to Guasco along the Camino Real to replenish their maize supply. There they were told of a river ten days "toward the west" (Robertson 1933:252). The people of Guasco said that they sometimes hunted deer in the mountains near the river, but they were not familiar with the people living there. Upon reaching the river, Elvas commented on the low population, their nomadic lifestyle, and on the fact that the Mississippi was 150 leagues away to the east. Biedma (1865:439) gave a distance of six days to the river, and the direction as south and southwest. He noted the people beyond Daycao lived on fish and flesh, and did not plant maize or any other crops. Both noted that the language of the local populations was unfamiliar to any of their guides.

The route taken by Moscoso to Daycao appears to be the Camino Real, which runs west southwest from the Neches River. In the seventeenth century, the Caddo were encountered several times hunting in the prairie lands of Texas. Each time, they guided the Spanish to their villages using the Camino Real. If this was the trail followed by Moscoso, the River Daycao is either the Brazos or Colorado River. This is based on the distance and on environmental and cultural changes. As noted previously, the River Daycao clearly marked an environmental and cultural change. If Biedma was correct about the six-day journey, the army marched 120 miles from Guasco; if Elvas was correct, they marched 200 miles from Guasco. Both are substantial distances. One hundred twenty miles is the approximate distance from the proposed location of Guasco to the Camino Real crossing of the Brazos River. The Blackland Prairie, located at or just before the Brazos, may represent the environmental change that was noted in the chronicles. In this zone topographic relief is low and few hardwoods can be sustained on the prairies. Elvas' estimate of 200 miles would indicate that the River Daycao is the Colorado River. The Camino Real crossing of the Colorado River in the vicinity of Austin and adjacent to the Edwards Plateau marks another environmental change. As noted earlier, the Edwards Plateau is an uplifted plateau covered by grasses and scattered oak and juniper trees. This region of the state has 53 percent of the state's deer (Cook 1984:460). This major uplift, then, may represent the mountains with deer noted in the Elvas (Robertson 1933:252) narrative. Either river may represent the River Daycao.

### Assessment of the Trammell's Trace Route

A brief assessment of the Trammell's Trace Route is in order. This route places the march in the midst of lands known to have been occupied by ancestors of the historic Caddo. Caddoan names, the custom of weeping as a greeting, references to heavy vegetation, and certain places with abundant maize all indicate Moscoso met the Caddo in Texas. In these regards, the Trammell's Trace Route fits the narratives. But in other respects Trammell's Trace does not fit the narratives. Distances between several towns are not given, so one must arbitrarily choose a dot on the map. There is no information on why, when, or if the army really crossed the Sulphur River and began their journey along Trammell's Trace. Nandacao is clearly a Caddoan province. But is the Hais, with reference to the bison, or Nisione, or Xuacatino with their low populations and little maize? Also, the twenty-day journey between Xuacatino and Guasco is difficult to explain by this route. In sum, there are a number of difficulties with the Trammell's Trace Route that cannot be satisfactorily explained by this reconstruction of Moscoso's route. Others have noted these discrepancies (Hudson 1989a), and the present attempt to reconcile these issues through comparison of the historical narratives to the archeological and geographical evidence is not solely the credit of the authors. For the purpose of this paper, we suggest an alternate, the Blackland Prairie Route, which we feel provides a better reconciliation of historical documentation with archeological and geographical facts.

## BLACKLAND PRAIRIE ROUTE

It is clear that the Spaniards were seeking native groups with supplies of maize that could be used to feed the soldiers. Since the presence or absence of maize supplies was of such critical importance for the expedition, we argue that the narratives, particularly the Elvas narrative, relatively accurately record the occurrence of this food source. We further assume that the relative occurrence of maize is an indicator of horticultural versus hunting and gathering economies of the native groups encountered. Since the expedition was traveling through eastern Texas during the summer, the year's maize crop should already have been harvested and stored for use during the remainder of the year. If present, the Spaniards should have encountered maize as they entered each province. This assumption is important for our comparisons with the archeological record since several macrobotanical studies have recently been conducted for northeastern Texas and offer a tentative assessment of the prehistoric dependence on maize (Bruseth and Perttula 1981; Perttula and Bruseth 1983; Perttula, Crane, and Bruseth 1983; Bruseth, McGregor, and Martin 1987; Martin, Yates, and Fritz 1988; Crane 1992).

Central to tracing any route through Texas is the point at which the expedition crossed the Red River. As outlined earlier in this paper, Schambach (this volume) presents a detailed and convincing argument that the Spanish army entered Naguatex and crossed the Red River at the Spirit Lake locality in the vicinity of Garland City, Arkansas (illustration 25). This fits well with the area archeology, since the Battle Mound, the largest in the Caddo area, is located in this area and several other mound sites and Caddoan farmsteads are also found here, many known to date to this time period (Schambach 1989:20).

## Naguatex

At Naguatex, the Spaniards stayed approximately twenty-eight days and left during mid to late August, guided by several Indians provided by the cacique of Naguatex (Robertson 1933:247). These guides, as became apparent several days later, were ordered to mislead the Spaniards and to get them lost. Schambach (this volume) suggests that the Indian guides led them down established trails along the Red to the Sulphur River.

## Nisione

The narratives are virtually silent on the route of travel, although they note that after three days they reached "a town of four or five houses, belonging to the cacique of that miserable province, called Nisione" (Robertson 1933:247). Travel down the Red River, as Schambach has suggested, would have prolonged the time that the Spaniards were within Naguatex province, particularly if the Spirit Lake complex identified as Naguatex includes the area from the Friday mound in the north to the Egypt site in the south—a distance of fourteen kilometers (Schambach and Miller 1984:168–69).

We would suggest that travel from Naguatex would more logically be directed west overland to the Sulphur River. If the goal of the Indian guides was to get away from Naguatex and to get the Spanish lost, heading directly west would most effectively accomplish this. Any movement in a northerly or northwesterly direction would have encountered other Kadohadacho allied tribes living along the Red River (cf. Swanton 1942). Travel to the southwest doubtlessly would have encountered Caddoan groups in the Cypress basin identified as the Titus phase by Thurmond (1981). For these reasons we propose that the "best" route to lead the Spaniards away from Caddoan farmsteads would have been due west, probably between present-day Texarkana and Wright Patman Lake. In this case, the poorly populated province of the Nisione encountered by the expedition would actually have been a few outlying farmsteads representing the southern extent of the Nisoni identified in the area during later explorations (e.g., M. M. Wedel 1978).

Assuming this westerly route, three days' travel from Naguatex would place the expedition somewhere in central Bowie County (illustration 25). Recent survey work in the Red River Army Depot in this area has identified relatively few Caddoan sites (Cliff and Peter 1990) and supports the inference of a poorly inhabited region. Immediately to the south along the Sulphur River, work by Jelks (1961) during salvage excavations in Lake Texarkana, identified sites of the Texarkana focus which temporally span the sixteenth century. Based on ceramic styles, Schambach (this volume) has suggested that the Texarkana focus represents the cultural equivalent of the historic Nasoni, and Chafe (this volume) has noted that Nisione is equivalent to Nasoni. Thus, on the Blackland Prairie route, this is the general vicinity of the Nisione.

## La Came

After leaving Nisione it becomes very difficult to trace the route of the expedition. Elvas (Robertson 1933:247) noted that "if they had to go to the west, [their Indian guides] guided them toward the east, and sometimes they went through dense forests ('thickets' in the edited translation by Lewis in 1907), wandering off the road." They spent two days moving in this fashion, and at the end of this time they hanged their guides and used a Nisione woman to guide them on. Two days later, after relocating the road they had been traveling on, they reached another "wretched land" called la Came.

Swanton (1939:276) argues that Lacane (la Came) is another name for Nandacao. The reasoning for this conclusion is tenuous at best (Chafe this volume), and we suggest that the la Came was a non-Caddoan group living along the Sulphur River. Assuming that the Spaniards, despite being misled by their guides, were continuing to move west, away from the Caddoan hamlets along the Red River and the Caddoan hamlets to the south along the Cypress Creek, we suggest a location of la Came along the Sulphur River somewhere near the confluence of the North and South Sulphur rivers (illustration 25). This area is the transition area from eastern forests to western prairies. The transition between forest and woodland is important, since from an archeological standpoint, this also represents a cultural dividing line separating Caddoan cultures (i.e., horticulturally dependent groups) from those groups based on a hunting and gathering adaptation.

Recent work at Cooper Reservoir provides useful data that bear on this issue. The lake is located on the South Sulphur River, and excavations have taken place at a number of sites (Perttula 1988; Moir, McGregor, and Jurney 1992). Although late prehistoric occupations are generally scarce in the reservoir, the data that exist show an adaptation based largely on wild plants and animals; maize is present but in very small quantities and much below the frequency that is found in late Caddoan sites further south

(Bruseth and Perttula 1981). Another important difference is in burial customs; at Cooper Lake burials are flexed and lack grave goods. In contrast and almost without exception, Caddoan cemeteries of northeast Texas are well known as containing extended skeletons and almost always possessing burial offerings of ceramic vessels and other artifacts. These archeological differences underscore the cultural differences between groups straddling the forest/prairie boundary.

## Nandacao

At la Came the Spaniards, obviously much concerned about locating villages with maize supplies and not finding them, were told that Nandacao was a very populous land with "the houses scattered about one from another as is customary in the Mountains, and that there was an abundance of maize" (Robertson 1933:248). This appears to be a comparison to the types of Caddo villages encountered in the western Arkansas portion of the route. Moreover, upon arriving at Nandacao, the cacique and his people greeted the expedition by weeping. This is a custom observed at Naguatex and at Tula, and certainly a Caddoan custom (Schambach this volume). We argue that the evidence suggests that the expedition is once again among the Caddo. Swanton (1939:276; 1942:32) and Chafe (this volume) consider the Nandacao to be the same as the later identified Nadaco, a tribe located in the seventeenth and eighteenth centuries variously on the Sabine River or to the south close to the Nasoni in the upper reaches of the Angelina River. Our proposed route, however, would place the Nadaco north of the Sabine River.

We use archeology to suggest the location of the Nandacao. Following the Sulphur River drainage westward, the closest archeological complex that would fit the description of the Nandacao would be the Three Basins subcluster of the Titus phase (Thurmond 1985). This subcluster is largely based on a few excavations of cemeteries by WPA crews in the 1930s, later excavation of a cemetery site (Scurlock 1962), and work at Lake Fork Reservoir (Bruseth and Perttula 1981; Hockensmith 1977). Of particular significance for this discussion are the excavations at the Steck site (Hockensmith 1977). This site is located along the Dry Creek drainage of Wood County, and extensive testing was undertaken including processing of several flotation samples. Carbonized maize was common and found in all thirty of the flotation samples and shows the ubiquity of this food remains in the archeological record (Perttula, Crane, and Bruseth 1983). A radiocarbon date of A.D. 1470–80 (calibrated A.D. 1376–1527 [Stuiver and Pearson 1986] using 2 sigma standard deviation) was obtained from a midden deposit at the site (Bruseth and Perttula 1981:Table 9-1). In our opinion, the Steck site is representative of late Caddoan hamlets in the Three River Basin subcluster, and this subcluster could represent the province of the Nandacao. If we are correct in linking up this archeological complex with the expedition, then we would suggest that the Spaniards traveled south or southwest about a day from la Came to reach Nandacao. The narrative of Elvas, the most useful for this portion of the route, is silent on the direction or distance the expedition traveled to reach this province, but the implication is a relatively short time was spent moving.

## Hais

The expedition left Nandacao sometime in late August and traveled five days to the province of the Aays (Elvas), or Hais (Biedma). Biedma recorded that the Indian guide took them through a "rough" country and ultimately indicated that he did not know where he was taking the Spaniards. They took another guide who then led them to the Hais. Here the Biedma narrative provides one of the most significant pieces of information for identifying the location of Moscoso. The narrative records, "We took another guide, who led us to a Province called Hais, where, in season, some cattle are wont to herd." As noted in the section on the Trammell's Trace Route, a retranslation of the Spanish by the senior author gives the following: "We took another guide, who led us to a Province called Hais, where some cattle are accustomed to going at times" (Biedma 1865:438). For purposes of the Blackland Prairie Route, either translation is significant in that reference is made to cows (bison) being present at certain times, perhaps seasons, of the year. From a geographical standpoint, this is important information in that bison herds do not occur at any season in deep east Texas (San Augustine) where Eyeish are found during the eighteenth century. In fact, the only location that would work from a biogeographical standpoint is the Blackland Prairie (illustration 25). Based on the archeological record of the Blackland Prairie (Lynott 1979) we know that bison were present in that biogeographical zone throughout much of the prehistoric time period, and a notable increase occurred in bison numbers between 1200 and 1600.

Historical accounts also support the presence of bison on the Blackland Prairie (e.g., Kirkpatrick 1963). Of particular note for this paper is the journal of Captain Anthony Glass (Flores 1985). Captain Glass embarked on a journey in July of 1808 from north of Natchitoches with the goal of reaching the Taovaya-Wichita villages along the Red River near present-day Spanish Fort. His mission was to conduct trade and to generally explore this region for the United States government. His route started north of Natchitoches and headed north along the Red River. He detoured east around the Great Raft, and turned overland into Texas midway between the Cypress and Sulphur rivers. Here he linked up with a trail that followed the southern side of the Sulphur River, and he progressed west along this trail. This trail and general direction of travel is similar to the route we are proposing for Moscoso. Glass began his journey on July 5, and sixteen days later encountered the first bison in small groups along the North Sulphur River in present-day Delta County, just into the Blackland Prairie (illustration 25).

It is important to note that the Garcilaso de la Vega account, which up until this time we have chosen not to use because of its historical inaccuracy compared with the other narratives, consistently references a "Province of the Herdsmen" and mentions the presence of beef and cowhides at sites in this area (Garcilaso 1951). While this work is undoubtedly a romanticized version of the expedition and is therefore not a reliable historical account (Lewis 1927:5), it does nonetheless provide some highly interesting information that corroborates the Biedma narrative. In particular, the account of the Province of the Herdsmen and the notation that this land had open forests and deserts fits with how the Blackland Prairie may have appeared to the expedition during late summer and after an apparent lack of rain for more than a month. All of this, we argue, suggests that the Hais must have been located in an area where bison seasonally were present, and this could only have been on the eastern fringes of the Blackland Prairie.

When the expedition encountered the Hais, Elvas noted that they had not heard of the Spaniards, and consequently a fierce battle broke out as the Spaniards entered their lands. This evidence suggests that the Hais were not communicating with the Caddo and likely were not a Caddo tribe, although the guides could interpret their language. The Hais have been commonly identified with the eighteenth- and nineteenth-century Eyeish (Swanton 1942; Chafe this volume), which were identified as living in eastern Texas near present-day San Augustine. The Eyeish were considered by the Hasinai (southern Caddo) to be outside of their confederacy (Casanas in Swanton 1942:250). Their dialect was different from the tribes making up the Hasinai, and their customs were generally regarded as inferior (Bolton 1908:255). A significant difficulty with the Blackland Prairie Route, however, is that we would place the Eyeish of 1542 somewhere in the upper Sabine drainage of northern Hunt or southern Fannin counties. While this would be consistent with a five-day trip during which the expedition was lost by its Indian guide and would, importantly, place it in the Blackland Prairie where bison can occur, such a location is over two hundred miles from San Augustine, Texas. Either this group moved significantly during the intervening years, or the Hais of Moscoso was a different group.

## Xuacatino

From the province of the Hais, the Spaniards proceeded to Xuacatino, and after two days' travel, during which time they were led off the road by their guides, they traveled another day to reach this province. The Nandacao reported that the people of Xuacatino had seen other "Christians." While admittedly speculative, the route we have constructed brings the Spaniards sufficiently far to the west that they could have encountered groups who had seen or heard of Coronado's expedition to the west. The name Xuacatino does not appear in later accounts of journeys through East Texas, and although it is a Caddo word (Chafe this volume), we tend to agree with Schambach (this volume) that the narratives suggest these people had little maize and were likely not Caddo.

Perhaps some clue to where the expedition might have encountered this group comes from the etymology of the word Xuacatino. Chafe (this volume) notes that part of the word, *ha-ti'-no,* is the Caddo word for red. The prefix, *xuac,* is unknown as to meaning. We suggest that this word could be the same as the Caddo word *Bah'-hat-te-no,* or Red River (Newkumet and Meredith 1988:6–7), and the designation is referring to a province along the Red River. Based on our placement of the Hais in Hunt or Fannin counties, three days of travel, even over a circuitous route caused by an unfaithful guide, could take the expedition to the Red River in the vicinity of Fannin or Grayson counties (illustration 25).

Although the archeology of this area is poorly studied, work at Fish Creek Reservoir (now H. H. Moss Reservoir) in neighboring Cooke County to the west provides us with evidence that sites of this time period existed and consisted of settlements with permanent houses much like that observed for the later Wichita (Lorrain 1969). Recent excellent work by avocational archeologist Ernest Martin (1990) at the Dillard site on the Red River in Cooke County provides one of our best reports of a late prehistoric site for this region. Careful excavations by Martin and others uncovered house patterns and associated burials, indicating a small hamlet. Nearby sites are known from Martin's work, and the survey of Fish Creek Reservoir (Lorrain 1969) indicates that several other sites of similar type and time are present, and the settlement pattern appears to have been a series of dispersed hamlets along the Red River and adjoining small tributaries. Martin's work shows that the people of the Dillard site subsisted on a wide variety of fauna, and, although some maize was observed, this consisted of a few burned cobs. The overall appearance is of a group subsisting largely from hunting and gathering. These people are clearly not Caddoan. The ceramic assemblage further supports a non-Caddoan affiliation, consisting almost entirely of *Nacona Plain* pottery. Although Martin dates the site to A.D. 1150–1350, this is based largely on a single radiocarbon date of 680 B.P. $^{+}$110 (TX-6179). The diagnostic tool assemblage, particularly the dominance of Fresno and Washita projectile points, argues for a more recent occupation, one that may well overlap into the sixteenth century. The description of Xuacatino as a "poor land" with a lack of maize (Robertson 1933:250) fits with what we know of the area archeology.

Additional evidence, albeit circumstantial yet highly interesting, comes from the archeological record of Dallas and Denton counties. Over the past fifty years, accounts have occasionally been published in the Dallas Archeological Society *Record* of possible de Soto artifacts being found in Dallas County (Crook 1988; Hanna 1940; Harris 1951). The artifacts include "an East Indies Tabar of the 15/16 century," a cache (burial?) of several Mississippian ceramic vessels, sherds, and other items of the type found in late sites along the St. Francis River of Arkansas, the head of a medieval halberd, and a silver alloy gauntlet. The Tabar and gauntlet were both identified by the Department of Arms and Armory at the Metropolitan Museum during the 1950s as dating to the fifteenth to sixteenth centuries, although the letter of authentication for the gauntlet is missing. All of the artifacts except the gauntlet were found on the south side of the Trinity River in Dallas. The gauntlet was found along the Elm Fork of the Trinity River northwest of Dallas. Specific locations are available on the ceramic vessels and Tabar; both came from the Honey Springs site in present-day Dallas. The authenticity of these items has sometimes been questioned over the years, and efforts are currently underway to have the items re-evaluated in light of today's better understanding of the age of such artifacts. The re-evaluation of these artifacts should offer an important test for the Blackland Prairie Route.

## Guasco

From this position, the Moscoso expedition traveled for twenty days. According to Elvas, they were looking for other "Christians" traveling to the south. As Biedma aptly suggested, the expedition was most likely tracking down rumors of its own wanderings.

Importantly, Biedma stated that the Spaniards traveled eastward, a direction discounted by Swanton (1939) and other researchers. But an easterly direction of movement, particularly southeasterly and following the Trinity River, would be exactly the route needed to reach the province of Guasco, which almost certainly has to be the Hasinai (Swanton 1942, 1939). Supporting this identification is Casanas' seventeenth-century diary, which identifies the Guasco as a tribe of the Hasinai in the 1690s (Swanton 1942:8).

The Spaniards traveled during the twenty days through a "poorly populated region where they endured great need and suffering; for the little maize the Indians had they hid in the forests and buried it" (Robertson 1933). In the Lewis (1907) editing of the Smith translation of Elvas, the forests are referred to as scrub; this is an apt description of the Post Oak Savannah biotic zone that occurs along much of the Trinity River. The description of the Indians fits well with the known archeological record of the Post Oak Savannah region, where a hunting and gathering existence has been documented, along with a very minimal use of maize (Bruseth, McGregor, and Martin 1987). Assuming for the present the authenticity of the de Soto artifacts from Dallas County, this would suggest that the expedition traveled south or southwest from the Red River vicinity, perhaps along either the East Fork or the Elm Fork of the Trinity River. Both are tributaries of the Trinity and flow southward toward the Dallas area. Either would have been a logical route for the Spaniards to take, and as Elvas (Robertson 1933:250) noted, they wanted to move to the south. Travel along the Elm Fork could also explain the occurrence of the gauntlet noted by Crook (1988), and also explain the other artifacts from the Honey Springs site in Dallas County. Twenty days' travel from the Red River would be an appropriate length of time for the expedition to have reached the proposed location of Guasco on the Neches River in Cherokee County. Upon reaching Guasco they found ample supplies of maize, and, we argue, have once again encountered a Caddoan group. From here the Blackland Prairie Route merges with the final leg of the Trammell's Trace Route.[3]

## ACKNOWLEDGMENTS

The authors would like to thank Robert Mallouf, Peter Thurmond, Daniel Prikyle, and LeRoy Johnson who read and commented on earlier drafts of this paper. We would also like to express our appreciation to the assistance provided by Daniel Prikryl, Bill Young, William Crook III, and Mrs. Henry Hanna. In addition we are grateful to the Smithsonian Institution for the opportunity to review the field notes of the late R. K. Harris in their files. All drafting was prepared by William A. Martin. Finally, the paper would not have been completed without the able assistance of Jan Murray and Deborah Smith.

# Notes

1. The authors are aware that El Camino Real was a network of Spanish roads rather than a single road. However, since this route in Texas has been popularized as the Camino Real, it is used here for simplicity.

2. The earliest Spanish documents are Terán de los Ríos (1690–92) and the 1716 Hidalgo (quoted in Swanton 1942:267). The Juan Pedro Walker map is in the Berlandier Collection, Yale University.

3. For further discussion on the subject published since the 1990 de Soto symposium, see Bruseth and Kenmotsu 1991.

# Identification of Ethnic Groups Contacted by the de Soto Expedition in Arkansas

Michael P. Hoffman

## INTRODUCTION

The identification of the Native-American groups encountered by the de Soto expedition in Arkansas is a strong and frustrating challenge in spite of the scholarly diligence of John Swanton and that of Colonel Fordyce (Swanton 1939) and the many investigators of the last forty years. The difficulties of relating de Soto expedition town and chiefdom names both to later ethnic groups on the one hand, and to archeological sites and manifestations on the other, remain as real today as in Swanton's time. Crucial to the problem is where the expedition crossed the Mississippi River, still a matter of legitimate debate by competent scholars. The disruptions of the post–de Soto protohistoric period of A.D. 1543–1700, which must have included tribal extinctions, migrations, and amalgamations, are still unmeasured, so it is difficult to know how A.D. 1700 tribal distributions relate to the mid-sixteenth century.

While these old difficulties and uncertainties remain, the data available through archeology have increased and improved considerably since Swanton's time. The Lower Mississippi Valley Survey (Phillips, Ford, and Griffin 1951; Phillips 1970; Ford 1961) and Jeffrey Brain's (1979, 1981, 1988) focus on the archeology of the Tunica are important works. In Arkansas, the work of the Arkansas Archeological Survey since 1967 and particularly Morse and Morse's (1983) epic treatise on the archeology of the central Mississippi valley, present a solid data base which was not present before. A renewed interest in tracing the de Soto route in Arkansas has developed because of improved archeological knowledge.

This paper will review what is known, what is probable, and what is uncertain about the ethnic or language group identities of the Arkansas Indians visited by the de Soto expedition. Several kinds of information will be used in making the review. First, what is known of the late seventeenth- and early eighteenth-century tribal distributions in Arkansas will be presented. Archeological cultures associated with these tribes will be discussed. Then, the relevant oral tribal traditions of several Indian tribes, including the Quapaw and the Tunica, will be discussed. The useful information provided by linguistic and ethnological clues in the de Soto narratives will be summarized.

Finally, archeological information linking protohistoric sites and phases to de Soto–era towns and chiefdoms will be discussed. Also, I will point out what I think might be strong points and weak points in the two major views about the crossing of the river and the route of the expedition. Several scenarios had to be constructed here because two or three routes of the de Soto expedition were being debated. I also will touch on some research on genetic relationships of skeletal populations of the late Mississippian and protohistoric period in eastern Arkansas.

## LATE SEVENTEENTH- AND EARLY EIGHTEENTH-CENTURY ARKANSAS TRIBES: 150 YEARS AFTER DE SOTO

Northeastern Arkansas above the locality of the Arkansas River mouth was devoid of a native Indian population, save for a short-lived Michigamea village in the late seventeenth century. If one takes the map prepared by the French cleric, Jacques Marquette, at face value, the lower, and perhaps, central Arkansas River regions were ethnically heterogeneous places at the time of his arrival in 1673, with Quapaw (Akansea), Tunica (Tonika), and Koroa (Akoroa) villages present. The Marquette map (illustration 27) shows the village of Paniassa some distance south of the Arkansas River in what might have been the Ouachita Mountains. Another village, also called Paniassa, was shown well to the north of Arkansas and west of the Kansa village in what probably was the eastern plains area of Kansas. These Paniassa presumably represented the Wichita or Pawnee, since Paniassa was sometimes used to refer to the Wichita. Dickinson (1980) takes this indication of a Paniassa village south of the Arkansas River as evidence that the Wichita lived in Arkansas in the 1600s (with another term, Mentou, also referring to them), but I think it more likely that the Michigamea interpreters who helped construct the Marquette map simply used Paniassa to refer to tribes which spoke a Caddoan language, as both the Wichita and the Caddo do. Paniassa has sometimes been used in this way.

In 1687, another Frenchman, Henri Joutel encountered the Caddoan Cahinnio along the Ouachita River in the Ouachita Mountains of southwest Arkansas and the Caddoan Kadohadachos near the great bend of the Red River in extreme southwestern Arkansas (Jeter 1986:44). Tunica and Koroa people were also present in Arkansas along the lower Ouachita River and Bayou Bartholomew drainages in the late 1600s (Jeter 1986:44), but both these groups were gone from the state by 1700. Apparently the Arkansas Ozarks did not have a resident Indian population in the late seventeenth century.

In summary, the ethnic groups in Arkansas when the French arrived in the latter seventeenth century included (1) the Caddo peoples in the Ouachita Mountains and West Gulf Coastal Plain, (2) the Algonquian-speaking Michigamea who had a village in northeastern Arkansas, and (3) the Quapaw, Tunica, and Koroa peoples along the lower Arkansas River, with the Quapaw territory extending a short distance up the Mississippi River from the mouth of the Arkansas River, and Tunica and Koroa villages in southeast Arkansas east of the Ouachita Mountains.

## ARCHEOLOGICAL COMPLEXES LINKED WITH ARKANSAS TRIBES

### THE CADDO

Mark Harrington (1920) of the Museum of the American Indian was among the first to postulate that a specific archeological manifestation could be linked to the historic Caddo people of Arkansas, and a great amount of subsequent research has demonstrated the correctness of his assertion. The archeological culture, called the Caddo or Caddoan culture, which is defined by settlement, architectural, ceramic, and mortuary characteristics, has roots in southwestern Arkansas which extend from before A.D. 800 until after 1700: there are unbroken archeological sequences in the several regions. Thus, the archeological data indicate that the Caddo people were in the area for a long time.

### THE TUNICA AND KOROA

The Tunica and Koroa people moved a good deal in the protohistoric and early historic eras and rapidly disappeared from the Arkansas scene. Using a variety of approaches, Jeffrey Brain (1979, 1981, 1988) has traced Tunica archeology from the known eighteenth-century Trudeau site near the mouth of the Red River in Louisiana back through time to the late seventeenth-century Haynes Bluff site near the mouth of the Yazoo River in Mississippi to sixteenth-century sites near Clarksdale in northwestern Mississippi. Brain has demonstrated that the archeological remains of the Tunica clearly are in a "real Mississippian" tradition rather than one similar to Caddoan or Natchesan traditions. The sixteenth-century archeological complex linked to the Tunica has significant similarities to the Quapaw phase in Arkansas. Marvin Jeter (1986) linked the late prehistoric and protohistoric Tiller, Hog Lake, and Glendora phases of southwestern Arkansas with the Tunica and Koroa peoples, based on geographical coincidence and some ceramic similarities with Trudeau site ceramics.

### THE QUAPAW

Until recently, the archeological identity of the Quapaw tribe seemed settled, with the protohistoric remains of the lower Arkansas River valley excavated by C. B. Moore (1908) linked to the tribe. This hypothesis began with the postulate of Samuel Dickinson and Samuel Dellinger (1940) that the so-called "Arkansas River Culture" represented the Quapaw. It was strengthened with James A. Ford's identification of the Menard site near the mouth of the Arkansas River with the early eighteenth-century Quapaw village of Osotouy (Ford 1961). Philip Phillips (1970) and M. P. Hoffman (1977) freely used the term "Quapaw phase" to emphasize the firmness of the identification of lower Arkansas River protohistoric remains with the tribe. I have since drawn back from this identification because there are major discordances between what is known of historic Quapaw architecture, village distribution, ethnology, and linguistics and the archeological remains of the Quapaw phase (M. P. Hoffman 1987a). As Dan Morse has recommended, I think the wise thing to do is to forget the term

"Quapaw phase" and talk about archeological complexes like the Menard complex in Arkansas River area, and then start from there to work out more clearly defined archeological phases.

Menard complex or Quapaw phase archeological remains bear strong resemblance, or at least some resemblance, to those thought to represent the Tunica in northwestern Mississippi and the protohistoric Mississippian phases in adjacent northeastern Arkansas such as Kent, Old Town, and Walls. Dan Morse (1986) offered a hypothesis linking the Nodena phase of extreme northeastern Arkansas with the Quapaw people based on the assumptions (1) that the Nodena phase was Pacaha and (2) Pacaha-Kapaha of the de Soto era was a Quapaw town. Reacting to this idea, I pointed out that there are no protohistoric archeological complexes in the area of the lower Arkansas River which have ceramics very similar to those of the Nodena phase (Hoffman 1988). I think we should regard the archeological identity of the Quapaw as uncertain at the present time.

In summary, the archeological identity of the Arkansas Caddo peoples is well established, that of the Tunica and Koroa likely but not as strong, and that of the Quapaw, uncertain.

## NATIVE ORAL TRADITIONS

The Quapaw, Tunica, and neighbors of the Tunica have oral traditions about their pasts. The tradition of the Quapaw, dating back at least to the early nineteenth century is that they moved to the area near the mouth of the Arkansas River from the north (Bizzell 1981). They believe that they encountered and defeated the Tunica below the St. Francis River and also drove out the Michigamea (Illinois Indians). The Quapaw oral tradition places the Tunica and Michigamea in the same area in which they were located on the 1673 Marquette map. Native Tunica accounts also indicate that the Tunica lived further north near the Mississippi River before they arrived at their late seventeenth-century location at the mouth of the Yazoo River in present-day Mississippi (Haas 1950). Also, Choctaw and Chickasaw peoples referred to Mississippian culture sites near Clarksdale in northwestern Mississippi as "Tunica Oldfields," an assertion which Brain (1979, 1981) has used to help locate the sixteenth- and early seventeenth-century area of the Tunica. Probably the name of Tunica County in extreme northwestern Mississippi is also relevant. In summary, the Quapaw say they moved into the lower Arkansas River locality from the north and drove out the Tunica and Illinois who were there. The Tunica say that they were in northwestern Mississippi before 1700.

## LINGUISTIC AND ETHNOLOGICAL CLUES FOR ETHNIC IDENTIFICATION IN THE DE SOTO NARRATIVES

The narratives of the de Soto expedition provide two basic kinds of information for identification of the native groups contacted, independent of geographical and historical considerations. Linguistic information consists of sounds and words which may be linked to Indian languages or language families. Ethnological data from the de Soto narratives provide information on settlement, subsistence, social and political organization, and religion which can be related to later groups in the Southeast. John Swanton (1911, 1939) provided the bulk of such suggestions. Swanton had a holistic knowledge of the ethnology, and to a lesser extent, linguistics of the Southeast, and his speculations and insights still must be respected. In many cases, Swanton made guesses about language family relationships without attempting further tribal identifications. He did not venture a guess about the identification of the chiefdom of Quizquiz near the point where the expedition crossed the Mississippi River (Swanton 1939:54). He believed that the peoples encountered before reaching the Caddoan-speaking town of Tula in the Ouachita Mountains spoke languages of the "southern division of Muskhogean" (Casqui), Tunican (Pacaha, Coligua, Tonica, Cayas), or Natchesan (Quiguate). With the exception of Casqui, however, he was extremely uncertain and predicated his guesses with the phrase "connections unknown" (Swanton 1939:54).

He thought linguistic affiliations were unknown for the towns reached by the expedition after Tula. He did suggest Natchesan languages for the towns of Quipana, Anoixi, Quitamaya, Utiangue, and several others. Linguistic evidence was stronger for the identification of Amaye, Naguatex, and Hacanac as Caddoan. While Swanton thought in 1911 that Pacaha (Capaha) was affiliated to the Quapaw language, by 1939 he had changed his mind and speculated that the town was Tunican, a conclusion with which Robert Rankin (this volume) concurs. Swanton also thought that the religious complexity of the temple at Pacaha was more similar to that of the historic Tunica than that of the Quapaw. Swanton was most definite that the chiefdom of Casqui in northeastern Arkansas was the group which later became the historic Kaskinampo and who later merged with the Koasati and Creeks (Swanton 1939:52). The town of Tanico on the River of the Cayas (which was the Ouachita River according to the 1939 De Soto Commission) Swanton related to the Tunica. Coligua (near Little Rock according to the commission) was related to the Koroa. In Arkansas, the de Soto expedition found these Indians engaged in the salt trade, still one of the specialties of the Tunica in the seventeenth and eighteenth centuries (Brain 1988).

Swanton's extension of the Natchesan language to northeast and east central Arkansas is very speculative and based on a few phonetic resemblances. The identification of Tula and other chiefdoms as Caddoan, however, is fairly strong, based not only on linguistic evidences in some cases, but also on distinctive attributes, such as a dispersed settlement pattern and the Caddo form of greeting by weeping.

Alice Fletcher, writing in the original handbook of North American Indians (Hodge 1910), linked some de Soto town names with languages different from Swanton's identification. Quipana, she says, is a Caddoan word which has been attributed to the Caddoan speaking Pawnee. She also thought it probable that the town names—Chaguate, Aguacay, Colingua—had caddoan links (Hodge 1910:183). Except for Coligua, her guesses are more logical than Swanton's because these towns were located in the Caddoan-speaking area of the seventeenth century. Brain (1979, 1981) argued that Quizquiz and Aquixo on opposite sides of the Mississippi River near the point where de Soto made his crossing can be identified with Tunican-speakers because of Indian oral traditions, and because of the Spanish observation that the men of Quizquiz worked the fields, an unusual practice characteristic of the later Tunica.

Dan Morse (1986), Morse and Morse (1983), and to some extent Brain (1985) revived the idea that the de Soto chiefdom of Pacaha represented the ancestors of the Quapaw, based on their interpretation of phonetic similarities and on the general southern movement of Mississippi Valley tribes which occurred in protohistoric times. Morse (1986) further postulated that northeastern Arkansas, in general, was a domain of Siouan language speakers (the language family of Quapaw) who amalgamated in the de Soto aftermath and moved southward.

Robert Rankin (1985:4), a bona fide linguist, wrote that none of these town names in Arkansas from the de Soto accounts is identifiably Siouian. That statement is important in assessing whether the Dhegiha Siouan-speaking Quapaw were among the groups encountered by the de Soto expedition in northeastern Arkansas. Other data which support the *absence* of the Quapaws during the de Soto expedition, or at least among the groups that were encountered by the expedition, include: (1) the absence of any mention of the distinctive bark-covered lodges which were described a number of times by the French in the late 1600s and early 1700s, and (2) the ethnological contrasts of the late seventeenth- and early eighteenth-century Quapaw with other peoples of the lower Mississippi valley and Southeast generally (i.e., M. P. Hoffman 1987a).

In summary, linguistic and ethnological clues for ethnic identification in the de Soto narratives are all too few. The case for Tula and other nearby towns as Caddoan is strong as is the Caddoan identification of towns in the Red River drainage. Quizquiz, Tanico, and Cayas were probably Tunican-speaking. Coligua may have represented the Koroa people and Casqui the Kaskinampo, but those are questionable. That is about all that can be said with even a little assurance.

## ARCHEOLOGICAL SITE OR UNIT LINKS WITH TOWNS NOTED BY THE DE SOTO EXPEDITION

Over the last fifty years, two scenarios of archeological site or phase identifications with de Soto town names have been postulated.

### The Southern Route

The first or southern route is identified with John Swanton and the 1939 De Soto Commission (see illustration 5). Samuel D. Dickinson (1980) argued strongly for the geographical logic of the route. Jeffrey Brain postulated a slight modification of the De Soto Commission route (Brain, Toth, and Rodriguez-Buckingham 1974; Brain 1985a). Also Richard Weinstein (1985) supported this route with a Sunflower Landing Mississippi River crossing. In discussing archeological site or phase identifications of de Soto towns in the alternative routes, I make no attempt to assess the geographical or historical features upon which much of the reconstructed route was based. Both Brain and Weinstein are interested primarily in the area of the crossing of the Mississippi River and the early part of the route in Arkansas. Thus, their archeological site or culture unit assessments are the most up-to-date there and are less so for western and southern Arkansas.

The southern route relevant for Arkansas begins at the chiefdom of Quizquiz which is identified with the Oliver, Alligator, and Sunflower Landing sites located in Coahoma County, Mississippi, west of Clarksdale (Weinstein 1985). The archeological evidence supporting this includes numerous sixteenth-century Spanish artifacts—one hundred turquoise beads, two quartz crystal beads, and five Clarksdale bells. The location of the Sunflower Landing site near where the Spanish are postulated to have crossed the River also strengthens the case. Brain related the several protohistoric sites in this area with the sixteenth-century Tunica for reasons already stated (Brain 1981). Swanton (1939) postulated the Mississippi River crossing at Sunflower Landing while Brain and Weinstein have the crossing a short distance to the north at Friar's Point.

Brain (1981) and Weinstein (1985) link the Old Town site (and phase) south of Helena in Phillips County with Aquixo. Then, the northeast Arkansas itinerary according to the Brain modification of the southern route included visits to Casqui (the Kent phase on the lower St. Francis River) and the province of Pacaha (the Walls phase including the Belle Meade site west of Memphis along the Mississippi River). In 1974, Brain, Toth, and Rodriguez-Buckingham thought it likely that people of the Walls phase (Pacaha) were ancestral to the Quapaw people (and presumably the Quapaw phase). Quiguate to the south was the Dupree site on the lower White River drainage not far from the Mississippi River in Arkansas County, Arkansas. The protohistoric occupation of Dupree is classified as Quapaw phase by Phillips (1970).

Since the de Soto Commission had the crossing of the Mississippi River a short distance south of Friar's Point, Swanton's version of the southern route had Casqui on the White River west of Crowley's Ridge and Pacaha near the mouth of the lower St. Francis (Swanton 1939:251). Swanton wrote before the archeology of the area was well known, so specific site assignments were not often given.

The famous Menard site on the lower Arkansas River near its mouth excavated by C. B. Moore in the early twentieth century (Moore 1908) and Ford in the 1950s (Ford 1961) was Swanton's candidate for Quiquate. The Menard site was later identified by Ford (1961) as the Quapaw village of Osotouy, and the protohistoric materials there have become the type sample for the Quapaw phase. Swanton thought a possible linguistic affinity of Quiguate was Natchesan. Menard site and Quapaw phase ceramics are closely related to the Old Town, Kent, and Walls phases to the north in Arkansas, to the Carden Bottom phase up the Arkansas River, and to late archeological materials across the Mississippi River in Coahoma County Mississippi (M. P. Hoffman 1987).

From Quiguate (the Menard site), the De Soto Commission (Swanton 1939) traced the southern route to Coligua in the vicinity of Little Rock. Coligua was thought by Swanton to be the Koroa, a Tunican-speaking people, a not unreasonable location considering the placement of them on the lower Arkansas River in the Marquette map of 1673. A critical part of the de Soto southern route was the location of the River of the Cayas and the town of Tanico on the upper middle Ouachita River in the Ouachita

Mountains. Swanton (1939:254) placed Tanico at Hot Springs (illustration 16) and the town of Cayas on the Ouachita River near Magnet Cove. Tanico and Cayas were postulated to have been Tunican. The archeological record as it is known in this area (Harrington 1920) makes it difficult to accept the Tunica here, for virtually all the late prehistoric remains known are of the Caddoan archeological tradition. By the Swanton scenario, the linguistic boundary between Tunican and Caddoan language groups was between Hot Springs and Caddo Gap, Arkansas (Tula). The late prehistoric remains at Caddo Gap excavated by Ann Early (1988) are clearly in the Caddoan tradition but so are those in the Hot Springs locality. From Tula the de Soto expedition traveled southward along the Ouachita River eventually leaving Arkansas. The town of Quipana (thought to have been where Antoine Creek joins the Little Missouri River), was a chiefdom believed by Swanton possibly to have been Natchesan. Fletcher (Hodge 1910, 1:216) identified the word Quipana as Caddoan, which would make more sense. Swanton's placement of other possibly Natchesan towns such as Anoixi, Quitamaya, and Utiangue along the Ouachita River (the River of the Cayas) runs into the same contradiction because of Caddoan archeological material found there.

## The Northern Route

The first modern archeologists to seriously discuss a northern route, locating the Mississippi River crossing near Commerce Landing in Mississippi a few miles south of the Tennessee state line, were Phillips, Ford, and Griffin (1951). More recently the Morses (1983) and Hudson (1985) have studied the route using archeological knowledge of the 1980s (see illustration 26). The Walls phase sites of Hollywood, Indian Creek, and Commerce Landing in Tunica County, Mississippi, are identified with de Soto's Quizquiz (Morse and Morse 1983). The Belle Meade site across the Mississippi River is the northern route candidate for Aquixo. None of these sites have yet produced Spanish-era trade goods, while the site candidates on the southern route for Quizquiz have a significant number.

The Parkin phase of the St. Francis River was Casqui in the northern route scenario. The Parkin site has yielded both a de Soto–era chevron bead and a Clarksdale bell. The Nodena phase of the extreme northeast corner of Arkansas and the adjacent Missouri bootheel represented Pacaha. Support for this view includes twenty-five Spanish chevron beads and other Spanish-era artifacts at the Campbell site. Dan Morse (1986) postulated that the chiefdom of Pacaha represented the ancestors of the historic Quapaw tribe primarily because of the sound similarities of Pacaha-Kapaha-Kappa-Ogaxpa (Quapaw).

Quiguate was linked to the Kent phase on the lower St. Francis River, where Spanish-era trade goods have been recovered by pothunters. In the northern route scenario, the town of Coligua was the Greenbriar phase near Batesville on the White River (Morse and Morse 1983). Charles Hudson (1985) postulated that the River of the Cayas was the Arkansas River and that Tanico, a Tunican locality, was at Carden Bottoms site, where a Clarksdale bell, protohistoric pottery, and early European trade goods have been found (Clancy 1985). Schambach (this volume) traced the northern route through the Caddoan area.

With respect to archeological and ethnic information, the northern route fares moderately well. The many Spanish-era trade goods of the sites in the Clarksdale vicinity are missing in the Walls phase sites in northwestern Mississippi, but Tunican place names in the Walls phase locality are present. The Spanish de Soto–era artifacts in the Parkin, Nodena, and Kent phases bolster the identification of Casqui, Pacaha, and Quiguate. The de Soto–era Clarksdale bell at Carden Bottoms site on the Arkansas River and the several protohistoric sites along the lower Arkansas which have yielded European trade goods support the idea that the River of the Cayas was the Arkansas River. The northern route places a major linguistic boundary between the Arkansas River (Tunican) and the Ouachita Mountains (Caddoan). In protohistoric sites there is an archeological boundary between the "real Mississippian" Quapaw and Carden Bottoms phases of the Arkansas River Valley and the Caddoan culture of the Ouachita Mountains. If Coligua were a Koroan town, it seems somewhat out of place near Batesville, Arkansas; I also don't think that the Greenbriar phase resembles very closely the other archeological phases linked to the Tunica or Koroa.

In summary, the archeological and ethnological relationships seem to correspond best with the northern or Commerce Landing route. It is possible, however, that now we just know the archeology better along the northern route because of the recent zeal of Hudson and the Morses.

## NONMETRIC CRANIAL COMPARISONS

A potential source of information useful in postulating ethnic identities and relationships is through comparison of nonmetric cranial characteristics. Ideally, if one had known skeletal samples from specific tribal groups, these could be compared to protohistoric samples to assess degrees of relationship. Federal and state grave protection and repatriation laws make such comparisons difficult, however. Some studies are possible, however. Katherine Murray (1989) has done nonmetric cranial trait comparisons of three Quapaw phase sites on the Arkansas River (Kinkaid-Mainard, Menard and Greer), a Parkin phase site (Cummings Place), and a Nodena phase site (Nodena). The Nodena and Parkin phase non-metric frequencies are close; frequencies of the Nodena or Parkin phase sites with the Quapaw phase sites are low. The Greer and Kinkaid-Mainard frequency similarities are weak but are closer than similarities to sites of the other units. These results do not support the idea that the Nodena phase was ancestral to the Quapaw phase. They also imply significant biological variation among Quapaw phase towns. The samples for Murray's studies were very low, and her results should be used only as hypotheses for further study.

## CONCLUSIONS

A few firm conclusions can be drawn. It is reasonably certain that Tunican-speaking people were encountered by the de Soto expedition. Tanico on the River of the Cayas is widely accepted as a Tunica town because of (1) seventeenth-century tribal distributions, (2) the Quapaw oral tradition of having driven the Tunica out of the area, and (3) the archeological similarities of the protohistoric phases of the lower and central Arkansas River with other archeological complexes thought to represent the Tunica. Jeffrey Brain probably had a pretty good case historically and archeologically for identifying Quizquiz in northwestern Mississippi as Tunican. I think a decent case can be made for relating many of the remains of the so-called Quapaw phase with Tunican speakers based on historical and archeological evidence. It seems to me that the Arkansas River as the River of the Cayas and the location of Tanico on that river fit better ethnologically, linguistically, and archeologically than the linkage of the Ouachita as the River of the Cayas and the placement of Tunica towns in the Ouachita Mountains. I also would postulate that other northeast Arkansas chiefdoms visited by de Soto, such as Quiquate, were Tunican speaking rather than Siouan or Natchesan. It is certain that the de Soto expedition met with Caddoan-speaking peoples (probably the ancestors of the Cahinnio and others) when it was in the Ouachita Mountains and along the middle Ouachita River in Arkansas and in the Red River drainage. There is no other late prehistoric or protohistoric evidence of non-Caddoan towns there, certainly not Tunican or Natchesan. Also historical, ethnological, and linguistic evidence support the Caddoan identity.

Other identities are questionable. The Coligua-Koroa link seems reasonable if the southern route location near Little Rock is accurate but not if a location near Batesville on the White River is used.

The enduring issue of whether the Quapaw were encountered by the de Soto expedition cannot be answered with certainty, but I interpret the evidence to indicate that it was unlikely. There are no recognizable Siouan names of towns encountered by de Soto according to linguists. No mention was made by the Spaniards of the distinctive Quapaw bark-covered long house. Historical, ethnological, and oral tradition data suggest that the Quapaw are latecomers to Arkansas who drove the Tunica out when they settled. I would guess that this took place after 1543. The identification by Swanton of Casqui as the Kaskinampo, a group which later merged with the Muskhogean Koasti and Creek, has not been challenged, but no one really knows much about the group. Nonmetric cranial comparisons relate Nodena and Parkin phase populations, as opposed to Quapaw phase peoples, but sample size is poor and unrepresentative. If the Parkin-Casqui-Kaskinampo links are valid, then the Nodena-Pacaha people might be related to the Kaskinampos and Muskhogeans also.

# Note

Since the de Soto Conference of 1988, I have published or given several more papers that further discuss the protohistoric period in eastern Arkansas. They include:

1991. Quapaw Structures, 1673–1834, and their Comparative Significance. In Hester A. Davis, editor, *Arkansas Before the Americans,* Arkansas Archeological Survey Research Series No. 40, pp. 55–68.

1992a. Protohistoric Period Tunican Indians in Arkansas. *Arkansas Historical Quarterly:* LI(1):30–53.

1992b. The Depopulation and Abandonment of Northeastern Arkansas in the Protohistoric Period. In James Stoltman, editor, *Papers in Honor of Stephen Williams* to be published in 1993.

1991c. Ethnic Identities and Cultural Change in the Protohistoric Period of Eastern Arkansas. Paper presented at 1992 meeting of the Southern Anthropological Society, Saint Augustine, Florida.

# Reconstructing the de Soto Expedition Route West of the Mississippi River: Summary and Contents

Charles Hudson

In the summer of 1984, I worked out a new reconstruction of the route of the de Soto expedition west of the Mississippi River (illustration 26). Using the same methods used in reconstructing the route east of the Mississippi River, I extracted from the documents a relatively full narrative of the activities of the expedition, and I fitted this information to the more easily accessible archeological and geographical information. But I was well aware that parts of the reconstruction were "soft." In the winter of 1984, I drove the route, as closely as I could get to it in my automobile, checking my narrative against geographical features.[1] I also conferred with archeologists along the way, and in so doing I modified and improved what I had worked out. But even after I had done this, several parts of the route remained "soft."

At the encouragement of Hester Davis, I prepared a synopsis of crucial elements in the route west of the Mississippi River for publication in *Field Notes, Newsletter of the Arkansas Archaeological Society* (Hudson 1985). My hope was that Arkansas archeologists, both professional and avocational, might be stimulated to adduce additional evidence for and against my reconstruction. This procedure has worked out very well, and my purpose here is to review this evidence as well as to discuss certain other issues that have come to the surface since 1985.

## THE CROSSING OF THE MISSISSIPPI RIVER: NORTH OR SOUTH?

The single episode in the de Soto expedition that has entered popular culture in the United States is de Soto's discovery of the channel of the Mississippi River. (From the vast quantity of fresh water coursing into the Gulf of Mexico, it was known long before de Soto's expedition that a great river ran through La Florida.) It is, therefore, ironic that the location on the river at which this discovery occurred is one of the most debated parts of the route. In brief, my contention is that the expedition crossed the river a few miles south of present-day Memphis, in De Soto County, Mississippi, while the U. S. De Soto Expedition Commission (Swanton 1939), Jeffrey P. Brain (1985), and Richard Weinstein (1985) contend that the crossing was to the south, in Coahoma County, Mississippi (illustration 5).

It is possible that at some time in the future this debate will be resolved on archeological grounds. De Soto and his army spent a considerable period of time camped near the Mississippi River building four *piraguas* in which to make their crossing to the western side. It is possible—though it is a remote possibility—that the archeological traces of this encampment could someday be discovered. Another kind of archeological evidence that can be brought to bear on the controversy is the mention in the narratives of an extensive wilderness, an area in which no native people were living in 1541. In traveling from Alibamo, a tributary of Chicaza, the expedition spent eight and a half days crossing such a wilderness, a distance of perhaps 130 miles. The archeological identification of a wilderness of similar dimensions has been of capital importance in working out the de Soto route from Apalachee to Cofitachequi in the present-day states of Georgia and South Carolina (Anderson 1990). What are the chances of delimiting a similar wilderness in the state of Mississippi? There is now a fairly good consensus among Mississippi archeologists that Chicaza and Alibamo were located west and northwest of present Columbus, Mississippi (Weinstein 1985). The Mississippi Department of Archives and History has compiled a map of all known late prehistoric sites in the state. Unfortunately, the version current in 1990 of this map shows the corridors which run from this Chicaza location to both De Soto County and Coahoma County to be virtually empty of late prehistoric sites. Thus, as it stands now, it is possible that wilderness lay both to the west and to the northwest of Chicaza. Perhaps future archeological survey work will settle the issue by showing that one of these two corridors was in fact occupied by native people in 1541.

But I contend that there are other kinds of evidence which decisively tip the scales in favor of the northern crossing. Elsewhere I have pointed out that the northern crossing is consistent with Biedma's statement that they took a northwestwardly direction when they departed from Chicaza, and that, moreover, this northern crossing is more consistent with the description of the terrain they traversed than would have been the case if they had gone west from Chicaza and Alibamo (Hudson, Smith, and DePratter 1990:201).

I have also pointed out that a crossing of the Mississippi River in the Coahoma County area lands one in a veritable thicket of geographical inconsistencies on the western side of the river. That is, with any crossing of the Mississippi River downstream from the mouth of the St. Francis River, one cannot propose locations for Aquixo, Casqui, Pacaha, and Quiguate that are consistent with the geographical features mentioned in the documents (Hudson, Smith, and DePratter 1990:201–02, 204–05; and see Akridge 1986). In contrast, a crossing of the Mississippi River at the northern location makes it possible to match on a day-by-day basis every town location and geographical feature mentioned in the narratives (Morse and Morse 1990:197–210; Dye this volume).

A second problem with the southern crossing is that a good match cannot be made with the three towns of Quizquiz. Ranjel wrote that the first three towns of Quizquiz were spaced out at about a league apart. This means that the distance from the first to the third was no more than about seven miles. This is reasonably close to the spacing of the Irby, Lake Cormorant, and Norfolk sites in De Soto County, but the spacing of sites near Sunflower Landing or Friar's Point in Coahoma County do not match this description.

A third problem with the southern route is that it places the domain of chief Quigualtam in the general vicinity of present Natchez, Mississippi. But if this location is accurate, then where is the location of the next large, late prehistoric polity downriver? It is clear that after the fleet of Quigualtam's war canoes ceased to attack the Spaniards who were fleeing downriver in their boats as they left in 1543, a second fleet of war canoes, smaller than the first, took up the attack (Hudson 1985).

In contrast, the northern crossing makes it possible to match the Quigualtam chiefdom and the unnamed second chiefdom with clusters of archeological sites on the eastern side of the river. And on the western side of the river, using the northern crossing, one can match the narratives with the locations of Aquixo, Casqui, Pacaha, Quiguate, Coligua, and Cayas. As the Morses have shown, one obtains an extraordinarily good archeological match with all of these polities (Morse and Morse 1990). And one can trace the day-by-day movements of the expedition from one of these polities to another. This is the case even if it should be determined that the crossing was somewhat further south, in Tunica County. But the requisite town and polity locations for the crossing can only be made by a crossing that is above the mouth of the St. Francis River.

## CONFIRMATION FOR THE ROUTE FROM QUIGUATE TO CAYAS

Research conducted since 1985 has firmed up several parts of the route from Quiguate to Cayas. On the first leg of this journey, in traveling from Quiguate to Coligua, de Soto crossed an extensive, swampy wilderness. At the time I wrote the "Synopsis" (Hudson 1985), I did not know whether the area between Kent phase sites and Greenbrier phase sites (illustration 7) was uninhabited. But on the basis of the survey of prehistoric sites by the Morses (1990:198) it is clear that this area was in fact unoccupied in the sixteenth century (see illustration 6).

Similarly, from talking with local people when I drove the route, I knew that mineral waters occur in the general vicinity of Bradford and Bald Knob, in White County, Arkansas, where my route indicated Calpista should be, but I did not know whether a saline capable of producing salt ever existed there. I was most gratified, therefore, when Scott Akridge (1986:5) unearthed a Civil War report of a Union army contingent that destroyed a Confederate salt works about two miles east of Bald Knob on August 10, 1864. And the Union commander specifically said that it was the only salt works in this area.

I am also grateful to Akridge for information that favors the northern crossing. The Gentleman of Elvas (Robertson 1933:189) noted that the town of Coligua was situated at the foot of a mountain range in a field alongside a river of medium size, half the size of the Caya (the Caia) River in Extremadura. In my location for Coligua, this river would be the White River, while the southern crossing places Coligua on the Arkansas River.

Akridge (personal communication, 1986) cites the following figures:

1. The Guadiana River (into which the Caia flows, and which is therefore larger than the Caia) has a basin of 60,883 square kilometers.
2. The White River has a basin area of 60,886 square kilometers.
3. The Arkansas River has a basin area of 409,741 square kilometers.

Thus, the Arkansas has a basin more than six times larger than that of the Guadiana, and it must exceed that of the Caia by an even larger factor. Similar results are obtained when the flow rates of these same rivers are compared. Again, the White River matches the Guadiana (and the Caia) more closely than the Arkansas River does.

When the Spaniards reached Cayas they also found Indian salt making in this area. I noted in the "Synopsis" (Hudson 1985) that this could have been the Sequoyah salt spring near Scottsville. Subsequently, Dan Morse (personal communication) informed me that a productive saline was located on the West Fork of Point Remove Creek, and this is closer to my proposed location for Cayas.

## WHERE WAS TULA?

Two of the chroniclers of the expedition gave contradictory indications of where Tula was located with respect to Cayas. Biedma (in Bourne 1904, 2:32), who is ordinarily to be trusted in directions, wrote that the people of Cayas told the Spaniards that they could go up the river and reach Tula. But the Gentleman of Elvas (Robertson 1933:194) stated that they were told that Tula was to the south, at a day and a half of travel from Cayas. Another geographical tidbit in Biedma (in Bourne 1904, 2:33) is his mention of the fact that when they first visited Tula to reconnoiter it, de Soto was worried about a "bad passage" in a ridge through which they had come and where he was afraid of being ambushed when they returned. Yet another piece of information is that of all the people de Soto and his army had encountered up to this point, there is the clearest evidence that the people of Tula possessed bison skins in such quantity that large numbers of bison had to have ranged nearby (Robertson 1933:197–99).[2]

In my initial reconstruction of the western route, I placed the most weight on Biedma, and I located Tula somewhere between present Ozark and Fort Smith, Arkansas. But I was later advised that sixteenth-century sites are not known to have existed in this area. At the same time, I learned that a substantial mound complex is located at Bluffton (see illustration 16). I reasoned that locating Tula at Bluffton placed it to the south of Cayas, and it could be thought of as being up the river if the Fourche la Fave and the Petit Jean Rivers (see illustration 4) were considered to be "arms" of the Arkansas River, a terminology that the chroniclers often use. This is why I placed Tula in the vicinity of Bluffton.

But there were problems with this interpretation. One is that I was hard put to locate the "bad passage." Neither the valley entrance near Ola nor the pass near Danville seemed wholly satisfactory. Another problem is that although the archeological coverage for the Fourche LaFave valley is far from copious, the archeological material that has been recovered there shows no evidence that the Indians in this area used bison as a major source of food.

Recently, Ann M. Early and Frank Schambach have brought to light information suggesting that my initial solution might have been closer to the mark. For one thing, the valley of the Arkansas River becomes sharply constricted at about present-day Ozark and this continues for several miles upriver. I suspect that the old trail would have followed on or near the present Missouri and Pacific Railroad. As Ann Early has suggested, this constricted valley could well have been the "bad passage" that had worried de Soto (Early 1990a:5).

Both Early and Schambach have pointed out that there is good archeological evidence that Fort Coffee phase people relied on bison for a substantial part of their diet. Moreover, very few Carden Bottom phase artifacts have been found in Fort Coffee phase sites, and vice versa, indicating that a sharp cultural boundary consistent with information in the documents existed between the two (Early 1990a:3, and this volume). Hence, if archeological survey proves that Fort Coffee phase sites do occur in the area between Fort Smith and Ozark, then this is the likely location for Tula.

All of this fits quite neatly with Early and Schambach's provocative hypothesis concerning the cultural affiliations of the Fort Coffee phase of the Arkansas River in the vicinity of Fort Smith as opposed to the Carden Bottom phase further down the Arkansas River. According to them, Carden Bottom phase is Mississippian (and the people were possibly Tunican speakers), and its closest affiliations are with cultures in the Lower Mississippi Valley. Fort Coffee phase, on the other hand, was a Caddoan culture, whose closest affiliations were to the culture of the Ouachita Mountains to the southeast. In contrast to the Mississippian cultures, the Caddoans had vacant ceremonial centers and populations living in dispersed farmsteads who were well adapted to upland environments (Schambach 1990, 1988). This hypothesis fits very neatly with the several indications of a sharp cultural divide between Cayas and Tula. Indeed, there may be no other instance of such a sharp difference on the entire de Soto route, unless it would be that between the Mississippian Apalachee on the western side of the Aucilla River of Florida and the several societies of Timucuan speakers on the eastern side of the Aucilla River.

If Tula does turn out to have been in this location, then certain adjustments must be made in the route. That is, from this location for Tula, de Soto and his army traveled southeast on October 19, 20, and 21, 1541, swinging down past Pisgah Mountain to pick up the valley of the Petit Jean River, then they passed east of Dutch Creek Mountain to reach the valley of the Fourche LaFave River on October 22, where they came to the province of Quipana. This would place Quipana in the general vicinity of present Nimrod Lake. Thus, Quipana also appears to be a part of Schambach's emerging Ouachita Mountain phase (Schambach 1990). This location for Quipana makes better sense of the Gentleman of Elvas' statement that when they were at Quipana, they learned that Autiamque was six days' travel to the east and Guahate (i.e., Chaguate) was a week's travel to the south (Robertson 1933:201).

This solution to the route means that when de Soto departed from Quipana he traveled down the valley of the Fourche LaFave River before turning south to reach Anoixi in present northern Saline County, and Quitamaya remains in the vicinity of present Benton. (An alternate location for Anoixi is in northern Garland County, as before.) It is possible to argue that the Spaniards traveled down the Fourche LaFave valley all the way from Quipana to Quitamaya, but such an argument will not hold up because this would place Quitamaya on the River of Cayas (the Arkansas), and they made no mention of again reaching the River of Cayas until they came to Autiamque.

## GUACHOYA, A COMPACT TOWN?

In 1985, I indicated what I thought was a difficulty with my location for Guachoya. Namely, from statements in the chronicles Guachoya appears to have been a compact palisaded town situated a crossbow shot from the Mississippi River. It was perhaps no more than a day and a half of travel from Anilco (now thought to be the Menard site).

The contradiction was that the best archeological advice I could get at the time indicated that dispersed settlement patterns prevailed in the area of the Hog Lake phase where I placed Guachoya. I offered the rather lame suggestion that Guachoya might have been the victim of a meandering river (Hudson 1985:8).

But I have since learned from Dan Morse (personal communication) that compact, multiple mound sites do occur in this area, including one (3DE14) four miles south southeast from present McArthur, in whose vicinity I had located Guachoya. Even if this particular site turns out to have been too far from the river, it is nonetheless encouraging that compact towns did occur in this area.

## A BETTER LOCATION FOR NAGUATEX

The route to Naguatex I proposed in 1985 has been substantially improved. My location for the central towns of Chaguate in the vicinity of the Bayou Sel site (3CL27) near Arkadelphia still appears sound, as does my location for Aguacay on the upper Little Missouri River, though Schambach (this volume) believes that the center of this polity may have been a bit further west, in the general vicinity of present-day Nashville, Arkansas. In reconstructing the route beyond Aguacay, I did not pay sufficient attention to Biedma's statement (Bourne 1904, 2:36) that from Aguacay the expedition went southwest and south. At the end of the Spaniards' first day of travel they came to a town near a salt marsh, subject to Aguacay (Robertson 1933:238), which Schambach argued was the Hickman salt site, an unusual salt marsh which closely matches descriptions in the narratives.

From 3SV69, Schambach (this volume) takes them to Pato, a polity located on the Little River. He argues that they traveled directly south from 3SV69, while I suspect, on the basis of travel time, that they may have proceeded westward to arrive at Pato on the Little River near present Horatio, Arkansas. The archeology of the Little River area is poorly known. Additional survey and excavation may make it possible to resolve this slight difference of interpretation. From 3SV69, Schambach (this volume) takes them to Amaye, which he identifies as Texarkana phase, whose eastern boundary lay near present Ogden, and from there to Naguatex, which he identifies as the Spirit Lake locality in the Belcher phase area. All of these identifications are consistent with incidents recounted in the documents.

Schambach's discussion of the Great Raft of the Red River is a major contribution to understanding the de Soto route. The Great Raft accounts for the mysterious, sustained rise of the Red River while the expedition was at Naguatex (Schambach this volume). In working out my 1985 reconstruction of the route, I had no knowledge of the manner in which the Great Raft affected the river, nor of the location of the upper margin of the lake the raft formed. Hence, I regard this as a kind of geological confirmation of my route that is on the same order as Scott Akridge's discovery of the Confederate salt works near Bald Knob.

## TO THE RIVER OF DAYCAO

Reconstructing the route of the expedition into eastern Texas was especially difficult because Rodrigo Ranjel's account of this part of the expedition has not survived. No other chronicler recorded the movements of the expedition on so consistently a day-by-day basis as did Ranjel. Moreover, on this segment of the journey the Spaniards were often anxious about obtaining food, and they were traveling as rapidly as they could, so that even the account by the Gentleman of Elvas is less detailed than for previous parts of the expedition. The most extreme instance of this was their return to the Mississippi River, which was described by him in only the sketchiest way.

There is now a good consensus among archeologists that the identification of the province of Naguatex with Belcher phase, and specifically with the Great Bend of the Red River, is correct. From Naguatex, as Kenmotsu, Bruseth, and Corbin (this volume) point out, the expedition could have followed two main avenues into east Texas: the Trammell's Trace Route and the Blackland Prairie Route. This general area of east Texas is known to have been occupied by Indians in the middle of the sixteenth century, and plausible archeological sites can be proposed to fit both of these routes. The question they ask is, which route best fits the total evidence?

The evidence that archeologists have assembled on modes of production in this general area is also consistent with the experiences of the expedition. Moscoso and his army found that the direction they wanted to follow—i.e., generally to the west—put them into difficulty because they soon reached the limits of adequate maize production. They had no choice but to travel where they could plunder native supplies of maize. The archeology of east Texas shows that such maize production existed only in areas adjacent to the Red River, the Cypress Creek drainage, and probably the upper Neches and Angelina rivers. Beyond this lay country occupied by hunter-gatherers: the upper and middle Trinity River and the middle Brazos River (Kenmotsu, Bruseth, and Corbin this volume).

One of the advantages claimed for the Trammell's Trace Route (see illustration 24) is that it follows a historic trail known from nineteenth-century documents.

However, it should be noted that in general there are no significant barriers to travel in eastern Texas, and the economic factors that determined nineteenth-century trails need not reflect those that determined sixteenth-century trails. Hence, a trail that was a thoroughfare in the nineteenth century need not have been one in the sixteenth century. A second advantage claimed for the Trammell's Trace Route was that it located the Aays (i.e., the Hais) near present San Augustine, Texas, where the Hais were located in the eighteenth century (Schambach this volume; Kenmotsu, Bruseth, and Corbin this volume). However, the assumption that eighteenth-century Indian towns were in the same locations they occupied in the sixteenth century is the selfsame assumption that so badly misled the U. S. De Soto Expedition Commission. The Commission, for example, assumed that Coosa was in the same location for the entire time between the sixteenth and eighteenth centuries, whereas evidence now shows that sixteenth-century Coosa was about 130 miles northwest of eighteenth-century Coosa (Hudson et al. 1985:723–24). In areas where the Spanish mission system prevailed—in Florida and Texas—there was more locational stability in place names than there was in the interior. But using eighteenth- or nineteenth-century place names to reconstruct the de Soto route is a hazardous enterprise.

In fact, what is notable about the Aays is that they lived at a place where bison could be hunted in some seasons of the year. As Kenmotsu, Bruseth, and Corbin point out (this volume), this could only have been the Blackland Prairie. This location for the Aays is consistent with several indications that Moscoso and his army desired to travel toward the west, which they believed was the way to New Spain (see esp. Biedma in Bourne 1904, 2:35). Perhaps they got this notion from the tales Cabeza de Vaca told after he returned to Spain (Nuñez 1962).

The location proposed by Kenmotsu, Bruseth, and Corbin (this volume) and Schambach (this volume) for Nissohone (or Nisione) in the vicinity of present Carbondale, Texas, is reasonable. Beyond this point Kenmotsu, Bruseth, and Corbin favor the Blackland Prairie Route. Beyond Nissohone the Spaniards still wanted to go west, but their guide seemed to mislead them for two days, sometimes leading them to the east. They executed him. Then a woman led them in two days' time to another miserable town, Lacane (or la Came). Kenmotsu, Bruseth, and Corbin locate Lacane farther west on Sulphur River, near the confluence of the North and South Sulphur Rivers. This is a distance of fifty-five to sixty miles from their location for Nissohone, a full four days of travel—too great a distance in my opinion.

Here, too, I believe that Kenmotsu, Bruseth, and Corbin were misled by linguistic considerations, i.e., their assumption that only Caddoan speakers were horticulturalists in east Texas in the sixteenth century. Because Lacane (or la Came) is not definitely a Caddoan word, they argue that the Lacane were probably located on the line separating horticultural societies from those based on hunting and gathering. But surely one should keep open the possibility that Indians who did not speak Caddoan were capable of practicing horticulture in east Texas. Moreover, in east Texas the possibility should be kept open that speakers of different languages might have aligned themselves together in multilingual paramount chiefdoms, which are well documented in the eastern part of the Southeast.

Kenmotsu, Bruseth, and Corbin identify Nandacao (or Nondacao), the next destination, with the Three Basins subcluster of the Titus phase (see illustration 25). But using a day's travel time of about fifteen miles, they locate Nandacao at a considerable distance from Lacane. This location places Nandacao at two and half to three days from their location for Lacane.

On the next leg of their reconstruction, Kenmotsu, Bruseth, and Corbin (this volume) get into serious trouble. That is, the expedition traveled from Nandacao to Aays in five days. As Kenmotsu, Bruseth, and Corbin point out, bison were present in the Blackland Prairie during the period from 1200 to 1600, and in 1808 a herd was documented in present Delta County, near Kenmotsu, Bruseth, and Corbin's location for Lacane. They are not very specific about their location for Hais. It may have been located in northern Hunt or southern Fannin County. There was no mention, however, of whether or not sixteenth-century archeological sites occur in this area.

Their location for Hais requires the expedition to have taken a notably northern direction, but there is no indication in the narratives up to this time that the expedition went in any direction but west, southwest, and south. In reconstructing their route from Hais to Soacatino (Xuacatino), Kenmotsu, Bruseth, and Corbin take the expedition even farther to the northwest, perhaps to Grayson County. And because the Nandacao reported to Moscoso that the Soacatino were reputed to have seen other "Christians," Kenmotsu, Bruseth, and Corbin (this volume) conclude that the said Christians must have been members of the Coronado expedition. Hence, this locates Soacatino where the people might have seen or heard of Coronado's expedition. Archeological research in this area shows very little evidence of horticulture, and Kenmotsu, Bruseth, and Corbin see this as consistent with the evidence that *Soacatino* is not a Caddoan word.

The Blackland Prairie route location for Soacatino places the trajectory of the expedition north of Denton and Dallas counties, where several early European artifacts—possibly dating to the sixteenth century—have been found. Thus, Kenmotsu, Bruseth, and Corbin took literally Elvas' (Robertson 1933:250) statement that after Soacatino they traveled for twenty days through a thinly populated country of little maize before reaching Guasco. In this way Kenmotsu, Bruseth, and Corbin (this volume) take the expedition from the Red River down the East Fork or Elm Fork of the Trinity River to present Dallas, and then presumably down the Trinity River to Guasco on San Pedro Creek.

The expedition most certainly could have traveled from Soacatino in Grayson County to Guasco in Houston County in twenty days. But it is dubious that they could have traveled for so many days without replenishing their supply of maize. Even though one can only estimate when they departed from Naguatex (it would seem to have been around August 18), the Gentleman of Elvas noted that on about the first of October, while at or near the River of Daycao, they decided to return to the Mississippi River. This indicates a total of about a month and a half of travel time between Naguatex and the River of Daycao, which is insufficient time to allow the twenty days of travel from Soacatino to Guasco.

Instead, it is more probable that the twenty days mentioned by the Gentleman of Elvas was an estimate of the number of days they spent traveling about as they went from Soacatino, to Guasco, to Naquiscosa and Nazacahoz, back to Guasco, and then to the vicinity of the River of Daycao. All of this travel was in an area where they found little maize.[3]

Let us return to Nissohone, a location on which all agree. Let us also put aside the linguistic identification or analysis of place names, or else call into question the assumption that in the sixteenth century the societies in this area were not as solidly Caddoan speaking as they were in the eighteenth and nineteenth centuries.

The overall trajectory of the expedition was to the southwest. Therefore, let us suppose that in the four days the Spaniards spent going from Lacane to Nondacao, sometimes deliberately misled by their guides, they came to Lacane in the Cypress Creek basin, where the presence of horticultural societies in the sixteenth century is documented archeologically. And let us suppose that Nondacao was also on Cypress Creek, to the west of Nondacao, a day or so away. This would place Nondacao in Titus or Camp County.

From Nondacao they set out in search of Soacatino, where they evidently expected to find a better supply of maize. But again they were deliberately misled by their guide into an area where they might have been expected to starve, and after five days they reached Aays (Biedma in Bourne 1904, 2:36). They were led astray from the trail for at least two days during this time (Robertson 1933:250). Because bison only occurred in the Blackland Prairie, it would seem that they traveled generally west from Nondacao. (Recall that west seems to have been their *intended* direction of travel.) This travel time would place them at the edge of the Blackland Prairie, near the forks of the Sabine River, in Rains County or possibly in Hunt County. This would seem to be a reasonable place to look for sixteenth-century sites identifiable as Aays. The later migration of the Aays (Hais) southeastwardly to the area of the Spanish missions may have been prompted by some of the same forces that caused Indians to move southward to the missions of Florida (Milanich and Hudson 1993).

From Aays, Moscoso and his army took a direction that was generally to the south (Robertson 1933:250) and to the east (Biedma in Bourne 1904, 2:37). From Aays they continued on to their original destination, Soacatino, a province that produced far less maize than they desired. I propose that Soacatino was on the upper Neches River. From here they proceeded southward to Guasco, probably on San Pedro Creek, from whence they made their disappointing foray eastward to maize-poor Naquiscoza and Nazacahoz in the Angelina River basin. Then they returned to Guasco.

Regardless of the route followed by the Spaniards from Naguatex to Guasco, their route beyond this point was to the south and southwest, probably along to the Camino Real (Kenmotsu, Bruseth, and Corbin this volume). The only question is, how far did they go? The Gentleman of Elvas stated that they were told at Guasco that the River of Daycao was a ten days' journey (Robertson 1933:252). Since Indians could easily travel twenty miles per day, this could mean that the River of Daycao was as much as two hundred miles away—the Brazos or even the Colorado. But this stated distance might also have referred to a round trip, in which case the River of Daycao would have been about a hundred miles distant, i.e., the Navasota or the Brazos.

Perhaps we should rely here on Biedma, who is generally to be trusted in matters of direction. He noted that from Guasco the Spaniards traveled for about six days across an uninhabited wilderness (Bourne 1904, 2:37). This would have allowed them to travel perhaps ninety miles, to about the Trinity or the Navasota River, just inside the oak-hickory forest zone. From here they sent out ten horsemen as scouts with enough food to last for eight or nine days. After an unreported length of time these scouts returned with some captive Indians who turned out to be hunter-gatherers who could speak no language spoken by their Indian interpreters (Biedma in Bourne 1904, 2:37–38).

It seems unlikely that the people of Guasco would have traveled farther than ninety or so miles to hunt deer. Hence, the River of Daycao was probably the Trinity (as the U. S. de Soto Commission concluded) or the Navasota.

## THE NORTHERN VERSUS THE SOUTHERN CROSSING AND "THE END OF THE TRAIL"

Earlier I argued that a crossing of the Mississippi River south of the mouth of the St. Francis River leads one into a plethora of geographical and archeological inconsistencies. The inconsistencies are so great the southern crossing advocated by the U. S. De Soto Commission cannot be sustained. Frank Schambach and others have similarly argued that the southern crossing of the Commission route leads to major inconsistencies in the final year of the expedition. For example, between Camden and Calion, Arkansas, where the Commission located the 1541–42 winter site of Autiamque, there are no large Mississippian towns. And in fact, hardly any maize was produced by Indians in the vicinity of present Camden and perhaps none at all around present Calion. Schambach (this volume) and Early (this volume) argue that if Moscoso and his army had wintered in this area, they would have starved to death.

## CONCLUSION

To some, the new reconstruction of the route of the de Soto expedition proposed by myself and some others has been profoundly disturbing, and in some places the reaction has been rancorous, generating more heat than light. Happily, this has not been the case in Arkansas. Whether this can be attributed to the abundance of the archeological information in Arkansas gained through the auspices of the Arkansas Archeological Survey, or whether it is because of the large number of professional archeologists in the state, or the high level of give and take between professional and avocational archeologists, it has made for a happy experience in reconstructing the de Soto route west of the Mississippi River.

The route west of the Mississippi River would now seem to be firmly enough established to justify surveys and excavations in specific locations. In coming decades, we can expect such research to further refine the route and, more importantly, to provide us with the kind of information on which a social geography of the sixteenth-century Southeast may be firmly established.

# Notes

1. For a popular account of this foray by automobile, see Joyce Rockwood Hudson, *Looking for De Soto: A Search Through the South for the Spaniard's Trail* (Athens: University of Georgia Press, 1993)

2. The James A. Robertson (1933) translation of the *Relaçam Verdadeiro* by the Gentleman of Elvas is used throughout this chapter.

3. For further discussion on the expedition route in Texas published since the 1990 de Soto symposium, see Bruseth and Kenmotsu 1991.

ILLUSTRATION 1. The Southeast Showing Native-American Groups and Spanish Settlements Mentioned in Chapter 1. Courtesy of Jerald T. Milanich.

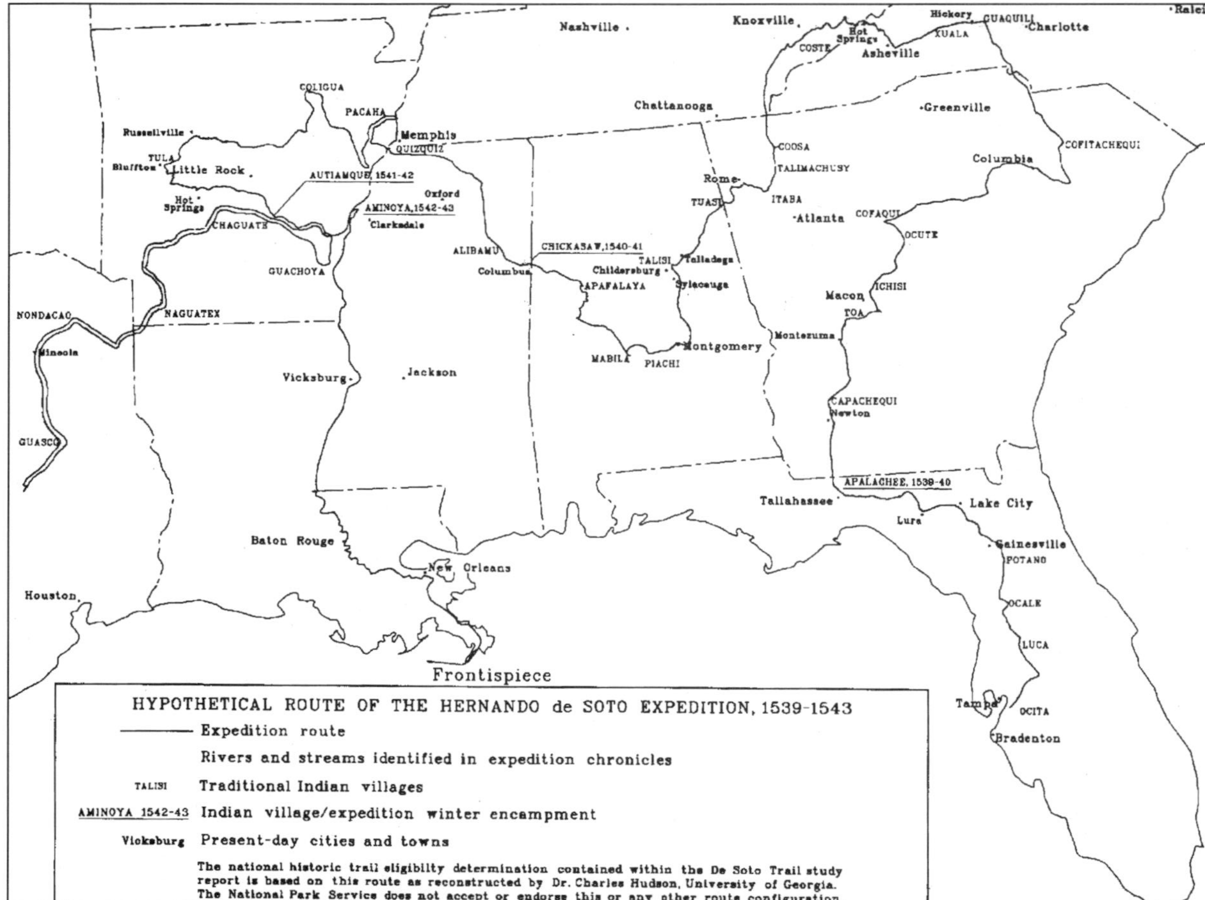


ILLUSTRATION 2. Hypothetical Route of the Hernando de Soto Expedition Proposed by Charles Hudson in 1988. Courtesy of Charles Hudson.

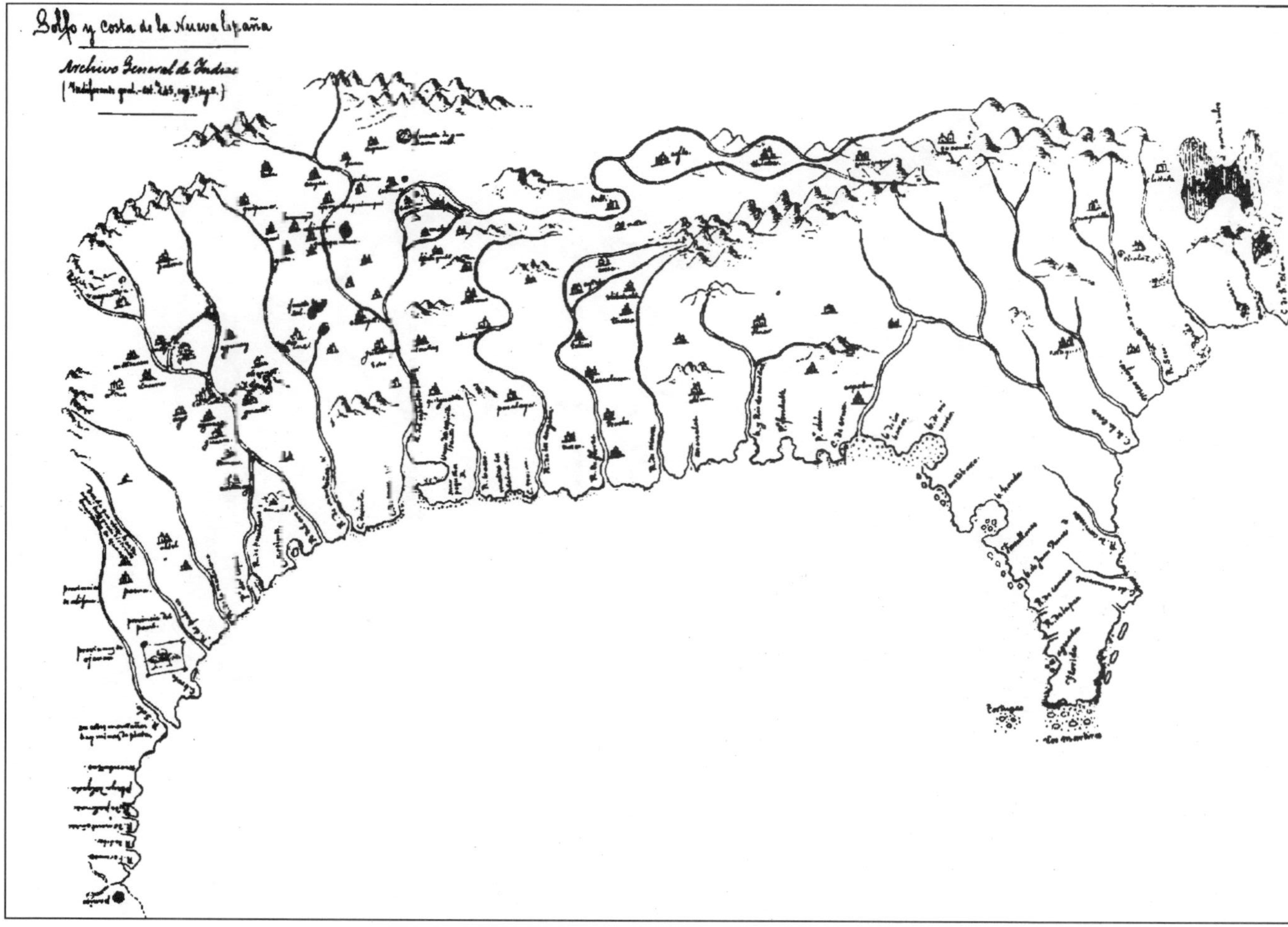


ILLUSTRATION 3. The "De Soto" or Santa Cruz Map. After Harisse 1892 (original at the Archives of the Indes, Seville).

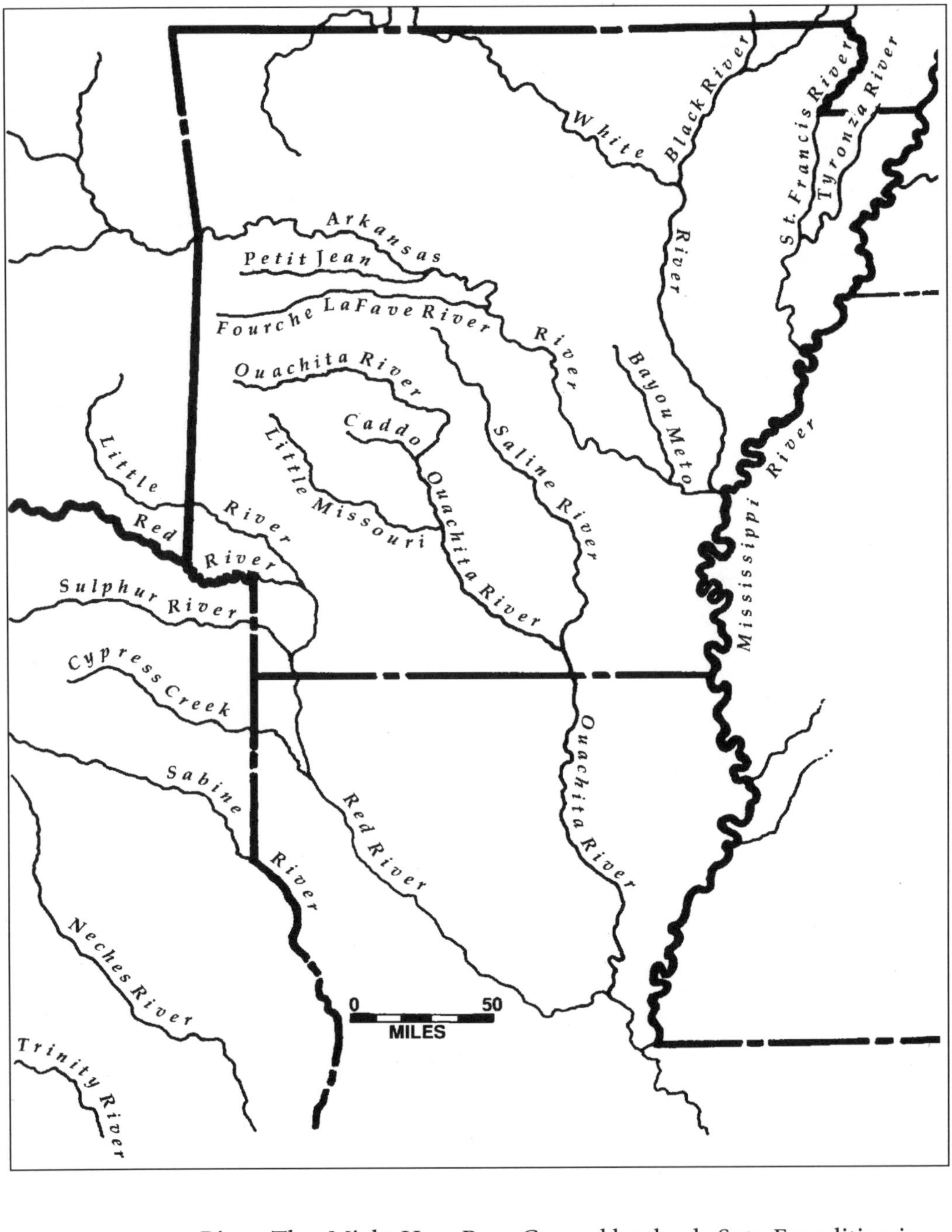


ILLUSTRATION 4. Rivers That Might Have Been Crossed by the de Soto Expedition in the Trans-Mississippi West.

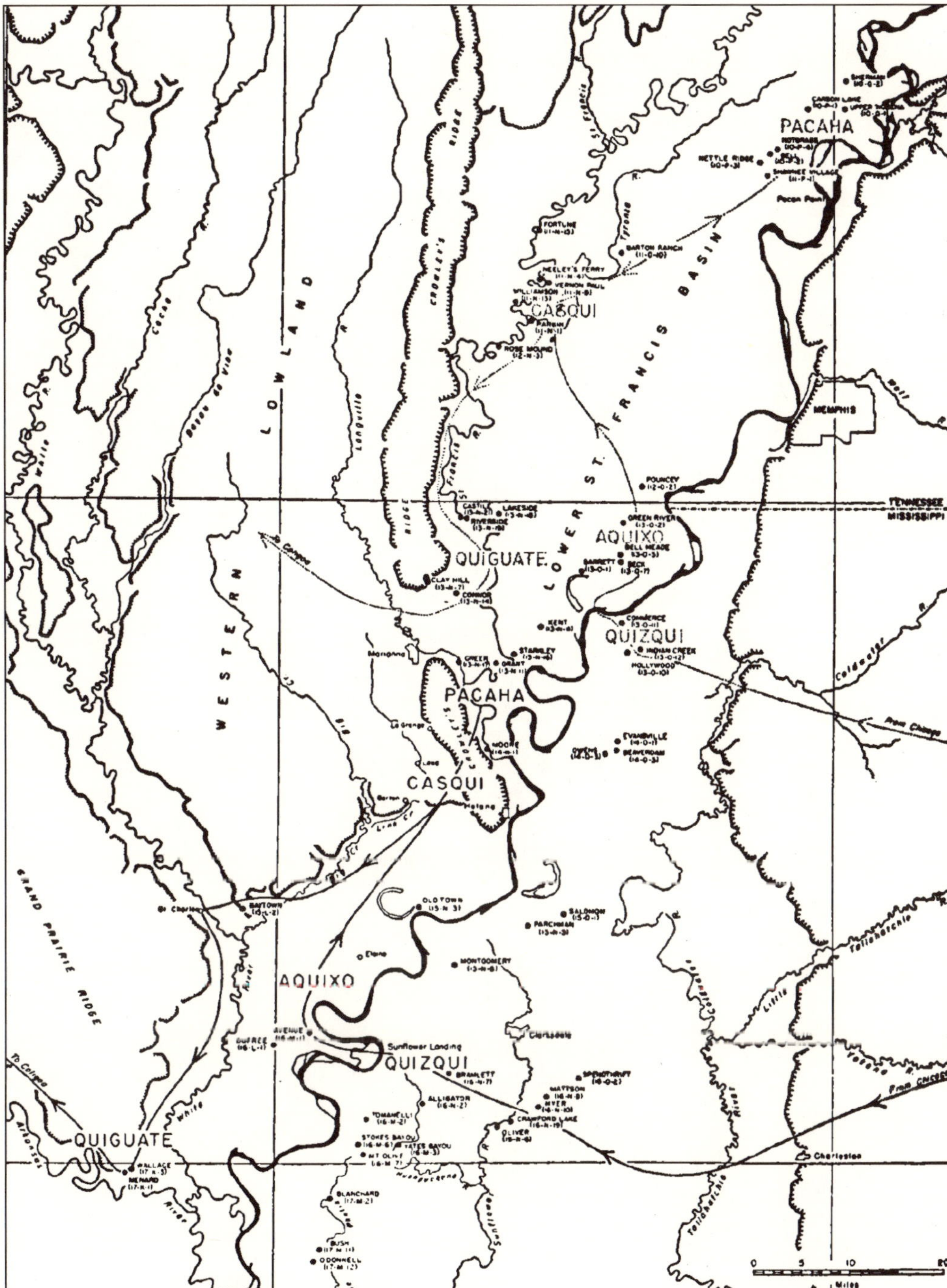


ILLUSTRATION 5. Hypothetical Routes and Mississippi River Crossings (after Phillips, Ford, and Griffin 1951).

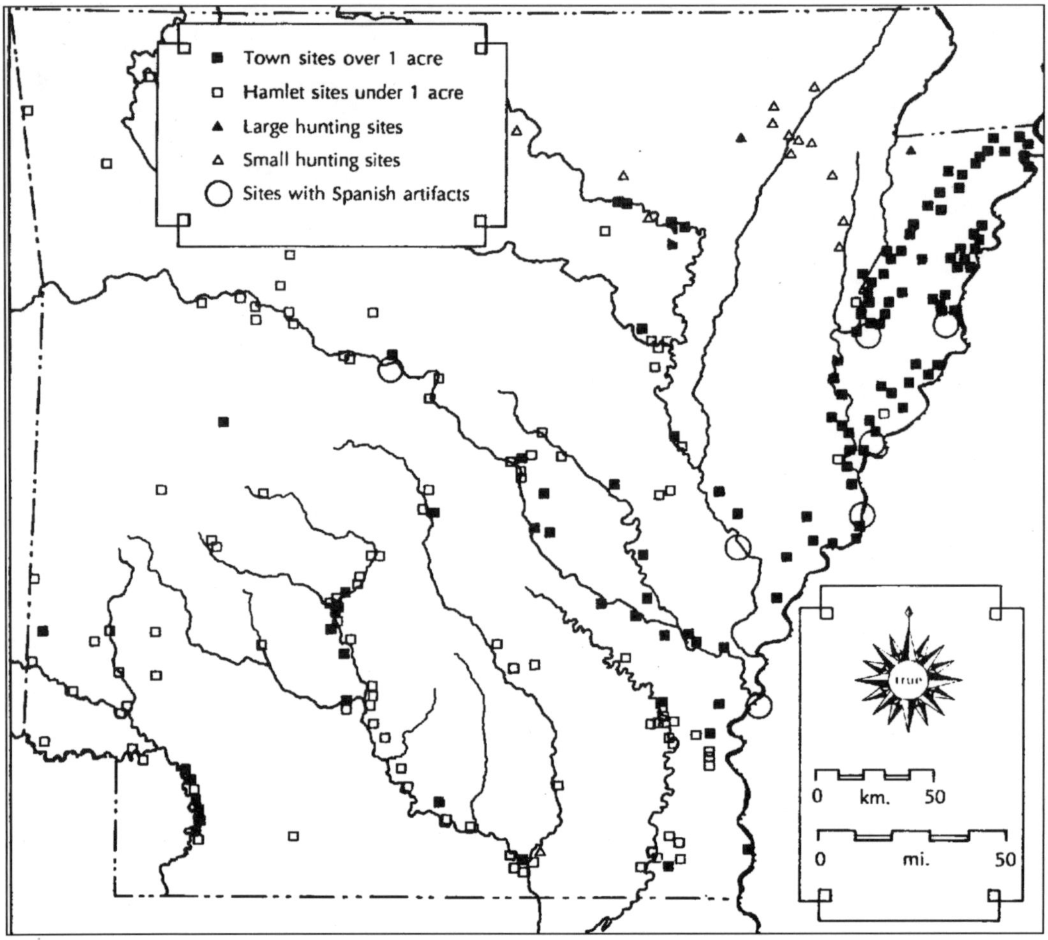


ILLUSTRATION 6. Protohistoric Archeological Sites in Arkansas (A.D. 1500–1700). Courtesy of the Arkansas Archeological Society and AMASDA.

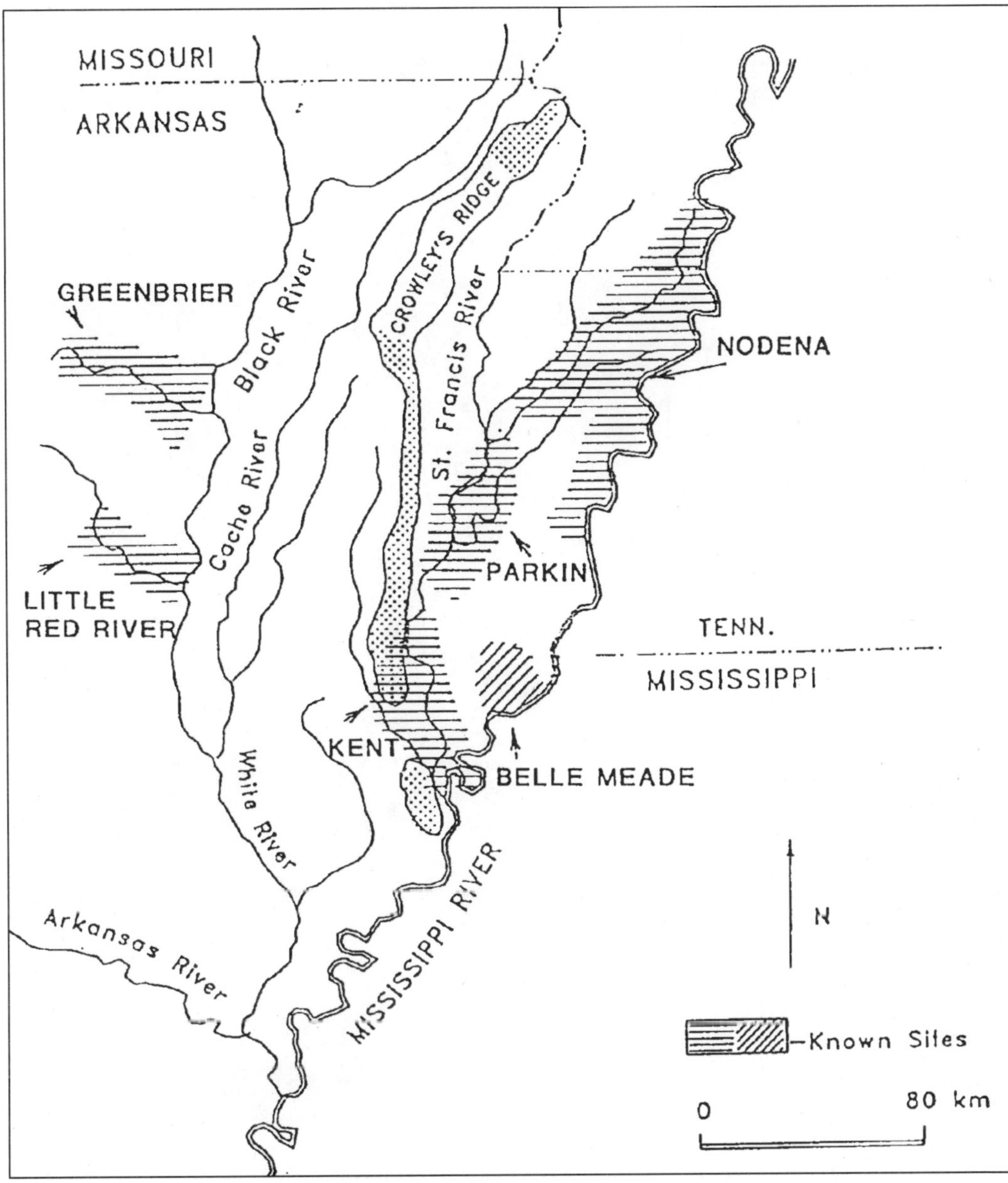


ILLUSTRATION 7. Sixteenth-Century Archeological Phases in Northeast Arkansas. Arkansas Archeological Survey Research Series No. 4.

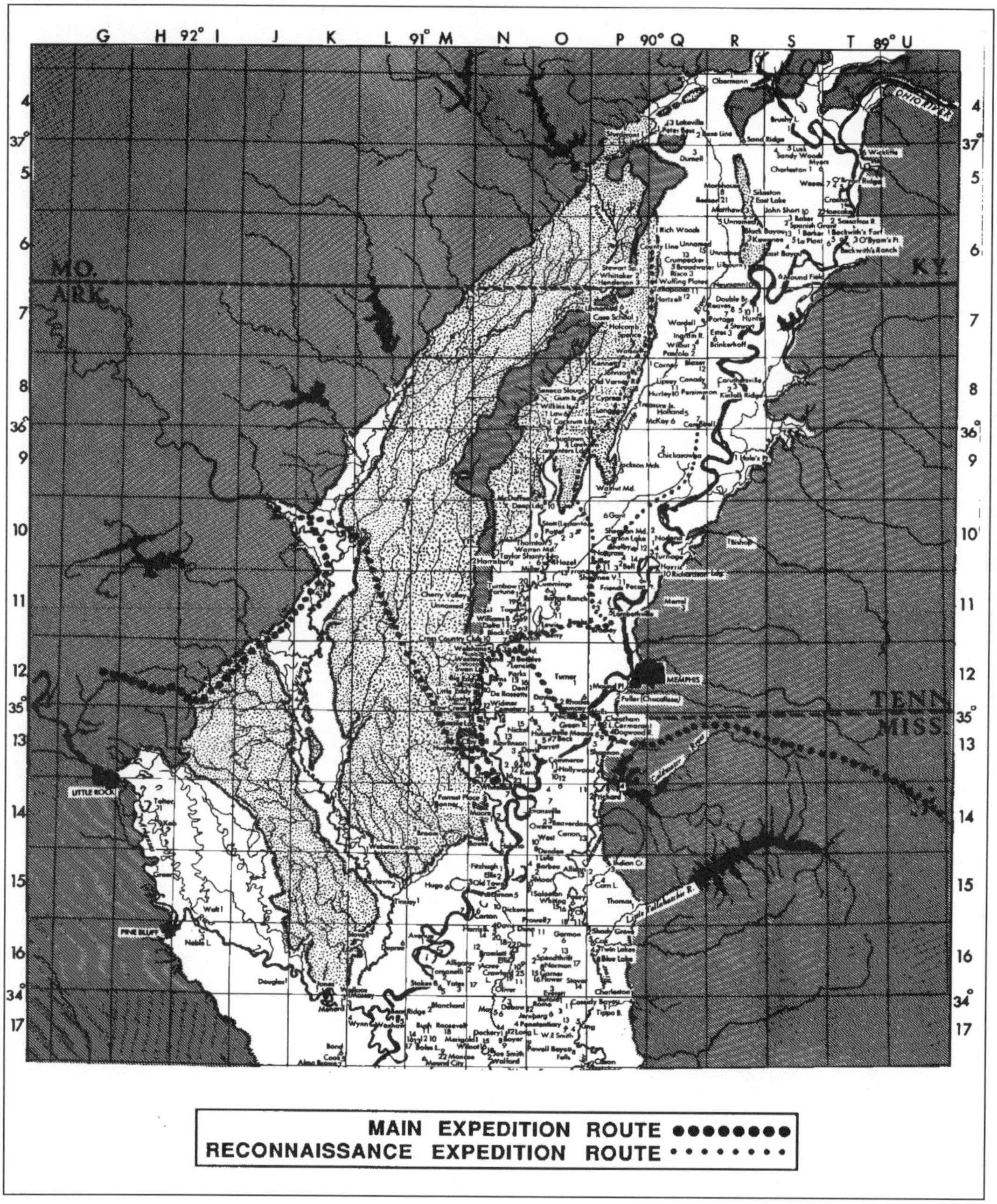


ILLUSTRATION 8. The Study Area and Hypothetical Route for the Expedition in the Mississippi Alluvial Plain. After Phillips 1970.

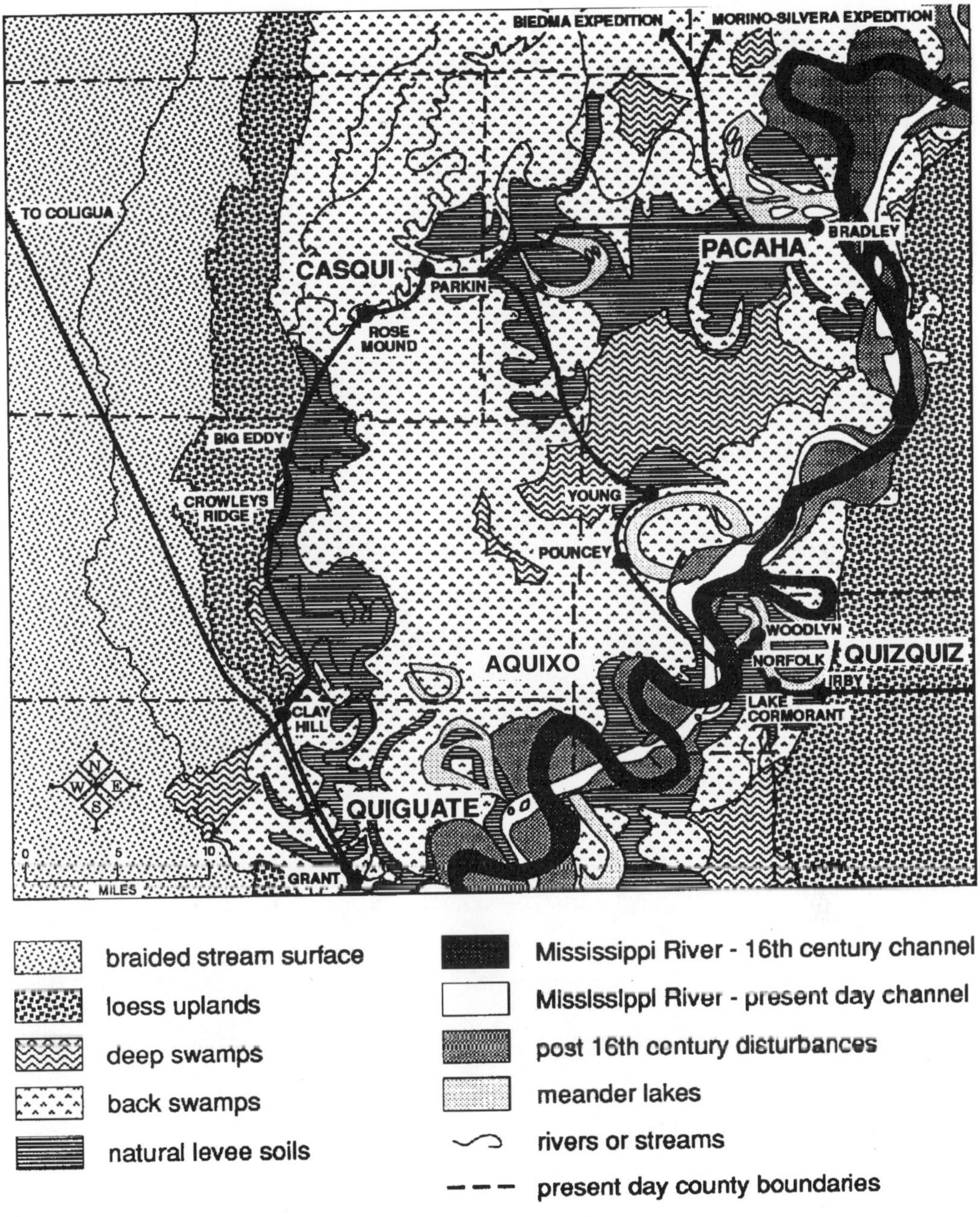


ILLUSTRATION 9. Physiographic Features of the Eastern Lowlands. Courtesy of David H. Dye.

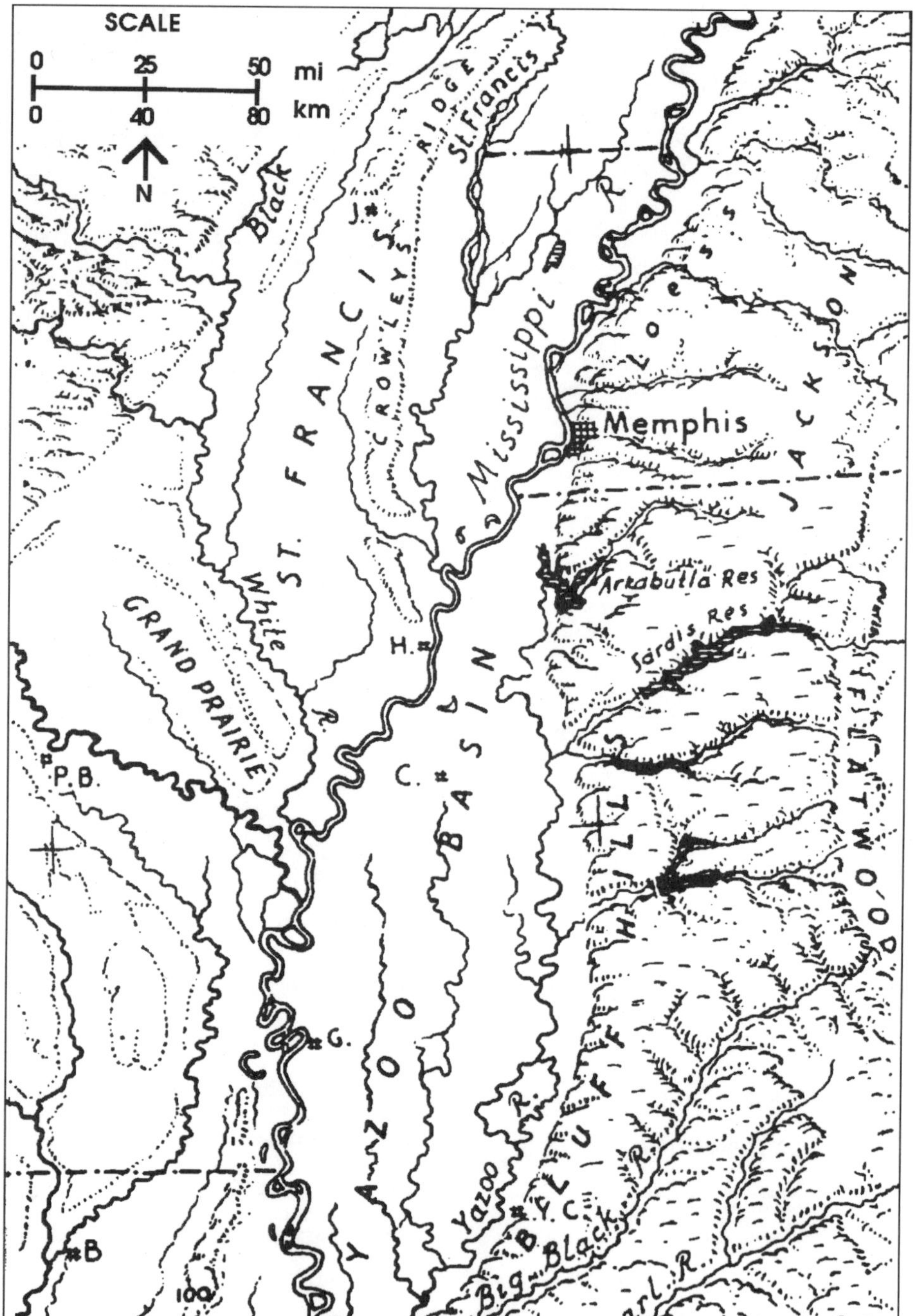


ILLUSTRATION 10. Physiographic Features of the Central Mississippi Valley. After Raiz 1957.

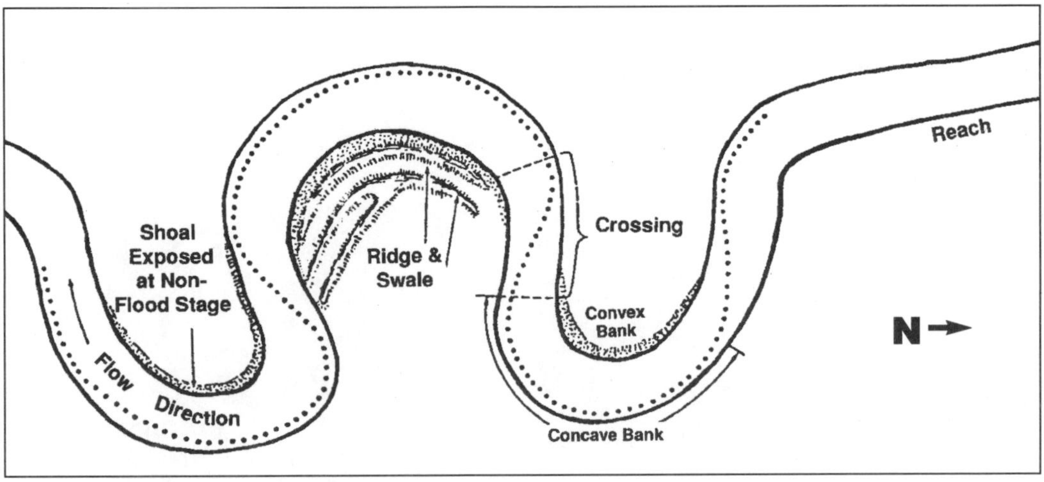


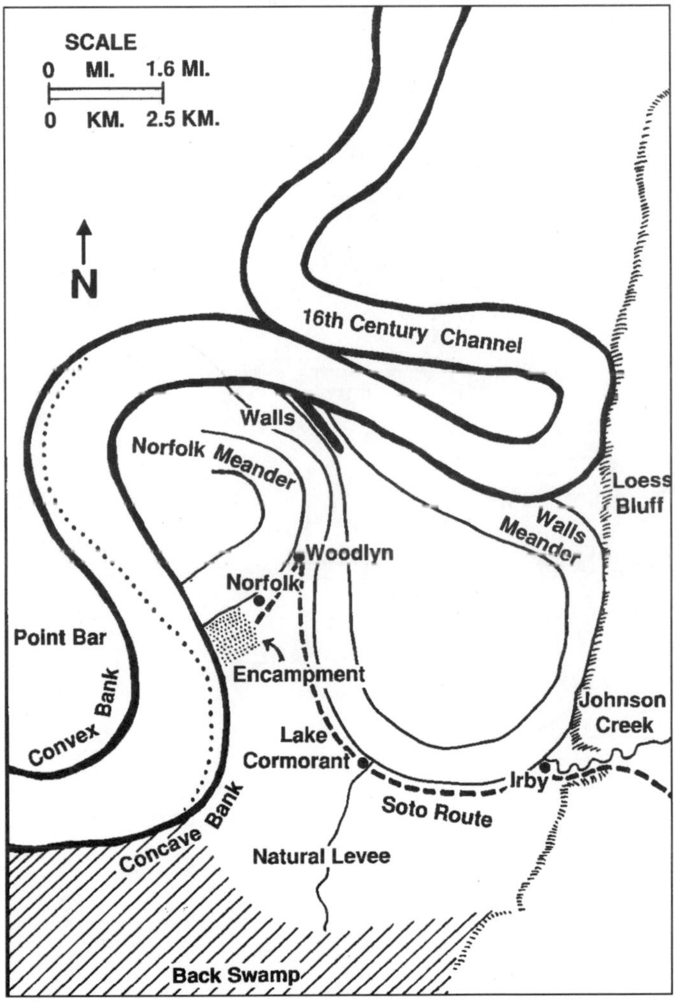


ILLUSTRATION 11.
Idealized Plan of the Mississippi River Channel. Courtesy of David H. Dye.

ILLUSTRATION 12.
Physiography of the Norfolk Crossing. Courtesy of David H. Dye.

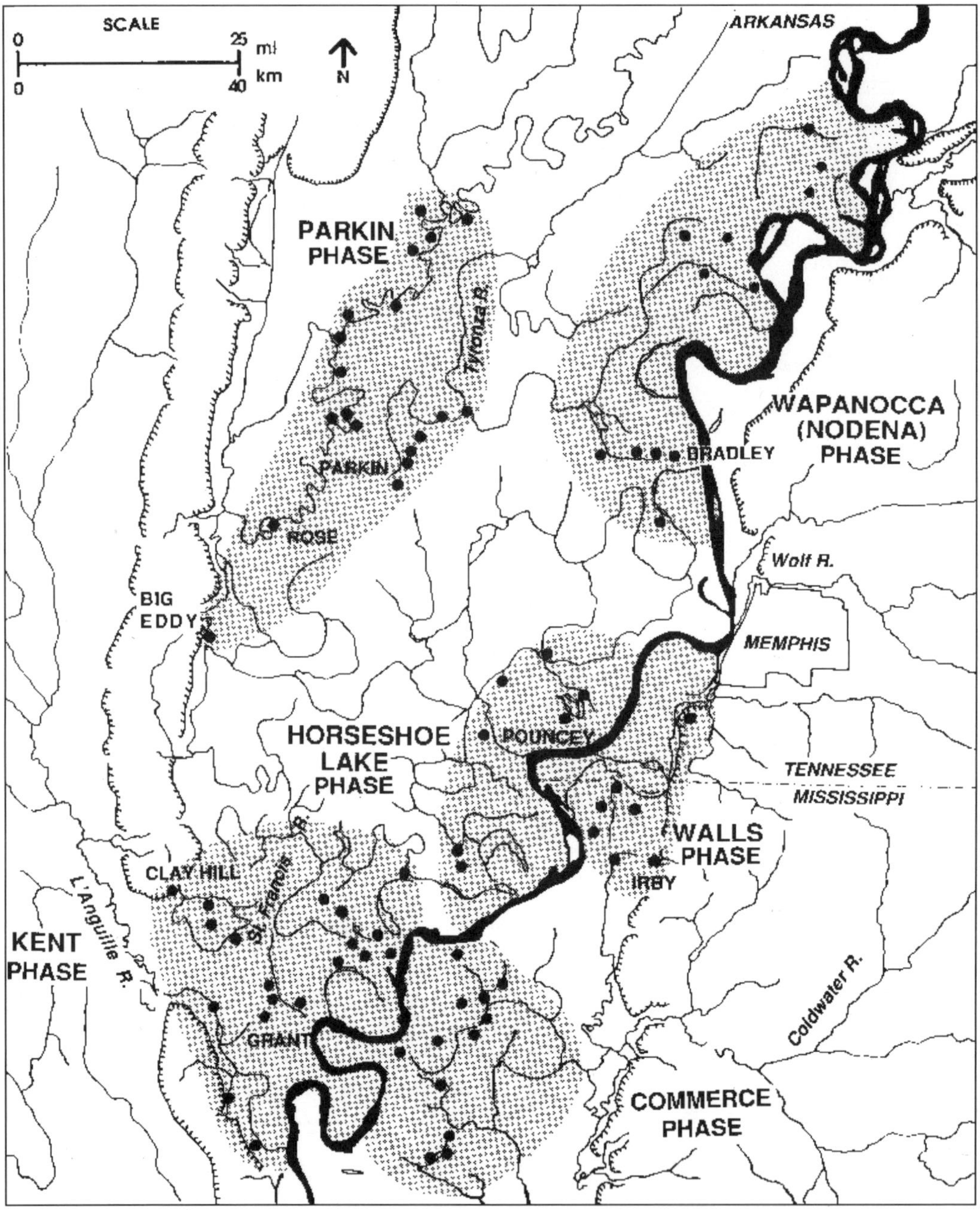


ILLUSTRATION 13. Distribution of Archeological Sites and Phases around the West Memphis Swamp. Courtesy of David H. Dye.

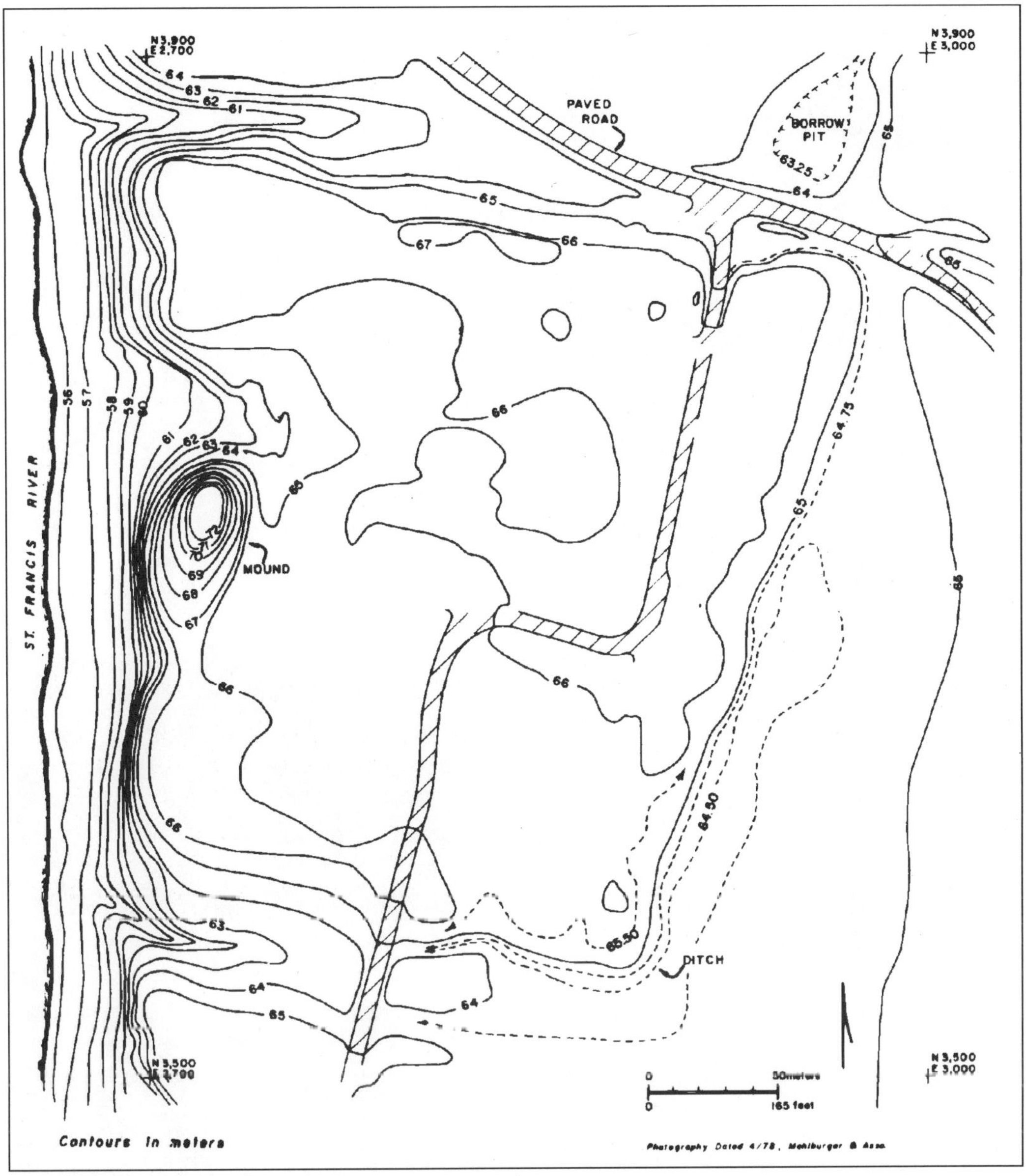


ILLUSTRATION 14. Parkin Archeological Site. Courtesy of the Arkansas Archeological Survey.

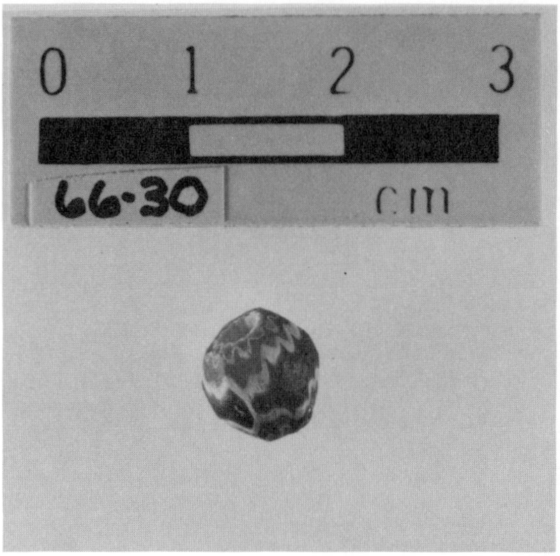


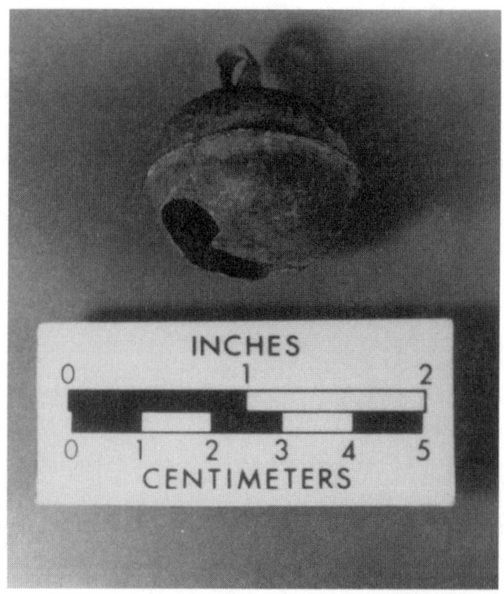


ILLUSTRATION 15. Artifacts from Parkin. Courtesy of the University of Arkansas Museum.

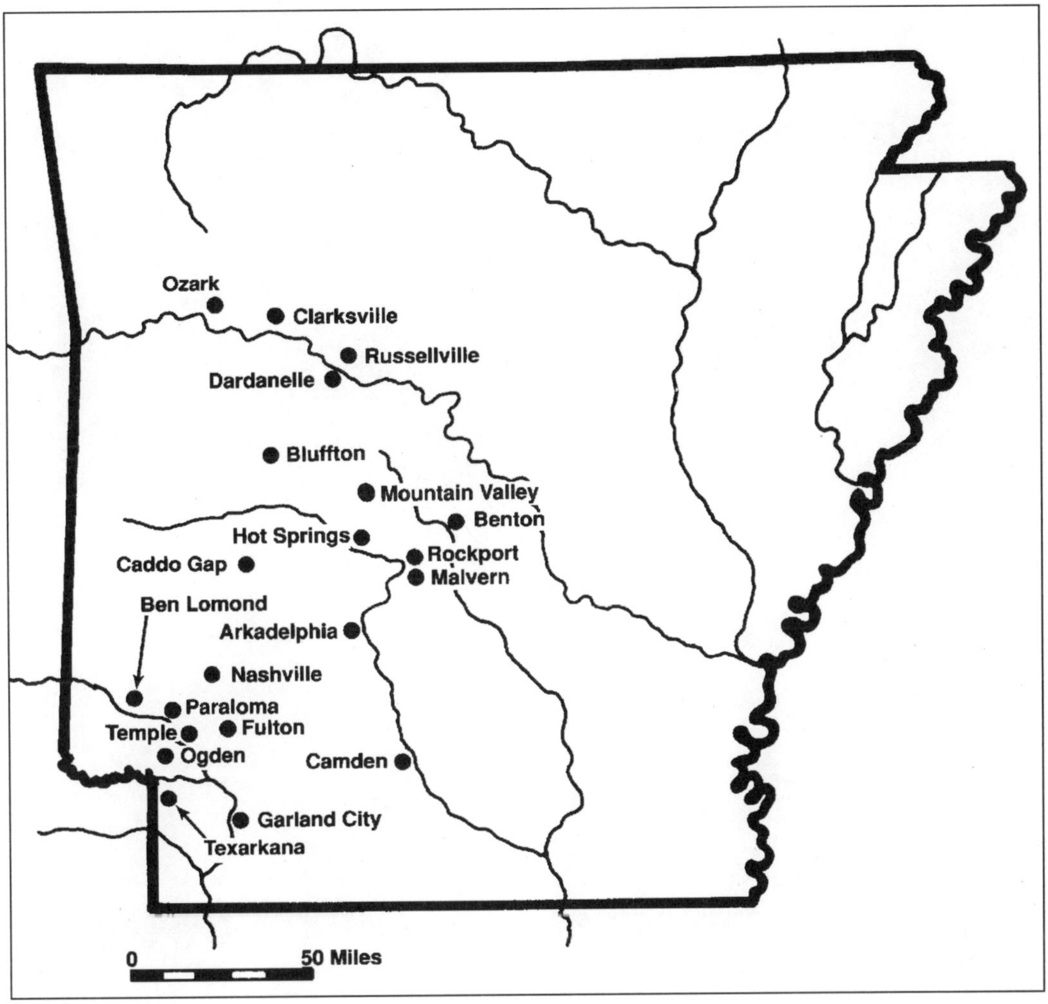


ILLUSTRATION 16. Present-day Cities in the Oauchita Mountain Uplands.

ILLUSTRATION 17. Carden Bottoms Phase and Fort Coffee Phase Pottery. Courtesy of the University of Arkansas Museum.

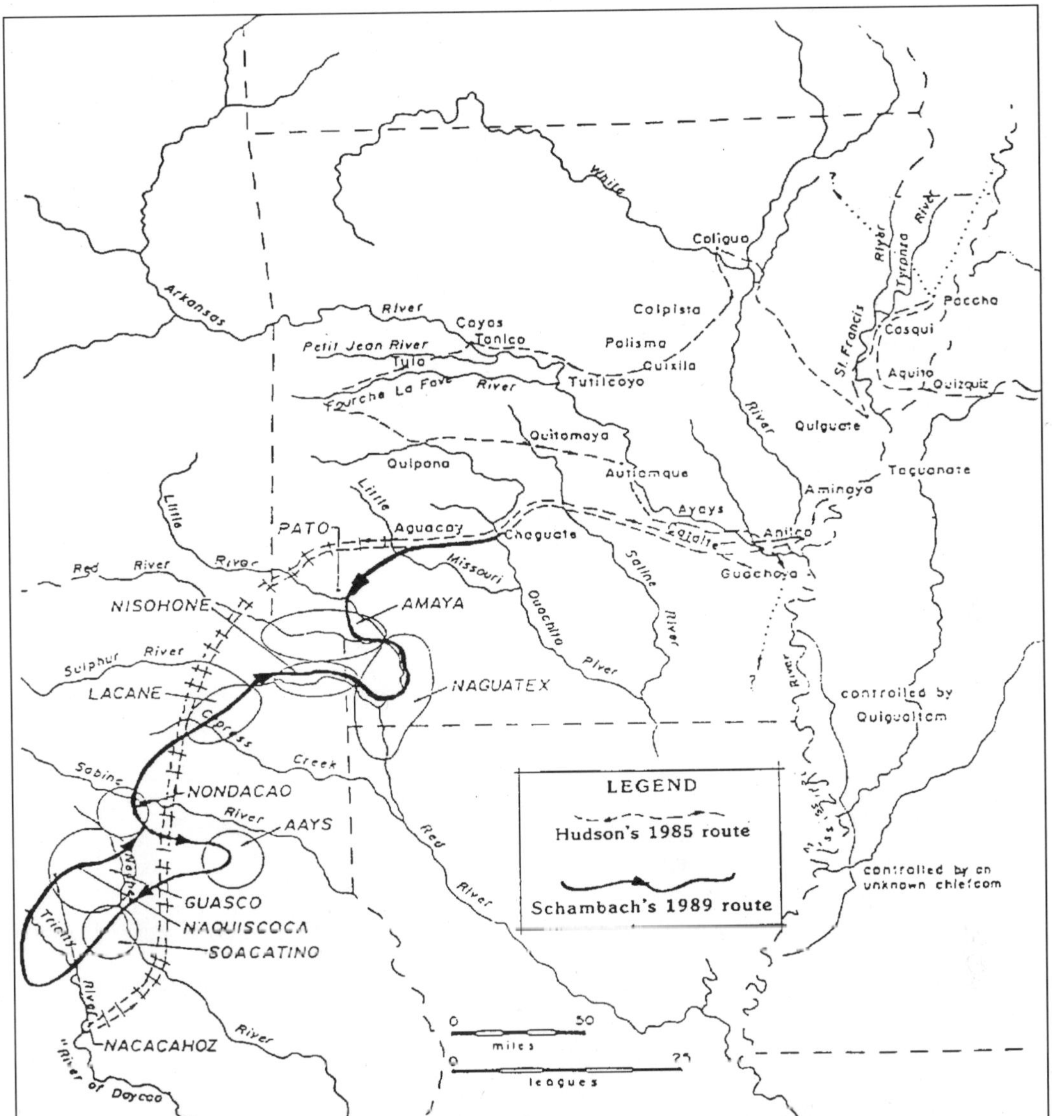


ILLUSTRATION 18. Schambach's 1989 Version of the Route through Caddo Country. Courtesy of *The Arkansas Archeologist* vol. 27/28.

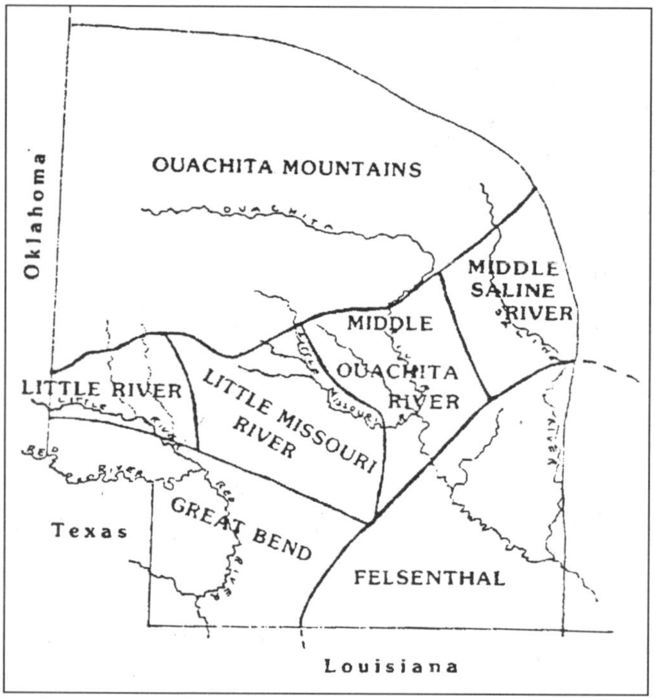


ILLUSTRATION 19. Archeological Regions in Southwest Arkansas. Courtesy of the Arkansas Archeological Survey.

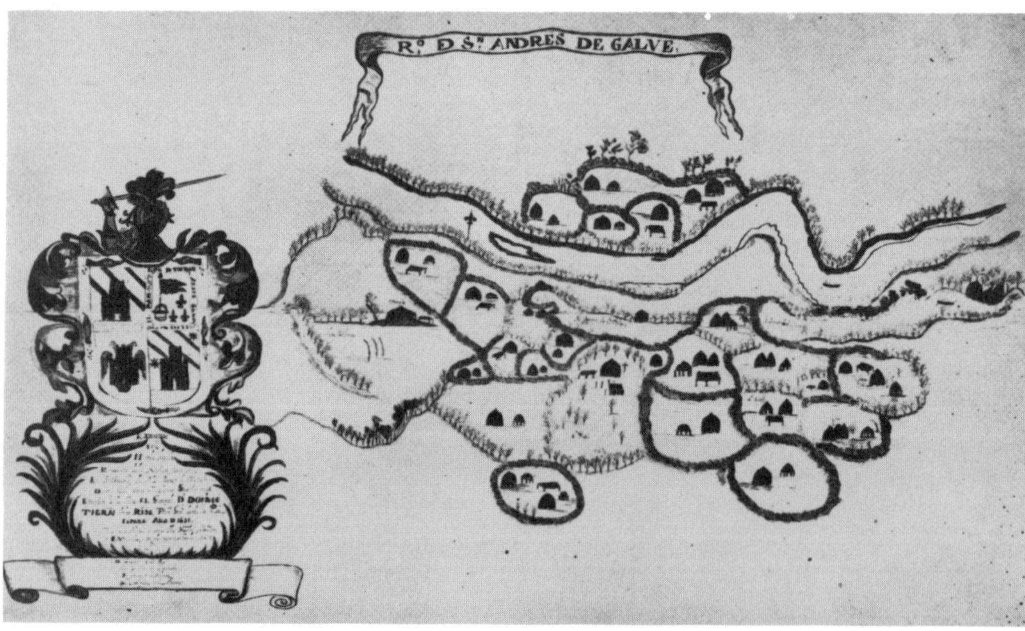


ILLUSTRATION 20. The Teran Map Showing a Caddo Community along the Red River. Courtesy of the Smithsonian Institution.

ILLUSTRATION 21. Long Hat's Camp: A Caddo Homestead in Western Oklahoma, 1868–72. Courtesy of the Smithsonian Institution.

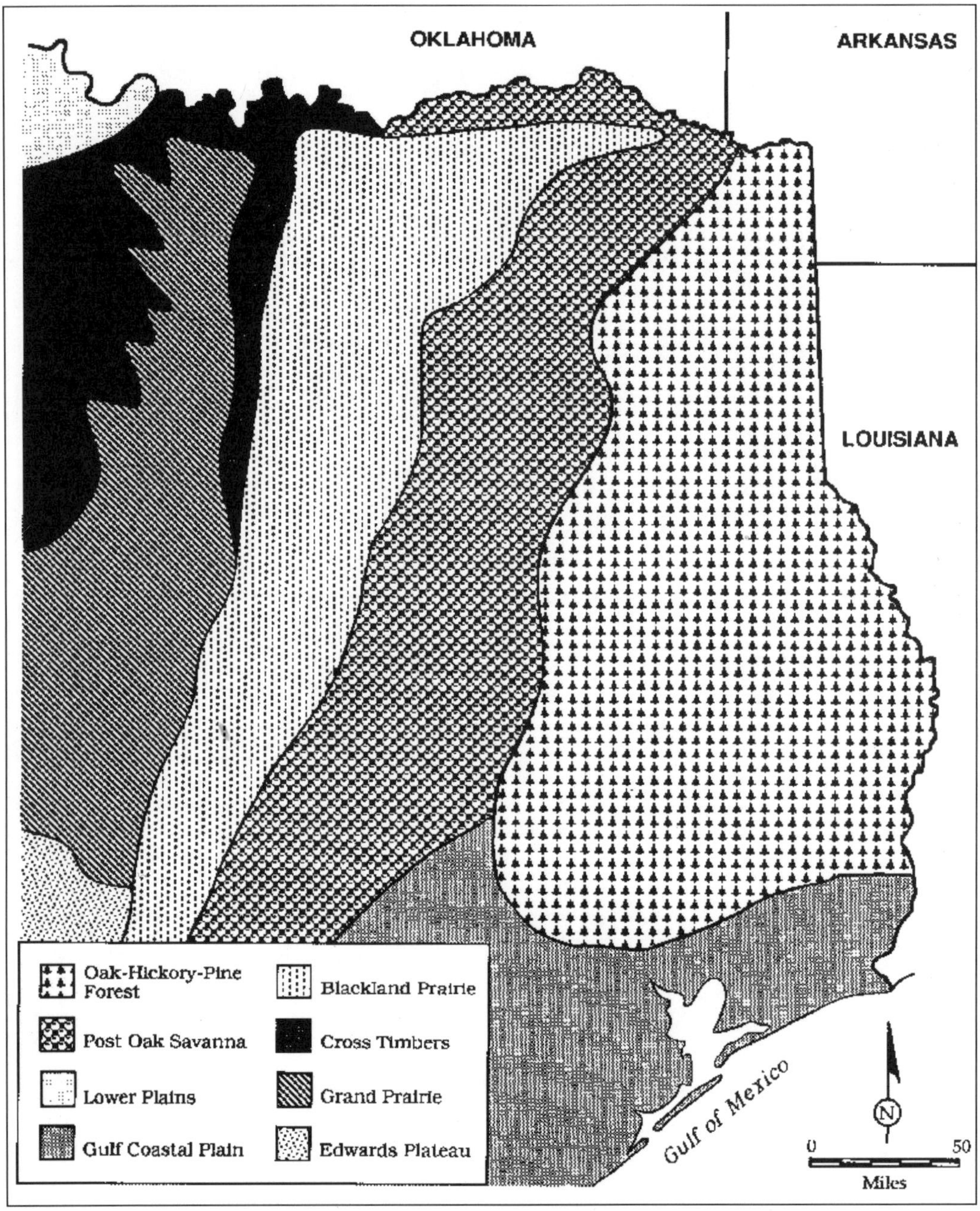


ILLUSTRATION 22. Biogeographic Zones of Northeastern Texas (after Kuchler 1964).

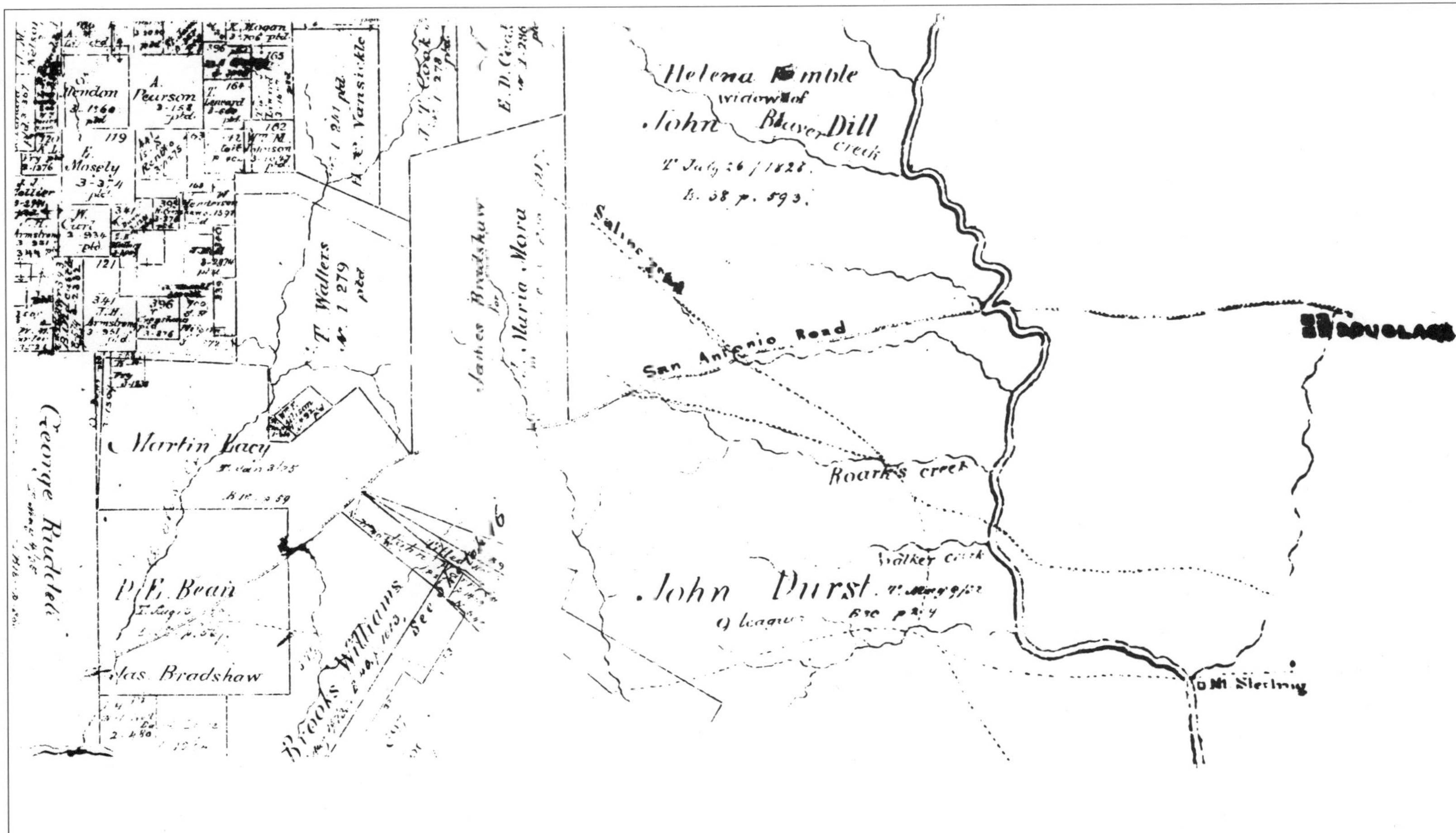


ILLUSTRATION 23. 1851 Map of Cherokee County, Texas, Showing Portions of the Camino Real (San Antonio Road), Saline Road, and Other Trails. Courtesy of the Texas General Land Office, Austin, Texas.

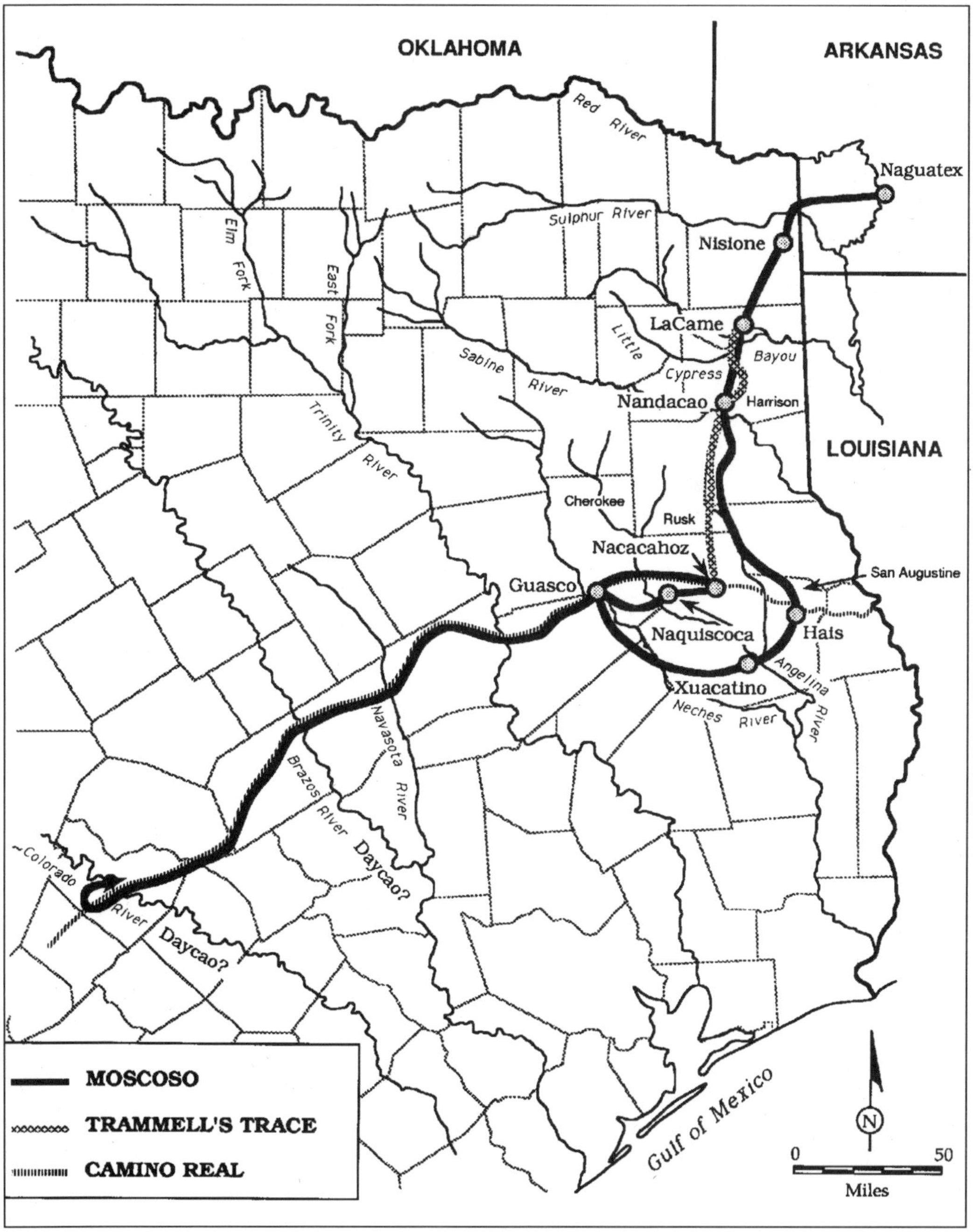


ILLUSTRATION 24. Trammell's Trace Route.

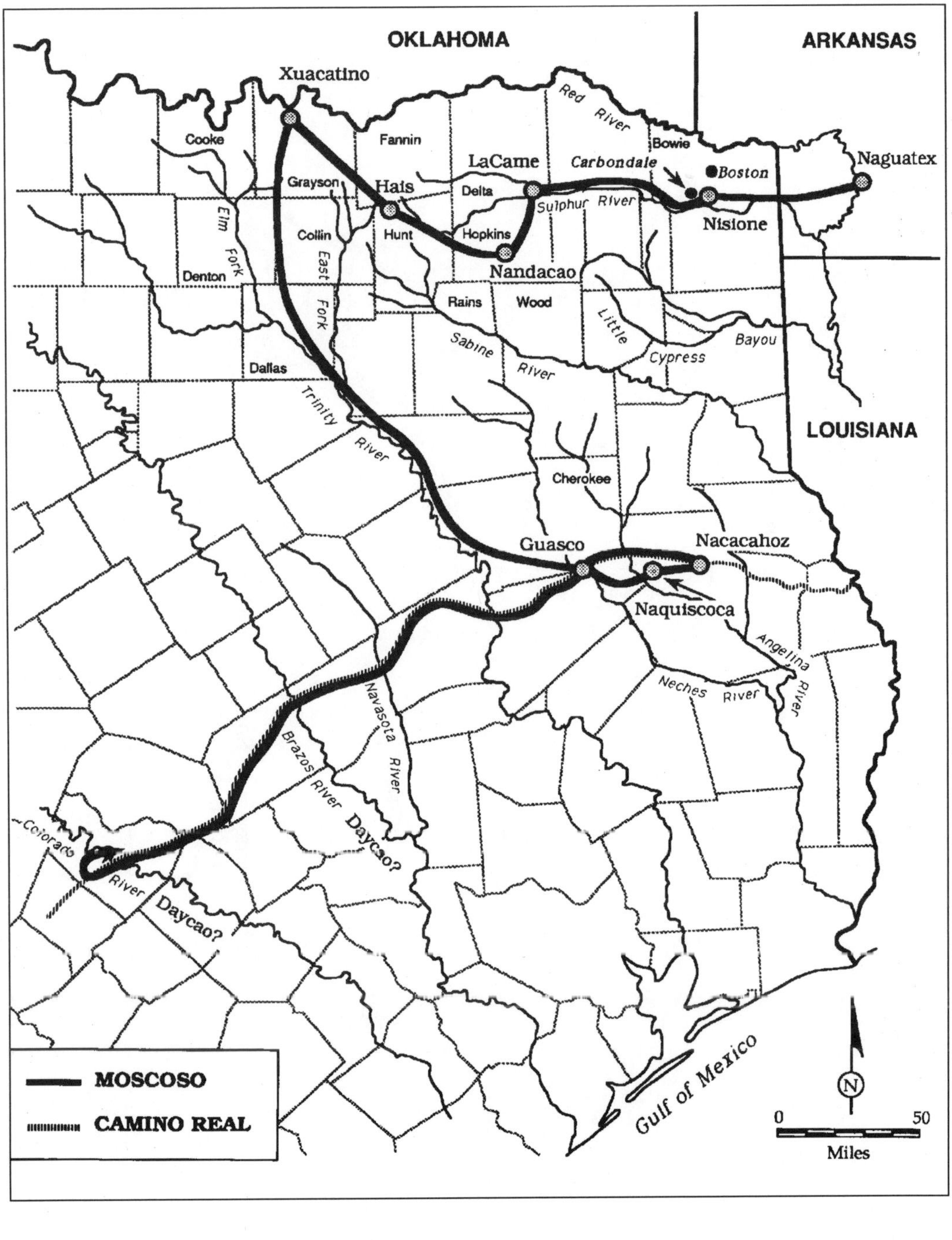


ILLUSTRATION 25. Blackland Prairie Route.

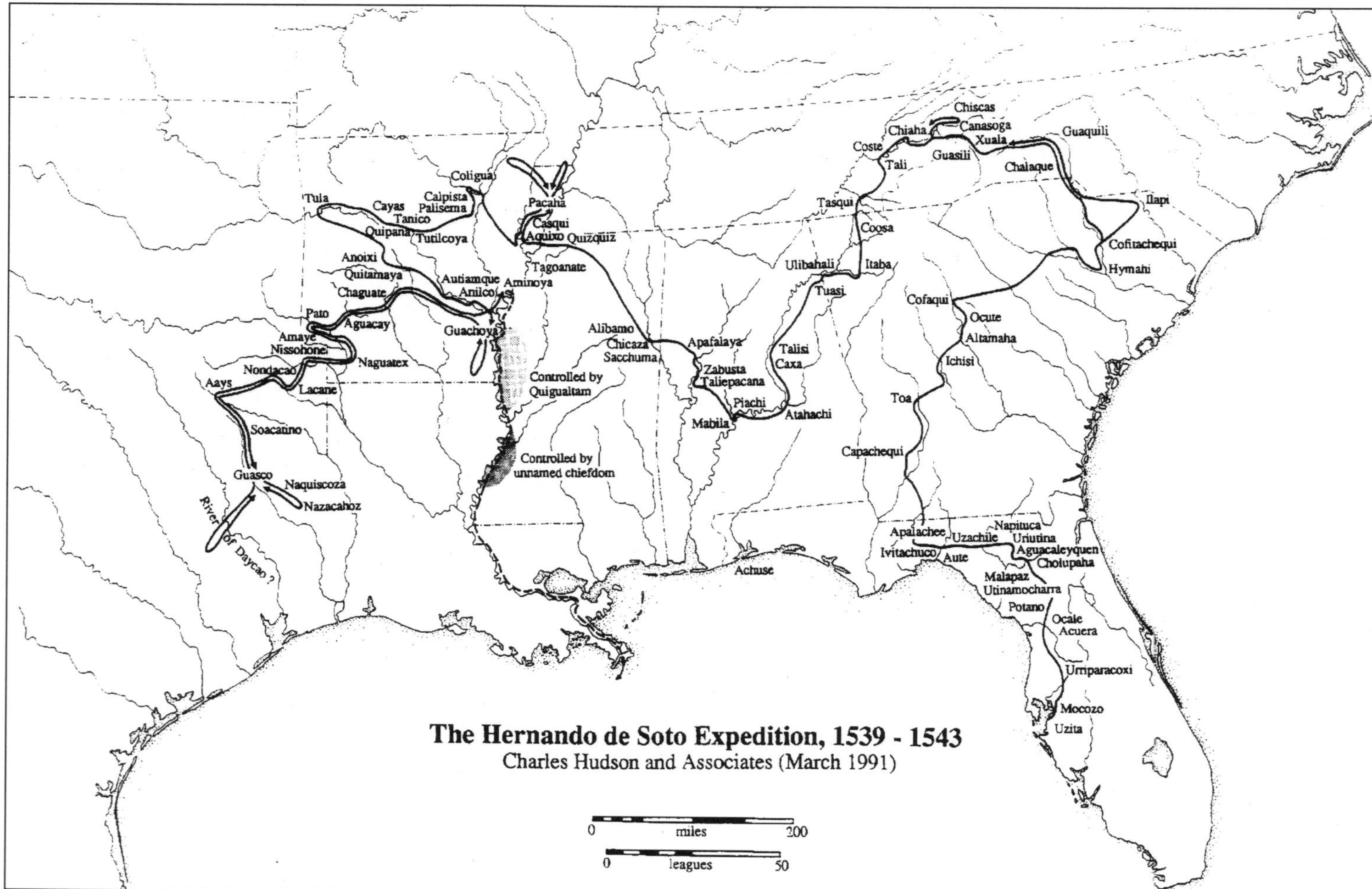


ILLUSTRATION 26. Hudson's Reconstruction of the Route through Arkansas and Texas. Courtesy of Charles Hudson.

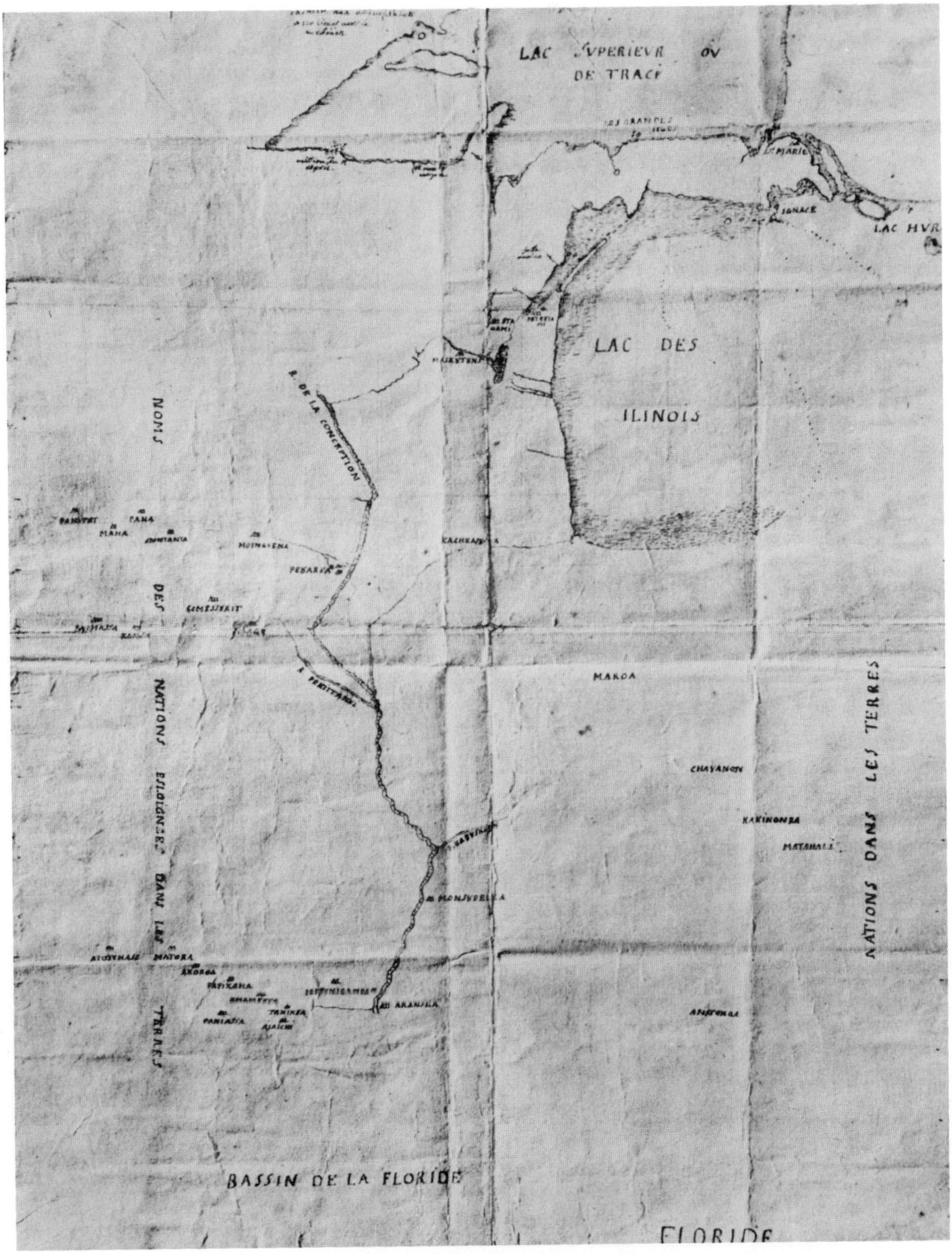


ILLUSTRATION 27. Marquette's Map Showing Tribal Locations in the Late 1600s. Courtesy of the University of Arkansas Museum.

ILLUSTRATION 28. De Soto and the Indians. Painting by Charles Hardman. Courtesy of the National Archives.

ILLUSTRATION 29. Burial of de Soto. In Samuel, Huber, and Ogden, *Tales of the Mississippi,* 1955.

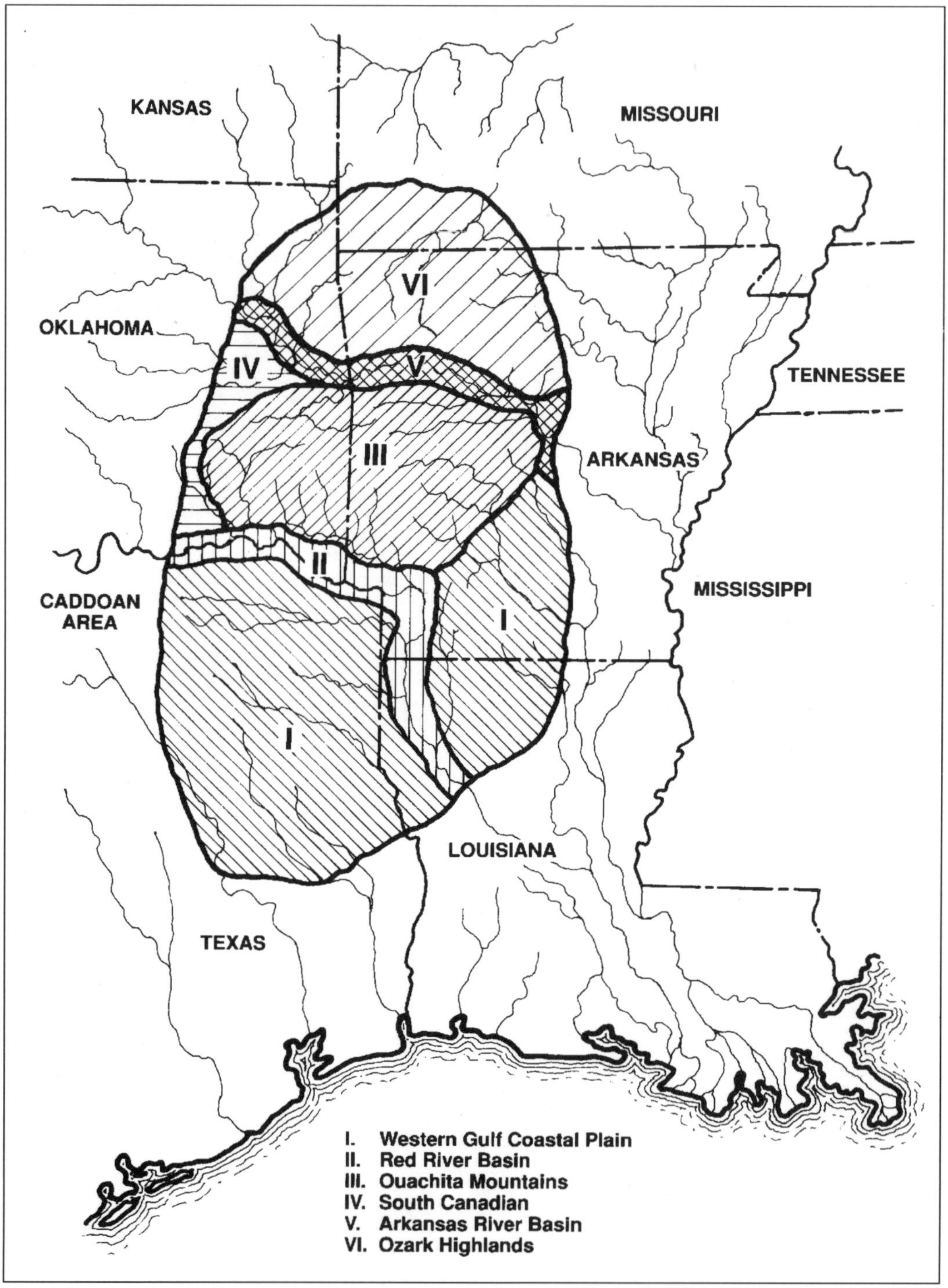


ILLUSTRATION 30. The Caddoan Area. Courtesy of Timothy K. Perttula.

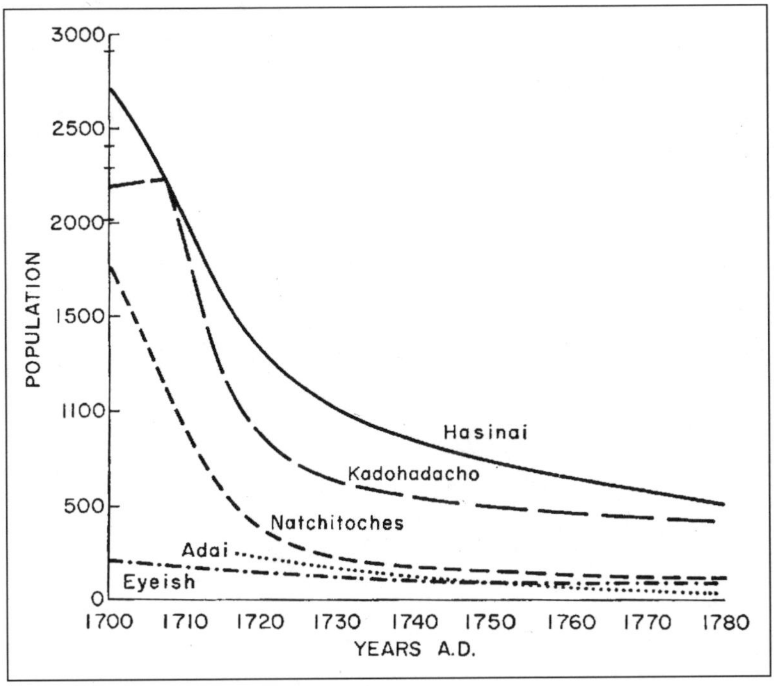


ILLUSTRATION 31. Populations of Caddoan Tribes, 1700–1780.

ILLUSTRATION 32. Schematic Differences in Depopulation Trends among the Caddo. Courtesy of Timothy K. Perttula.

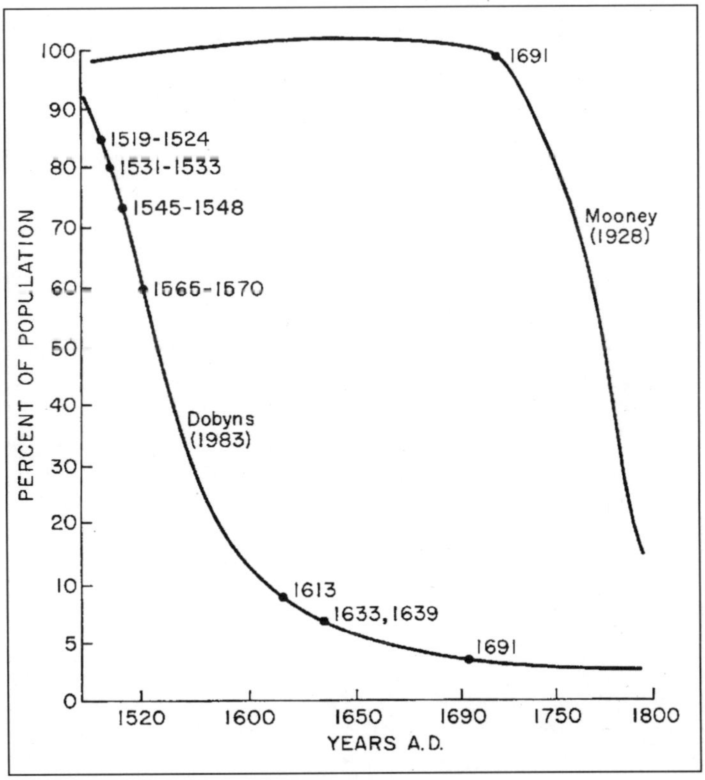

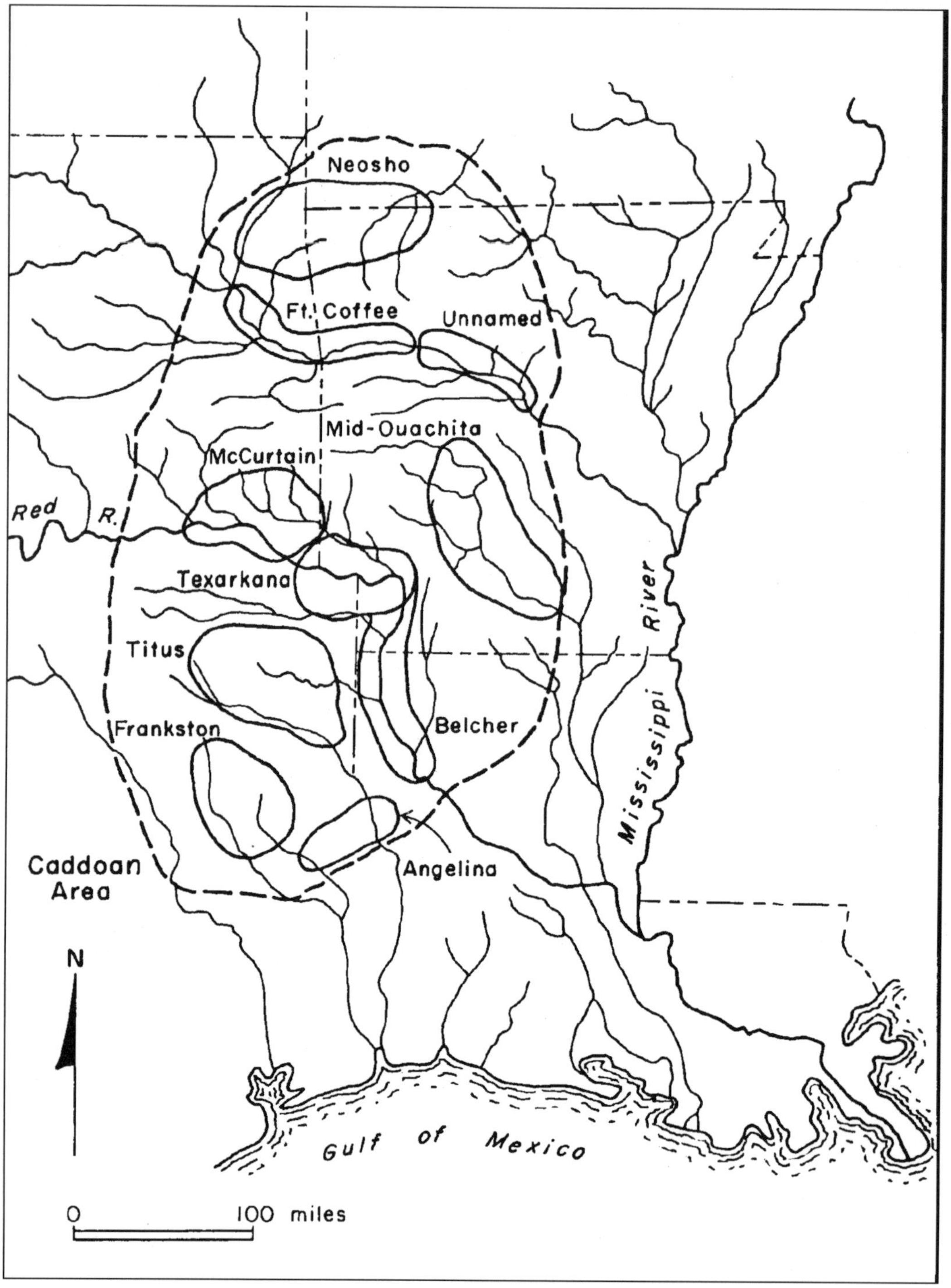


ILLUSTRATION 33. The Distribution of Caddoan Phases at Initial Contact (ca. 1520). Courtesy of Timothy K. Perttula.

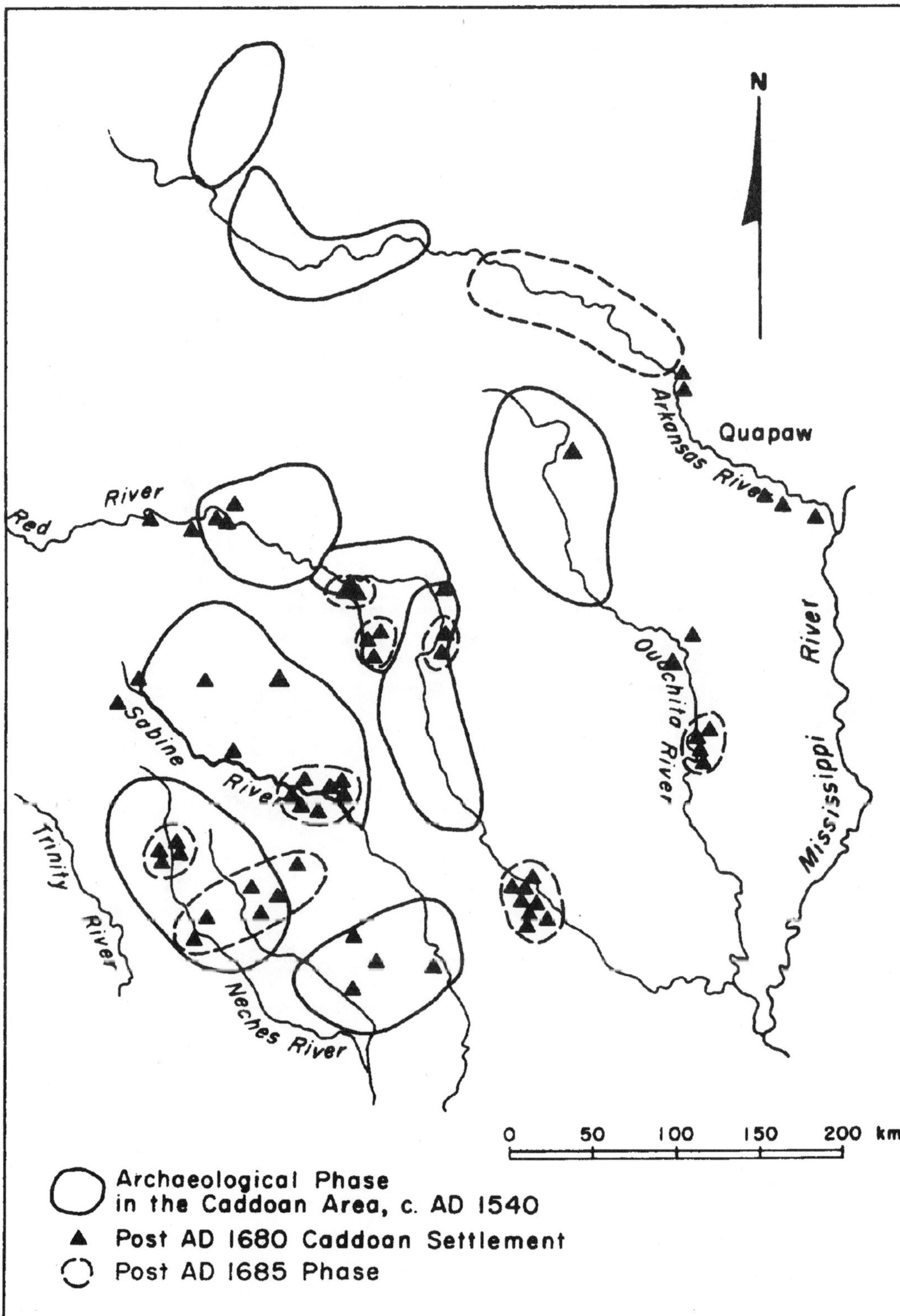


ILLUSTRATION 34. Spatial Relationship between 1520 and 1685 Phases and Caddoan Settlement after 1685. Courtesy of Timothy K. Perttula.

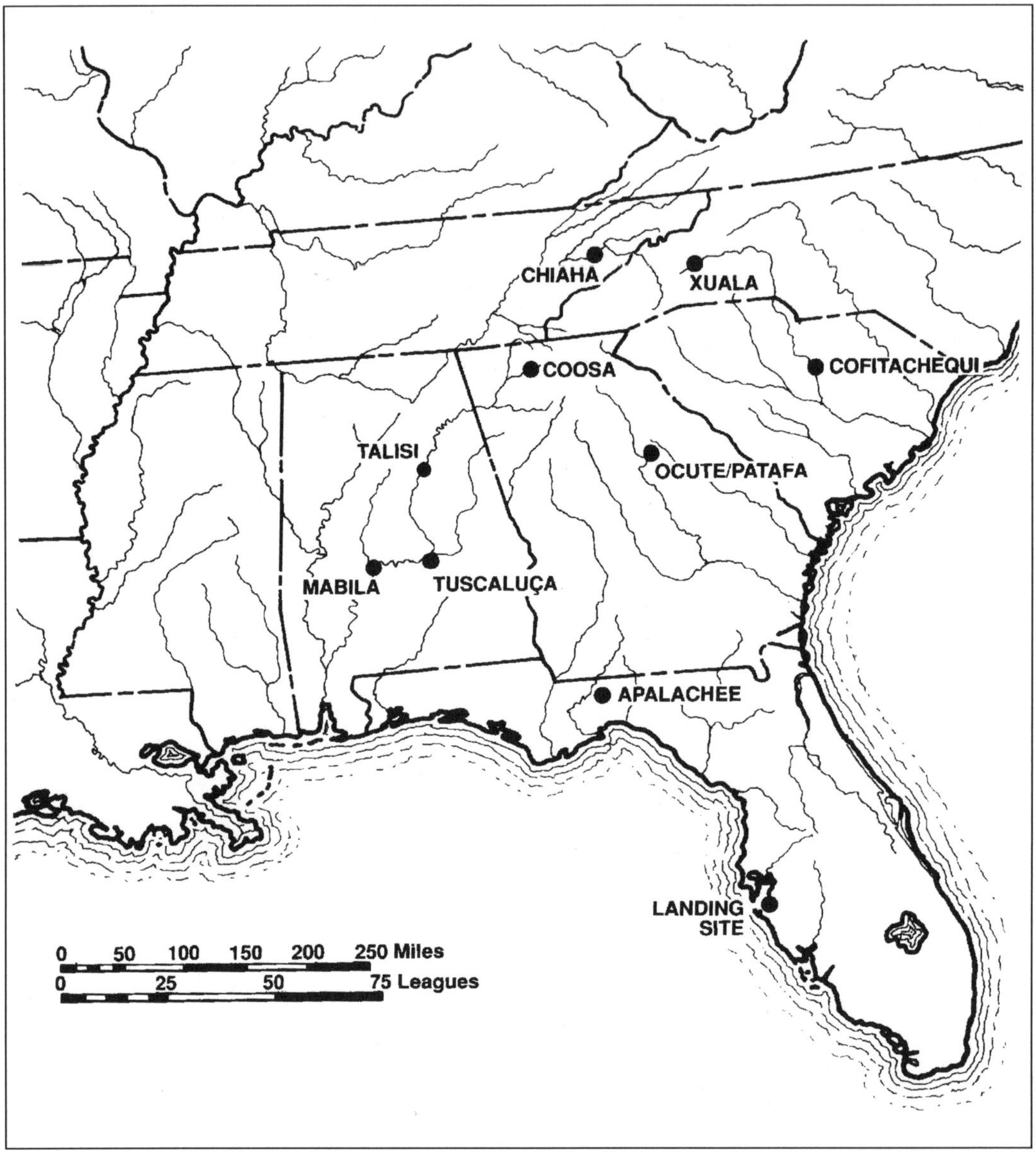


ILLUSTRATION 35. Native Polities in the Southeast. Courtesy of Charles Hudson.

# Proxy Data, Historical Method, and the de Soto Expedition

David Henige

*. . . distrust is a necessary qualification of a student of history. Distrust quickens his discernment of different degrees of probability, animates his search after evidence, and, perhaps, heightens his pleasure at the discovery of truth. (S. Johnson 1825:5–6)*

The florescence of de Soto studies in the 1980s seems destined to quicken in the 1990s, perhaps to culminate in 2000, the quincentenary of his birth (Albornoz 1971:23–24).[1] The interest is hardly new, of course. By 1935 controversy over de Soto's route had reached the point that the U.S. Senate created a commission of experts charged with providing the final answer to the matter of de Soto's itinerary. In due course this commission produced a monumental report in time for the quatercentenary of the expedition (Swanton 1939). Its answer has proved to be anything but final, however, and a good deal of recent activity has been dedicated to disputing its conclusions from beginning to end (see Brain 1985:xii–lxxii).

Two new dimensions are associated with this recent research: (1) the contribution of archeology to solving the question, and (2) the impact of the expedition on the Indian societies through which it passed, as well as any ripple effects throughout the southeastern United States. In the latter regard, the expedition's possible epidemiological consequences have so far attracted the greatest attention (most noticeably Dobyns 1983; Ramenofsky 1987a; M. T. Smith 1987).

In this paper I look at the characteristics and interpretation of the written sources for the expedition, as well as the role that archeology can be expected to play in throwing light on the course and implications of de Soto's four-year peregrination. In addition, and as an ineluctable part of this consideration, I remark on the nature of the argumentation itself. The reconstruction of past events using proxy data is a delicate operation and full of traps for the unwary. I propose to look at these issues with rather a cold eye, following Johnson in concentrating on their limitations rather than on their purported strengths.

## THE SURVIVING ACCOUNTS OF THE EXPEDITION

*Now, remember, I write down all that I hear and the next day, if I hear that it is not so, then I write down the contradiction, too.* (Chesnut 1981:360)

Surviving participant accounts of the major activities of the Spanish in the New World are, not surprisingly, rather sparse. We have nothing more than a late, third-hand, edited, and abridged account of Columbus's first voyage.[2] For the conquest of Mexico there is one early participant account (Cortés), another very late participant account (Bernal Díaz), and a few shorter ones in the form of reminiscences, and Gómara's hybrid and derivative work. We fare little better for the conquest of Peru and for expeditions into the American Southwest. The available accounts for the Southwest, particularly those of Cabeza de Vaca and Niza, have been subjected to particularly hostile scrutiny lately, and many think them to be little more than fiction disguised as chronicle, a popular genre of the times.[3] On the whole, though, the tendency has been, perhaps inevitably, to grant these sources considerable credit, with grateful acceptance replacing grudging analysis.

In contrast to this typical exiguity, students of de Soto's activities seem to be endowed with no fewer that four firsthand accounts, ranging from the laconically notarial account to the monumentally detailed narrative in which no opportunity to include helpful circumstantial details appears to have been overlooked.[4] The result of this is a plenitude of evidence ranging from the persuasively austere to the persuasively circumstantial. This situation has prompted students of the expedition to plumb these sources repeatedly.

This is a silver lining with a cloud, however. I have argued, for example, that Garcilaso de la Vega's (1605) rococo *La Florida del Ynca* bears innumerable hallmarks of being largely a work of tautological fiction based on the *Relaçam* (1557) of Elvas, the only account of the expedition published in the sixteenth century; on other since-lost sources; and on revivified and embellished oral recollection (Henige 1986).[5] I concluded that it would be fatuous to rely on *La Florida del Ynca,* whether in ostensible corroboration of other evidence or as a repository of data not to be found elsewhere. The work doubtless has a great deal of historiographical interest, but no demonstrable historical worth.[6]

This brings us to Elvas' *Relaçam,* published anonymously in Portugal in 1557, presumably by one of the Portuguese members of de Soto's army. We know no more about the circumstances of its publication than about its author(s), and so get little help in answering the fundamental question: was it an entirely independent account or did it too rely on other reports (Biedma, Ranjel, and others) then in circulation? First we note that an important reason why Elvas' work is so much longer than either Biedma's or Ranjel's (although it hardly rivals *La Florida*) is that it adopted the technique, so widely used by Garcilaso later, of introducing irrelevant, and presumably unmemorable, detail and an orgy of speechifying. This ominous circumstance is made all the more inauspicious by the little we do know about its publication. Patricia Galloway notes that André de Burgos, Elvas' publisher, had done business in Seville (where, interestingly, he had published an edition of Oviedo's *Claribalte*) before removing to Evora several years before Elvas' *Relaçam* appeared there (Galloway, forthcoming). This inclines us to suspect (as we must in any case) that in Elvas' work we do not have independent corroboration of other accounts of the expedition, already or yet to be written.

Problems with the two earliest—and shortest—accounts, those of Ranjel and Biedma, are rather different, being more of a textual nature. Biedma's is the only account known to survive in manuscript, but, although it has been published and translated several times since the mid-nineteenth century, this brief text has never been accorded a diplomatic edition, nor even a simple facsimile treatment, which would enable students better to judge the tenor, content, and composition of the work.[7]

Much the same is true of Ranjel's account, albeit at one step removed. This survived only as it is embedded in Oviedo's (1851–55) massive *Historia general y natural de las Indias* as an example of Oviedo's Autolycan habits in compiling that work. Very unfortunately for historians, Ranjel's version, although accepted by common consent as the most trustworthy of our sources, stops abruptly on November 2, 1541. Despite Oviedo's intimation that he intended to include the balance of Ranjel's account later in his work, nothing more survives in any of the extant manuscripts of Oviedo's *Historia general.*

Oviedo's own work has failed to receive the textual attention it deserves and desperately needs. While several manuscripts, often only partial, of the *Historia general* are known to survive, not one of them has been treated to a critical transcription or edition.[8] Before we can hope to have a realistic picture of what Ranjel wrote (or rather of what Oviedo wrote that Ranjel wrote or said) we need a critical edition of the *Historia general.* Several problems accruing from this situation are discussed below.

While we have no idea of what other accounts of the expedition might have been in circulation from the 1540s on, we would be unwise to discount either their existence or their influence. Some hint of the profusion of participant accounts available at the time is gained from the surviving records of the unsuccessful attempt of Tristán de Luna to colonize Alabama in the late 1550s. Not only did several veterans of de Soto accompany Luna, but Luna took with him "a relation of the route [de Soto] followed." Later the viceroy of New Spain sent him yet another "relation of the country [de Soto] traversed." Another copy of this latter had also been sent to the Spanish court. Rodrigo Ranjel apparently remained in (or possibly returned to) New Spain after de Soto's remnants returned there in 1543, for he was *alcalde mayor* of Pánuco in 1557.[9] If his account in Oviedo was based, as is widely assumed, on a written account, then it too might well have had a currency among interested parties, if indeed it was not one of the "relations" used by Luna. None of this can for the moment be more than speculation, but hardly unlikely speculation just the same.

Looked at in this way, the picture of four contemporary participant accounts of de Soto's expedition that were also independently derived loses much of its credibility and luster. But in invoking this approach, I am asking no more than historians normally demand of their preferred sources. In fact most would agree that the more germane, the more detailed a source, and the more congenial it seems to modern hypotheses, the more urgent the need to visit on it the closest possible textual and contextual scrutiny. To date this kind of preliminary step has not been carried out for any of the accounts of de Soto's travels.

## MODERN ARCHEOLOGICAL SITES AND THE EXPEDITION: CAN THERE BE A CORRELATION?

> *These lacunae upset all the calculations of the geographer, who cannot make use of the distances and directions when some are missing. (Cavelier 1938:12)*

In no field, whether we consider it a science, a social science, or an art, is the scholar more obliged to extrapolate than in archeology, which is the quintessential science of the silent. Each site that is discovered and excavated adds to an existing database, of course, but never really allows us to measure progress toward a once-existing database, because most of that will long since have disappeared. Even worse, we can never be sure that what we happen to discover is particularly representative of this larger unknowable whole.[10] As a result, archeologists are inclined—virtually find it necessary—to advance claims that require some suspension of disbelief on both their part and on the part of their readers. The archeology of de Soto's expedition is no exception.

One of the more doubtful working assumptions of many archeologists seems to be that artifacts (or what become artifacts with the passage of time) fall to the ground immediately on being introduced into a new environment, there patiently to remain until uncovered by modern excavation. As a result, when certain artifacts are found *in situ,* it is assumed that they must represent evidence that some events related to them occurred at that very spot. It is this principle, or operational assumption, that has guided recent attempts to fix de Soto's route by means of archeological interpretation, as though the members of de Soto's army were so many Hansels and Gretels in armor, but there were no birds. The practice is commonplace but, at least for the moment, let one recent example serve as surrogate for the others.

Hudson, DePratter, and Smith (1989:91) note that "a sixteenth-century two-edged sword has been found at the King site" (near the Georgia-Alabama line), which they describe as "the last town [i.e., Piachi] that de Soto visited before leaving the Coosa River and heading south into what is now Alabama." Indian burials at the site show wounds that could have been inflicted by weapons such as this sword. From this the authors conclude that "we are confident that these people were wounded and killed by de Soto's soldiers" (Hudson, DePratter, and Smith 1989:93).

The source of this poorly simulated confidence is not at all clear. To suggest just one alternative scenario, could not Indians anywhere in the southeast have come into possession of such weapons by way of trade, tribute, or battle? And could they not themselves then have used them to kill other Indians? In other words, why this reflexive but undocumented assumption that European weapons were used exclusively by Europeans? The Indians of the western United States were only too happy to resist modern weaponry by acquiring their own modern weaponry, and the same pattern was repeated by various societies in west Africa and numerous other parts of the world. We cannot with any plausibility claim that the odds favor the general argument that artifacts remain wherever they are first deposited, and this must particularly be so for weapons once their effectiveness has been made obvious.[11] In the circumstances it is injudicious to use such artifacts to attempt to localize any part of de Soto's route with any precision.[12]

This leads us to wonder about the frequent identification of places mentioned in the de Soto chronicles with modern archeological sites.[13] One problem with this procedure is simply that it is not always possible to distinguish the use of nomenclature in the various sources, that is, to know whether descriptions of size, population, location, and material resources refer to politics in whole or in part, or even just to particular towns. More on this later.

Beyond this issue, we must ask with what epistemological validity we can argue that the population centers mentioned in the sources invariably, and luckily, conform to large and small archeological sites since discovered. Doing this assumes, for instance, that few sites remain to be discovered, clearly a view at variance with its own experience. Even worse, it implies strongly that given time, modern ingenuity can recover, one way or another, any site mentioned in early sources (Hudson 1987a:5–6, Hudson 1990a:75–109). This seems at odds with common sense, or at least with the laws of probability that govern all modern attempts to recapture the past.

It would be more reasonable to assume instead that many of the sites mentioned in the sources have since disappeared without a trace, perhaps in some cases were little more than temporary settlements happening to exist when de Soto was in the neighborhood. By this line of reasoning, any ability to equate ancient sites with modern ones with any degree of certainty is wrenched from the archeologist. Withal, in the lack of any written records to tie together the past and the present, this apparently must be so.

## TIME, DISTANCE, THE CHRONICLES, AND ARCHEOLOGICAL SITES

*I was with you, until I heard your argument. (Gore-Browne 1953:123)*[15]

To assess the degree to which the chronicles have been excavated, as well as to test certain archeological assumptions, I look at recent attempts to trace de Soto's route during 1540, when he made his way from northern Florida to (for the sake of argument) Mississippi by a very circuitous route, always in search of precious metals to rival those of Peru. Using this segment of de Soto's travels has two advantages: all four sources cover the year, and the journey was so eventful that it has attracted an unusual amount of modern speculation.

In terms of exploiting historical evidence, the very existence of many sources puts on the researcher the additional burden of deciding how best to choose among them for particular data designed to support a line of argument. Despite covering the same set of activities, the discrepancies and differences among these sources are undoubtedly serious. This requires anyone seeking to assimilate them into a coherent account (that can have the advantage of exploiting the "best" evidence for each segment) constantly to make judgments as to the relative reliability of conflicting evidence. In this exercise the modern scholar will often find it necessary to choose one version over others as well as to justify using evidence in one source even though it is absent from the others.

The love-hate relationship between Inca Garcilaso and modern students of de Soto's route is well exemplified in the treatment that Hudson, Smith, DePratter, and others accord him, but it has a much longer history, extending well back into the nineteenth century. Hudson and others continue this tradition by adopting a *modus operandi* that ignores Inca Garcilaso only when other sources are available or when his own grand eloquence surpasses all bounds of plausibility, while citing him unhesitatingly whenever he is the only witness or when his information suits.

This procedure is amply illustrated in their study of de Soto's route during the first part of 1540. After reminding us again that Garcilaso's *La Florida* is "remarkably unreliable," particularly for the stretch from Apalachee to Cofitachequi, Hudson and his colleagues relent by claiming, predictably but paradoxically, that he still provides "valuable [*sic*] details" (Hudson, Smith, and DePratter 1984:65). This Janus-like posture is manifested in their citations to the chronicles. Inca Garcilaso is cited no fewer than twenty-two times (only twice in conjunction with other sources), often to make points crucial to their reconstruction.[16] In contrast, neither Biedma nor Elvas is cited as often. Although Ranjel, rightly so, remains their preferred source for those parts of the journey covered by his account, it is all too clear that *La Florida del Ynca*'s prolific detail continues to beguile.

This curious reliance on Inca Garcilaso culminates in the authors' statement that disease near Cofitachequi shortly before de Soto arrived there had caused "great loss of life" (Hudson, Smith, and DePratter 1984:73).[17] In fact, of course, of the four chroniclers only Inca Garcilaso mentioned any deaths. Elvas noted that a "pest" had forced inhabitants of certain villages to flee elsewhere (Elvas 1557:lv$^{r}$). Ranjel and Biedma, the earliest sources, have nothing at all to say, which itself is surely worthy of notice (Biedma 1971:224; Oviedo 1851–55:560). None is forthcoming. No doubt Inca Garcilaso's typical, but idiosyncratic, penchant for the dramatic and cajoling detail serves well the aims of those who would prefer to infer high mortality owing to the introduction of European diseases from the very first moment of contact, but contradicted Inca Garcilaso is the epitome of worthless historical evidence.[18]

Normally, as noted, when there is a choice between taking *La Florida del Ynca* at its florid word and accepting the testimony of one or more of the other chronicles, Hudson, Smith, and DePratter wisely ignore the former.[19] Thus they accept the date of March 3, 1540, for the breaking of the winter camp at Apalachee against the testimony of Inca Garcilaso that it occurred "in the last days of March" (Garcilaso 1605:140). With somewhat less justification perhaps, they also agree with those who state that de Soto forced the ruler of Cofitachequi to accompany him for several days, even though Garcilaso explicitly stated otherwise.[20] What is lacking in all this enterprise is an explicit attention to the contradictions and differences among the four sources. The casual reader is in danger of concluding that Hudson and others chose from among their sources on the basis of best evidence, whereas in many cases it is merely because it is the only evidence.

It would have been helpful for instance, if Hudson, Smith, and DePratter had noted that Garcilaso declined to provide any dates whatever in his version of this leg of the journey, but only the duration of some marches and sojourns. Unhappily, even this reluctant arithmetic of Garcilaso fails in the aggregate. In discussing events that occurred shortly after the expedition left Cofitachequi early in May, Garcilaso recorded that "unless he had counted badly," de Soto had so far spent fifty-seven days "on the road" ("*de camino*") (Garcilaso 1605:178). If, by this, he meant only the days spent traveling rather than resting, he was several days awry. If, on the other hand, he was referring to elapsed time (which seems more probable), then by his own expressed cumulative daily counts, they had been traveling more than eighty days.[21]

The number of leagues covered by the expedition during this period also proves troublesome. Elvas calculated (or at least asserted) that it was 130 leagues from Ocute to Cofitachequi, and no less than 250 leagues from the latter place to Xuala, a distance reached in about a week (Elvas 1557:lix$^{r-v}$). Although in this case Elvas stands condemned by both his own testimony and that of the other sources, it reminds us that numbers are the most likely candidates for untraceable transcriptional error.[22]

The fitting of modern interpretation with evidence preserved from the past is a necessary, but often delicate, operation, with the questions always being the degree to which modern interpretation should be permitted to overturn this evidence. On the basis of data from outside the direct sources for de Soto's journeys, Hudson and his colleagues decide, in contrast to most earlier opinion, that the sources meant by "legua" a distance of 3.45 miles, the *"legua común"* rather than the shorter distance of 2.63 miles, the *"legua legal"* (Hudson et al. 1987:848). Not only Ranjel and Biedma then, but Elvas, who was Portuguese (distance measures were often nationally bound in those days), and Garcilaso, who wrote half a century later, all meant the same thing—a "league" that was 3.45 miles in length.

The question as to which league length (and there are more choices than just these two) was used in what place and at what time in the early modern period is a particularly vexed one. It remains, for instance, at the heart of the enterprise to pinpoint Columbus's landfall and is unlikely ever to be settled conclusively.[23]

The issue of how distances were computed and recorded during the expeditions should be even more liable to a thoroughgoing analysis. Boyd and Schroedl do raise this issue, and in response Hudson et al. are forced to suggest rather lamely that, somehow it was done, had to be done, and was done with a sufficient degree of accuracy, perhaps by counting paces each day (Boyd and Schroedl 1987:841, Hudson et al. 1987:848–49). This is an issue to which we shall certainly never have the answer (or know it if we do), but this is insufficient reason to shrug the problem off. Given the terrain the expedition traversed, it is hard to imagine that pace counting, or any other quasi-mechanical technique, could possibly produce accurate results for even a few days over rough ground, let alone consistently for nearly one thousand days over every conceivable terrain.

In reconstructing an itinerary which contains as many distinct segments as that of de Soto, it is clearly necessary to have virtually complete data on both distances and directions. While our four sources are fairly generous in providing the former (usually measured in days rather than leagues, however), if less congenial about agreeing with each other, it is striking how seldom they provide concrete information on direction. For the period in question—Apalachee to Chiaha—Biedma and Ranjel provide at most two or three indications of directions traveled, and not always in the same cases. Elvas provides none at all. In his turn Garcilaso provides only one direction explicitly, as usual different than either Biedma or Ranjel, and twice mentions that the expedition went "upstream," once in apparent contradiction to information that Biedma and Ranjel provide for what appears to be the same occasion (Biedma 1971:221, Oviedo 1851–55 1:557).

At first glance this seems much too little on which to reconstruct an itinerary except by a series of inferences based on one another, each inevitably more tenuous than its predecessor. Surprisingly then, in one recent account of the expedition we find directions provided no fewer than fourteen times, or more often than all the sources combined (Hudson, DePratter, and Smith 1989:86–88). On inspection we find that the impetus for this modern insinuation of so much extrinsic information is largely archeological, as the authors seem intent on marching de Soto from one modern archeological site unerringly to the next. There is, of course, as we have seen, no way to be sure in even one instance that any modern site corresponds to any particular site mentioned in the sources.

Hudson and others cite several eighteenth- and nineteenth-century sources to indicate scattered and intermediate toponymic stages. This would help if only we could be certain that names stayed attached to one site whenever we want them to, and moved about when we prefer that they do that.[24] Regrettably, as we will see, it is certainly too much to expect this kind of cooperation, or, as Hudson, Smith, and DePratter (1990:197) put it "[o]ne of the lessons learned in our recent researches is that eighteenth-century ethnic locations in the Southeast do not necessarily coincide with sixteenth-century locations."

## THE CASE OF THE ELUSIVE "CHIAHA"

*I'm not denying anything. I'm very careful not to. It's you who feel the need of precise facts, documents and so forth. So you can affirm or deny. (Pirandello 1954:59)*

A major axis in most modern reconstructions of de Soto's route springs from the analysis of documents surviving from two journeys carried out by Juan Pardo into the interior Southeast between 1566 and 1568. These suggest that, if each place name in these sources refers to the same location as similar names in the de Soto chronicles, de Soto reached farther north than previously believed. Hudson and others routinely make such identifications. To test the validity of this approach ($X$ in de Soto = $Y$ in Pardo = $Z$ modern site), I look at the case of Chiaha, where de Soto spent twenty-three days in June of 1540, and where both Pardo expeditions also spent considerable time.

DePratter, Hudson, and Smith have repeatedly identified the "Chiaha" of the sources with Zimmerman's Island in the French Broad River in Tennessee, about thirty miles east of Knoxville (DePratter, Hudson, and Smith 1983:145–46; DePratter, Hudson, and Smith 1985:110; Hudson, Smith, and DePratter 1990). They see many similarities between the two, at least as Elvas described Chiaha. Elvas located it on an island, with the main town on one side abutting one of the branches of a large river, two "shots" distant from the upstream end and one league from the other (*Relaçam* 1557:lxii$^r$; Bourne 1904, 1:74). In other words, according to Elvas the island on which Chiaha was located (or which was itself Chiaha) was somewhat over one league long. Moreover, there was a "vale" transecting the island, which itself was from one to two "shots" wide (Bourne 1904, 1:74).

Apparently Zimmerman's Island, now submerged, comes close to matching these requirements, if we first accept that Elvas meant a crossbow shot and then that such a shot was typically "on the order of about 300 yards" (DePratter, Hudson, and Smith 1983:146). On the other hand, Zimmerman's Island is unfortunately only some 2½ miles long, as opposed to Elvas's estimate that it was more like 4 miles long (using Hudson, DePratter, and Smith's league), an estimate Elvas had over three weeks to confirm by measurement.[25] Nonetheless, DePratter, Hudson, and Smith conclude that "[n]o other island with a large mound [a feature of Chiaha not mentioned in any source] in the Tennessee-French Broad River matches Elvas's description as closely as Zimmerman's Island."[26] Such arguments are seldom sufficient to make cases as strong as these authors make this one out to be, and this alone encourages us to look at some aspects of the argument.

In their discussion, DePratter, Smith, and/or Hudson fail to note that Garcilaso described Chiaha as five leagues (fifteen to eighteen miles) in length, and added that its chief town was at one end ("*a la punta*") of the island (Garcilaso 1605:182). It is unwise to privilege Garcilaso's description here, of course, although by its very existence it becomes, or should become, part of any arguments sustaining any interpretation of Chiaha's location. It is easy enough to entertain doubts about Garcilaso's estimate of the size of Chiaha, but his placing of the main settlement at one end of the island makes better strategic sense than placing it along one side, particularly if it were the upstream end.

At any rate DePratter, Hudson, and Smith (1983:145) flatly identify Pardo's Chiaha as a "very strong town because it was on an island surrounded by a river." But was it? DePratter and his co-authors never present a clear idea of what the Pardo sources say about the location of Chiaha, and with good reason, since these accounts are no less puzzling than those for the de Soto expedition. Francisco Martínez, who accompanied the first Pardo expedition, described Chiaha as situated on "a mountain ridge" ("*cabo de la sierra*") and "between two great rivers" (Ruidíaz y Caravia 1893, 2:479; Hudson 1990:318).

In turn, Juan de la Bandera (Vandera), the notary for Pardo's second expedition, seemed to agree. Bandera submitted two reports sometime after he returned to Santa Elena. In his shorter abstract, Bandera characterized Chiaha as a large village "surrounded by beautiful rivers" (Ruidíaz y Caravia 1893, 2:484, Hudson 1990:299). In his larger report, the most detailed extant account of either Pardo expedition, Bandera was at once more precise and more vague. Chiaha was, he wrote, "on a very strong site because it is an island surrounded by copious rivers." In fact, in order to reach Chiaha, Pardo was forced to cross "three copious rivers" (Hudson 1990:221, 268).

All in all, these are very peculiar, and very pointless, circumlocutions for the word "island," which by itself would have sufficed if this Chiaha were the same as that mentioned in the de Soto chronicles. Biedma, Ranjel, even Garcilaso, were all satisfied to use the word "island" to describe Chiaha, while Elvas, though he did not use that word, made it clear in various ways that he was referring to an island (Garcilaso 1605:182; *Relaçam* 1557:lxii$^r$; Biedma 1971:225; Oviedo 1851–55 1:563). Zimmerman's Island could hardly be the locus of the descriptions in all the Pardo accounts. Before being submerged, it was a long narrow island clearly within a single river's flow.[27] An island is not ordinarily surrounded by, or in the midst of, more than one river.[28]

These descriptions in the 1560s can lead us only to suspect that in the intervening thirty years the name "Chiaha" had migrated from one place to another.[29] The problems in the nomenclature of Chiaha in the chronicles and therefore necessarily in modern interpretations lend credence to this notion. Hudson and others prefer to distinguish between Chiaha (which they treat as the polity as a whole) and Olameco (for them the capital). In this they appear to disagree, at least in part, with their sources, which in turn seem to disagree with one another. For the de Soto chroniclers this place (polity, capital, chief) had only one name, Chiaha, but the Pardo chroniclers perceived a more complex situation. Pardo himself wrote that "the other name" of Chiaha was "Lameco" (Ruidíaz y Caravia 1893, 2:471; Hudson 1990:308). In his turn Bandera, in his short report, wrote of "the large village called Solameco, and by another name Chiaha" (Ruidíaz y Caravia 1893, 2:484; Hudson 1990:299). In his longer report, on the other hand, he gave a different account of local nomenclature: there we read of Chiaha as the place and of its cacique, "who is called Ola mico" (Hudson 1990:221). Later in the same report he mentioned that the expedition departed from "the place called Olameco" (Hudson 1990:222). Later still we find mention of "Olameco, which by another name is called Chiaha" (Hudson 1990:223). A few days later the expedition "returned directly to "Olameco" but then arrived at "a [*sic*] place which is called Chiaha" whose ruler was called, not "Ola mico" but "Chiaha Orata" (Hudson 1990:226).

Of course it is just possible that in every case Pardo and Bandera were referring to the same place and the same cacique, but if they were, they were exceedingly indifferent to saying so. It is rather more likely that both Chiaha and Olameco happened to be places where the local ruler was at any particular time and thus that the name moved as frequently as he did. The Chiaha of the de Soto chronicles and the Chiaha (Olameco of the Pardo records) might have been near one another, or they might not have been, but on the basis of the surviving descriptions it seems clear enough that Pardo's Chiaha[30] was not Zimmerman's Island or for that matter any other island, normally defined, in the southeastern United States (Henige 1991a).

Finally, there is another slight problem with respect to identifying Chiaha. Bourne translated Elvas' "*averzea*" as "vale," and Hudson and others follow suit since they rely on Bourne rather than on Elvas. But a more probable meaning of the word (modern "*várzea*") is simply a stretch of flat land suitable for cultivation, which is less precise and does not imply a search for hilly environs[31] (Bourne 1904, 1:74; Costa 1958, 4:2306; Bueno 1963–67, 8:4197). The issue of translations of earlier terms for landforms is obviously central to any attempts to follow de Soto around, and this instance reminds us how extraordinary it is that so little modern recourse to the chronicles is to them in the original languages.

## THE USE OF NEGATIVE EVIDENCE IN ARCHEOLOGY

*The cruellest lies are often told in silence. (Stevenson 1925:83)*

The fourth and final cornerstone of Hudson, DePratter, and Smith's arguments relates to the leg of de Soto's itinerary between Ocute and Aymay/Hymahy in April of 1540. The chronicles are at one in characterizing this stretch as proceeding through an uninhabited wasteland. The writers argue that "[t]he areas where there are no protohistoric sites are fully as important as the areas where there are sites" (Hudson, DePratter, and Smith 1989:83). No one is likely to want to disagree with this premise in principle, but it is legitimate and necessary to wonder about the ontological status of the word "no" in this sentence.

In any case Hudson, DePratter, and Smith go on to affirm that the chroniclers could have been talking *only* about the area around Augusta, Georgia, and the Savannah river valley, since "it is now well established" that these areas were "vacant" at the time of the de Soto visit (Hudson et al. 1987:846, Hudson, Smith, and DePratter 1984:72, 75). One of the sources on which they rely (the other is unpublished) is rather more cautious: "[t]he upper Savannah River south of Lake Hartwell *appears* to have been *largely* abandoned after ca. 1450." The basis for the cautious assertion is simply that "there are no late-Lamar sites *known* from this area" (Anderson, Hally, and Rudolph 1986:42, emphases added). This impoverished argument from silence is further weakened by the observation that research in this area "is still in its infancy in many ways," and the authors can point to only one area (the Russell Reservoir) where "fairly intensive surveys have been carried out" (Anderson, Halley, and Rudolph 1986:32). Thus it is far from "well established" that the area in question qualifies for the pivotal role that Hudson, DePratter, and Smith confidently bestow on it.

This example underscores an important point of method. It is probably safe to say that, for various reasons—none of them strong—the argument from silence is too seldom and too feebly exploited in historical argument. In archeology, however, much the reverse is the case. The failure of modern archeology so far to discover appropriately dated sites is just that, and by no means testimony that the sites are not there, let alone that they never have been.[32] As its own history so amply testifies, drawing positive historical conclusions prematurely from negative archeological evidence is definitely risky business. In archeology the argument from silence is almost always presumptuous and always dangerously susceptible to being refuted.[33]

## PROBLEMS OF HYPOTHESIS AND ARGUMENTATION

*It's one of my most tiresome principles that I don't accept everything wholly as it first appears. And not later either without something to support it. (Ross 1989:89–90)*

In defending the reconstructability, as well as their particular reconstruction, of de Soto's route, Hudson and his co-authors note that their "general plan of research" is to "condense information" in the various sources "into a series of interconnected narrative accounts" of de Soto's expedition and those of Juan Pardo thirty years later. Their goal is, they state, to "achieve a 'fit' with a minimum of inconsistencies and contradictions" (Hudson et al. 1987:846). This conforms with the hopes of all students of the past that they will be able, on the basis of whatever evidence has happened to survive and come into their hands, to reconstruct a picture that faithfully reflects past general patterns, or at least to escape being shown not to reflect such patterns.

In order to achieve their "fit" the writers find it necessary to recruit the chroniclers in a most extraordinary way. We can see this clearly by looking at their circumstantial but lapidary interpretation of de Soto's route from Mabila to the Mississippi (Hudson, Smith, and DePratter 1990). Here, as elsewhere, their *modus operandi* is to refer very frequently to the sources—no fewer than seventy-five times in fact. This might strike readers as an impressive attempt to tie hypothesis to surviving evidence, but, before we agree, it might be well to look at the pattern which this citational structure assumes (B = Biedma; E = Elvas; G = Garcilaso; R = Ranjel):

EBEREBRREREEGGRE(ER)RRERRBERE(ER)(ER)GEEE(ER)GGEBREEE(ER)ERGREE (BG)G(EGR)GR(BREG)GGR(BE)(ER)(BG)BEBGG(BE)BBE(BER)BEGEG

The letters in parentheses represent those few cases where Hudson and his co-authors cite more than one source for a particular statement. These are only 17 percent of the total, which means that in more than four-fifths of the cases they have been unable to secure support from more than one of the chronicles, as they string together variant, and often disparate, if not discrepant, information to create their account while re-creating this leg of de Soto's journey.[34]

The thirteen occasions in which they cite more than one source are interesting in themselves; in not a single one of them have they been able to marshal agreement, either between the sources cited or between these sources themselves. In these cases their procedure is merely compressed, with sentences now instead of paragraphs harmonized and woven together from the tenuous fabric of the sources to provide a series of sums that are truly greater than the aggregate of their parts.

Readers will pick out their favorite examples in this respect, and I will cite only one here. Hudson, Smith, and DePratter (1990:188; emphasis added) tell us that "[i]t is clear that 'Apafalaya' was the name of the chief, *and* of the province (Elvas 1866:91), *and* of the river (Ranjel 1922:130)."[35] In devising this statement they imply not only that both Ranjel and Elvas were correct, but that by being correct in different ways, actually passed down to posterity twice as much information. This habit of heaping together snatches of information as if they were complementary rather than, as in this case, discrepant can only be abhorrent to proper historical method.

With this passage there is another problem as well. Contrary to Hudson, Smith, and DePratter's translated source, Ranjel did not in fact refer to the river as bearing the name Apafalaya, but instead wrote that "this creek ["*ribera*"] is called the river ["*rio*"] *of* [chief?] Apafalaya" (Oviedo 1851–55, 1:570; Bourne 1904, 2:130). Thus, whereas Hudson and colleagues would have three entities called Apafalaya, their sources count at most two and possibly just one.

The delicate and intricate tolerances that control reconstructions of past experiences are exposed all too clearly when the writers attempt to defend their conclusions as to the length of the league used in the sources and the "average" daily march of the expedition. Arguing that de Soto's force, "as a whole body," traveled at "about the same rate of speed" as the Pardo expedition, they continue:

> This appears to be confirmed on the next leg of journey, on which Pardo spent 10 days in going from Cofitachequi to Joara (De Soto's *Xuala*), which we have located near present Marion, North Carolina. This was a distance of 175 miles, and the average day's travel was *therefore* 17.5 miles. Because an ambiguity in Ranjel's account makes their day of departure uncertain, De Soto spent either 8 or 9 days going from Cofitachequi to Joara. De Soto *evidently* traveled by the slightly shorter route of 158 miles which Pardo had taken on his first expedition. Hence, if De Soto spent 8 days on the trail, he averaged 19.7 miles per day. If he spent nine days, *as is more likely*, he averaged 17.5 miles per day—the same as Pardo. Even with 9 days, De Soto was traveling somewhat faster *than usual*, and the reason he did so was probably because of the fact that he was finding insufficient food in the area. (Hudson et al. 1987:848–49, emphases added)

This passage crystallizes arguments that are implicit throughout recent reconstructions of de Soto's route. Here we see the untenable practice of juggling three hypotheses, mere assertions really, in support of one another, the classic, if intensified, structure of *petitio principii*. The hypothesis that Cofitachequi and Xuala are 175 miles apart is supported by the hypothesis that de Soto's chroniclers all used a league that was 3.45 miles long, *and* that de Soto averaged five leagues a day, no matter what the conditions or the terrain. The latter hypotheses in turn are held to gain credibility from the further hypothesis that de Soto traveled 158 miles in nine days *because* that averages out to 17.5 miles per day![36]

In this passage Hudson and his colleagues assume *ex hypothesi* that de Soto and Pardo must have averaged much the same distance every day even though they traveled at different times of the year. Yet in the very next paragraph they turn the circle into a helix by arguing (again, because it is required *ex hypothesi*) that de Soto probably traveled more slowly than Pardo since his force was nearly five times as large (Hudson et al. 1987:849). In fact of course we have no grounds for judging either the distances traveled by de Soto or by Pardo on particular days, or for assuming that Pardo's movements can serve as a guide in this respect for de Soto's as well.

Any number of factors could have, and certainly did, affect the rate of travel along particular segments of both itineraries. Most important of these would have been the weather, which receives virtually no attention in sources. Dry, mild weather (or shortage of food, as Hudson et al. 1987 note) would allow or force all or part of the expedition to travel more rapidly. Conversely, stretches of extremely hot or wet weather would slow down the march, as would rough terrain, wooded areas, rivers, and the like. So too would fatigue, and problems with equipment or the animals.

In short, it is illicit to use Pardo's experience (to the extent that we can know it) as a handy template to fit over de Soto's. It is even less valid to heap hypothesis on hypothesis in hopes that, by their very proliferation, they will in some way transform themselves into proofs susceptible of demonstration rather than reiteration. Neither historical method generally, nor these data in particular, permit this. But without resorting to such reasoning, it will prove impossible to reconstruct de Soto's route, leaving us with the question as to what degree proper method is to be subordinated to the goal of placing de Soto and his men in very particular places at very particular times.[37]

## FROM HYPOTHESIS TO ORTHODOXY

> *If the [De Soto] Commission's report had a fatal flaw, it was its authoritative and comprehensive tone which caused the public to accept its theories as fact. (National Park Service 1990:27)*

This observation, offered by a nonparticipant in the attempts to localize de Soto's every move, leads me to offer a few final remarks on the discursive style and strategies of recent studies of de Soto's route, for it is these, rather than the quality, or even the disposition, of the evidence that gains victories in the scholarly battlefield. Many of these strategies epitomize remarkably the points that Fahnestock raises in her superb analysis of the rhetoric characterizing the debate in American archeology over when the first Indians arrived in the Americas (Fahnestock 1989:26–42).[38] We see, for instance, the standard but token mobilization of skepticism, which then quickly disappears, overwhelmed in the flood of declarative sentences that take firm possession of the discursive battleground.[39] The resulting composite account devours and digests even contradictory evidence with an eclectic, but undiscriminating, appetite. We then see hypothesis slowly being transformed into orthodoxy by dint of constant reiteration in place of new evidence or of new means of testing and exploiting present evidence. Moreover, and this is crucial, this gradual metamorphosis occurs in both the scholarly and the popular press, with the latter serving as both a catalyzing and a sanitizing or simplifying agent.[40] Throughout this process, both the ambiguities of the evidence and contrary opinion are studiously ignored.

In the case of the studies of the de Soto expedition, we meet another practice, already noted several times in passing: the amazing aversion to using the sources in the language in which they were composed, despite the well-demonstrated fact that, at best, all translations are low-grade interpretations and, at worse, outright betrayals of their presumed originals. The notion that detailed remonstrations of any complex past event can be accomplished without the recourse to the sources *as they are* is dismayingly ingenuous.[41]

In his useful survey of post–de Soto Commission work, Brain observed, paradoxically but absolutely correctly, that "if one thing is certain, it is that we are far more uncertain about the itinerary than the Commission was" (Brain 1985:xlvi). To judge from the record, Brain's "we" does not include a number of recent students of de Soto's route, and, all things considered, perhaps it is time that de Soto studies partake of the best, rather than the worst, discursive, textual, and intertextual strategies. Until they do, there is no good reason to say that "de Soto slept here."[42]

# Notes

1. De Soto is thought to have been born in or close to 1500. Albornoz (1971) was certain that it was in 1500, and this is now the consensus.

2. See Henige 1991 for an extended discussion of the character and value of this source, the so-called *diario.*

3. See Henige 1986a and the sources cited there for details on the fiction-as-truth temper of the times. For Cabeza de Vaca's account, see Núñez 1962. For Cortés's account of the conquest of the Aztec empire see Guzmán 1958 and Guzmán 1989; for Bernal Díaz del Castillo's very different account of many of the same events see Díaz del Castillo 1982; Brody 1987; and Boruchoff 1991; for yet a third version, this time by a non-participant, Francisco López de Gómara, see Gómara 1943; Iglesia 1980:96–215; and Valcárcel Martínez 1989. Finally, for the very peculiar, but still influential, account of Marcos de Niza, see Niza 1539; Weber 1988:19–32; and Ahern 1989.

4. The discursive spectrum (from few details to many details) is Biedma 1971, 14:211–61; Ranjel in Oviedo 1851–55, 1:544–77; Elvas in *Relaçam* 1557, and Garcilaso 1605.

5. A recent and very relevant study on Herodotus is Detlev Fehling (1989).

6. C. Clifford Boyd, Jr., and Gerald F. Schroedl (1987) are willing to grant Garcilaso derivative and corroborative credentials, but even this is unwarranted. Brain (1988) believes that "some details in *La Florida del Ynca* appear factual." No doubt they are, although it is unclear what is meant by "some" or by "factual," or for that matter by "appear." More on the relationship between scholars and Garcilaso is discussed below at various points. It is true of course that Garcilaso is plausible almost as often as he is not, but then most fiction depends on plausibility in order to be successful.

7. But Biedma (1971) is a facsimile of a copy made for Martín Fernández de Navarrete in 1793. It differs in many respects from later printed transcriptions.

8. One such partial manuscript, at the Huntington Library, appears to have been a working copy since it is characterized by changes, corrections, and other additions (Kathleen Myers, personal communication).

9. Priestley (1927, 2:129, 155, 259, 265, 343n. 7) improbably thought that the information sent to Luna was "very possibly a ms. copy of the account . . . credited to the Gentleman of Elvas," although conceding that it could have been the narrative of Biedma or an "an abridged [*sic*] journal" of Ranjel. See also Fairbanks (1985:128–39).

10. On the epistemological status of archeological interpretation see among others Salmon (1982), Kelley and Hanen (1988:225–74 *et passim*).

11. For a similar and even broader argument see Hudson et al. (1987:852).

12. Boyd and Schroedl (1987:842–43) also make this fairly obvious but constantly overlooked point. In their reply, Hudson et al. (1987:852) retreat somewhat, while declaring that they feel that the odds favor European artifacts remaining at the spots at which Indians first secured them, rather than "one hundred miles away." Somehow, this imputes somewhat zombie-like behavior to the Indians. Brain (1985a:96–107, 205–07) exhibits reservations about the diagnostic value of such *in situ* arguments. In an entirely different context, Redford (1981:5–16) shows the fallacy of this kind of argument for the Ancient Near East. Hudson, Smith, and DePratter (1990) are more willing to concede (largely because their argument requires it) that "small [*sic*] articles could easily have been carried from one place to another."

13. Morse and Morse (1983:306) make this very point for the Mississippi valley, but nonetheless frequently succumb to the temptation to argue otherwise. For the likelihood of finding sites in the Mississippi valley from this early period see Neuman (1989:9–18).

14. Brain (1985:xlvii–xlviii) goes so far as to assert that archeology "is ultimately the only source for proving without doubt [*sic*] a De Soto presence."

15. Edward, Baron Thurlow, to Sir John Scott.

16. In the discussion in Phillips, Ford, and Griffin (1951:349), the authors of this generally tempered analysis of the possibilities of de Soto's route from Chicasa to Quiquate, freely admit that Garcilaso is "commonly regarded as completely unreliable, used only in cases of desperate necessity when one wants very much to prove a point." They then proceed to prove their own point throughout their discussion by relying time and again on information only in *La Florida del Ynca,* particularly as it relates to mounds in Indian towns. They do this on the grounds that *La Florida del Ynca* can somehow be "carefully screened for exaggeration and sheer invention," after which it can be "very useful."

17. Hudson, Smith, and DePratter continue that "many of the old people [at Chalaque] were blind." This statement they leave unreferenced, but they speak of "all the chroniclers" in the same paragraph. In fact, only Garcilaso records this titbit, which is doubtless useful information for pandemicists, but otherwise merely a curio.

18. Marvin T. Smith (1987:54–85) is so far the most ardent, besides Dobyns (1983) in using Garcilaso to support archeological claims to precipitous population decline.

19. In fact, most recently Hudson (1990:103) concedes that *La Florida del Ynca*'s evidence is "negligible . . . in reconstructing De Soto's route" and then does not explicitly cite the work at all, which is a marked departure.

20. That is, given Garcilaso de la Vega's (1605:176) propensities, we might expect the reverse pattern.

21. These accounts, of course, belie Garcilaso's earlier statement that de Soto departed his camp *late* in March, but they also contradict the testimony of the other chroniclers that it occurred *early* in March.

22. For the effects of taking this figure seriously, see Boston (1939:277–97).

23. Eubanks (1989:374–76) makes a stronger case for a 2.63-mile league. Hudson and Smith (1990:37–38) defend themselves and at the same time throw the importance of league length overboard, although they are probably well advised to abandon that particular ship. Still, this does not help their cause, nor does the fact that the longer league militates strongly against a Tampa Bay landing, which Hudson (1990:79) espouses.

24. Hudson, Smith, and DePratter (1984:74) posit that a place called "Guasili" in de Soto's time had changed its name to "Cauchi" by the time Pardo happened on it.

25. This length of four miles assumes that Elvas meant to say that the river "reunited" a league from the town, not the other end of the island. Hudson (1990:38) believes otherwise. Both the original text of Elvas and modern translations are unclear enough to prohibit a solution.

26. DePratter, Hudson, and Smith (1983:146) go so far as to claim that "the placement" of the mound apparently on Zimmerman's Island "agrees with Elvas's description" despite the fact that Elvas mentioned no mound at all. Hudson (1990) is written in the same vein.

27. See the aerial photograph of Zimmerman's Island in Hudson (1990:37) where this island is accompanied by several smaller islands also not mentioned in any of the early sources.

28. There are exceptions, of course, e.g., Manhattan Island.

29. Of course this hypothesis would apply to most other sites mentioned by either the de Soto or the Pardo chronicles.

30. In 1628, a Spanish delegation visited whatever place was then called Cofitachequi, and was told that "[it] was 82 [*sic*] years since Hernando de Soto was there and until [the present] occasion no Spaniards had come." (Eubanks 1991:125). If true, this would seem to suggest that Juan Pardo's expedition of 1568 had reached a different place with the same name, unless the Indians

were lying (but why?) or unless the Spanish had misinterpreted the message (possible but ominous for those wishing to use these kinds of sources). Whatever the case, this statement lends support to any notion that Indian place names tended to move more frequently than modern scholars would prefer to believe. For details of this incident, see Eubanks 1991/92.

31. Translating "avarzea" as "vale" would better fit Martínez's description of Chiaha as being on a mountain, or so it would seem.

32. An additional problem in this case is that the silence itself appears to be illusory and that there are sites in the area that can be dated to the sixteenth century. See Eubanks 1989:369–74; Brain 1985.

33. This is less to suggest that extensive archeological work has not been carried out in the southeastern United States than to point out that, even in areas (e.g., the Nile valley, Israel, Greece, southeast England) that have been subjected to intensive archeological investigation for generations, new discoveries requiring new interpretations are still frequently made.

34. By no means, though, are Hudson and his colleagues alone in this means of re-creating de Soto's activities. For Florida there is Schell (1966) and, more generally, R. S. Weddle (1985:208–26), who uses material from all four de Soto chronicles without discrimination.

35. The writers are citing twentieth-century translations. Cf. Hudson (1990:90). "Elvas 1866" refers to B. Smith 1866; "Ranjel 1922" is Ranjel in Bourne 1904, 4.

36. Compare this discussion of the distance from Cofitachequi to Ilapi in Hudson, Smith, and DePratter (1984:73).

37. T. C. Chamberlain (1890) remains the classic study of the relationship between hypothesizing and argumentation. Others may prefer Agassi (1973), who proposes less rigorous criteria.

38. A similar study is Veldink (1989).

39. It is interesting to compare the two parts of Hudson's 1990a. In the first, a narrative interpretation of de Soto's route, Hudson expresses few doubts, whereas in the second, a site-by-site probability evaluation, the reader learns that most identifications of sites mentioned in the chronicles with modern equivalents are rated only "possible" or "problematic."

40. Recent writings on de Soto's route aimed at a mass audience include, in addition to Hudson's (1990a) "Synopsis," "Hernando de Soto's Expedition Through the Southern United States," by Hudson, DePratter, and Smith (1989), and "Tracking the Elusive de Soto," by Hudson and Hudson (1989). The very format of these presentations does not permit reasoned arguments, nor is the audience in most cases likely to welcome them.

41. Note the strange advice of Jerald Milanich (1989a:311): "[a]dditional translations of all three of the narratives [Biedma, Ranjel, and Elvas] now exist and the interested scholar should consult all of them." There is not one word about consulting these in the originals, nor are there any citations to such originals in Milanich's bibliography.

42. Since this paper was presented in 1990, studies of the de Soto expedition have continued unabated, in fact have increased in both volume and interest. Their appearance has largely been in clusters. No fewer than fourteen papers have been collected in D. H. Thomas 1990. *En ensemble* these offer the rare advantage of presenting together several differing views of the weight and nature of both the archeological and the documentary evidence, as well as strong bibliographies. Patricia Galloway (1993) has assembled a collection of more than a dozen essays which address the fullest spectrum of issues to date, ranging from the written sources to the perennially pesky issue of league length to the means by which the expedition measured its progress to the intellecutual context of the occasion. See as well DePratter (1991), which leans heavily on *La Florida del Ynca* and uses all four chronicles only in translation. Finally, readers should be aware of *The Soto States Anthropologist,* which began publication as a quarterly in 1990, and which serves as a clearing-house and forum for what must be termed heterodox views of the expedition's routes and its effects.

# Legends of the Adelantado

George E. Lankford

## INTRODUCTION

In 1539 Hernando de Soto, the newly appointed Adelantado (governor) of La Florida and Cuba, set out to explore his territory with some six hundred cavaliers, infantrymen, and slaves, putting ashore at Tampa Bay. Four years later, in 1543, the survivors floated into Tampico in their makeshift boats, having floated down the Mississippi River and along the coast.[1]

There were several accounts of the voyage written by various survivors. Four chronicles were published; there is evidence of at least two unpublished ones; and it is not unreasonable to hope for more to surface.[2] The longest and most controversial of the chronicles was the second to appear in print. It was written by Gómez Súarez de Figueroa. He was the illegitimate son of an Inca noblewoman and one of the Spanish conquerors of Peru, Capt. Sebastián Garcilaso de la Vega Vargas, who was born in 1539, the very year of the start of de Soto's expedition. In later life, after his father's death, he went to Spain and adopted his father's illustrious ancestral name, "Garcilaso de la Vega," with a personal addition, "The Inca." Under this name he published in 1605 a lengthy and well-written account of the de Soto journey, *La Florida del Ynca,* of which he claimed only to be the editor (Garcilaso 1605, 1951). The real author, he said, was an anonymous Spanish cavalier, but he left copious textual clues to identify that member of de Soto's army, Gonzalo Silvestre, who had died in Spain in 1592. It is quite clear from the text that Silvestre was not the author, however, but rather the informant with whom Garcilaso worked for many years in preparing the narrative. In addition to the anonymous cavalier, Garcilaso claimed, he had two other sources, brief written accounts which he had come upon shortly after the first draft had been completed. He claimed general support of Silvestre's account from them, and he incorporated in *La Florida del Ynca* additional information from them. They were Alonso de Carmona and Juan Coles, about whom nothing is known from other sources.

This paper seeks to assess the work of Garcilaso and his three sources from the viewpoint of the legends contained in them. Such a study can offer little to the already lengthy debate concerning whether Garcilaso's account should be read as history or as literature, but it may provide a slightly different vantage point for considering the issues. Garcilaso claimed to be writing history—rather vehemently, in fact. John G. Varner (1968), one of El Inca's major biographers, strongly supported that claim and provided a good biographical base for it. Garcilaso de la Vega laid great stress on the poor treatment of his father by the Crown after the civil wars in Peru, the major problem being the interpretations by historians of his father's behavior during a battle. In the wake of Garcilaso's father's death by depression and the loss of financial support for him and his mother, Varner argued, the young mestizo (half Spanish, half Inca) dedicated himself to correcting the errors of the historians about the conquest of Peru and the nature of the indigenous peoples. This commitment ultimately resulted in his masterpieces, the *Comentarios reales de los Incas* (Garcilaso 1609) and volume two of that work, the *Historia general del Perú* (Garcilaso 1616).

Garcilaso's history of Peru offers strong contrast to the other contemporary histories, perhaps because he based much of his presentation on information gathered from the actors in the civil wars. Many of the Spaniards were visitors in his father's home, and he grew up surrounded by the lore of the conquistadors' world. The very year Garcilaso was born, 1539, had seen the beginning of a fabled disastrous expedition into La Florida. He heard much about it through the years from his father's friend Gonzalo Silvestre, a cavalier who had both accompanied Hernando de Soto and fought through the Peruvian civil wars on the side of the Crown. Silvestre lived to tell about them both, and one of his favorite listeners was Garcilaso, who later claimed that their friendship began in 1552, when he was only thirteen and Silvestre was in his forties (Varner 1968:114f.) In 1556 Silvestre had an altercation with the governor and was sent to Spain, and Garcilaso made the same journey in 1560, after his father's death. The impoverished Silvestre became a major source of information for Garcilaso as he worked on the *Comentários*. It may have been that connection which led Garcilaso into an enthusiasm for producing yet a different work, a history of the de Soto expedition.

There was certainly room for such a work, because only one printed version of the journey had been produced, the 1557 *Relaçam* of the "Gentleman of Elvas." Moreover, there might be an audience for such a work, for Spain was in the thrall of a literary movement, the romances. Spain's literary masterpiece *Don Quixote* was composed as a parody of the romances which had so little to do with the real world of sixteenth-century Spain, but the world of the conquistadors was not far removed from the courtly, dangerous life of the romances. In fact, it is the strong similarity between the romances, such as *Amadís de Gaula* (Thomas 1920) on the one hand, and the stories of the New World adventures, such as the *Naufrágios* of Cabeza de Vaca (Nuñez 1962)[3] and Garcilaso de la Vega's *La Florida del Ynca* on the other, which gives rise to the question of whether such works are not really to be read as literature rather than as history. Any reader of *La Florida del Ynca* knows there is a certain plausibility to the idea, for there is a literary quality in that work which the other three narratives of the de Soto expedition do not possess. Even the strongest supporter of the historical reliability of Garcilaso must recognize that the literary romances had an impact and that the consequences of that impact must be assessed by the historian.

A different approach to the issue of historical reliability lies in the realm of folklore. The historians would prefer to have an official daily journal from an expedition, and the popular theory is that Oviedo's (1851–55) account is based on just such a journal, written by Ranjel, who was de Soto's secretary. Apart from such a document, however, the story of the expedition would have been kept primarily in the oral tradition. Each member of the de Soto army, including the historically silent peasants, slaves, and women, had his own set of memorates—those stories which express what that person experienced individually, quite apart from the general event and its meaning. After a significant battle, for instance, each person would have several strong memories which were expressed to his comrades as memorates. In the general exchange some memorates would be picked up and retold by others, either for the quality of the story or for its importance in imparting some sense of significance for the understanding of the larger event. Those retold stories are by definition "legends," and the core legends of the full collection will eventually come to characterize the event, at least in the oral tradition if not in the documents. The result is a corpus of legends known generally by all the participants in the expedition. Each expedition member would also have a set of personal memories to augment that general legendry.

In the interviewing process for oral history, the historian hopes for the sort of memorate which is an accurate reflection of the event in which the informant participated, albeit many years earlier. Unfortunately, there is frequently an admixture of those general legends, the events that are supposed to have happened, even if the informant did not personally see them in particular. The historian must determine which is being collected. Adding to the problem is the tendency for an oft-told memorate to assume a more story-like format, if only to smooth out the delivery. On an expedition such as de Soto's, in which some six hundred Spanish speakers were encapsulated in an alien world for four years, the process of daily life might well be expected to produce the storytelling environment within which even one's own memories might begin to make the subtle shift from memorate to legend. In short, I believe the survivors of the de Soto expedition emerged from their cocoon in La Florida with a common set of legends about most of the important events they had lived through, and any oral historical hopes should be modest. If that was already the case in 1543, what can be said about the historical accuracy of testimony gathered decades later?

## THE LEGENDS

The length of Garcilaso's *La Florida del Ynca* is not the only thing which sets it apart from the other chronicles. There is a literary quality to it which makes it simultaneously interesting reading and suspicious history. It is, in fact, that quality which has led to so much of the criticism and distrust of the book as an accurate historical source. To a folklorist, that literary quality is more accurately identified as the incorporation of many legends. It is possible to see the account as essentially a long series of legend narratives—a "string of beads," if you will—strung together with a running description of the journey. These legend narratives are "authenticated" in a way characteristic of oral legendry: they are carefully located in space and time and attributed to a known person who is purported to be a participant, and frequently with claims to pass on the *ipsissima verba* of the informant. Henige (1986a:8) and others have seen such authentication techniques as indications of literary fraud, but they are equally strong indications of legends.[4]

The problem lies in the fact that Garcilaso attempts to convince the reader that he is but the editor of a collection of Gonzalo Silvestre's memories. If these were indeed memorates, then the debate would have to focus on the accuracy of the memory of Silvestre and the degree of professionalism in the oral historical approach of Garcilaso. The questions we would have to raise would include how many times Garcilaso had heard each story, how he recorded them (verbatim? in outline?), whether he cross-examined Silvestre to catch him in internal inconsistencies or to jog his memory further, whether he used outside standards to channel Silvestre's memories (such as Elvas' *Relaçam* or other manuscripts from the survivors), and so on. In fact, however, it is clear that the narrator throughout *La Florida del Ynca* is Garcilaso, and the removal of Silvestre to the position of informant behind the narrator moves the discussion into the realm of legend. This does not mean, of course, that *La Florida del Ynca* may not be exactly what Garcilaso claimed it to be, namely, a carefully researched history based on remarkably precocious professional oral historical interviews with an extraordinary informant. It does mean that such a conclusion cannot be reached with assurance, and that the narrative can be examined fruitfully as a collection of legends even if the oral historical claims are true.

If it is correct to view the army of de Soto as a legend-generating group, then it ought to be possible to make an educated guess at the corpus of legendry which had been created by the entire party to describe to themselves the events they had lived through together. In an attempt to do so I have identified eighty-two legends from *La Florida del Ynca* (see table 1). There is a certain amount of subjectivity in such a list, of course, but I have used the following set of standards to sift through the narratives: To be selected, a legend text should (1) be in story form (or point to a story behind its present brief form), (2) be nonessential to the historical narrative (can the account get along without it?), (3) have a focus on a named figure (or, alternatively, describe a wonder not associated with a particular person), and (4) present strong visual images (or provide a strong belief problem). Even though the entire narrative—the journey itself, with all its marvels—can with justification be seen as a legend, I decided not to include the hundreds of observations made en route unless they took story form (with a few exceptions, as will be seen).

This is not to de-emphasize the importance of the overall structure, however. From one view, it may be argued that the narrative of Elvas has provided Garcilaso with the basic framework, but it may also be argued that one of the reasons for the power of the stories of the conquistadors is their structure along the lines of the heroic quest—the hero sets out against insuperable odds, but by gaining the support of the right companions along the way, he overcomes several different types of ogres to receive the treasure at the heart of the quest. In the case of the de Soto entrada, the search for riches and the way to the Orient becomes the Quest, the great cavaliers and the freed captive, Juan Ortiz, become the helpful companions, the battles against Taskalusa, Chicasa, and Tula become the confrontations with the enemy, and the Temple at Cofitachequi fills the role of the Treasure. The *Märchen*-like structure has to yield to the classic legend theme of the death of the hero and the loss of the treasure, but that certainly would not have reduced its fascination in the world of oral tradition.

TABLE 1: Legend Sequence in Garcilaso de La Vega. Courtesy of George E. Lankford

| | Silvestre | Carmona | Coles | Pages |
|---|---|---|---|---|
| 1 | Two ships collided | | | 24-27,626 |
| 2 | | Soldiers drowned | | 28 |
| 3 | | Dog swam miles | | 28 |
| 4 | | Hidalgo drowned | | 28 |
| 5 | Ship struck rock at Santiago | | | 30f |
| 6 | Fight between Spanish/French | | | 31-37 |
| 7 | Bishop almost drowned | | | 39 |
| 8 | | Añasco cast away on island | | 45 |
| 9 | Ponce attempted to defraud de Soto | | | 48-53 |
| JUAN ORTIZ | | | | |
| 10 | Saved by chief's wife | | | 63 |
| 11 | | Worms in wounds | | 81 |
| 12 | Lucky spear cast | | | 65-68 |
| 13 | Became captain general | ◊ | ◊ | 72 |
| 14 | "Sevilla!" | | Sign of cross | 81 |
| 15 | | | Velvet suit | 81 |
| APALACHEE | | | | |
| 16 | | | Dog returned Indians | 126 |
| 17 | | | Dog killed Indian | 126 |
| 18 | De Soto sprang trap | de Soto signal: trumpet | | 146 |
| 19 | Indians tread water | | | 148ff |
| 20 | European saints legend | | | 151 |
| 21 | Vitachuco hit de Soto | | knocked out teeth | 163f |
| 22 | Apalachee defended self | | | 165f |
| 23 | Apalachee defended self | | | 167 |
| 24 | Indian died well | | | 187-90 |
| 25 | Indians addled soldier | | | 229f |
| 26 | Indians took Spaniard | | | 230f |
| 27 | Indian killed horse | | | 233f |
| 28 | Indian held off seven | | | 250ff |
| 29 | Indian killed two horses | | | 254ff |
| 30 | Indian killed two men, one horse | | | 256ff |
| 31 | Indians fought chivalrously | | | 264ff |
| 32 | Indian attacked by demons | | | 280 |
| 33 | Indian punished by drinking water | | | 289f |
| 34 | Jokes about maize | | | 290f |
| COFITACHEQUI | | | | |
| 35 | The Lady of Cofitachequi | | | 299ff |
| 36 | Indian killed self | | | 304-308 |
| 37 | Temple of Cofitachequi | pearls/pest dead | statue/ruby | 315-325 |
| 38 | Soldier discarded pearls | | | 334f |
| 39 | Soldier killed comrade | | | 339f |

TABLE 1 *continued*

| | Silvestre | Carmona | Coles | Pages |
|---|---|---|---|---|
| MAVILA | | | | |
| 40 | Taskalusa a giant | giant | horse too small | 348,356 |
| 41 | | Dancing women | | 356 |
| 42 | Gallegos slashed Indian | | | 359f |
| 43 | Gallegos killed son | | | 360f |
| 44 | Fr. Gallegos wounded | | | 363f |
| 45 | Death of Don Carlos | ◊ | | 364 |
| 46 | De Soto wounded | ◊ | | 367 |
| 47 | Arrow split Tovar's lance | ◊ | | 368 |
| 48 | Death of Diego de Soto | ◊ | | 370f |
| 49 | Indian killed self | | | 373 |
| 50 | Spanish death: coward | | | 378 |
| 51 | Spanish death: hero | | | 378f |
| CHICASA | | | | |
| 52 | De Soto lost his saddle | ◊ | ◊ | 402 |
| 53 | | Friar saved day | | 407 |
| 54 | Swine lard flowed | | ◊ | 404 |
| 55 | Soldier lived, teased | | | 403f |
| 56 | Horses died of arrows in hearts | | | 405 |
| 57 | | Indians had 3 cords | | 405 |
| 58 | | Saved from attack by rain | | 407 |
| CASQUI | | | | |
| 59 | Adoration of cross brought rain | rained 15 days | | 431ff |
| 60 | Soldier drowned | | | 440f |
| 61 | Indians debated ranking | | | 447f |
| TULA | | | | |
| 62 | Women held soldier by genitals | | | 455f |
| 63 | Indian defeated Spaniard with staff | | | 456 |
| 64 | Indians defeated Spaniard with staff | | | 459 |
| 65 | Indian showed skill with ax | | | 460ff |
| 66 | Tula boy showed warrior skill | | | 465f |
| 67 | Spaniard deserted for woman | ◊ | | 479ff |
| 68 | Crosses adopted from Cabeza de Vaca | | | 482 |
| 69 | Indians sneezed in universal way | | | 490f |
| 70 | Death of de Soto | ◊ | ◊ | 501ff |
| 71 | Indian joined Spanish | | | 511f |
| 72 | Indian killed two women by accident | | | 516f |
| 73 | | Discovered lost sow | | 530 |
| 74 | Warriors challenged Spanish | | | 518f |
| 75 | Spanish healer healed self | | | 523ff |
| 76 | Indian killed two horses | | | 526ff |
| 77 | | Woman predicted flood | | 534f,554 |
| 78 | Spanish killed an Indian | | | 549ff |
| 79 | Spaniard led boats into trap | ◊ | | 583ff |
| 80 | | | Indian/final shout | 595 |
| 81 | | Añasco threw chart overboard | | 600 |
| 82 | | Xaramillo took in 18 | ◊ | 622 |

Table 1 lists the eighty-two legends and their page numbers, but it also separates the contributions of Alonso de Carmona and Juan Coles from the basic collection from Gonzalo Silvestre. The accounts of the first two were so brief that their contributions were minimal, but there were still a few legends peculiar to them which hint at a flavor of their interests. In the opening sequence, which caught up various events before arrival at La Florida, the different perspectives of the cavalier Silvestre (or Garcilaso?) and the plebeian Carmona are displayed. Silvestre tells stories about the ineptitude of the sailors and nobility, international warfare, and the underhanded dealings of Ponce de León, partner of de Soto (#1, #5, #6, #7, #9), while Carmona seems more interested in telling about three accidental drownings (#2, #4), a marvelous dog story (#3), and a story which ridicules Juan de Añasco, de Soto's lieutenant (#8). In the latter, although Añasco was supposed to be out surveying the Florida coast, he managed to get stranded on a desert island for days and was so glad to return to Cuba that he and his men crawled on their knees to mass to give thanks. This story critical of Añasco stands alone, apparently rooted in an unexplained animosity toward the high-ranking cavalier, an observation which is strengthened by the fact that Carmona alone also has an unflattering story about him at the end of the saga, one in which Añasco, laughed at by the men for pretending to be a navigator, threw the instruments overboard in pique. Carmona's other contributions are congruent with the interests of a soldier. He added a subordinate detail to the Juan Ortiz legend in which the roasted flesh of Ortiz produced worms before it healed (#11); to the battle of Mabila he added the detail of the presence of dancing women before the outbreak of hostilities (#41). To the Chicasa battle account he added a significant story of how one of the religious rallied the panicked men and saved the day (#53), an observation of the three cords worn by the Indians (#57), and a miraculous delivery from disaster in the form of a sudden rain shower (#58). He also remembered the discovery of a lost sow and her offspring on the return from Texas (#73), and he contributed the story of the old Indian woman who correctly predicted the Mississippi River flood (#77). Juan Coles, by contrast, in his brief account contributed only two dog stories and a wild yarn about his taking a ruby from a statue in the temple at Cofitachequi (#16, #17, #37). Despite his suggestion that no one else knew about it, the last story is so implausible that it manages to confer a perverse legitimacy on Coles as a teller of legends from the de Soto journey.

The second chart may be more useful in examining the de Soto legend corpus (See table 2). In the Garcilaso column all three of his sources have been coalesced, with cross references to the other three narratives listed alongside. The indication of the presence of the legend in another source does not necessarily signal more than a reference to the event; in most cases, it in no way approaches legend status. It is fair to say that Elvas, Biedma, and Ranjel show little interest in passing on legends, for only a few entries, interpolated in the sequence without numbers, indicate legends found in them which are not included in Garcilaso. Thus Biedma included a one-liner about the Indian town where they shouted birds out of the sky, without any explanation or expansion into the full legend which must have circulated among the soldiers. Elvas, on the other hand, tells several legends which Garcilaso did not incorporate into his work, which could be used to support the argument that he did not use Elvas. Elvas alone of the chroniclers tells of pre-Florida events with two interesting legends. In one, the Portuguese report to a preliminary military muster correctly outfitted, earning de Soto's praise and leading him to chastise the Spanish cavaliers, a story which arises somewhat naturally out of the interests of the Portuguese writer. In the other legend, he offers the gratuitous story of how a cruel overseer of Vasco Porcallo's slaves stopped them from committing suicide in Cuba by threatening to kill himself so he could continue their persecution beyond the grave—surely a story of wider distribution (but other examples of which I have not been able to locate). Of even greater interest is the story of the trick the men played on de Soto: when he condemned some Spaniards to death for looting without permission, their comrades got the interpreters to lie to de Soto, telling him that the Indians themselves were pleading for mercy on the thieves; de Soto relented. This is a curious story on several counts. For one thing, with the possible exception of Carmona's Añasco legends, it is the only indication of different bodies of legendry circulating among the ordinary soldiers and the nobility. If there is historical basis to the legend, it is an important story which testifies to insubordination by the men, manipulation of de Soto and their ability to do so, and to an ethical code to which de Soto ascribed which is seldom visible in the chronicles. It seems strange that Elvas thought his revelation would not cause concern in official quarters, even after the death of de Soto, but it may have stemmed from his Portuguese bias—that is, the legend may have been intended to show up the Spanish military in yet another way, a companion piece to the story of the mustering of the troops.

Other than these stories, and a few more brief references, Garcilaso's fellow chroniclers avoided telling the legends of the de Soto expedition, and most of the references are merely comments that the event did happen, albeit without the full details or interpretation given by Garcilaso/Silvestre. Those references, however, are important in providing evidence that Silvestre's stories are more than the idiosyncratic imaginary maunderings of an old soldier. We can get a feel for the differences in the treatment of events by the chroniclers by looking at the legend of Juan Ortiz in some detail.

The death of Juan Ortiz toward the end of the journey is one of the great tragedies of the de Soto expedition, for with him died information about the Timucua which would now be of great importance. Had he lived to return to New Spain, he would have been hailed as a second Cabeza de Vaca—the fifth survivor of the Narváez expedition—and would almost certainly have had his romantic story enshrined in print. (On the other hand, however, Garcilaso told the story of two Spaniards who were kidnapped in Florida and returned to the Spanish world a decade later; in that case, no books were written (#25, #26). As it happened, de Soto had tried to get Cabeza de Vaca to accompany him on his journey. Although he failed, some of Cabeza de Vaca's kin did make the trip. All of the Spaniards were thus well aware of the story of Cabeza de Vaca, and the legends of Juan Ortiz would have circulated rapidly throughout the de Soto army after he was found among the Timucua early in the entrada (#10–#15). His treatment by Oviedo/Ranjel was disconcertingly brief: Ortiz was identified by his calling out in the name of "Holy Mary," and the Spanish were delighted to have an interpreter. None of Ortiz's story is given, and even the Narváez connection is omitted. This is brevity to the point of throwing away the story altogether. Biedma gave little more: Ortiz was identified by his calling upon "Our Lady," and he had been there for twelve years, but the Narváez expedition was not mentioned. Biedma's interest in the Ortiz legend seems to have been limited to the difficulty of repatriation; Ortiz, he noted, had trouble speaking Spanish. Elvas, as the other legend-teller of the chroniclers, told this sequence: Ortiz was saved from burning by the chief's daughter, then by a lucky spear throw he killed a wolf who had stolen a dead body from the ossuary temple he was guarding. Warned by the friendly chief's daughter of his impending death, he fled to another town where he was allowed to become a warrior and eventually to go to meet the Spanish under de Soto. Garcilaso tells pretty much the same sequence of legends, but at greater length. It was the chief's wife who saved the roasting Ortiz, and Carmona supplied the worms in the wounds. The same spear cast saved Ortiz's life, but it was a "lion" which was killed instead of Elvas' wolf. Garcilaso includes details such as the charge that Narváez had cut off the chief's nose and fed his mother to the dogs (the only source of that information), and that Ortiz felt his spear cast in the darkness had been good because his hand felt salty, an interesting folk belief in its own right. All three of his sources, Garcilaso said, insisted that Ortiz rose to high warrior rank in the second Timucua town, and Coles supplied the interesting note that de Soto gave Ortiz one of his own velvet suits, but that Ortiz found it too uncomfortable to wear. Under Garcilaso's pen Elvas' four-page narrative became a twenty-page saga.

On the basis of this brief comparison of the Juan Ortiz legend as presented by the chroniclers, it is difficult to argue for the independence of Garcilaso from Elvas. The brevity of Biedma and Ranjel—brevity to the point of strangeness—removes them from consideration as sources, at least in this case, but it is noteworthy that Garcilaso does not add anything substantial to the legend as given by Elvas other than a few details and a greatly expanded exposition. Such agreement between Elvas and Garcilaso is seen several more times. They agree that one of the Spaniards deserted to the Indians because of a woman (#67). The legend of the Indians who tread water in the pond until de Soto took pity on them and had them pulled out in exhaustion (#19) was told also by Elvas and mentioned by Ranjel. The incident of the Indian interpreter who had a fit was also told by Elvas, Ranjel, and Garcilaso (#32). There is general agreement that Taskalusa was a giant (#40), that Gallegos began the fighting at Mabila (#42), that Don Carlos Enríquez died in the battle (#45), that de Soto lost his saddle at Chicasa (#52), that adoration of the cross at Casqui brought rain (#59), that the two chiefs of Casqui and Pacaha debated their hereditary ranking (#61), and that a foolish Spaniard led several boatloads of his comrades to their deaths on the trip down the Mississippi (#79).

In these cases the legends are generally ratified by all of the chroniclers, and Garcilaso can be seen as an embellisher of the legends of the other chroniclers as well as the editor of Silvestre, Carmona, and Coles that he claimed to be. There are other cases, however, which cast a different light on Garcilaso, for there are several instances in which he told stories which were not included in Elvas, but which were ratified by Biedma or Ranjel, documents which presumably were not available to Garcilaso. In the battle of Mabila, for example, Garcilaso told of the arrow which split the wooden lance

TABLE 2. Legend Sequence in the Chronicles. Courtesy of George E. Lankford.

| | Garcilaso de la Vega | Elvas | Biedma | Ranjel |
|---|---|---|---|---|
| | | Muster (12f) | | |
| | | Porcallo's slaves (17) | | |
| 1 | Two ships collided | | | |
| 2 | Soldiers drowned | | | |
| 3 | Dog swam miles | | | |
| 4 | Hidalgo drowned | | | |
| 5 | Ship struck rock at Santiago | | | |
| 6 | Fight between Spanish/French | | | |
| 7 | Bishop almost drowned | | | |
| 8 | Añasco cast away on island | | | |
| 9 | Ponce attempted to defraud de Soto | | | |
| JUAN ORTIZ* | | | | ___*begin* |
| 10 | Saved by chief's wife | Daughter (30) | | |
| 11 | Worms in wounds | | | |
| 12 | Lucky spear cast | Δ(30) | | |
| 13 | Became captain general | | | |
| 14 | "Sevilla!"/sign of cross | Call (27) | "Our Lady" (232) | "Holy Mary" (57) |
| 15 | Velvet suit | Δ(33) | | |
| APALACHEE | | | | |
| 16 | Dog returned Indians | | | |
| 17 | Dog killed Indian | | | Δ(70) |
| 18 | De Soto sprang trap | | | Δ(74) |
| 19 | Indians tread water | Δ(42f) | | Δ(75) |
| 20 | European saints legend | | | |
| | | | Shout birds down (232) | |
| 21 | Vitachuco hit de Soto/ knocked out teeth | Δ(45) | | Δ(76) |
| 22 | Apalachee defended self | | | |
| 23 | Apalachee defended self | | | |
| 24 | Indian died well | | | |
| 25 | Indians addled soldier | | | |
| 26 | Indians took Spaniard | | | |
| 27 | Indian killed horse | | | |
| 28 | Indian held off seven | | | (cf. 80) |
| 29 | Indian killed two horses | Δ(48f) | | |
| 30 | Indian killed two men, one horse | | | |
| 31 | Indians fought chivalrously | | | |
| | | | | Altamaha chief (89f) |
| 32 | Indian attacked by demons | Δ (58) | | Δ (91) |
| 33 | Indian punished by drinking water | | | |
| 34 | Jokes about maize | | | |
| COFITACHEQUI | | | | |
| 35 | The Lady of Cofitachequi | Δ(62) | Δ(239) | |
| 36 | Indian killed self | | | |
| 37 | Temple of Cofitachequi | Δ(63) | (239) | Δ(100f) |
| 38 | Soldier discarded pearls | | | |
| 39 | Soldier killed comrade | | | |
| MABILA* ** | | | | |
| 40 | Taskalusa a giant/ horse too small** | Δ(81) | Δ(242) | |
| 41 | Dancing women | | Δ(243) | |

TABLE 2 *continued*

| | Garcilaso de la Vega | Elvas | Biedma | Ranjel |
|---|---|---|---|---|
| 42 | Gallegos slashed Indian | Δ(85) | Δ(244) | Δ(124) |
| 43 | Gallegos killed son | | | |
| 44 | Fr. Gallegos wounded | ?(87) | | |
| 45 | Death of Don Carlos* | Δ(89) | | Δ(126) |
| 46 | De Soto wounded | | | |
| 47 | Arrow split Tovar's lance | | | Δ(127) |
| 48 | Death of Diego de Soto* | | | Δ(128) |
| 49 | Indian kills self | | Δ(245) | Δ?(127) |
| 50 | Spanish death: coward | | | |
| 51 | Spanish death: hero | Δ(90) | | |
| | | Men lied to save comrades (94f) | | |
| CHICASA* ** | | | | |
| 52 | De Soto lost his saddle | Δ(96) | | Δ(134) |
| 53 | Friar saved day | | | |
| 54 | Swine lard flows | Δ | | |
| 55 | Soldier lived, teased | | | |
| 56 | Horses died of arrows in hearts | | | |
| 57 | Indians have 3 cords | | | |
| 58 | Saved from attack by rain | | | |
| | | Woman burned (96) | | |
| CASQUI | | | | |
| 59 | Adoration of cross brought rain | Δ?(139ff) | Δ?(109) | Δ(250f) |
| 60 | Soldier drowned | | | |
| 61 | Indians debated ranking | Δ(116) | Δ(253) | Δ(143f) |
| TULA | | | | |
| 62 | Women held soldier by genitals | | | Δ?(78) |
| 63 | Indian defeated Spaniard with staff | | | Δ?(126) |
| 64 | Indians defeated Spaniard with staff | | | |
| 65 | Indian showed skill with ax | | | |
| 66 | Tula boy showed warrior skill | | | |
| 67 | Spaniard deserted for woman | Δ(153) | | Δ(165) |
| 68 | Crosses adopted from Cabeza de Vaca | | | |
| 69 | Indians sneezed in universal way | | | *end* |
| 70 | Death of de Soto | Δ(147f) | Δ(257) | |
| 71 | Indian joined Spanish | | | |
| 72 | Indian killed two women by accident | | | |
| 73 | Discovered lost sow | | | |
| 74 | Warriors challenged Spanish | | | |
| 75 | Spanish healer healed self | | | |
| 76 | Indian killed two horses | | | |
| 77 | Woman predicted flood | Δ?(173) | | |
| 78 | Spanish killed an Indian | Δ(132) | | |
| 79 | Spaniard led boats into trap | Δ(178f) | Δ(260) | |
| 80 | Indian/final shout | | | |
| 81 | Añasco threw chart overboard | | | |
| 82 | Xaramillo took in 18 | | | |

* Also in Argote  ** Also in Cañete  Δ datum present

of Nuño de Tovar, forming a cross (#47). Elvas did not tell that legend, but Ranjel did. So, too, did Ranjel confirm the death of Diego de Soto, Hernando de Soto's nephew, in the battle (#48), and both Ranjel and Biedma mentioned the suicide of the last Indian at Mabila (#49), stories which were not included in Elvas. There can be no definitive conclusion drawn from these correspondences, but the pattern suggests that either Garcilaso had access to all three of the other chronicles (which seems unlikely), or that his informants told him legends from the general body of de Soto legendry which were also known to the others.

TABLE 3. Legend Categories. Courtesy of George E. Lankford.

| | Garcilaso de la Vega | Elvas | Biedma | Ranjel |
|---|---|---|---|---|
| DE SOTO'S ADVENTURES | | | | |
| 9 | Ponce attempted to defraud de Soto | | | |
| 18 | De Soto signal: trumpet | | | Δ (74) |
| 21 | Vitachuco hit De Soto/ knocked out teeth | Δ (76) | Δ(45) | |
| 46 | De Soto wounded | | | |
| 52 | De Soto lost his saddle | Δ(96) | | Δ(134) |
| 70 | Death of de Soto | Δ(147f) | Δ(257) | |
| MARVELS | | | | |
| 54 | Swine lard flowed | Δ | | |
| 73 | Discovered lost sow | | | |
| JUAN ORTIZ | | | | |
| 10–15 (see Table 2) | | | | |
| DEATHS | | | | |
| 2 | Soldiers drowned | | | |
| 4 | Hidalgo drowned | | | |
| 39 | Soldier killed comrade | | | |
| 45 | Death of Don Carlos Enriquez | Δ(89) | | Δ(126) |
| 48 | Death of Diego de Soto | | | Δ(128) |
| 50 | Spanish death: coward | | | |
| 51 | Spanish death: hero | Δ(90) | | |
| 60 | Soldier drowned | | | |
| 79 | Spaniard led boats into trap | Δ(178f) | Δ(260) | |
| DOGS | | | | |
| 3 | Dog swam miles | | | |
| 16 | Dog returned Indians | | | |
| 17 | Dog killed Indian | | | Δ (70) |
| RELIGIOUS | | | | |
| 7 | Bishop almost drowned | | | |
| 14 | "Sevilla!"/sign of cross | call (27) | "Our Lady" (232) | "Holy Mary" (57) |
| 20 | European saints legend | | | |
| 32 | Indian attacked by demons | Δ (58) | | Δ(91) |
| 44 | Fr. Gallegos wounded | ?(87) | | |
| 47 | Arrow split Tovar's lance | | | Δ(127) |
| 53 | Friar saved day | | | |
| 58 | Saved from attack by rain | | | |
| 59 | Adoration of cross brought rain 15 days | Δ?(139ff) | Δ?(109) | Δ(250f) |
| 68 | Crosses adopted from Cabeza de Vaca | | | |
| 77 | Woman predicted flood | Δ?(173) | | |

TABLE 3 *continued*

| | Garcilaso de la Vega | Elvas | Biedma | Ranjel |
|---|---|---|---|---|
| NUMSKULL | | | | |
| | | Muster (12f) | | |
| | | Porcallo's slaves (17) | | |
| 1 | Two ships collided | | | |
| 5 | Ship struck rock at Santiago | | | |
| 6 | Fight between Spanish and French | | | |
| 8 | Añasco cast away on island | | | |
| 34 | Jokes about maize | | | |
| 38 | Soldier discarded pearls | | | |
| 55 | Soldier lived, teased | | | |
| | | Woman burned (96) | | |
| 67 | Spaniard deserted for woman | Δ(153) | | Δ(165) |
| 75 | Spanish healer healed self | | | |
| 78 | Spanish killed an Indian | Δ(132) | | |
| 81 | Añasco threw chart overboard | | | |
| 82 | Xaramillo took in 18 | | | |
| INDIAN PROWESS | | | | |
| 19 | Indians tread water | Δ (42f) | | Δ (75) |
| 22 | Apalachee defended self | | | |
| 23 | Apalachee defended self | | | |
| 24 | Indian died well | | | |
| 25 | Indians addled soldier | | | |
| 26 | Indians took Spaniard | | | |
| 27 | Indian killed horse | | | |
| 28 | Indian held off seven | | | (cf. 80) |
| 29 | Indian killed two horses | Δ (48f) | | |
| 30 | Indian killed two men, one horse | | | |
| 31 | Indians fought chivalrously | | | |
| 42 | Gallegos slashed Indian | Δ(85) | Δ(244) | Δ(124) |
| 43 | Gallegos killed son | | | |
| 49 | Indian killed self | | Δ(245) | Δ?(127) |
| 56 | Horses died of arrows in hearts | | | |
| 57 | Indians had 3 cords | | | |
| 62 | Women held soldier by genitals | | | Δ?(78) |
| 63 | Indian defeated Spaniard with staff | | | Δ?(126) |
| 64 | Indians defeated Spaniard with staff | | | |
| 65 | Indian showed skill with ax | | | |
| 66 | Tula boy shows warrior skill | | | |
| 72 | Indian killed two women by accident | | | |
| 74 | Warriors challenged Spanish | | | |
| 76 | Indian killed two horses | | | |
| 80 | Indian/final shout | | | |
| INDIAN CUSTOMS | | | | |
| 33 | Indian punished by drinking water | | | |
| 36 | Indian killed self | | | |
| 35 | The Lady of Cofitachequi | Δ(62) | Δ(239) | |
| 37 | Temple of Cofitachequi | Δ(63) | (239) | Δ(100f) |
| 40 | Taskalusa a giant/horse too small | Δ(81) | Δ(242) | |
| 41 | Dancing women | | Δ(243) | |
| 61 | Indians debated ranking | Δ(116) | Δ(253) | Δ(143f) |
| 69 | Indians sneezed in universal way | | | |
| 71 | Indian joined Spanish | | | |

Another way in which we can examine the de Soto legends is to look at their themes, since legends usually reflect beliefs of the tellers, or at least concern discussion of them. The third chart is a reorganization of the legend list by category (table 3). Without the context of the telling of these legends it is not always possible to determine how they were intended, and thus how they should be categorized. Even so, the general categories seem sound, although any specific legend's location in the schema may be arguable.

The first in the list is the obvious one: the army of de Soto would have told many stories about de Soto. The general legend category one would expect is that of the hero, and Gonzalo Silvestre's stories do not disappoint. In fact, what is clear in *La Florida del Ynca* is that Silvestre either did not know any negative stories about de Soto or did not choose to tell them. Material which could easily be used for negative legendry, such as burning Indians to death or having them attacked by the dogs, is told matter-of-factly as part of the expedition narrative rather than as legendary highlights, a treatment which is matched by the other chroniclers. This bias, of course, could simply reflect the fact that there would be a cool reception in the Spanish literary market for attacks on the Adelantado himself, or that it was simply bad form to speak ill of the dead, but de Soto's complimentary treatment may equally well reflect the honest opinion of Silvestre, who was, after all, a conquistador. Most of the stories are of military exploits, just the sort of thing one would expect Silvestre and his friends to talk about: the ingenuity of de Soto in launching a counterattack even before the Indians can attack (#18), the Indian who struck de Soto in the face (#21), the time de Soto was wounded but sat on his horse throughout the battle (#46), the time de Soto lost his saddle and took a tumble, a major embarrassment for a *caballero* (#52), and his death, marked by a romantic double burial (#70). Garcilaso is the only source for de Soto's wound (#46) and for the fascinating prologue about Ponce de León's attempt to defraud de Soto financially (#9), but both seem plausible, if only because both would have been too widely known for Garcilaso to have risked contradiction by publishing them if they were not true (or believed to have been true). It may be significant that there are not more stories about de Soto, for one of the characteristics of Garcilaso is the distant view of de Soto himself, who remains throughout a two-dimensional character.

As might be expected, the general category of marvelous events is well filled. Even in the present day, human beings like to tell stories about occurrences which challenge normal beliefs or push against the accepted limits of possibility. The range of legend topics is broad, from the simple observation of the life and death of swine (#54, #73) and dogs (#3, #16, #17) to divine miracles (e.g., #59). As already discussed, the entire story of Juan Ortiz is a marvel, and its components stress the marvelous, from the miraculous reprieve by the Indian woman to the lucky spear cast to the recognition scene. Among the topics which could be expected to lead quickly from memorate to legend on the expedition is the death of soldiers, and they are well represented here. Carmona was struck by the tale of two soldiers who died needlessly by fighting on board ship and falling overboard, and with the story of the *hidalgo* who accidentally got pushed overboard (#2, #4). Silvestre continued the theme with the soldier who accidentally speared a comrade (#39) and the soldier who fell into the river and was drowned (#60). The drownings probably reflected the concern of all soldiers of that day, who were well aware that the weight of their armor could easily mean death in the water, a concern which was strongly highlighted in the story of the deaths of so many of their comrades at the very end of the expedition, when a foolish Spaniard attacked the Indian armada of small boats on the Mississippi (#79). The deaths of de Soto's kin are told probably more because of their relation to him than because of anything inherent in the stories (#45, #48), but that is not true of two Spaniards who died with no apparent reason. It is intriguing that Silvestre preserved the rationale for their deaths which apparently emerged in the process of legend formation during the expedition: one was a coward, so his unexplained death was interpreted as a failure of nerve (#50), while the other was known as a heroic knight, so his virtually identical death was judged to be a result of excessive zeal (#51). What is worthy of note is the small number of deaths which are reported, both as legends and as simple recording, because the enormous number of deaths (more than three hundred, regardless of whose figures are used) should have made it possible to include many more stories than appear in any of the chronicles.

The religious stories, as might be expected, provide some high points of the sense of the marvelous in the legend collection. The more mundane of the stories deal with the life of the religious on the expedition—the bishop who almost drowned (#7), the wounding and retreat of Fr. Gallegos (#44), and the friar who saved the day in the surprise attack by the Chicasa (#53). These legends are less marvelous than they are simply giving recognition to the participation of the religious in the dangers of the expedition, a theme which would have appealed to The Inca, who became a priest in the latter years of his life. The marvels include the saving of Juan Ortiz by his "pious ejaculation" at the moment of danger (#14), the arrow which split Nuño de Tovar's lance, transforming it into a cross (#47), and the crosses already adopted by Indians who had met Cabeza de Vaca (#68). The major miracles, however, deal with rain. There is the Old Testament–like downpour which God sent just in time to wet their bowstrings and stop a second and final attack by the Chicasa (#58), and there is the challenge of the pagan Casqui for the Christian God to demonstrate his power by sending rain to the parched region (#59). De Soto raised a cross on the mound at Casqui, and the natives participated in the adoration of the cross, which was then followed by heavy rains. This legend caught the fancy of more than Garcilaso, since all of the chroniclers mention the incident in varying ways. This was not an unusual theme for the time, by the way. Almost the identical legend was told twice about one of de Soto's successors as Adelantado of La Florida, Pedro Menéndez de Avilés. Both occasions were in 1566, one in Guale and one among the Timucua, and the point is the same, a miraculous vindication of the power of God in winning converts to the True Faith. (J. G. Johnson 1924:293f.).

In an age in which Europeans were surrounded by the legends of the saints, such stories are hardly even to be wondered at. In fact, it is a reasonable judgment that Garcilaso has acted with some restraint in his incorporation of legends of the miraculous, a restraint not exercised by all historians of the day. Witness, for example, a related theme which is missing from the legendry of *La Florida del Ynca*—the divine retribution. Just thirteen years before the publication of Garcilaso's book, Ribadeneyra published his biography of the general of the Society of Jesus, Francisco de Borja. In it he told of the massacre of the Jesuits at Axacán (Virginia) in 1568. When the Powhatan attackers opened the mission's box of paraphernalia and looked upon the crucifix, they fell dead (DePuy 1920:68). Johnson (1924:297, 299) told two more similar legends drawn from Barcia's *Ensayo Cronológico.* In one, during the Guale Revolt of 1597 a dog touched the dead body of a priest and fell dead; in the other, the Spanish pilot of a ship carrying Jesuits from Florida cursed them for bringing bad luck, and on the return trip he and his ship went down at that very spot. Such stories were not unknown to Garcilaso, for he gratuitously included a European religious legend he learned from his Spanish uncle, a story of how a Protestant was defeated in the religious wars because of his sacrilegious treatment of a statue of the Virgin (#20).

Although not overtly religious, marvelous prophecies were a common theme of the legendry of that day as well as in modern times. Silvestre apparently was struck by the knowledge of the Indian woman who predicted that the Mississippi would flood that year, because it always did so every fourteen years and that was the fourteenth (#77). He also remembered that a knight who drowned had told them about a prediction by an astrologer who had said he would die by drowning (#60). That legend makes a fine companion piece to similar prophecies both in the *Naufrágios* of Cabeza de Vaca (Alvar Nuñez 1962) and the history of the Mexican conquest by Bernal Díaz del Castillo: "Botello, a necromancer, had warned of a tragic event four days prior to the 'Noche Triste' . . . Botello is killed during the escape from the city of Tenochtitlán; he tragically predicted his own death" (Bost 1983:10).

"Numskull" may not be the best label for the next group of legends, but it does catch up the idea of most of them—that they are stories which highlight stupid behavior which seemed amusing enough to remember and retell. Garcilaso alone of the chroniclers tells of the ineptitude of the sailors who took the army to La Florida, how two ships collided, and how one struck a rock, and how the Spanish and French got involved in an incredible marine altercation (#1, #5, #6). The stories which defamed the abilities of Añasco have already been mentioned, but there were also legends of a common soldier who discarded a fortune in pearls because he grew weary of carrying them. There was another about a Spaniard who deserted the army to live with an Indian woman (#8, #81, #38, #67). Silvestre even recalled his jokes to his starving comrades, in which he convinced them to think of their few grains of maize as pastries (#34). One of the more interesting numskull legends is about the Spaniards' folk healer who stopped his medical aid for much of the journey because he lost his special ingredients; he resumed shamefacedly when he discovered that any of the local materials would do as well (#75).

The longest category on the list deals with the prowess of the Indians, and its nature is no surprise, given Garcilaso's strong personal concern to grant to the New World natives the respect they were so often denied by Europeans. The legends deal primarily with the military prowess of the Indians—their skill with the bow and arrow, their courage, their willingness to die well, their military sagacity, and their non-equestrian chivalry. Garcilaso makes it quite clear that the de Soto expedition should bear witness to the basic equality of Spaniard and Indian in personal qualities; the disastrous difference lay in the technology of the former. Since this theme is repeated in 30 percent of the total legend content, even the casual reader of *La Florida del Ynca* is struck by Garcilaso's insistence on the "noble savage." The very number of the legends in this category and the repetitious nature of some of the stories—far beyond anything included in the other chroniclers—make this group of legends the best candidate for the direct authorship of Garcilaso. While some of the details, such as the use of staffs as weapons against the horses by the Tula, seem to bear the mark of Silvestre, it is not implausible that Garcilaso coaxed these legends out of Silvestre's memory and augmented them with legends of his own creation.

It is the final category, "Indian Customs," which is of importance for the anthropological students of the de Soto journey, for these stories are clues to social structure of the native Americans. Some are obviously important, such as the matrilineal structure of Cofitachequi, producing a woman chieftain and a niece who seems to be the heir apparent, and the details of the temple at Cofitachequi shed some light on burial practices (#35, #37). The basic facts of these legends are attested to by the other chroniclers, but the details differ from one to the other. So, too, all are agreed that Taskalusa was a giant of a man, and there were dancing women at Mabila (#40, #41). In an extraordinary legend from Arkansas, two rival chiefs debated their hereditary ranking, seeking to determine who had primacy, and thereby hinting at patrilineality (#61). That is a story which would quickly be rejected as a fantasy of Garcilaso, were it not also found in the other chroniclers. More problematic are Garcilaso's stories of how an Indian was punished by drinking massive amounts of water and of the "noble" who killed himself at Cofitachequi, apparently because he was being forced by the Spanish to betray an express command of his woman chief (#33, #36). Even though they are found only in Garcilaso, however, there is no basis for automatic rejection, especially since they seem less fantastic than some which are presented by all the chroniclers.

## CONCLUSIONS

These lists bear out what those who interview people for their memories are well aware of—that most of us remember our past in story form, and that the closer stories are to tellable legends, the more memorable they are. These legends in Garcilaso are what we would expect if Garcilaso's claim to be recording the memories of an old soldier is true. These legends in Garcilaso's text suggest another important insight, however. Garcilaso seems to have deliberately collected such legendary materials and incorporated them quite prominently in the full narrative of the journey. The reason is not hard to divine; if we delete all these legend narratives from his account, we are left with a bare-bones story not significantly different from Elvas and Ranjel in tone, although the details may vary. It is the legend corpus, in fact, which gives Garcilaso's work the novelistic quality which has led some scholars to conclude that *La Florida del Ynca* is a fictional work by a literary scholar. While the view of the de Soto legends as recorded oral traditional material does not gainsay that, it does argue that the category of folklore rather than literature is a more reasonable way to characterize this work.

If we follow this line of thought, then the majority of the legends may be attributed to Gonzalo Silvestre, with the exception of ones noted otherwise by Garcilaso and those about Indian nobility which might well have sprung from the mind of Garcilaso or from Silvestre under the urging of Garcilaso. What, then, can be said about the other material, which comprises the major portion of the book? It is here that Garcilaso's claim to be the amanuensis for another may be most doubted, for this material is not in the memorable form of stories, and it contains most of the details, structure, and chronology which is most needed by researchers. Even the friendliest critic of Garcilaso, it seems, must posit the existence of other sources for this information. I believe, but without evidence, that Garcilaso has functioned as an oral historian in this work—that he interviewed many of the survivors, particularly those he could locate in Spain, that he used the written sources, both those he named and Elvas, and that he then labored to re-create the chronology and details of the expedition as the matrix into which he could incorporate the legendary material of Silvestre and the others. Even this most sanguine of interpretations, however, leaves the hard data in question, for it merely broadens the oral sources for Garcilaso's narrative without strengthening its trustworthiness. Indeed, many oral historians and folklorists would argue that the detailed information, particularly statistical information, is precisely the sort of stuff that is poorly remembered, if at all, and is therefore the least trustworthy in a work of oral history and legend. Not so easily dismissed, however, are the memorates and legends told by the survivors of the de Soto journey, for they may be—if not acceptable historical documentation for the modern academician—the only way the details of the historic events were actually preserved by the sixteenth-century adventurers.

# Notes

1. This paper has benefited greatly from the comments of colleagues who heard or read earlier versions of it. My thanks especially to Charles Hudson, Marvin Smith, V. J. Knight, Jr., Patricia Galloway, John Dahlquist, and Barbara Allen.

2. I am indebted to V. J. Knight, Jr., for information on the "Cañete fragment" and the Argote document, neither of which has yet been published.

3. For a critical view of the historicity of this work, see Lewis (1982).

4. For studies on folklore in relation to oral history, see Montell (1970); Allen and Montell (1981); and Dorson (1971).

# Indians and Spaniards in Arkansas: Symbolic Action in the Sixteenth Century

George Sabo III

## PRELIMINARIES

The epic journey of Hernando de Soto is perhaps the most well-known example of early Spanish explorations in southeastern North America. It was not the first attempt by Spaniards to explore this continent in search of prosperous Indian civilizations, but it was the largest by far of several sixteenth-century expeditions that penetrated the interior from Atlantic and Gulf coast landfalls. That de Soto died in this attempt to add to his already considerable wealth and fame added further notoriety to an undertaking already brimming with numerous tales of adventure and tragedy.

It is hardly surprising, therefore, that the story of de Soto's journey looms as large as it does in our modern retelling of European exploits in North America. Yet, for all that has been said about de Soto's expedition, scholarly attention has centered on surprisingly few of its aspects. Beginning with the investigations of the late seventeenth- to early eighteenth-century French mapmaker Guillaume de L'isle and continuing to the present, a major concern has been to trace the route that de Soto followed on his fateful trek (e.g., Swanton 1939). As Charles Hudson has pointed out, accurate reconstruction of the route itself is an important step toward a larger goal of understanding the social geography of sixteenth-century native North America, which could serve in turn as a valuable benchmark for studies of prehistoric cultural evolution as well as for studies of post-contact cultural change among societies indigenous to the region (Hudson, Smith, and DePratter 1984; Hudson 1987). Another area of scholarly interest, represented most often in anthropological studies, concerns the effects of de Soto's army on the indigenous populations of the sixteenth century Southeast (e.g., M. T. Smith 1987). The effects of Old World diseases upon Indian populations and the consequences of Indian participation in European economic institutions, especially trade in deer skins and slaves, have been the major issues dealt with here.

In contrast to these subjects, concerning which an extensive list of titles could be cited, only a few studies have examined the Indians' role in the events of the contact era (see Hudson 1988), and it is accurate to say that we still very poorly understand the significance of Indian cultural influences in the early development of Euroamerican institutions in colonial North America (Axtell 1982).

The purpose of this chapter is to examine the extent to which Southeastern Indian cultural themes are represented in European accounts of the de Soto expedition. The four narrative accounts will be examined in an effort first to determine the nature of indigenous participation in events that typify the sixteenth-century conjunction of Spanish and Southeastern Indian cultural systems. Second, major themes will be identified that emerge in the cross-cultural discourse that is preserved, however imperfectly, in the various accounts of de Soto's expedition. By this means, I hope to determine how Spaniards and Southeastern Indians perceived each other and to explore how these perceptions were symbolized in the actions each group took in response to the other.

For this study, I have used the English translation of the Ranjel and Biedma narratives in Bourne (1904, 2), Robertson's (1933) translation of Elvas, and the widely available translation by the Varners of Garcilaso de la Vega (1951). A number of problems confront any attempt to use these accounts to reconstruct indigenous cultural systems and to assess their impact on sixteenth-century Spanish actions and perceptions. First, it is often very difficult to know exactly where de Soto was when an encounter with a particular Indian group took place. The names attributed to those Indians often are not mentioned in later European accounts, making it difficult to correlate those groups with subsequently identified tribes. Second, ethnohistorical information in these accounts is both limited in extent and heavily inflected with European cultural biases. Finally, the literary genres represented by these accounts introduced yet additional colorations to observations concerning Indians (Auerbach 1957). In sum, it is foolish to use these accounts without a detailed critical analysis. Yet, despite these problems, I suggest that these accounts can, under appropriate study, provide extremely valuable information about the sixteenth century Indians and the consequences of their encounters with the Spaniards.

This analysis is based on several premises. First, I follow Paul Ricoeur's (1971) suggestion that human actions (especially ritualized encounters) can be "read," much like a written text, because they encode meaningful information concerning the actors' views of a situation in which the action takes place. Human actions are symbolic, and what actions symbolically express are the assumptions and motivations the actors bring to a particular situation.

A second premise derives from the work of Marshall Sahlins (1985), who observes that in contact situations the assumptions one group holds concerning another group are based on culturally derived systems of classification. These moreover are subject to change as an inevitable result of experiences gained during the process of interaction. Thus it may be argued that the recorded actions of de Soto and his men reflect symbolically the attitudes concerning Indians that the Spaniards brought with them to the Southeast, many of which were transformed as a result of their encounters with Indians during the course of their expedition. Analysis of the recorded experiences of the Spaniards should, therefore, provide at least some information on the impact of Indian beliefs and practices on Spanish perceptions.

A third point, made by James A. Boon (1982:173), is that European accounts of encounters with exotic cultural "others" do not simply convey received impressions of the contact experience, but rather they articulate a "web of meanings—simultaneously domestic and exotic, we/they" that is built up from the European's "reading" of native "texts" (whether written, spoken, performed, or otherwise represented) that contain perceived similitudes to themes prominent in the cultural milieu of the European chroniclers. In short, European accounts of contacts with indigenous populations inscribe a cross-cultural (or two-way) discourse from which themes epitomizing the conjuncture can be discerned. In a somewhat related vein, Roland Barthes (1977:124) has written about narrative texts in general that:

> The 'reality' of a sequence lies not in the 'natural' succession of the actions composing it but in the logic there exposed. . . . Narrative does not show, does not imitate; the passion which may excite us in reading . . . is not that of a 'vision.' . . . Rather it is that of meaning, that of a higher order of relation which has its emotions, its hopes, its dangers, its triumphs.

In summary, it is possible to suggest that many of the actions performed in the context of encounters between de Soto and Southeastern Indians brought to the surface of a cross-cultural discourse the categories and themes each group used to convey intended meanings that concerned specific events. Since these "meaningful actions" symbolized elements of both Spanish and Native-American cultural systems, it should be possible to identify through critical analysis these Indian cultural themes that significantly influenced these Spanish perceptions of the contact situation.

To identify native cultural themes, it is necessary to examine carefully selected examples of interaction that reflect what Sahlins has referred to as "structures of the conjuncture," or the matrix of cultural categories expressed in the actions of participants in intercultural encounters (Sahlins 1985:xiv). The strategy I employ is to examine key passages of the narratives that describe, in detail, action-packed events in which Indians were prominently involved and that also represent crucial turning points in the fate of the Spaniards. It is important to note that I am not primarily concerned with the issue of whether the events identified actually took place; rather, I am interested specifically in the telling—that is, in the images the Spaniards set about to convey to a reading audience. Real or imaginary, these stories condense, encapsulate, and dramatize longer-term historical and cultural processes, and so they may be regarded as "epitomizing events" (Fogelson 1989:143).

Since this analysis entails a rather detailed consideration of specific epitomizing events, for the sake of brevity I shall circumscribe the focus of this paper to the portion of the expedition that follows de Soto's crossing of the Mississippi River, and, furthermore, I shall center my analysis on three key sets of events that transpired, respectively, in the native provinces of Casqui/Pacaha, at Guachoya, and at Naguatex. This strategy is intended in part to draw attention to the Indians then living in the present states of Arkansas and Texas, who until recently have been largely ignored in scholarly works treating sixteenth-century North America. A second consideration is that this focus will permit comparison of the interactions of Spaniards with two distinctive sixteenth-century Indian cultural systems: the central Mississippi Valley polities represented by the provinces of Casqui, Pacaha, and Guachoya, on the one hand, and the Red River Caddoan polities represented in the events that took place at Naguatex on the other.[1]

## SIXTEENTH-CENTURY SPANISH AND INDIAN CULTURAL PERSPECTIVES

Interpreting the cultural meaning of human actions, whether enacted in a ritual or in some other context, is difficult even under the most favorable circumstances of direct observation. The veracity of such interpretations can only be as firm as the ground upon which they are made, and this is a particularly important point to recognize when interpretation of the meaning of actions observed in the historical record is being attempted. In all cases, interpretive frameworks must consist minimally of an understanding of the cultural rules, assumptions, and organizing principles that apply to the case at hand, along with some grasp of the sociocultural context of the actions under consideration. In contact situations, it is also necessary to recognize that each group brings to the encounter independent sets of rules, assumptions, and expectations, and each group may define in somewhat different terms the nature of the circumstance that brings them together. Thus, we have a conjunction of elements representing distinctive cultural systems—this is the essence of Sahlins' concept of "structures of the conjuncture."

In *New Worlds for Old,* William Brandon (1986:ix) draws the following broad contrast between European and Native-American cultural systems:

> This study suggests that the one greatest dividing difference fell in the attitude toward property, the usual Old World tendencies summed up in the word *dominium,* the New World's in the word *communitas;* that these two differing tendencies led on the one hand to preoccupation with business, competition, adversarialism, authoritarianism, and the ultimate act of dominium, total war—on the other hand to preoccupation with group relationships, lack of interest in the acquisition of property, and frequently to a lack of central authority resulting in a seeming masterlessness.

The Old World idea of property, according to Brandon, is well expressed by the Latin *dominium,* from *dominus*: "one who has subdued," thus signifying "master, possessor, lord, proprietor, owner." The sense of this notion is best conveyed in the concept of "absolute ownership," which applied legalistically refers to the right of absolute property ownership; that is, ownership by one implying lack or loss of ownership by another—if necessary, even through the use of force. Property rights are therefore based on an assumption of the necessity of adversarial relations between competing parties. By contrast, the Latin *communitas* expresses a sense of "the ruling idea of community, of masterless cooperation requiring each [individual] to be as free as the other: the idea of liberty for others as well as for one's self [as] a basic philosophy for living." It was this philosophy, Brandon (1986:121–22) suggested, that drove the reciprocating social machinery common to Native-American societies.

Brandon may have overstated the concept of masterlessness as applied to Native-American cultures, especially those found in southeastern North America. Our understanding of the organization of many Southeastern societies acknowledges the existence of a hierarchical social structure in which institutions of authority are fairly well developed. Indeed, in some societies, such as the Natchez (de Josselin de Jong 1930) and the Hasinai (Griffith 1954; Bolton 1987), some elite leaders wielded a supreme power of life or death over their subjects. Moreover, the political subjugation of some native polities by other, more powerful, ones has also been identified for the sixteenth-century Southeast (Hudson et al. 1985), and frequent adversarial relations between these polities, including chronic warfare, is a well-known aspect of the cultural history of this region. A major point of distinction between European and Native-American cultural systems, however, does seem to lie in the notion of property ownership and its relation to adversarialism. In lacking a concept of absolute property ownership, interaction among Southeastern Indian societies did not, indeed could not, carry with it the assumption that relations (political, economic, or otherwise) must necessarily be adversarial, nor did adversarialism itself carry the implication of a necessary deprivation of the adversary's basically egalitarian status. Despite whatever hostilities might erupt between groups, over the long run these hostilities did not alter the basic status of equivalence and autonomy that most neighboring Indian polities had in relation to one another.

The basic differences in cultural organization implied by the *dominium/communitas* dichotomy can be examined further by considering several important characteristics of Spanish cognitive frameworks employed to understand the New World. As the historian J. H. Elliott (1970:41) has suggested, early modern Europeans maintained a dual classification of mankind born of Christian and Classical Greek heritages. In this classification, the peoples of the world were categorized according to their religious affiliations as well as by their degree of civility (Elliott 1970:41). The resulting dichotomies were: Spanish Catholics (representing the one true faith) versus heathens or infidels on the one hand, and civilized Spaniards versus uncivilized savages or barbarians on the other. This classification, moreover, referred not just to diametrically opposed categories but to points along a continuum, for in early modern European thinking, savages and barbarians were generally considered to represent variants of the civilized state: either antecedent, representing stages through which all societies passed on their way up to civilization, or degenerate, representing lower stages to which formerly civilized peoples had fallen. Elliott (1970:43) added that "[the] Christian tradition defined man in terms of his receptivity to divine grace; [while] the classical tradition defined him in terms of his nationality." Native Americans under these criteria were generally regarded by Europeans as humans capable of receiving divine grace and being elevated to civility. Therefore, a twofold project motivated Spanish exploration of the New World: 1) the acquisition of wealth (that is, the attainment of absolute ownership of property), and 2) the extension of Catholicism into the New World through conversion of the indigenous peoples (thereby attaining absolute ownership on both material and spiritual levels, emphasizing yet another categorization underlying early modern European attitudes and perceptions). In summary, "For all their [individual] differences [Spaniards] were the products of a society united by certain strongly defined attitudes—Christian in its values, legalistic in its outlook, corporate and hierarchical in its organization" (Elliott 1973:106–07).

Southeastern Indians also speculated about the humanity of the Europeans, especially vis-à-vis the world as defined by their own systems of belief. Europeans were real enough in a corporeal sense, but whence had they come? The obvious "other worldly" origin of the Europeans, beyond the known spatial boundaries of Native-American experience, plus their novel and demonstrably powerful technological capabilities, justified categorizing these individuals, at least initially, with the rest of the "other worldly" beings populating the Native-American cosmos—namely, supernaturals whose powerful capabilities gave force to the elements of nature and whose actions restored balance to the organization of relationships among all living beings inhabiting the reality of existence (Helms 1987). Furthermore, in Southeastern Indian belief, supernatural forces sustained life and well-being in the context of webs of reciprocal relations binding humans, other earthly beings (animals, plants, certain weather conditions, etc.), and supernaturals into one large system of ongoing interactions. An important feature of this system was the negotiability and manipulability of these relations along a continuum from complementary reciprocity to oppositional retribution (which, incidentally, provided the motivation for much of the adversarialism witnessed among Southeastern polities). Europeans were incorporated in these systems of relationships for several reasons, one of which was to advance native interests through manipulation of the capabilities and powers these foreigners possessed. Europeans typically were integrated within native systems through various social mechanisms that served to create fictive or ancillary kinship relations, since it was indeed the obligations stemming from kinship relationships that cemented the ties Indians recognized within and between their own communities.

This latter point requires amplification. Southeastern Indian societies were organized along lines of kinship and reciprocity in significantly different ways than were European societies at the time of contact. Kinship and marriage was a "metainstitution," in the sense that kinship principles underpinned the organization of economics, politics, religion, and so forth (Boon 1982:229). The most fundamental notion of life in the Southeast was based on the concept of conjunction between universal male and female life forces, creating a fundamental reciprocal unit that served as a building block for the elaboration of other categories of social relationships. Thus, the categories and principles that structured the institution of kinship also underpinned the organization of economic systems, political systems, and religious beliefs, including ideas about the nature of relations between humans and supernaturals and between Indians and those whom they identified as cultural others (see Schneider 1972).

Encounters between members of Hernando de Soto's expedition and the native inhabitants of the Southeast thus took place at the intersection of two fundamentally different cultural perspectives. The basic principles underpinning these two cultural systems—hierarchy, Catholicism, and materialism for the Spaniards and hierarchy, reciprocity, and kinship for the Indians—provided the key elements of a sixteenth-century "structure of the conjuncture." By examining the narrative accounts describing these encounters, it should be possible to explore the symbolic imagery and transformations that arose as a product of interaction within this structural framework.

## SYMBOLIC ACTIONS: DE SOTO WEST OF THE MISSISSIPPI

In the summer of 1541, de Soto moved his camp from Quizquiz (located somewhere in present-day northeastern Mississippi) to a spot along the Mississippi River just across from present-day Arkansas. At this location, the first encounter with Indians from the opposite side of the river took place. According to Elvas:

> Immediately the Indians came down the river, and told the governor that they were vassals of a great lord called Aquixo, who was lord of many towns and people on the other side of the river. (Robertson 1933:159)

In this account, the first description of Indians from Arkansas was described using categories of social hierarchy (vassals and lords) familiar to sixteenth-century Spaniards. Elvas employed a model of Spanish feudal society, where vassals were subservient to property-owning lords, to portray Indian emissaries sent by their cacique (leader) to greet the Spaniards. In a similar fashion, Garcilaso in describing this meeting employed the term *curaca* to designate the Indian leader Aquixo. This term is derived from a Quechua word for the leader of an Incan kin group that holds certain property rights for the lineage. In both accounts, therefore, the Spaniards attributed to Indian social organization their own notion that authority structures must necessarily emanate from a basis of property ownership.

Garcilaso also interjected a putatively Indian point of view into his version of this encounter. We pick up his narrative as the emissaries sent by Aquixo arrive in de Soto's camp.

> Stationing themselves before him . . . they turned their faces to the east and with a profound reverence made a bow to the sun; then turning to the west, they made a second but lesser bow to the moon; and finally addressing themselves to the Governor himself, they made a third and even less pretentious gesture. And everyone present took note of the degree of respect by the manner in which it was expressed. (Garcilaso 1951:428)

Here, the Indians were portrayed as responding to the Spaniards from the perspective of their own cosmology, deferring to de Soto with something less than the reverence accorded the Sun and the Moon. The Indians next were described attempting to establish relations with the Spaniards according to indigenous social rules. Upon learning that the Spaniards, too, were led by an elite leader, Aquixo himself visited de Soto, presenting the governor a gift of fish and plum loaves. This act may be interpreted as an attempt to create an alliance between the two groups that would be based on a reciprocal relationship between the two leaders, a type of intergroup alliance often observed in hierarchically organized societies (Sahlins 1983). However, de Soto's actions after accepting Aquixo's gift violated the latter's expectations based on indigenous protocols of gift-giving.

> . . . upon seeing that the governor and his men were on guard, [the Indians] began to withdraw from the land. With loud cries, the crossbowmen who were ready, shot at them and struck five or six. They withdrew in splendid order; no one abandoned his paddle even though the one near him fell. Flaunting themselves, they retired. (Robertson 1933:161)

The Aquixo Indians, after this encounter, chose to avoid further direct interaction with de Soto, but commenced to harass the Spaniards both before and after their crossing of the Mississippi River. As a result of his violent rejection of Aquixo's offer to join in a mutually beneficial alliance, the Indians' perception of de Soto shifted from viewing him as a supernatural (albeit one less powerful than the Sun and the Moon) to relegating him to the status of a common human enemy. As will become apparent, this categorical shift was but a hint of more far-reaching changes in Indian perceptions that would be incorporated into Spanish accounts.

A few days after they crossed the great river, de Soto led his men into the province of Casqui. As the Spaniards approached the main village after plundering several of the bordering settlements, de Soto sent word to the cacique that he came "for the purpose of procuring . . . friendship and of considering him as a brother" (Robertson 1933:167). Casqui was then said to have replied that he would welcome de Soto and receive him with special pleasure. As the Spaniards drew near the village, Casqui sent out a gift of fish and hides and then, accompanied by many Indians, met the Spaniards on the road a half league from the village. According to Biedma, Casqui claimed that he had heard of the Spaniards for a long time, and "that he knew we were men from heaven, whom their arrows could not harm; wherefore, he desired to have no strife, and wished only to serve us" (Bourne 1904, 2:26). Elvas incorporated into his account a more lengthy welcoming speech attributed to Casqui, in which the Indian leader first admonished de Soto for entering his lands and killing and taking captives, but then pledged to serve the Spaniards in whatever manner de Soto wished (Robertson 1933:167–69). This part of the narrative illustrates use of a literary device frequently employed by sixteenth-century chroniclers that praises native fortitude and nobility in order to underscore the innocence of the so-called savages against patently savage acts perpetrated by the supposedly civilized Spaniards (Elliott 1970:26). Speaking through a native voice, the writer inscribes apologetics considered necessary in order to maintain a history of positive accomplishments that accrue upon a society through the achievements of its noble and glorious sons. The occurrence of this device in the Elvas account (here and elsewhere, such as in Elvas' portrayal of de Soto's attack on Anilco mentioned below) gives us pause to wonder who the writer of this account actually was and what motives shaped this particular narrative.

Casqui's actions portray a willingness on his part to negotiate an alliance with de Soto based on the familiar rule of reciprocity, or mutual obligation. However, the two societies were held apart, literally and symbolically, when de Soto decided to set up his camp in an open field some distance from the Indian village. The interaction between the two groups permits us to trace the route this discourse took across the boundaries of dissimilar cultural systems. Now some Indians debilitated by blindness were brought before the de Soto, who claimed to be the "son of the Sun." The Elvas account continues:

> . . . since he [de Soto] was the son of the sun and a great lord, he [Casqui] begged him to do him the favor of giving health to those blind Indians. The blind men immediately arose and with great earnestness begged this of the governor. He replied saying that in the lofty heaven was He who had power to give then health and everything they might ask of Him; whose servant he [de Soto] was. . . . (Robertson 1933:169–70)

An important symbolic element in this exchange is the attribution of de Soto's powerful capabilities to a heavenly source of power, a feature prominent also in the native cosmology. De Soto, adhering to the tenets of Catholicism, represented himself as merely a humble servant of the infinitely more powerful Christian God. This admission did not lessen the claim to power de Soto knew he was making—his status as the "servant" of the Christian God would be congruent with the identity he also claimed as son of the Sun, the earthly representative of the Indians' primary source of life and well-being. A fascinating account of how de Soto's claim to this status might have been profoundly demonstrated in practical action is contained in the following story. The native crops were in desperate need of water because of a prolonged drought, Casqui asked de Soto to request of his God the favor of sending rain. Below is Garcilaso's colorful and no doubt greatly exaggerated version of what then happened, giving the reader a sense of Garcilaso's literary style.

> To these words, the General responded that even though he and his entire army were but sinners, they would pray to God Our Lord, as the Father of mercy, to grant them this grace. Then in the presence of the Cacique, he ordered Maestro Francisco . . . to fashion a cross from the highest and thickest pine to be found in the whole of that region . . . This cross was placed at the summit of a lofty mound . . . overlooking the river . . .
>
> Two days were spent in completing and planting the cross, and then on the third day a solemn procession was ordained. The Governor participated in this ceremony along with his captains and people of most consequence. . . . The cacique walked at the Governor's side and many of his nobles were scattered among the Spaniards. In front and off to themselves was a chorus of priests, clerics, and friars, who sang the litanies while the soldiers made the responses. So it was that more than a thousand persons, including both Christians and infidels, proceeded a goodly distance to the site of the cross. Here in front of that symbol, all sank to their knees while two or three of the prayers were said. When they had arisen, the priests advanced two by two and, kneeling in adoration, kissed the cross. They in turn were followed by the Governor and the Cacique, and the latter, having come for the purpose and of his own accord, emulated his companion in all that he saw him do, even kissing the cross. Next came the rest of the Spaniards and finally the Indians, who also imitated the Christians in each of their acts of reverence.
>
> Fifteen or twenty thousand human beings of both sexes and all ages had assembled on the opposite bank of the river where with arms outstretched and hands uplifted they stood watching the Christians. . . . Thus on both sides of the river all of this ceremony and ostentation was being rendered for the purpose of adoring the cross. . . . When all had worshiped in the manner we have described, they returned as they had come, observing the same order of procession. . . . Only after four long hours was the ceremony of that day concluded.
>
> Now God in His mercy desired to reveal to these pagans that he heeds those of his people who truly call upon him; for at midnight of the same day, a heavy rain began to

> fall and it did not cease for two more days. This circumstance afforded the Indians much happiness, so the Curaca and his cavaliers organized a procession such as they had seen formed to worship the cross, and in this manner went forth to thank the Governor for the great favor they had received through his intercession. (Garcilaso 1951:432–33)

As noted above, Garcilaso's rendering of this event is surely exaggerated, but what spectacular images it creates! The main act by the Spaniards of setting a cross on the Indians' temple mound and the subsequent rainstorm was, however, repeated in the other three accounts. Biedma further reported that the Indians even encircled the cross with a fence of cane stalks, perhaps in order to delineate an area of sacred space around this newly emplanted icon of the extraordinary powers to which de Soto evidently had access. In any case, through this quirk of fate de Soto made two important statements in the context of a grandly symbolic public event. First, he validated the efficacy of his ability to manipulate supernatural powers and to bring them favorably to bear upon his own endeavors (and, by extension, upon those of his allies/kinsmen). In other words, he demonstrated that he did indeed merit the status of the "son of the Sun." Second, he responded reciprocally to Casqui's acts of hospitality in permitting the Spaniards to reside at the village and to provision themselves from Casqui's stores.

That Casqui perhaps had ulterior motives in cooperating with the Spaniards is suggested in subsequent events when de Soto decided to push on to Pacaha, a large province to the north where the Spaniards hoped to resume their quest for discovery of riches. Casqui offered personally to serve as guide, and he supplied warriors and servants to assist de Soto's army. Casqui's men even erected a bridge across a deep channel that provided the Spaniards access to Pacaha's village. Important here is the indication in all four accounts that Casqui and Pacaha were leaders of rival polities. Pacaha controlled a more extensive territory and had a larger number of warriors at his call than did Casqui. Casqui, evidently, had suffered many losses to Pacaha while inflicting comparatively few acts of retribution. It thus appears that Casqui's motive in aiding the Spaniards was in fact to gain revenge upon Pacaha. Convinced of the powerful capabilities of de Soto, Casqui hoped to bring these demonstrably "other worldly" powers to the assistance of his own objective of taking vengeance on Pacaha.

As the combined force of Spaniards and Casqui Indians approached the main village of Pacaha, the latter cacique led a number of his people into hiding on a nearby island. De Soto set about taking captives and plunder, as was his wont, and the Casqui were permitted a share of the booty. Garcilaso provided the following account of the manner in which the Casqui defamed their enemy.

> . . . the Casquins moved on to the temple in the large public plaza, which is the burial place of all who had ever ruled that land . . . [Realizing] how much Pacaha . . . would resent their daring to enter and desecrate this place, they not only proceeded within but committed every infamy and affront they could. Sacking it of all ornaments and riches, they took the spoils and trophies which had been made from the losses of their own ancestors. Then they threw to the floor each of the wooden chests which served as sepulchers, and for their own satisfaction and vengeance as well as for an affront to their enemies, strewed upon the ground the very bones and bodies the chests enclosed.

> Afterward not content with having cast these remains to the ground, they trod upon them and kicked them with utter contempt and scorn. (Garcilaso 1951:438)

As always, Garcilaso's account of this event is considerably more embellished than the others. Even so, the enmities described between Casqui and Pacaha provide important clues concerning Spanish perceptions of Indian social organization and belief systems. For example, the acts of sacrilege committed by the Casqui upon the ancestral remains of the Pacaha are consistent with belief systems of many Southeastern Indian societies that possessed a social organization based on hereditary lineages. In these belief systems, the ties that a group maintains with its ancestors serve to transmit down through the lineage the sacred powers or "mana" that ancestor spirits acquired through heroic deeds performed in some former era (i.e., in "myth time"). These sacred powers, with which the living group attempts to augment its own endeavors, are accessible via rites in which participants (who usually are the contemporary leaders of the lineage, descendants of the mythic ancestors, and/or other ritual specialists) are transported out of the everyday temporal state of being into a sacred "time out of time" in which contact with the ancestors and transmission of ancestral powers takes place. If access to the ancestors were to be impeded or disrupted, through desecration of remains of the ancestors or of other ritual spaces or paraphernalia, then the effects upon the living community could be devastating and might include such consequences as loss of social identity, loss of community solidarity, and loss of social control. Thus, the acts of retribution attributed to the Casqui in the de Soto accounts may be indicative of the degree of animosity that existed between these two neighboring polities.

Another characteristic of these societies that may be inferred from the description of events at Pacaha is that kinship systems did indeed play a fundamental role in structuring relations between native groups as well as between the Indians and the Spaniards. As the preceding example shows, adversarial relations between Casqui and Pacaha were expressed in the idiom of kinship relations connecting members of living communities with their sacred ancestors. It is also at this metainstitutional level of kinship relations that both of the native leaders, Casqui and Pacaha, are portrayed as attempting to take advantage for their own rival purposes of de Soto's perceived superordinary capabilities. At one point during the Spaniards' pillaging of Pacaha's village, Casqui is said to have returned to his own village without de Soto's permission, evidently in order to oversee the safe transport of the Casqui's share of the booty. This enraged de Soto, who then convinced Pacaha to return to his village and join the Spaniards in an alliance against Casqui. When Casqui learned of this pact, he hastened back to Pacaha's village bearing gifts for de Soto along with an apology and an explanation for his actions. He lectured de Soto further that if the Spaniards laid waste to Casqui's lands, then de Soto would in effect be destroying his own people and his own property, because of the reciprocal relationship that existed between Casqui and de Soto.

De Soto consequently arranged an uneasy truce between Casqui and Pacaha, but the two Indian leaders continued to vie for his favor. For example, a scuffle broke out at one point when all three leaders sat down to a meal, and Casqui, who had enjoyed the longer association with the Spaniards, attempted to sit in the position of highest rank at de Soto's right hand. Pacaha, who claimed to represent a more ancient lineage than Casqui, refused to tolerate Casqui's presumptuous move. The shoving match that followed, by all accounts, much amused the Spanish soldiers. Later, the contest was resumed when Casqui offered de Soto one of his daughters, claiming that "his greatest wish was to unite his blood with that of so great a lord as [de Soto] was" (Robertson 1933:180). Pacaha, according to Elvas, then presented de Soto with two of his sisters, although Ranjel indicated that Pacaha gave one of his wives, one of his sisters, and another "woman of rank" (Bourne 1904, 2:144).

Casqui's presentation of his daughter and Pacaha's giving of his sisters would seemingly indicate a patrilineal system of descent and inheritance. On the other hand, if Pacaha offered his wife, then patrilineality would not be indicated. Nothing can be determined of Pacaha's possible offer of "another woman of rank" without further information on the relationship between this woman and Pacaha. The fact that the Spaniards themselves possessed a strongly patrilineal system of descent and inheritance, especially among the noble classes, raises the possibility that their perception of Indian descent systems may have been colored by their own practices.

After their stay in Pacaha, which lasted for roughly a month, de Soto returned with his army to the province of Casqui and then undertook an extended journey through other parts of Arkansas (according to Hudson's version of the route of travel). This portion of their journey took the Spaniards through a number of provinces and settlements along a route that looped through central, western, and southeastern Arkansas until, once again approaching the Mississippi River but now from the west, they decided to spend the winter of 1541–42 at a village called Autiamque. I wish to pass over this portion of the expedition, except to mention that during these months the Spaniards' situation became increasingly desperate due to loss of men, horses, and supplies both through attrition and through increasingly violent encounters with Indians, particularly with the Tula. The Spaniards' goals of conquest and attainment of glory and riches appeared to slip farther and farther from reach as it became increasingly difficult even to satisfy basic subsistence needs. Finally, at Autiamque, the interpreter Juan Ortiz died, making it now tremendously difficult for the Spaniards to gather strategic information from the Indians.

De Soto's only hope at this point was to return to the seacoast and send word back to Hispañola to obtain fresh supplies. So, in the spring of 1542, de Soto led his bedraggled company into the town of Guachoya, having passed through Anilco and having found both towns abandoned and stripped by their residents of food stores. Subsequently, however, the cacique of Guachoya returned to his village, bringing with him a considerable quantity of gifts. De Soto welcomed the cacique and questioned him concerning what knowledge he might have of the sea. The cacique replied that he had no such knowledge, but indicated that farther down the river there was a province called Quigualtam, whose cacique was "the greatest lord of the region" (Robertson 1933:216). De Soto sent several of his men to explore in that direction in the hope that they might find a route to the sea. A week later, the men returned and reported that during the entire time they had traveled not more than fourteen or fifteen leagues due to the many rivers, canebrakes, and woods that had hindered them. De Soto received this news with considerable grief because it dashed his last hopes for obtaining help from Hispañola. He fell ill. Elvas noted:

> . . . before he took his bed he sent an Indian to tell the cacique of Quigualtam that he was the son of the sun and that wherever he went all obeyed him and did him service. He requested him to choose his friendship and come to where he was, for he [de Soto] would be very glad to see him; and in token of love and obedience that he [Quigualtam] should bring him something of what was most esteemed in that land. By the same Indian, he [Quigualtam] answered . . . saying that with respect to [de Soto's claim] about being the son of the sun, let him dry up the great river and he would believe him. With respect to the rest . . . , he was not accustomed to visit anyone. On the contrary, all of whom he had knowledge visited and served him and obeyed him and paid him tribute, either by force or by their own volition. Consequently, if he [de Soto] wished to see him, let him cross there. If he came in peace, he would welcome him with special good will; if he came in war, he would await him in the town where he was, for not him nor any other would move one foot backward. (Robertson 1933:217–18)

This passage reveals interesting and significant changes in the Spaniards' view of their interactions with the Indians of the central Mississippi Valley. De Soto's persona as the "son of the Sun," demonstrated powerfully to the Indians at Casqui, had been rejected by everyone but de Soto himself. This once-shining image appears to have dimmed as de Soto's actions toward the Indians continued to violate their expectations of reciprocity and as his abilities even to provide for his own endeavors diminished through time. The cacique Quigualtam rejected de Soto's lofty claim, recasting him and his followers as merely common human enemies. From this point on, the Spaniards were no longer able to compel the respect and authority typically accorded those with access to great supernatural powers.

There followed a very tense period for the Spaniards during which their paranoid leader, fearing that Quigualtam—aided by Guachoya—would soon attack, kept guards ever alert and at the ready for battle. Finally, the tension mounted to an unbearable degree. A surprise attack was ordered upon Anilco, an attack which turned so brutal that hints of shock and bewilderment even infused the Spaniards' own accounts (e.g., Elvas in Robertson 1933:222).

On May 21, 1542, de Soto died at Guachoya. This event heightened the fears of the Spaniards, who now were certain that the Indians would attack. Consequently, de Soto's men attempted to conceal his death, first by secretly burying him and then by surreptitiously dumping his weighted corpse into the Mississippi River. But the Indians were not fooled: Guachoya is said to have promptly sent two Indians to be sacrificed so that their souls might accompany and serve de Soto in his other worldly journeys.

Luís de Moscoso took charge of the expedition following de Soto's death, and the decision was quickly made to attempt an overland retreat to New Spain (Mexico). The path followed by the Spaniards brought them soon into the Red River region inhabited by Caddoan Indians (Schambach this volume). Here, interactions with the Indians took on a significantly different character than those that had taken place in the central Mississippi Valley.

## THE EXPEDITION AMONG THE CADDOANS

In the province of Amaye, Moscoso learned that the province of Naguatex was nearby, only about a day-and-a-half journey away (Robertson 1933:239). Moscoso led his troops half that distance and set up camp alongside a pleasant brook, where soldiers soon encountered Indians sent from Naguatex to spy on the Spaniards. Two Indians captured by Moscoso's men admitted that they had been sent by their leader, the cacique of Naguatex, to find out what manner of people the Spaniards were. Additionally, Moscoso learned from these two Indians that the cacique of Naguatex and other caciques who were his allies were planning to attack the Spaniards that day.

In short order, two bands of Indians attacked the Spaniards' camp from different directions. Turning in flight when the Spaniards retaliated, the fleeing Indians succeeded in drawing away a number of soldiers. The exposed camp was then attacked by two more bands. In the ensuing battle, Moscoso's men eventually gained the upper hand. After questioning some of the captives taken in battle, the Spaniards learned that the attackers had been sent by the caciques of three provinces—Naguatex, Maye, and Hacanac—and that the cacique of Naguatex was the leader and chief of them all (Robertson 1933:241).

On the following day, the Spaniards marched into the village of Naguatex, which they described as being very extensive. They also learned that the village of the cacique was located on the opposite side of the large river (the Red River) that ran through the province. Unable to find a crossing place, Moscoso set up camp. Over the next several days reconnaissance parties searched for a place to cross the river. Two days later they crossed to the other side and observed a large village with many provisions (Robertson 1933:242).

Moscoso sent a message to Naguatex, inviting the cacique to visit him. Two days later the messenger returned with news that the cacique would arrive the next day. Before the cacique appeared, however, a number of other Indians, including some "principal men," visited the Spaniards' camp to measure Moscoso's demeanor. Then,

> The cacique came two hours later well attended by his men. They all came after his manner, one ahead of the other in double file, leaving a lane in the middle through which the cacique came. They reached the place where the governor was, all weeping after the manner of the Tula which lay to the east not very far from that place. The cacique paid his respects fittingly. . . . (Robertson 1933:244)

Although the speech Elvas recorded and attributed to Naguatex is similar to those attributed to other Indian leaders in its apology for past transgressions and its offer of service henceforth, it is perhaps significant that no mention was made of any gifts presented to Moscoso. Instead, the cacique remained for four days and then departed, later refusing to meet a second time with Moscoso. When the Spaniards, in retaliation, began to burn the province's villages and take captives, Naguatex sent six principal men and three guides to lead the Spaniards on to their next destination (Robertson 1933:246–47).

From Naguatex, the Spaniards traveled through a number of other Caddoan settlements—Nisohone, Nondacao, Aays, Soacatino, Guasco, Naquiscoca, and Nacacahoz. Along the way they encountered only resistance on the part of the Indians, and their prospects for reaching New Spain by overland route became increasingly doubtful. Finally, the Spaniards decided to retrace their steps back to the Mississippi River, which they would attempt to descend to the Gulf coast. On their return, they passed back through the lands they had so recently devastated, and consequently they found very little food. Only at Naguatex had the houses been rebuilt and the stores of maize replenished.

## DISCUSSION AND CONCLUSIONS

The thesis guiding this study is that accounts of the de Soto expedition embody a discourse of actions symbolizing cultural categories and principles brought to encounters between sixteenth-century Spaniards and Southeastern Indians. The interpretations of "epitomizing events" given above permit us now to identify several important cultural themes reflected in these accounts.

The first theme apparent from the nature of interactions portrayed in the de Soto narratives is that *relationships between hierarchically organized societies were secured via alliances or pacts between the elite leaders of those societies.* This is a theme that reflects both Spanish and Southeastern Indian cultures of the sixteenth century. It is interesting, furthermore, that both Spanish and Native-American models of social hierarchy and elite leadership are represented in the events examined in this analysis. For example, the narratives describing the initial contacts between de Soto and Aquixo, frame the encounter in terms of the Spanish feudal system as well as Southeastern Indian social hierarchies (incorporating both humans and supernatural beings). Moreover, in virtually every intercultural encounter that occurred for the portion of the expedition examined in this study, interactions between Spaniards and Indians proceeded in terms of specific relationships (whether positive or negative) between de Soto or Moscoso and their counterpart in the native society.

A second theme reflected is that *relationships between groups were motivated by competition.* This again is a theme that reflects both Spanish and Southeastern Indian cultural systems. However, the nature of competition as portrayed in the accounts represents two different kinds of adversarialism that correspond to the *dominium/communitas* dichotomy discussed earlier in this chapter. The actions of the Spaniards as portrayed in these accounts clearly reflect the primary characteristic that Brandon (1986) attributes to his conceptualization of *dominium*: namely, conquest of other people and control of their material resources. In contrast, the kind of adversarialism that is evidenced by the Spaniards' portrayal of Indian actions is one that perhaps can be best characterized as a competition for prestige. This is true whether the competition is between rival Indian groups (e.g., Casqui versus Pacaha), or between the Indians and the Spaniards (e.g., Quigualtam versus de Soto). In both cases, competition for prestige reflects a structural opposition between reciprocity and retribution, which accords well with Brandon's conceptualization of *communitas* in native American societies.

A third cultural theme is that *relations between groups were structured according to the idiom of kinship*. The centrality of this theme in the accounts of the de Soto expedition is clearly the product of Indian cultural influences. This theme can be identified in actions that portray relations between separate Indian groups, as evidenced, for example, in the series of interactions between Casqui and Pacaha, which included attacks on ancestral shrines and explicit claims concerning the priority of Casqui's lineage over Pacaha's. It is also reflected in accounts of interactions between the Indians and the Spaniards, as in the attempts by Casqui and Pacaha to mingle their blood with de Soto's through the offer of Indian women that de Soto might take for wives. The fact that the idiom of kinship is seen in these accounts as operating in the context of such diversified domains as political alliance, economic interaction, and intergroup hostilities lends further support to the observation that kinship relations served in a "megainstitutional" capacity among sixteenth-century Southeastern Indian societies.

The fourth cultural theme reflected in epitomizing events is that *positive interactions between groups were dependent upon the fulfillment of reciprocal obligations.* Reciprocity was another important institution among Southeastern Indian societies reflected in the pivotal role that gift giving played in relations between de Soto and elite Indian leaders. In all instances in which Indian leaders wished to interact with de Soto in any positive way, gift giving was an important part of the proceedings. Conversely, where Indian leaders wished to have as little to do with the Spaniards as possible, as in the Caddo area, gift giving was mentioned only in circumstances that clearly indicated that the Indians' motivation was to give the Spaniards a false impression of friendliness. It is furthermore the case that where gifts were presented to de Soto, there was a clear expectation that he would return the favor in kind. Examples of reciprocal actions on de Soto's part include the rainstorm fortuitously brought on by raising a cross at Casqui and the reward and booty the Casqui gained by accompanying de Soto to Pacaha. Both Casqui and Pacaha also hoped to advance their own rival aspirations through their separate alliances with de Soto. Conversely, when de Soto came to be perceived by the Indians as no longer living up to reciprocal obligations, his stock as the "son of the Sun" quickly plummeted.

A fifth theme reflected in the de Soto accounts is that *achievement of goals required the sanction of supernatural powers.* Both Spanish and Native-American versions of this theme are represented. The Spaniards believed in the efficacy of the Christian God while the Indians maintained the belief in the powers of sacred beings populating their cosmos. That both versions of this theme are represented indicates, once again, the significance of Indian cultural themes in shaping the Spanish narratives.

These five themes reflect sixteenth-century Native-American culture. Two represent the most fundamental aspects of Southeastern Indian cultural systems—kinship and reciprocity, leading to one inescapable conclusion: that Spanish perceptions of the events considered in this chapter were shaped to a significant degree by the actions of the Indians. Indeed, the Indians' actions in response to the Spaniards were such that indigenous cultural themes were incorporated into the Spaniards' own accounts of their encounters with the Indians. Far from being passive figures, the Indians engaged their visitors in a symbolic discourse that gave rise to changes in orientation within both cultural systems. These changes, in turn, had profound effects on the literary representation of these encounters in the de Soto expedition narratives. Whether or not the events actually occurred as described, the consequences of these events were decisive in shaping Spanish perceptions of the New World and its native inhabitants.

An additional set of conclusions may be suggested on the basis of this analysis. These conclusions concern differences in cultural patterns that may be attributed to the various Indian societies described in the accounts of the de Soto expedition. Although a finer-grained comparison than the one that will be given here would undoubtedly disclose more specific findings, some general differences can be identified by comparing the Indian polities of the central Mississippi Valley (as represented by Casqui, Pacaha, and Quigualtam) and the Caddoan polities of the Red River Valley (Naguatex, etc.).

At least one important difference between these two areas involves the nature of indigenous sixteenth-century political organization. Although paramount chiefdoms (that is, an organization of several polities, each with its own leader or chief, all of whom are subject to a single, paramount leader) are mentioned in the central Mississippi valley (Aquixo, Pacaha, and Quigualtam are all referred to as paramount chiefs), the accounts provide no examples of leaders actually functioning as paramount chiefs. Instead, the existence of independent hereditary lineage societies is indicated. Competition between these groups seems to have been endemic. An example of this is the rivalry between Casqui and Pacaha, who both attempted to secure an alliance with de Soto in order to gain the advantage of the Spaniards' support in contests for ascendancy over neighboring polities. Conversely, these internecine rivalries provided a clever man like de Soto with opportunities to manipulate these contests for his own purposes.

In contrast, the Caddoan polities encountered by Moscoso clearly represented paramount chiefdoms as seen in the alliance between Naguatex, Amaye, and Hacanac, in which the cacique of Naguatex was unambiguously identified as the paramount chief. Perhaps because of the greater social solidarity this form of political organization provided the Caddoan tribes, Moscoso found no opportunity to manipulate rival caciques against one another. More significantly, not one of the Caddoan leaders was described as attempting to secure an alliance with the Spaniards in hopes of furthering a specific project: the only cacique mentioned as providing gifts to the Spaniards is Nondacao, who, according to the Elvas account, had only hoped to secure the Spaniards' trust long enough to strand them in the wilderness.

# Notes

1. This study employs the reconstruction of the expedition route through Arkansas presented by the authors in this volume.

# Language Affiliations of Some de Soto Place Names in Arkansas

Robert L. Rankin

This is a propitious time to re-examine the place names of the de Soto expedition, not only because of the 450th anniversary of the trek, but also because the last several decades have seen a welcome resurgence of interest by linguists in the native languages of the Southeast. Since the early 1970s we have seen fieldwork in every one of the extant Muskogean languages, including Mikasuki, Seminole, Creek, Alabama, Koasati, Choctaw, and Chickasaw. Two book-length treatments of the Mobilian trade jargon have appeared, and Muskogean comparative work has been undertaken. There has also been additional important work on Caddo, Cherokee, and Quapaw and philological work on the extinct Catawba, Ofo, and Biloxi Indian languages. Thus there are now many new reference tools that were not available to earlier linguists and ethnographers such as Gatschet, Swanton, or Haas.

This efflorescence of linguistic work should be good news both to linguists and to practitioners of related disciplines. However, once we reach the Arkansas of the de Soto era and attempt to draw a linguistic map of the native cultures encountered by the Spanish explorers, we enter a *terra* which, compared with other areas of the Southeast, is still relatively *incognita.* The languages and peoples of proto-historic Arkansas are, unfortunately, not covered as well as they might be by the recent advances in linguistic documentation.

One of the difficulties is diversity. Protohistoric Arkansas was at the crossroads of a number of quite distinct native cultures and linguistic groupings. The Siouan linguistic family stretched from perhaps near the mouth of the Arkansas River northwestward all the way to the Rockies. Tunican and Natchezan languages extended southward, Muskogean-speaking peoples probed from across the Mississippi, and Caddoan languages were probably spoken in the southwest, extending into the eastern plains and thence northward. Unraveling the linguistic threads using only the Indian place and personal names mentioned by the chroniclers of the de Soto expedition is no easy task. Every scrap of information we can glean from analysis of such names is important if we are to be able to produce a moderately accurate ethnographic map of the southeast in de Soto's time. Such a map is important because, by the time the French and English turned their attention to the region over 130 years later, there had been an immense amount of change.

Natchez grammar and lexicon are unfortunately still very poorly known, although Mary R. Haas has a great deal of material in her personal files that may someday see publication. Nor is there a full treatment of Caddo grammar, although Wallace Chafe's (1976) short published grammatical sketch and his typescript Caddo lexicon are very helpful. Although there is now a Quapaw (Siouan) lexicon (Rankin 1986), which includes the vocabulary from my own fieldwork as well as that assembled by previous scholars, there is as yet no publishable grammar or text collection. The Tunica, Biloxi, and Ofo languages are all extinct and known only from limited materials collected from the last generation of speakers or, in some cases, from the very last speaker (Haas 1940; Dorsey and Swanton 1912).

Nevertheless, it is now possible to make a few new points, clarify a few old ones, disprove one or two old claims, and pose at least a couple of new questions that future scholarship may actually be able to answer.

The study of ethnonyms—and in the Southeast this means mostly town names—especially as they are filtered through the spelling systems of the various colonial languages of the Americas, has had a checkered past. Linguists and ethnographers have always perceived the need to make maximum use of any native words mentioned in the journals of early explorers or on the maps that emerged from their quests, since such words are often among our only clues to the identity of the native populations with whom they dealt. But, unfortunately, the study of place names has always attracted more than its share of amateurs, some quite talented but many given to unrestrained speculation. And even for the best of these, the lack of good reference materials has been a constant problem.

Linguists have learned to be very conservative when attempting to establish etymologies for native names of the sort we must deal with in the de Soto accounts. We run serious risk if we uncritically accept native statements about the meanings of place names or permit easy substitutions of letters in order to render place names similar to known words in Indian languages. The former frequently turn out to be folk etymologies, while in the latter instance we are catering to our own wishful thinking. And once we begin transposing entire syllables in our attempts to make sense of things, the thread of truth has usually been lost and we have entered the realm of arid speculation.

If a name cannot be analyzed or interpreted easily, disguised in its sixteenth-century Spanish or Portuguese spelling, or if it does not conform to the known *grammatical* patterns of the language it is alleged to be from, or if it fails to conform to known *naming* practices in a given culture or culture area, then we must generally resist the temptation to believe that we have successfully explained it or established an etymology for it.

It is also the case that most of the communication between the de Soto expedition and the Indians was conducted through an interpreter, and often through multiple interpreters, so possible interference from the interpreters' native language(s) must be taken into account. All things considered then, conservatism has to be the order of the day in place name studies such as these.

Applying this to our particular problem, we should perhaps be a little careful about accepting some of the linguistic identifications of John R. Swanton (1939), the most prominent of our predecessors, as well as those of other scholars. Swanton had an amazing capacity for detail and was a prolific writer. His ethnographic work in the Southeast and Mississippi Valley is, and should remain, highly respected. But, as a linguist, he sometimes jumped to conclusions that today seem unwarranted. Some of Swanton's proposed etymologies rely on ungrammatical word orders or on unlikely meanings, and some of his identifications of the language family affiliation of de Soto town names are little more than educated guesses. All in all though, were it not for Swanton's work, we would be far behind where we are today in our understanding of the linguistic aspects of the de Soto chronicles. Even this paper is derivative, in many ways, from his work.

At this point, although there is relatively little that can be said about many of the Arkansas place names on the de Soto inventory (but see Chafe this volume), I hope to make up for the lack of quantity by saying something intelligent about such important and problematic names as *Casqui, Pacaha,* and *Tanico,* and will also say a few words about *Coligua.* Beyond these, it is best to urge caution and point out one or two areas that may be fruitful for future research. The names will be considered in roughly the order in which we encounter them in the published accounts.

## CASQUI

The first of the towns that de Soto encountered after crossing the river into Arkansas was probably *Casqui* (Ranjel *Casqui/Quarqui,* Elvas *Casqui,* Biedma *Icasqui,* Garcilaso *Casquin*). Some scholars, notably Swanton (1939:52), have tied this name to the *Kaskinampo* of later accounts. There is really no way to confirm this hypothesis, but if it is correct, then the town was clearly named by the Koasati, in whose language *Kaskinampo* means "the warriors are (so) many" (Kimball 1985).

Among the Muskogean languages *Káskí* is "warrior" only in certain Koasati dialects. The related Choctaw and Chickasaw have *taska,* Apalachee *taskaya*; Hitchiti *tastênáki*; Creek *tastanaki.* The passage of the initial phoneme *t* to *k* is such a rarity that no linguist would postulate its having happened independently in two Muskogean languages. Moreover, the remainder of the name, *nampon,* is Koasati for "to be (so) many." So the town of *Kaskinampo* was presumably named by Koasatis, although this alone would not necessarily imply that it was inhabited by them.

Use of the word *warrior* in town names was not uncommon elsewhere in the Protohistoric, Muskogean-speaking Southeast, so the name certainly falls within known southeastern naming practices. Spanish explorers also encountered towns named *Kaski* or *Taski* and *Taskiki* (Tuskegee) with the similar meanings elsewhere (Booker, Hudson, and Rankin 1992). Kimball (1985:4–5 and per litt.) stated that in late prehistoric times Koasati was spoken in four dialects: *Koasati* proper, *Kaskinampo, Tuskegee,* and *Alibamu.* Note that two of the four, *Kaskinampo* and *Tuskegee,* specifically contain the Muskogean root for "warrior."

We will probably never know whether *Casqui(n)* and *Kaskinampo* were one and the same. And even if we did, it is not obvious from the name alone whether the Koasati were describing one of their own towns, in which case the name would refer to "warriors," or whether they were describing a town inhabited at the time by enemies, in which case *Casqui* (or even *Kaskinampo*) would refer to someone else's warriors. The form of the name recorded by Biedma, *Icasqui*, appears to show the Koasati third person possessive prefix and would mean "his warriors," presumably referring to a chief, or "their warriors," perhaps referring to the people. This is the third person possessive prefix not just in Koasati but in virtually every Muskogean language. So the prefix itself could just as easily have originated in one of the languages spoken by de Soto's interpreters.

Note that if the identification of *Casqui* as a Koasati-speaking town is correct, it would mean that, in the early sixteenth century, people speaking dialects of this Muskogean language were to be found from the mountains of Eastern Tennessee (see Booker, Hudson, and Rankin 1992; Kimball 1985:4) all the way to Arkansas. Kimball (1985:4–5) states, "At the beginning of the historic period, the Koasati inhabited the upper Tennessee valley from above the mouth of Hiwassee River downstream to the northward bend of the Tennessee. The middle section of the Tennessee valley seems to have been inhabited by the Tuskegee (also spelled Taskigi or Casquigi . . .), and the lower Tennessee valley by the Kaskinampo. . . ."

Whether any sort of archeological correlation for this hypothesis can be found remains to be seen. The Koasati are linked to the Dallas phase in eastern Tennessee. If no progression of archeological material across Tennessee into Arkansas or no other archeological confirmation is forthcoming, the question of the final identification of Casqui must be left open.

## PACAHA

After his visit to Casqui, de Soto left the Muskogean-speaking Southeast and moved on to the controversial Pacaha. Various linguists and historians over the years have equated Pacaha with the Quapaw. Baird (1980:228) attributes the first mention of this theory to Father Charlevoix in 1721, but it has often been repeated since then in the linguistic and cultural literature. It has permeated both the technical and popular literature on the Quapaw people. Some examples are as follows:

> The Kwapa or Quapaw tribe of Indians are identical with the Pacaha or Capaha who were met by De Soto when he discovered the Mississippi River. (Dorsey 1895:130)

> The descriptive name *Omaha* (*umoⁿ´hoⁿ*, 'against the current' or 'upstream') had been fixed on the people prior to 1541. In that year De Soto's party met the Quapaw tribe; *quapaw*, or *uga´xpa*, means 'with the current' or 'downstream,' and is the complement of *umoⁿ´hoⁿ*, or *Omaha*. (Fletcher and La Flesche 1911:36)

> The chronicles of De Soto's expedition in 1541 report the Quapaw as the 'Pacaha' or 'Capaha,' located on the west bank of the Mississippi River about forty or fifty miles north of the mouth of the Arkansas River. (Wright 1951:219)

> If the Quapaw were the same as the Capaha encountered by De Soto in 1541, they apparently had moved down the Mississippi during the intervening century and a half. (Crawford 1975:56)

There are a great many other such references, especially in the archeological literature (see, for example, the discussion in Jeter 1986), so it is important to clarify if possible the widely held view that Pacaha was Quapaw.

Let me anticipate my conclusion here and state that, though I am myself a Siouanist with a special interest in Quapaw and would like to see the Quapaws receive mention earlier than any other Siouan people in western literature, I am forced by the evidence to conclude that Pacaha was *not* Quapaw and *not* Siouan in linguistic affiliation. The evidence, as in all of these place name lists, is slim but qualitatively important and, I believe, now conclusive.

Much of the existing evidence was pointed out by Swanton and others over the years scattered through various publications. I shall try to bring it together here and then add a bit to it. Originally Swanton equated Pacaha and Quapaw (Swanton 1911:186), but his detailed investigation for the 1939 De Soto Commission Report to Congress, celebrating the four hundredth anniversary of the expedition, apparently convinced him that he had been wrong.

As we know, there are four written accounts of the expedition that mention this village. Three of them, those of Ranjel, Elvas, and Biedma, are firsthand accounts; the fourth, that of Garcilaso, was composed from secondhand accounts several decades after the expedition and is acknowledged to be the least faithful to the facts. There is also a map sometimes attributed to the expedition (reproduced in Swanton 1939:343, discussion, 11).

All three firsthand accounts agree on the spelling Pacaha (Swanton 1939:57), and the Spaniards stayed in the village for approximately a month, so there is no reason to assume that they experienced any confusion about its name. Yet, if we look at the name by which the Quapaws call themselves, *okáxpa* (Anglicized to *ogáxpa* by some of the last generation of speakers), which is supposed to be what the chroniclers were attempting to reproduce here, we can see that only by ignoring the three reliable accounts and comparing *okáxpa* to Garcilaso's spelling of the village name, *Capaha,* (with the transposition of the syllables) can we hope to see any real similarity.

| | | | | |
|---|---|---|---|---|
| Firsthand accounts: | | pa | ca | ha |
| Garcilaso's account: | | ca | pa | ha |
| In the Quapaw language: | o | káx | pa | |
| Early French accounts: | | kap | pa | |

Neither sixteenth-century Spanish nor Middle French had any way to render the Quapaw sound [x] (a voiceless velar fricative similar to the *ch* of German *ach*) in their spelling systems, so if Garcilaso's spelling were accurate, he would have been as close to the actual pronunciation of the Indian name as, say, Marquette or LaSalle's *Kappa* over a century later, which we know did represent the Quapaw. But we have seen that the other three chroniclers, all of whom lived in the village a month, agreed on the spelling

*Pacaha*, which is not at all like *okáxpa*. So the evidence in favor of the meaning *Quapaw* for the name was never strong, and without the demonstrably less reliable Garcilaso, the equation of *Pacaha* with *Okaxpa* probably would never even have been proposed.

Nor is it possible to assume that the Indians themselves transposed the syllables in their tribal name between the time of the de Soto expedition and the arrival of the French, because the Kansa, Osage, Omaha, Ponca, and other cognate Siouan tribes share the Quapaw's designation, *okáxpa*. So the term in its present form is almost surely older than the split of these Siouan tribes, an event which took place well back into prehistoric times.

There is more evidence that bears on the ethnic identity of Pacaha. At Pacaha the Spaniards met, and in fact were offered as gifts, two sisters of the chief. (In Garcilaso's account they are described as wives.) These women's names are given by Biedma, written *Mochila* and *Macanoche*. And Swanton (1939:61) pointed out that one of these, Macanoche, is very close to Tunica for "beloved-woman."[1]

Tunica is a language isolate spoken in recent times only much farther south along the Mississippi. There is evidence, both in the de Soto accounts and in early French descriptions of the area, that the Tunica had villages at least as far north as Arkansas in the sixteenth and seventeenth centuries, however. Haas's (1953:234, 242) *Tunica Dictionary* confirms the identity of the constituent morphemes in this compound.

| | | | | | |
|---|---|---|---|---|---|
| Biedma: | ma | ca | | no | ch e |
| Haas: | m á h | k a | + | n ú h | č i |

I have arranged the names here in such a way that the reader can easily see the correspondence of the Tunica words with the Spanish spellings. Haas (1940, 1950, 1953) does not discuss the name at all as far as I am able to determine, nor does she compound the two words as I have done here. The putative compound is found only in the de Soto accounts and in Swanton's discussion of them.

Spanish spelling conventions had no way to render syllable final *-h*, so those are missing, as they are everywhere in all the accounts, but otherwise the fit is as good as we find between Indian names and Spanish vowels and consonants anywhere in the Southeast. The full Haas (1953) entries are:

máhka adj. high in price, expensive, dear
-máhka st(ative verb). G-S to love. (p. 234)
núhči f. female, woman. (p. 242)

In Tunica it is not possible to treat this construction as an ordinary noun-adjective compound as Swanton does, since adjectives must invariably follow the noun they modify (Haas 1940:75ff.). There are, however, deverbal nouns in Tunica, and máhka can be analyzed as a nominalized stative verb, "one who is beloved" (Haas 1940:78).[2] *Núhči*, then, may be interpreted either as an adjective, "female," or another noun "woman." The name, in any event, appears to pass the grammaticality test mentioned above.

Regarding the meaning of *Macanoche,* although I am still researching the question, there is evidence that this name, a compound of "beloved one" and "female," was an attested woman's name or (perhaps equally likely) a woman's title in other native southeastern cultures. Swanton (1939:61) mentions the existence of the similar name in Natchez, and there is additional evidence from the Apalachee language, where the compound *beloved-woman* actually meant "wife" (Kimball, personal communication). The words are different, of course, since Apalachee was a Muskogean language, but the meaning of the compound is the same, so the Tunica term is not at variance with known southeastern naming practices. And this name *is* the best linguistic evidence we have for the actual linguistic identity of *Pacaha.* If Swanton's identification of the woman's name was correct, and I tend strongly to believe that it was, then Pacaha must have been a Tunican-speaking town.

Here it should be pointed out that, whatever the exact meaning of these names, the real Quapaw language lacked any sound approaching our ch [č], yet the women's names *Mochila* and *Macanoche* both contain this sound. The *ch* sound has developed only recently preceding front vowels, *i* and *e,* in Kansa and Osage, two closely related Dhegiha Siouan dialects, but there was little or no parallel Quapaw development.[3] In addition, *l* is not a Quapaw speech sound either, so the name *Mochila* is doubly unlikely to be Quapaw.

Furthermore, the one other word of the Pacaha language that was recorded, the name of the so-called "second province" of Pacaha, called *Caluç* or *Caluça* by Elvas, also contains an *l,* once again, not a speech sound in Quapaw. This is true as of our earliest sample of real Quapaw, the vocabulary recorded by Gen. George Izard, territorial governor of Arkansas in the mid 1820s.

The name Caluça was interpreted by Swanton (1939:229) as representing *okalusa,* "Black Water," an obviously Muskogean (most likely Chickasaw) name. This may be a legitimate interpretation. It may also have been a loan-translation by de Soto's interpreters, who, at this point in the trip, may well have been Chickasaw-speaking. If the town or "province" was really Muskogean-speaking, then the chiefdom of which Pacaha was the seat of power was bilingual. Multilingual chiefdoms seem to have been fairly common in the late prehistoric Southeast (see Booker, Hudson, and Rankin 1992). So, phonologically speaking, what little we have of Pacaha vocabulary seriously violates Quapaw and Dhegiha Siouan pronunciation norms. All of the sounds found in the words *Pacaha, Mochila, Macanoche,* and Caluç(a) are, however, regular speech sounds (phonemes) in the Tunica language.

Thus far we have seen that the name Pacaha, as reliably recorded, does not really resemble the Quapaw self-designation, that one of the Pacaha proper names mentioned in the accounts seems transparently Tunican, and that several of the sounds present in the few Pacaha words recorded are not normal speech sounds in the Quapaw language but are normal in Tunica. There are one or two further points worth mentioning.

On the Marquette map of 1673–74 (Tucker 1974), the Quapaw villages are clearly labeled with the ethnonym provided by the expedition's Illinois Algonquian-speaking interpreter, *Akansea,* but on the same map, up the Arkansas River from the known

Quapaw villages, sandwiched between the Tunica and Koroa villages, is an unidentified town named *Papikaha.* The French did not ascend the river, so the name represents secondhand knowledge at best. I have seen little research that even attempts to make anything of this name, but if *Papikaha* and de Soto's *Pacaha* are the same, then there is evidence that these people (Pa(pi)kaha) and the Quapaw (*Akansea*) were perceived as separate and distinct ethnic entities in Marquette's time.[4] And geographically, at least, *Papikaha* was associated with the non-Siouan Tunica and Koroa.[5]

*Papikaha* appears on a couple of other (derivative) French maps, then disappears totally from history along, ultimately, with the neighboring Koroa and any other northern offshoots of the Tunica that there may have been. My only real point here is that the French recorded *Papikaha* and the Quapaw towns as quite distinct from one another. The identity of de Soto's *Pacaha* and the later *Papikaha* cannot be proved, although we would have to admit that the similarity is great. Table 4 is a list of towns extending up the Arkansas River on three French maps.

TABLE 4. Order of Town Names on Several Early French Maps of the Arkansas River Valley.

| "Jol(l)iet" 1674 | Marquette 1673-74 | "Randin" 1674-81 |
|---|---|---|
| Paniasa | Atotchasi | Paniassa |
| Aiahichi | Matora | |
| Tanik8a | Akoroa | Tanik8a |
| Papikaha | Papikaha | Apapikaa |
| Enamoueta | Emam8eta | Emamoueta |
| Akoroua | Tanik8a | Akoroua |
| Matora | Paniassa | Matora |
| | Aiaichi | |
| Akansea | Akansea | Akansea |

Although the order of some of the names is different, *Papikaha* is sandwiched between the Tunica and Koroa towns in both listings. Actually all three maps are most likely derived from a single source of information. The Randin map was probably copied from one of the Joliet tracings (Tucker 1974), and later French maps (LaSalle, Franquelin, etc.) show Tunica and Koroa towns only much farther down the Mississippi Valley. The earliest maps do show a Tunican presence on the Arkansas River however, and it is not surprising to find *Papikaha* upriver among these towns.

## TANICO

We need to look now at these names that resemble the English tribal name *Tunica.* Ranjel and Elvas recorded *Tanico,* while the Marquette expedition recorded *Tanika.* If these spellings do not represent the same town, they almost certainly represent the same name. That they could be the same name but different towns follows from the way the name *Tunica* is put together in the Tunica language.

The name in Tunica means "the people," and it is put together from several elements described by Haas (1950:18–19n.).

| | |
|---|---|
| ta- | 'the' (definite article) |
| óni | 'people' |
| -ku | 'gender/number suffix' (masc. sing. and collective in this case) |

This yields *ta-óni-ku* 'the people', which, depending on speed of utterance, etc., may undergo a regular contraction whereby the two vowels, *a* and *o* fall together. These contractions are described by Haas (1940:21), and it is clear from her examples that instances of *o* and *a* coming together frequently yield an intermediate vowel that she writes as the phoneme /ɔ/ and describes as similar to the English vowel of *fought.* In fact, this seems to be the phonetic outcome of several back rounded vowels including *u* and ɔ when contracting with *a.*

Since ɔ was not an orthographically distinct speech sound in either 16th century Spanish or Middle French, speakers of those languages would have written it with their nearest equivalent, either *a* or *o.* And that, I believe, accounts for the variation in the writing of the initial syllable vowel. Additional elements may be placed between the article, *ta-*, and the noun *'óni* "people"; for example, the name the modern Tunica often called themselves is *tá yoroníku,* where *yor* (meaning unknown) modifies *'óni* "people." Note that Haas also cites the name *Toniku,* where *a* + *o* shows *o* simply "winning out" over the *a* of *ta.* Whatever the precise meaning of the modern term (with-*yor-*), *Tanico* is an excellent rendering of "the people" in a Tunican language, and I believe we should regard the linguistic identity of these people as relatively well established now.

## COLIGUA

Unfortunately it is harder to say the same for the *Koroa* and *Coligua/Colima* equation made by many scholars. *Coligua* (Ranjel and Biedma), *Coligoa* (Elvas), and *Colima* (Garcilaso) was visited soon after Pacaha, so it was relatively close by. I cannot deny that the names are similar to the Koroa of the French nor that they may be related. The problem is simply that all four de Soto accounts agree on the medial vowel *i,* while all subsequent accounts insist on *o* or *ou.* Additionally, Tunica has both *r* and *l* sounds, so if Koroa is related to Tunica, the fluctuation of *r* and *l* in this name would have to be explained. For the moment, it seems to me that we must still consider the identification of *Koroa* and *Coligua* only a strong possibility.

Here we begin to reach the point of diminishing linguistic returns. There are obviously a number of Caddoan names on the de Soto lists. They are found further along in the narrative, beyond the apparent Tunican entries, and a number were spotted by Swanton (1939:61).

## UTIANGUE

Between our putative Tunican area and the Caddo were a number of unidentified towns. Many of these Swanton believed might be Natchezan, that is, either Natchez proper or some now-extinct group that spoke a closely related language. A number of these share a final element that should be identifiable when and if we obtain better Natchez lexical materials (assuming, of course, that the language turns out to be Natchezan). This ending had the pronunciation *-anke* or *-yanke,* and it is found disguised in a number of slightly divergent Hispanic spellings. Table 5 contains the names with the pertinent ending in emphasized italics.

TABLE 5. Town Names from the de Soto Accounts with the Suffix *(y)anke.*

| Ranjel | Elvas | Biedma | Garciliaso | "de Soto" map |
|---|---|---|---|---|
| | | | | Epavaqu***ianqui*** |
| Uti***angue*** | Aut***iamque*** | Vir***anque*** | Ut***iangue*** | Vt***ianqúj*** |
| | Aut***ianque*** | | | |
| | (A)nilco | Anico***yanque*** | Anilco | |
| | Guachoya | Guacho***yanqu***e | Guachoya | Guachoya |
| Quigudta | Quigualt***am*** | | Quigualt***anqui*** | Quigualt***anq̃*** |

The identity of the ending is obscured by the frequent shifts among the letters *i, e,* and *j* common in Hispanic renderings of place names in the de Soto and other chronicles, plus the fact that, in the native languages of the Southeast (including Natchez), the sounds *k* and *g,* so different to our ears, represented conditioned variants of a single speech sound (phonetic variants of a single phoneme), which can be written unambiguously using just *k.* The ending seems detachable, since some writers include it while others do not on the various occasions that it appeared. At *Utiangue,* where the group wintered, however, the ending appears on all versions of the name. When we identify this ending, we should at least know the language in which these towns were named.

Swanton (1939:54, 61) proposed tentative Natchez etymologies for a number of these names, identifying the suffix, which he wrote *-ngue, nege,* as meaning "it is like." Swanton did a certain amount of fieldwork on Natchez, but most of his proposed translations seem fairly unlikely as town names, and it is here that I believe his proposed etymologies to be most vulnerable. He was careful to mark them as uncertain, however. It is very doubtful that Natchez *nege* would have been so consistently mistranscribed by all four Hispanic chroniclers. Apparently Swanton did not spot the fact that we are dealing with a single suffix rendered into writing in different ways. An examination of the Natchez lexicon of Van Tuyl (1979) so far fails to turn up any convincing source in that language for the suffix *-(y)anke.*

## SUMMARY

In summary, I feel that, even using more conservative standards than Swanton, I can reiterate and strengthen his conclusion, published in 1939, that Pacaha might be Tunican, and was, in any event, certainly not Siouan-speaking. I also believe that deeper linguistic analysis of the name Tanico further confirms its Tunican identity as well. Early but secondhand French accounts tend to corroborate the presence of a cluster of Tunican-speaking villages on or near the Arkansas River, but upstream from the Mississippi during the protohistoric period.

Where the Quapaw were in 1541 we do not know, but as things stand now, it does not appear that de Soto encountered any Siouan-speaking peoples during his trek through Arkansas. My best guesses would be either that de Soto missed the mouth of the Arkansas and only encountered the upstream Tunican villages, or that the Quapaw moved to the mouth of the Arkansas only after 1541, probably from the North, as both Illinois Algonquian and Quapaw ethnohistorical accounts independently state, and that they settled in an area (and perhaps even on specific village sites) that already had a long history of occupation by southern Mississippi Valley groups. It is quite apparent to me that the Quapaw were not in the vicinity yet to meet de Soto, and that he met the Tunican-speaking people who lived there earlier.

# Notes

1. Swanton (1939:61) also mentioned that "*Makanadzi* is said to have been an ancient name in (Natchez)." So both Tunican and Natchezan cultures may have had variant pronunciations of the name. The Natchez term cited by Swanton presumably does not break down into "beloved one" and "women, female" in the Natchez language, however. It is, in any event, not Quapaw.

2. Haas only included discussion of active verbs in compounds of this kind. Tunica was never documented thoroughly enough for me to be certain whether stative verbs also participated in such constructions. There is no reason to believe they would not have, but the matter is moot in any event, since we are dealing here with a language that was probably closely related to Tunica proper but was not Tunica.

3. Quapaw [čh] developed in isolated instances via retroflexion as a variant pronunciation of aspirated /th/ preceding back rounded vowels. Both of the Pacaha women's names show *ch* before front vowels, however. So what little we have of Pacaha vocabulary seriously violates the Quapaw phoneme inventory and sequence restrictions.

4. In spite of the evidence, Dorsey, in a Quapaw dictionary slip file in the National Anthropological Archives, included the following under his entry for Uká-qpa-qti. "Real Kwapas: The name of one of the five ancient Kwapa villages, known to the early French writers as Cappa, Capaha, *Papikaha*, etc." (emphasis mine).

5. This name looks as though it might be a reduplicated or partially reduplicated form of *Pacaha*. Haas (1940:45) reported that the Tunica language used reduplication to form the repetitive aspect of verbs. These she normally translated with "to keep on" doing the action. Other Tunican languages might have used reduplication in other ways, but there is no way to know this.

# Caddo Names in the de Soto Documents

Wallace Chafe

John R. Swanton (1942:8) listed the following names, mentioned in the de Soto documents, with the comment that they represent "tribes or 'provinces' . . . which were undoubtedly Caddo":

(1) Tula
(2) Amaye or Maye
(3) Naguatex
(4) Hacanac
(5) Nissohone
(6) Lacane
(7) Nondacao
(8) Hais or Aays
(9) Soacatino or Xuacatino or Xacatin
(10) Guasco
(11) Naquiscoça
(12) Naçacahoz

As with many lists of this sort, these words are both intriguing and frustrating. A few are clearly recognizable as Caddo words, others are partly recognizable, and some are not recognizable as Caddo words at all. In this last category there are several that *cannot* be Caddo words. Swanton, of course, was not saying that all twelve of these words belonged to the Caddo language, but only that they were used to refer to Caddo people or places. I will discuss them in turn, moving from the most identifiable to the least.

## NAGUATEX

The one word in this list that presents no problems whatsoever is the third item, *Naguatex.* Given a Spanish orthography in which *gu* represents *w,* and *x* represents the sound spelled *sh* in English, this is clearly the name *Nawidish* "the place of salt" or "the people of the place of salt."[1] It is derived from *widish* "salt," with the addition of the locative prefix *na-*. The primary function of this prefix is to designate a "place of," but it is also used to refer to the people residing at that place. The name *Nawidish* is still known to Caddo people today. There appears to have been a Caddo dialect in which *w* was replaced by *m*. In that dialect, therefore, this name was pronounced *Namidish*, a form that sometimes appears in later documents, presumably with reference to the people whose language had undergone this change. Since salt was present in various locations, it is not surprising that the names *Nawidish* and *Namidish* were sooner or later used to refer to more than one community.

It is interesting to observe that the importance of salt to traditional Caddo culture is manifested in several ways in the language. For one thing, although the basic meaning of the word *widish* is "salt," it also means "soup." By metaphorical extension, the same word is used to refer to a person who is a "show-off." It appears with the diminutive suffix *-tiitiʔ* to form the word *widishtiitiʔ* "cute." When it is followed by the adjective *habitsaw*, "sweet" in the phrase *widish habitsaw*, the resulting meaning is "sugar," literally "sweet salt." A concept that lends itself to such a variety of extended meanings is clearly one that played an important part in the lives and thoughts of these people.

Although the name *Nawidish* must have originated with reference to one or more communities associated with a source of salt, it is not impossible that the people to whom the name was attached had moved from that place by the time they were encountered by Europeans in the sixteenth century. That is, although the connection between salt and the name is obvious, one does not necessarily have to conclude that the place where these people lived when they were encountered by the de Soto expedition was a place of salt, even though that seems the most likely possibility.

## NONDACAO

Almost as certain as *Nawidish* is the identity of the seventh item on the list, *Nondacao*. It is probably equated with the source of the name *Anadarko*. The Caddo word is *Nadáákuh* "the place of the bumblebee," or the people of that place. It is derived from the word *dáákuh* "bumblebee." Puzzling, however, is the *n* at the end of the first syllable. The most likely explanation is that the vowel of this syllable was at least slightly nasalized because of the initial *n*, and that this nasalization was heard by the Spaniards as a syllable-final consonantal *n*.

I know of no good explanation for the extra *A* at the beginning of the English name *Anadarko*. The name *Nadáákuh* is well known to members of the present-day Caddo tribe as the name of one of their former bands. It is not, however, the name presently applied to the city of Anadarko, Oklahoma, which in the Caddo language is called Nawáshitah, referring to the Washita River that flows through it.

## HAIS OR AAYS

The only other name on this list that is familiar as a name to the Caddo today is Hais or Aays. The Caddo name is *Háish*. It is not surprising that the Spanish, and later the

French, should have neglected to write the initial *h*. The word has no obvious etymology, but is simply a name.

What is at least clear, then, is that the de Soto expedition encountered the ancestors of people later known as the *Nawidish*, the *Nadáákuh*, and the *Háish*, all of which words are still familiar to the Caddo as names for divisions of the Caddo people.

## SOACATINO OR XUACATINO OR XACATIN

There is no doubt that this name too belongs to the Caddo language. What is clear about it is that it consists of two words, the second of which is *hatinuʔ* "red." The identity of the first word is not clear. One possible guess is that it was *shiwáh* "squirrel," the entire phrase having been *shiwáh hatinuʔ* "red squirrel." The Spanish spellings, however, suggest a pronunciation *shiwák hatinuʔ*. While the word for "squirrel" no longer ends in a *k*, it is possible that it did so in the sixteenth century. In fact, a change from *k* to *h* at the ends of syllables can be internally reconstructed throughout the Caddo language. It should be emphasized that *shiwák hatinuʔ* "red squirrel" is only a guess, but that the name definitely comes from a Caddo phrase in which the second element was the word for "red."

## NAQUISCOÇA AND NAÇACAHOZ

There are only two other words about which anything positive can be said concerning their relation to the Caddo language: Naquiscoça and Naçacahoz. The fact that these words both begin with the prefix *na-* makes them almost unmistakably Caddo, but unfortunately the elements that follow that prefix are no longer recognizable.

## HACANAC AND NISSOHONE

These two names are possible as Caddo words. Most adjectives in Caddo begin with the syllable *ha-*, and therefore *Hacanac* gives the appearance of being a Caddo adjective, though it is no longer recognizable. *Nissohone* might possibly be another word that begins with the locative prefix *na-*, and one thinks of the possible name *Nasunah*, which would mean "the place of money." No such name is known today. One wonders about the original meaning of the modern word *sunah* "money," which presumably once referred to something that was used as money.

## AMAYE OR MAYE AND GUASCO

Although less obviously so, these words might also belong to the Caddo language. Swanton (1942:8) says that "Amaye or Maye seems to contain the Caddo word signifying a male human being," but it is not clear what he had in mind. The current word for "man" is *shúúwiˀ*, which bears no resemblance to *Amaye* at all. The word for "human being" or "person" is *háyáánuh,* which is perhaps slightly closer. The other name would evidently have been something resembling *waskuh* if it were a Caddo word, but there is no such word today. It is quite possible that these two words did not come from the Caddo language.

## TULA AND LACANE

In any case, these last two words quite certainly came from a different language, since the Caddo language does not contain the consonant *L,* although the similarity between *lacane* and *Hacanac* is intriguing. It is interesting that *Tula* was the first allegedly Caddo town that was encountered by de Soto. In all likelihood this was the name given to it by his guide, perhaps a speaker of a Muskogean language.

## SUMMARY

In short, of the twelve words on the list, eight are certainly or almost certainly Caddo names, two (*Amaye* and *Guasco*) are uncertain in that regard, and two (*Tula* and *Lacane*) are not Caddo. Of the eight that are Caddo, three are still known as names to the Caddo today (*Nawidish, Nadáákuh,* and *Háish*), and one other contains a clear Caddo word (*hatinuˀ* "red"). The remaining four names (*Naquiscoça, Naçacahoz, Hacanac,* and *Nissohone*) contain what appear to be Caddo elements.

# Notes

1. Caddo phonology is described in Chafe (1976:55–64). Here I am using the spelling *sh* for the palatal sibilant [š], and *ts* for the affricate which I sometimes write with the letter *c*. I show long vowels by doubling them. Caddo distinguishes between high-pitched and low-pitched syllables, and the acute accent mark over a vowel or vowel sequence indicates high pitch.

# Death, Drought, and de Soto: The Bioarcheology of Depopulation

Barbara A. Burnett and Katherine A. Murray

## INTRODUCTION

This study addresses the critical issue of depopulation and/or disappearance of the Late Mississippian people from northeast Arkansas. It has long been assumed that the disappearance of these densely populated chiefdoms was initiated through epidemics introduced by de Soto's entrada (Morse and Morse 1983, 1990; Ramenofsky 1987; Phillips, Ford, and Griffin 1951). Unlike previous studies, this analysis employs protohistoric paleodemographic data gained from numerous skeletal series to address this intriguing question. We will reconstruct the mortality profile of all extant protohistoric skeletal collections and will compare these statistics both temporally and spatially. This treatment of paleodemographic data is an invaluable tool for evaluating the mechanics of depopulation.

Using demographic data, archeological data, and historic accounts, three questions are addressed here.

1. What evidence is there for demographic collapse due to epidemics introduced by the de Soto entrada?
2. What evidence is there for epidemic-based demographic collapse in later protohistoric times?
3. What alternative suggestions would explain depopulation in Arkansas?

The Protohistoric period in Arkansas dates from A.D. 1500 to 1700. Historical documentation of this area begins with the crossing of the Mississippi River by the de Soto entrada in June of 1541. The expedition spent approximately two years in what is now known as Arkansas, and is believed to have explored along the St. Francis, Mississippi, White, Arkansas, and Ouachita rivers (Hudson 1985; D. Morse 1989; Schambach 1989). Morse and Morse (1990:197) believe that approximately three-fourths of the Indian polities present in 1541–43 were visited by the Spanish explorers. The de Soto chronicles provide a description of a culturally rich and diverse area. The chroniclers noted, during their explorations through what is now northeast Arkansas, that this region was highly populated and that many towns were located within sight of one another. For example, they estimated that five thousand people gathered to watch as the Spaniards raised a cross on a mound in one of these villages (Garcilaso 1951). These descriptions have given the impression that these Late Mississippians maintained highly organized chiefdom-level societies (Bourne 1904; Quinn 1979, 2). Based upon these chronicles and the archeological record, Dan Morse (1989:112) speculated that these Late Mississippian societies may represent the most highly developed Indian societies existing north of Mexico.

The archeological reconstruction of settlement patterns also indicates that northeast Arkansas was highly populated (Morse and Morse 1983, 1990; Ramenofsky 1987; Phillips, Ford, and Griffin 1951). Several archeological phases are thought to represent chiefdoms visited by de Soto. The skeletal data representing two of these phases, Nodena and Parkin, are included in the present analysis. Morse and Morse (1983) reported that at least thirty-four Nodena phase sites cluster together in Arkansas and Missouri. Three large Nodena sites (all in Arkansas) range between eleven and fourteen acres. The Parkin phase is represented by twenty-one sites, and Morse and Morse (1983:292) stated "Sites are literally strung like beads, with the two rivers (the St. Francis and Tyronza) representing the connecting cord." Morse and Morse (1990) estimated that some of these towns had populations ranging up to two thousand people.

One hundred and thirty years after the Spanish entrada, French exploration of the area provided the next historical description. The highly populous and culturally distinct societies described by the de Soto chronicles appear to have disappeared by the time of the French explorers. Three separate expeditions, Marquette and Jolliet in 1673, La Salle in 1682, and de Tonti in 1686, traveled down the Mississippi River passing through northeast Arkansas. In sharp contrast to the earlier Spanish descriptions, the only native Americans the French encountered were the Quapaw near the junction of the Mississippi and Arkansas rivers (Shea 1852; Thwaites 1900). The French did not report seeing large fortified villages in northeast Arkansas, they reported only a few widely spaced and sparsely populated villages at the mouth of the Arkansas River. Thus, areas that had been described as heavily populated between 1539 and 1542 appeared to have been virtually abandoned by the 1670s. Anne Ramenofsky's (1987:54) archeological reconstruction of the time period (Period II maximum time range 1541–1699) indicated a decrease in settlement counts. Her analysis tends to confirm the current interpretation of the French documents pertaining to northeast Arkansas.

The period between the departure of the Spanish and the arrival of the French (from 1543 to 1673) is referred to as the "Protohistoric Dark Ages" because little is known and much is speculated about (Dye 1986). This period of 130 undocumented years is thought to have been a time of major cultural disruptions resulting in the abandonment of northeast Arkansas. It has often been assumed that the devolution of these prehistoric native cultures came about through contact not only with Europeans and their technology, but also and perhaps most significantly with European disease (Morse and Morse 1983, 1990; Phillips, Ford, and Griffin 1951; Ramenofsky 1987).

Based on the historical accounts and archeological reconstruction, the dense Late Mississippian populations de Soto encountered were ripe for epidemic crowd disease. These people lived in clustered and highly aggregated communities. Epidemic crowd disease could have been rapidly transmitted within and between villages (Jorde,

Pitkanen, and Mielke 1989). More importantly, these native Americans lacked prior immunity to European diseases. If a pathogen had been let loose among them, it would have spread rapidly and without discrimination. Morse (1989) estimated that the population in Arkansas fell from 75,000 in 1541 to 15,000 by 1673, and he attributed this decline to European disease epidemics introduced by de Soto's army.

Despite the prevailing contention that disease was the major factor leading to the sociopolitical and demographic collapse during the Protohistoric period, the timing and origin of the disappearance of these societies are still not fully understood. This chapter offers a re-examination of the role that the de Soto entrada and/or European disease played in producing demographic collapse among the native American societies living in Arkansas between 1541 and 1673. This study uses a bioarcheological approach to reconstruct the population dynamics of the Protohistoric period in Arkansas. The protohistoric population profiles are based upon all analyzed collections from the time period in question (Burnett 1990a, 1990b; Powell 1989; Murray 1985, 1989; Hrdlicka 1908; Ford 1961; Rose 1984, Clancy 1985).

Robert L. Blakely (1977) has stated that the main objective of bioarcheology is to understand the integration of ecological, cultural, and biological systems that contribute to human behavior. Changes in these systems across temporal and spacial proximity allow scholars to assess the quality of lifeways in individual societies. Bioarcheology can contribute to the reconstruction of past lifeways by assessing the "adaptive efficiency" of a particular culture. Adaptive efficiency is a measure of how successfully a cultural system protects its members against environmental stressors and enables successful maturation to adulthood and production of viable offspring. Adaptive efficiency is ultimately a measure of reproductive success. Measuring and interpreting changes in the adaptive efficiency of various cultures can be approached by using paleodemographic data as an indicator of reproductive potential.

The fertility of women directly effects the reproductive potential (and thus the adaptive efficiency) of any given society (McFalls and McFalls 1984). Population studies in extant societies indicate that reproductive ability of women can vary widely. Generally live births range from only one to eight children per woman (Bongaarts 1976). However, several factors—genetic, disease, nutritional, environmental, or psychopathological—can interfere with a woman's (or man's) level of fertility. These factors all exist in modern societies and were undoubtedly present in past societies. In addition, reproductive potential is also sharply affected by age. Two studies (Schwartz and Mayaux 1982; Hendershot, Mosher, and Pratt 1982) indicate that less than 40 percent of women maintain their ability to reproduce by the time they reached their late thirties. Studies of developing societies indicate that fertility rates drop even faster than developed societies for the same age group (Cassen 1978; Population Reports 1979).

While there is no historic documentation available to establish fertility rates among the past societies discussed in this paper, paleodemographic analysis can provide the best method of evaluating the reproductive potential of these groups. Reproductive potential is used here to measure demographic collapse. In particular, it is the presence or absence of young adult females which determines the potential of population growth or, conversely, decline.

## ANALYSIS

Paleodemographic statistics are compared and contrasted across temporal and geographic proximity to the European presence in order to measure the reproductive potential of three protohistoric cultural manifestations.

This study employs the bioarcheological analysis of 391 burials from 13 sites representing 5 specific archeological manifestations or phases during the Arkansas Protohistoric period. These data, which represent the entire analyzed protohistoric skeletal sample of Arkansas, offer a unique opportunity to assess both the short-term and long-term biological consequences of initial European contact in Arkansas. Information is derived from the existing literature as well as from more recent investigations by the authors (Burnett 1990a, 1990b; Powell 1989; Murray 1985, 1989; Hrdlicka 1908; Ford 1961; Rose 1984, Clancy 1985).

All 391 burials are dated between A.D. 1450 and 1750, and have been divided into three broad cultural manifestations (table 6). The Nodena and Parkin material from northeastern Arkansas represents Late Mississippian manifestations. These populations date between A.D. 1450 and 1600. The sample from east-central Arkansas represents the Menard complex of the Arkansas River valley (formerly the Quapaw phase; see Jeter, Cande, and Mintz 1990), and is dated between A.D. 1600 and 1700. The southwestern Arkansas sample includes the late Caddoan cultural manifestations of the Red and Ouachita drainages. These populations are dated between A.D. 1650 and 1750.

TABLE 6. Protohistoric Bioarcheological Samples.

| Drainage | Phase/Site |
|---|---|
| LATE MISSISSIPPIANS | |
| Mississippi | Nodena Phase |
| St. Francis | Parkin Phase |
| Arkansas | Menard Complex |
| LATE CADDOAN | |
| Ouachita | Deceiper Phase |
| | Gordon Site |
| Red | Cedar Grove |

Total Individuals = 390

The route of the de Soto entrada is based on the work of Charles Hudson (Hudson and Hudson 1989). Although much of the route covers the same geographic locations addressed in this chapter, only the northeastern sites belonging to the Nodena and Parkin phases are thought to represent native American populations which came in contact with the Spanish conquistadors. Those samples from the Arkansas River Valley and the Ouachita and Red River drainages represent the time period from A.D. 1600 on and are dated well after the de Soto entrada.

The panregional protohistoric paleodemographic data are analyzed by age-specific mortality estimates and are crudely separated into three large demographic subsamples (see table 7). Subadults are individuals under 18 years at death, young adults are under 30 years at death, and older adults are those over 30 years at death. Of the 391 individuals, 304 or 78 percent are aged as adults and 44 or 11 percent are subadults (less than 18 years of age). There are 43 or 11 percent for whom ages could not be determined. These statistics provide the basic data for paleodemographic inference. The proportion of adults to subadults and the proportion of young adults to older adults are indicators of reproductive potential.

Table 7 presents the overall mortality profile of the 3 skeletal samples. The total protohistoric subadult sample, from 13 sites, makes up only 11 percent of the total protohistoric series. A normal biological population should contain between 30 and 50 percent subadults. Subadult material has traditionally been overlooked in the field and the recovery rate is low. This is due in large part to the excavation strategies in place during the turn of the century when many of these sites were excavated. The research priorities of the times tended to select against subadults (Moore 1908, 1910) (table 8). Rather than indicating low subadult mortality among the protohistoric populations, it is thought these statistics are the result of poor preservation and/or selective recovery. The analysis of subadult mortality is a sensitive indicator of overall population stress and adaptive efficiency. Due to the biases noted above, we are unable to incorporate childhood mortality statistics into the present study. We will measure population growth by comparing the percentage of young to old adults to determine what proportion of the adult population was available for reproduction.

Looking at the regional statistics from 304 adults (table 8), each geographic/cultural unit has a unique pattern of adult mortality. These proportional statistics indicate that over half the adults in the Late Mississippian northeastern group and over 75 percent of the adults in the Late Caddoan southwestern group could be expected to have survived past their primary reproductive years. Thus, these populations had the highest potential of reproductive success within the Protohistoric period of Arkansas. Conversely, the statistics representing east-central Arkansas indicate that the Menard complex people were not so fortunate. Almost twice as many young adults died as old

TABLE 7. Mortality Profile by Age.

| Archeological Component | Total | <18 | Age at death <30 Mean | >30 Mean | ? |
|---|---|---|---|---|---|
| NORTHEAST ARK 1450-1600 | 271 | 5.5 | 44.3 | 42.4 | 7.8 |
| EAST-CENTRAL ARK 1600-1700 | 72 | 25.0 | 40.3 | 20.8 | 13.9 |
| SOUTHWEST ARK 1650-1750 | 47 | 23.4 | 19.1 | 55.3 | 2.1 |

adults. The Menard complex data (East-central) strongly suggest that populations living between 1600 and 1700 in the Arkansas River Valley experienced a dramatic decrease in reproductive potential. The overwhelming majority of the adults was dying during their primary reproductive years (table 9).

While the Late Mississippian populations who lived in northeast Arkansas and the Late Caddoans who lived in southwest Arkansas both had a reasonable proportion of adults surviving past their primary reproductive years, their respective potential for reproductive success was not the same. Far fewer Late Mississippian adults were surviving into old age. These statistics indicate that the Late Caddoan populations enjoyed a much higher level of adaptive efficiency.

A closer examination of the mortality statistics representing just the Menard complex clearly illustrates the mechanics of depopulation. The mean statistics per age group show that there were far more younger adults dying than older adults. If we compare by gender alone, we can speak directly to the issue of reproductive potential. The majority of Menard complex females were dying during their peak reproductive years. Although these young males and females were dying in similar proportions, we know males, in general, retain the potential of reproduction long after thirty years of age. Thus, the Menard complex pattern of male mortality is not as significant. Conversely the female capacity for reproduction decreases after thirty years (Schwartz and Mayaux 1982; Hendershot, Mosher, and Pratt 1982).

TABLE 8. Mortality Profile: Aged Adults Only.

| Archeological Component | Total | Age at death <30 Mean | Age at death >30 Mean |
|---|---|---|---|
| NORTHEAST ARK 1450-1600 | 225 | 48.9 | 51.1 |
| EAST-CENTRAL ARK 1600-1700 | 44 | 65.9 | 34.1 |
| SOUTHWEST ARK 1650-1750 | 35 | 25.7 | 74.3 |

TABLE 9. Mortality Profile by Age and Sex for Adults Only.

| Archeological Component | Total | Death occurring <30 years of age M | F | ? | Mean | Death occurring >30 years of age M | F | ? | Mean |
|---|---|---|---|---|---|---|---|---|---|
| NORTHEAST ARK 1450-1600 | 225 | 17.3 | 28.9 | 2.7 | 48.9 | 19.1 | 21.3 | 10.7 | 51.1 |
| EAST-CENTRAL ARK 1600-1700 | 44 | 31.8 | 27.3 | 6.8 | 65.9 | 20.5 | 13.6 | 0.0 | 34.1 |
| SOUTHWEST ARK 1650-1750 | 35 | 14.3 | 11.4 | 0.0 | 25.7 | 42.8 | 31.4 | 0.0 | 74.3 |

These data offer a picture of depopulation. The vitality of the young female group is critical to the growth potential of succeeding generations. With a female population exhibiting reduced longevity, the reproductive potential for viable offspring would be severely impacted, leading to depopulation. This pattern of mortality is a critical aspect of our discussion.

The mortality data from northeast Arkansas reveal that there are proportionately the same number of older and younger adults (table 7). However, between the young and old female samples there exists a discrepancy. Here we see a slightly higher proportion of young females dying than older females. On the other hand, the younger and older males seem to have been dying in equal proportions. These data indicate that the reproductive potential among the Late Mississippian groups slightly diminished.

The mortality statistics representing the Late Caddoan population of southwestern Arkansas maintain a high potential of reproductive success. Far fewer younger females died than older females. The pattern of gender mortality among these groups indicates a high level of adaptive efficiency.

These three bioarcheological samples not only represent geographically defined units, they also represent temporal units. Based upon temporal variation in these mortality statistics we can track the pattern of depopulation across Arkansas. The earliest population, the Late Mississippians of northeast Arkansas, were maintaining an adequate adult life expectancy and a satisfactory level of adaptive efficiency between 1450 and 1600. However, we do see the beginnings of a slightly diminished reproductive potential among the female groups.

The adult inhabitants of the Arkansas River date later in time, between 1600 and 1700, and had the lowest adult life expectancies as well as the lowest reproductive potential of the entire study area. Following this pattern we should expect to see the most recent group, the Late Caddoans (1650–1750), with an even greater reduction in reproductive potential. However, this is not the case. Not only do they have the greatest adult longevity they also retained the greatest potential for reproductive success.

Perhaps the regional adult mortality statistics measure the increasing impact of European intrusion into the southeast United States. It is hypothesized that this intrusion into native cultures not only increased with time but, perhaps more significantly, was also dependent on geographic location (Burnett 1990a, 1990b). Evidence for European contact, in the form of trade items or historic accounts, has been found within the Late Mississippian and Menard complex populations (Morse and Morse 1983; Ford 1961; Jeter, Cande, and Mintz 1990), while comparable evidence is not present at the sites representing the Protohistoric era within Red and Ouachita drainage basins of Arkansas (Trubowitz 1984; Early 1990).

Comparison of the paleodemographic data of the Late Mississippians, up until 1600, indicates that these populations apparently enjoyed a fairly well-adapted biocultural system. However, when the data are compared to that of the Caddoan groups, there is some indication that these people may have experienced a slight reduction in reproductive potential. Evidence of reduced adaptive efficiency is clearly illustrated by the Menard complex data.

Apparently the populations living along the Mississippi River, its nearby tributary, the St. Francis, and the Lower Arkansas River, all major communication links between peoples, experienced reduced adult longevity which decreased further as time progressed. Perhaps this reduction in adult life expectancy is symptomatic of increasing cultural disruption due to the increasing European presence in the Southeast. Conversely, it appears that the protohistoric residents of the Ouachita and Red River drainage basins continued their aboriginal lifestyle, seemingly unaffected by the major cultural instability and accompanying depopulation that plagued their neighbors to the northeast. Perhaps, these Late Caddoan populations, living in dispersed settlements and in more remote areas, were buffered more completely from the European intrusion and consequently suffered less disruption of their biocultural systems (Burnett 1990b).

## ALTERNATIVE SUGGESTIONS

Prior to our analysis, the evidence supporting depopulation was drawn from both the archeological and ethnohistoric records. Based upon ethnohistoric descriptions of disease outbreaks among virgin populations, European disease has long been held responsible for the dramatic population losses in the Southeast (Dobyns 1983; Ramenofsky 1987). Based upon reproductive potential, the biological evidence provided here supports the view that dramatic depopulation occurred within at least *some* protohistoric groups of Arkansas.

The remaining question now is what caused the depopulation among other protohistoric populations of Arkansas during the "Dark Ages"? Was it the result of European disease? As previously stated, it has often been assumed that the depopulation of northeast Arkansas came about through contact with European disease carried by de Soto's army. However, our paleodemographic analysis of the these Late Mississippian populations does not support this speculation. The paleodemographic data provides little evidence for reduction in reproductive potential among the Late Mississippians in northeast Arkansas. In addition, several lines of negative evidence support our hypothesis. First, the skeletal series representing the northeastern Late Mississippians are dated between 1450 and 1600, indicating the area was still inhabited after de Soto's visit. If the de Soto entrada introduced European disease into these highly populated areas, the disease epidemics would have been rapidly disseminated leaving a wake of death. George R. Milner (1980) has suggested that mass graves or a change in mortuary practices might result from such a catastrophic event. Yet neither mass graves nor changes in mortuary practices are evident in the archeological record. Secondly, and perhaps most significant, is the lack of mention of disease outbreaks by the Spanish chronicles during the time the entrada was in this area. The Spanish were in Arkansas long enough to have witnessed an epidemic if one had occurred. Furthermore, the Spanish had recorded epidemic outbreaks among the native Americans in Mesoamerica (Smith 1974). The onset of smallpox symptoms occurs approximately nine days after infection with death typically following within a few days (Hopkins 1983). Knowing that the Spanish did observe and record the horrendous effect epidemics had on aboriginal groups, it is reasonable to presume that they would have made similar mention of such a dramatic event had it occurred in the Mississippi River Valley. In fact, it is thought by some scholars that two of de Soto's chroniclers recorded what has been interpreted as an epidemic in the area now known as South Carolina (Dobyns 1983; M. T. Smith 1987). However, this interpretation has been questioned (see Henige this volume). The Spanish spent approximately two years in Arkansas, and, if the region was as densely populated as has been projected (Morse and Morse 1990), the Spanish would surely have seen the ravages of an epidemic as they wove their way back and forth across the state.

The evidence indicates a reduction in reproductive potential is clearly in progress during the 1600s in the Arkansas River Valley. The historical documentation provided by the French indicate that populations living along the Arkansas River were visited by at least one epidemic in the very late 1600s. Father St. Cosme described a smallpox epidemic among the Quapaw in 1698 (Kellogg 1917:359). However, we do not know if the reduction in reproductive potential, that began well before 1698, among the Menard complex peoples can be related to European epidemics and/or to some other factor. There is some bioarcheological evidence to suggest that early Menard complex people were experiencing chronic malnutrition which could have influenced population growth (Burnett 1990a).

At present, it appears unlikely that European disease epidemics initiated the depopulation evident among the northeastern protohistoric groups which de Soto visited. However, we know that by 1673 these Late Mississippian populations were gone from the area. So why then did the Nodena and Parkin cultural manifestation cease to exist prior to 1673? Perhaps the answer lies within a totally different avenue of investigation.

Stahle, Cleveland, and Hehr (1985) reconstructed the drought cycle in northeastern and east-central Arkansas for the years between 1531 and 1980. Their analysis was based upon the Palmer Drought Severity Index and reconstructed both dry and wet periods for 450 years. They found that for the period between 1549 and 1577 negative index values occurred in 22 out of 29 years. They stated that this may represent the worst drought period in Arkansas during the past 450 years. This time period corresponds to the beginning of the "Dark Ages" of the Protohistoric period. Interestingly, these findings are underscored by the historic account of drought the people of the province of Casqui were experiencing when the de Soto entrada arrived. It will be remembered that de Soto and his men made a large wooden cross and placed it on a mound in order to pray to God for rain (Garcilaso 1951; Quinn 1979).

The bioarcheological reconstruction of the northeastern group does not offer a biological basis for depopulation and/or evidence of European epidemics during the Protohistoric period. The Late Mississippian people were essentially well adapted. However, we do know that these same people disappeared. Perhaps the explanation lies in the findings presented by Stahle, Cleveland, and Hehr (1985). According to archeological, bioarcheological, and ethnohistoric records we know that the Late Mississippian populations practiced intensive agriculture, supplemented by hunting and gathering (Morse 1989; Powell 1989; Murray 1985, 1989). The prolonged period of drought spanning twenty-nine years would not only have severely diminished agricultural productivity, but would also have had a profound effect upon the availability of wild food resources. These conditions most probably contributed to the disappearance of the Late Mississippian populations from northeast Arkansas.

## CONCLUSIONS

We would like to offer the following scenario. We still do not have evidence suggesting that the de Soto entrada had much biological impact on the northeast Arkansas groups. However, the prolonged period of drought, which occurred between the departure of de Soto's army and the arrival of the French, could have been a major contributor to the disappearance of the Late Mississippian populations by destroying their subsistence base. By the time we pick up the story again, with the Menard complex populations in the Arkansas River Valley, the inhabitants in this area were experiencing depopulation. It may be that during this time European disease had begun its movement through the major waterways linking the Arkansas River Valley to the rest of the southeastern United States. Conversely, the Late Caddoan people living in the Ouachita and Red river drainages seem to have escaped the tremendous upheavals seen in the Menard complex. The Late Caddoans remained healthy due in large part to their more isolated geographic location.

Abandonment of northeast Arkansas and the depopulation of east-central Arkansas cannot be associated with any single factor. The evidence strongly suggests that de Soto entrada did not bring epidemics with it. The major depopulation of this area occurred afterward and may have been initiated by a significant environmental disaster, the drought between 1549 and 1577, and later accelerated by further intrusions of Europeans and their diseases.

# The Long-Term Effects of the de Soto Entrada on Aboriginal Caddoan Populations

Timothy K. Perttula

## INTRODUCTION

> *The angel of death seems to have preceded rather than followed the white man, and testimony is practically unanimous that the aborigines decreased steadily and in many instances rapidly from the time of their first appearance. (John Swanton 1911)*

The first European explorers of the Caddoan Area were the two hundred or so ragged and exhausted members of the de Soto-Moscoso entrada in 1542. In their search for treasure and great wealth, the de Soto entrada aimed to discover native civilizations to exploit in La Florida like those encountered in Mexico and Peru (Quinn 1979, 2:93–96). That no such civilizations were discovered does not lessen the importance of the de Soto entrada and its various chronicles for the archeologist and ethnographer concerned with aboriginal life in the southeastern United States (Hudson et al. 1985, Hudson, DePratter, and Smith 1989).

At this time of initial European contact, the Caddoan-speaking groups lived in areas adjacent to, and between, the Arkansas and Red rivers, in the present-day states of Texas, Oklahoma, Louisiana, Arkansas, and Missouri. The Spanish chroniclers noted that the Caddoans shared similarities not only in language, but also in material culture and patterns of behavior and custom which differed from other aborigines previously encountered (Swanton 1939). The Caddoans were bison hunters as well as maize horticulturists. The Spanish chronicles provide a great deal of information about these aboriginal populations who "were still in the full state of their indigenous developments" (Brain 1985:xlviii) and who came to play a significant part in the Euro-American settlement of the area in the eighteenth and nineteenth centuries (see Perttula 1989). The long-term effects and consequences of contact and interaction between these Caddoan peoples and Europeans during the latter part of the Late Caddoan Period, recently defined by Story (1990:334) as lasting from A.D. 1520 to 1680, is the focus of the following study.

# THE QUESTION OF CONTACT

In the Caddoan area, periods of European contact can be divided into (1) a period of indirect and intermittent direct contact between European and Caddoan peoples, and (2) a subsequent period of direct, sustained, and continuous contact between both populations (Perttula 1989a).

## THE PERIOD OF INTERMITTENT AND INDIRECT CONTACT

It is clear that a focus on the Protohistoric period (A.D. 1520-1680) is of singular importance in the study of "initial changes brought about by European contact" (Trigger 1985:118). In general, episodes of indirect and intermittent direct contact with Europeans are characteristic of the years between 1520 and 1680.

Steward (1954:296) has noted that "even limited contacts with Europeans . . . may affect Indian society in a very fundamental sense." However, the duration or intensity of interaction between different cultural systems is only one part of the process of episodic contacts between Europeans and Native Americans. The magnitude or consequences of European influences can be initiated even while these groups are independent tribal or socio-political entities, substantially altering aboriginal societies prior to the actual onset of direct face-to-face European contact. Because the effects of European contact were well underway before the compilation of the earliest written records, archeologists and ethnohistorians are confronted with a "traumatic historic rupture in the evolution of culture in North America . . . like an archaeological Grand Canyon, more easily looked across than spanned or jumped" (Mason 1976:335).

Therefore, the extent to which European contact affected or changed aboriginal Caddoan societies in the Trans-Mississippi South will be underestimated if the archeological record is disregarded. Focus on written documents alone and the traits and particular cultural practices described there, rather than on the context of these traits, precludes the description of systemic discontinuity (major transformations in the cultural system) and of the processes responsible for the alterations and changes in culture traits (or their persistence) that created the ethnic groups described in the written documents. Trigger (1983:440) noted that an "increasing number of ethnologists and ethnohistorians are beginning to recognize that only archaeological data can provide a true base line for measuring changes brought about by a European presence in North America."

Thus, to consider the long-term effects of European contact on Caddoan groups, we must explore the processes, causation, and change embedded in the archeological record of the Late Caddoan period. To do this, archeologists must have already:

> detailed the changes in material culture that occurred during the protohistoric and early historic periods. This alone produces sufficient continuity in the archaeological record to permit archaeological and ethnohistorical data to be compared in detail for the early historic period, and the resulting understanding of the archaeological record to be used as a basis for interpreting earlier periods. (Trigger 1983:440)

European influence on Caddoan material culture during the Intermittent period has not been conclusively proved (Dickinson 1987; M. P. Hoffman 1986; Schambach and Early 1982:115), unlike in the Mississippi Valley and interior Southeast (Brain 1985a; Hudson, Smith, and DePratter 1984; Mitchem 1989; Morse and Morse 1983). However, an intriguing possibility for contact-related goods (albeit goods made by Caddoan peoples) are the "chalice-like" vessels found at three mid sixteenth-century Titus phase sites in the Cypress Creek drainage of East Texas (Turner 1978:98; Thurmond 1990).

R. L. Turner (1978:100) suggested that the ceramic "chalices" were copies of stemmed wine glasses, stemmed cups, or stemmed goblets in the possession of individuals in the de Soto entrada. Deagan (1987:127–55, and Figures 6.2a–b, 6.33a–b, 6.37b, 6.42, and 6.45) illustrated sixteenth-century Hispanic bottles, goblets, decanters, vases, and *almorratxa* which have a similar form to the stemmed vessels recovered in the Titus phase sites. These Titus phase sites are in the general vicinity of the province of *Lacane* (see Schambach this volume; Perttula 1989; Thurmond 1990) visited by Moscoso. Swanton (1939:348 and Map 9) equated the *Lacane* with the ethnographically recorded *Nacao,* a poorly known Caddoan group loosely affiliated with the Hasinai confederacy (see also Perttula et al. 1986:186–89; Chafe, this volume).

## Continuity and Change during the Intermittent Period

The intriguing evidence from the Cypress Creek should serve as notice that the archeological material remains which offer evidence of the entrada are likely to be subtle in character. Similarly, evidence of the transmission of epidemic diseases during this first phase of contact may be difficult to find. Nonetheless, smallpox, some form of tuberculosis (see Clark et al. 1987), and certain zoonoses (typhus, plague, and malaria) could all have been introduced to the area by the de Soto expedition (Ramenofsky 1982:255–59). Thus, it is important to note that while the effects of the de Soto entrada were probably not particularly significant in the sense of European goods and products being made available and introduced to the Caddo peoples, the biological effects of the entrada are manifold and cannot be easily overlooked. This is because in "virgin soil" conditions such as the Caddoan area, the introduction of an exotic virus such as smallpox can result in high mortality rates (Ramenofsky 1987a; Upham 1986; Crosby 1986).

This view of drastic change differs from a prevailing assumption of Caddoan resistance to European influence. The interpretation of the Caddoan archeological record in the periods following initial European contact has been consistently based on a systemic continuity between prehistoric, protohistoric, and historic Caddoan manifestations. In a review of the Caddoan historic archeological record, Gregory (1973:293–94) summarized that view, namely that:

> Certain patterns, established by the 1400s, were still functional in the eighteenth century. . . . This paper has attempted to remodel the eighteenth-century data in such a manner that these continuities are reflected in the interpretations and so the various Caddoan enclaves can be seen in a systemic way. . . . Consequently, the "changes" in Caddoan culture so often attributed to European influence merely reflect the adaptability of traditional economic strategies.

As a result of employing an assumption of continuity to link pre-contact and post-contact Caddoan tribal histories, the contact period archeological record has been conceptualized as a single entity comparable to written accounts beginning in the 1680s. Further, the presumed strength of the continuity has been accepted as demonstrating a resistance to European cultures that other native cultural groups did not possess (see C. H. Webb and Gregory 1978).

While not denying the historical record and the picture it paints of the political relationships and alliances of the time, an objective consideration of the changes to North American aboriginal peoples brought about by Europeans is negated by relying solely on the testimony of then-active participants embodied in the written documents to depict the "contest of cultures" (cf. Axtell 1985; Trigger 1983:440). As noted above, many changes took place long before the first in-depth accounts of aboriginal peoples were recorded by European explorers and settlers. Thus, the study of the archeology of this general period is essential to the comprehensive consideration of native history in the contact period, and the further integration of the ethnohistorical and archeological records as comparable or complementary data sets (see Story 1990:322–24).

## THE IMPLICATIONS OF DISEASE DURING THE INTERMITTENT PERIOD

### Demographic Issues

In what ways did Caddoan society and culture change as a result of European contact and interaction?

How is it possible to discuss, measure, and evaluate cultural change during the time period between 1520 and 1680 using the archeological record?

A key issue is the timing and magnitude of population declines in Caddoan groups caused by the introduction of European acute epidemic diseases (Perttula 1989; Ramenofsky 1987a; Trubowitz 1984).

Henry Dobyns (1983) has argued that periodic epidemics or pandemics (epidemics spread over wide geographic areas) caused dramatic population declines among North American Indians prior to 1565. After thoroughly reviewing the documentary evidence, David Henige (1986:303–05) has rather convincingly refuted the value of documentary sources as a means of demonstrating population reduction during this early period (see also Milanich 1987:174). Instead, Henige (1986) proposes that "arguments of silence," in this case the archeological record of the sixteenth and seventeenth centuries, be employed to independently demonstrate the timing and magnitude of such a population decline or demographic collapse, and thereby corroborate and extend the historical record.

Recent archeological and bioarcheological research in many regions of North and South America has shown that the lifeways of most aboriginal peoples were significantly "altered by changes produced by a European presence . . . long before the first detailed accounts of those groups were recorded" (Trigger 1983:439–40). In addition to changes which seemingly have occurred because of differences between Europeans and native Americans in social and political organization, religious beliefs, and technology, the impact of European-introduced diseases on aboriginal populations has become increasingly more significant (Dobyns 1983, 1988; Milanich and Milbrath 1989: 1–26; D. H. Thomas 1989).

Historians, demographers, and anthropologists have provided important comparative data on the reduction in population sizes among aboriginal groups across the world, including South America, Mexico and Central America, Australia, New Guinea, and New Zealand with the aid of written documentation (see Crosby 1986). Alaska and diverse regions within the North American continent have also been studied from this perspective (Thornton 1987; Crosby 1987; Ubelaker and Jantz 1986).

Archeologists and bioarcheologists, however, have begun to give attention to the demographic issue only recently. Both disciplines bring important insights to the interpretation of the record of contact period cultural change in the New World in light of European-introduced diseases and their diffusion (Trigger 1985; Milanich 1987; Ramenofsky 1987a). Re-evaluations of the sixteenth- and seventeenth-century archeological and bioarcheological records have been completed for South America, California, the Greater Southwest, the Great Plains of North America, the Northeast, Florida and the Caribbean, the Gulf Coast, South Texas, and the Southeastern United States (see for example Walker, Lambert, and DeNiro 1989; Merbs 1989; Trimble 1985; Snow and Lanphear 1988; Deagan 1985; Aten 1984; Miller 1988; Blakely 1988; Larsen 1987, 1987a; Ramenofsky 1985; Smith 1987, 1989).[1]

## Consequences of European Acute Diseases on Caddoan Populations

Significant diseases introduced in the Caddoan area included smallpox, measles, plague, diphtheria, whooping cough, trachoma, and influenza, among others, none of which were present in North America before the arrival of Europeans (Crosby 1986:197–98). The introduction of infectious diseases into non-immune or virgin soil populations would result in epidemics characterized by high morbidity and mortality figures and by abnormal age mortality distributions (Palkovich 1981). According to Ramenofsky (1982:80):

> (1) Exposure and infection for most of the diseases result in permanent or long-term immunity.
> (2) Therefore, if populations lack familiarity to such parasites, they have no immunity and are virgin colonizing territories for the reproduction of parasites.
> (3) In such populations, the parasite infestation is acute and epidemics erupt.

The increased mortality of adolescents and young adults from virgin soil epidemics results in decreased population fertility. Additionally, subsequent episodic infectious pathogens kill off those who, because they were born between epidemics, have no previous exposure or immunity. In the Texas area, epidemics at "least once each generation from 1731 to 1877" (Ewers 1973:107) are known from existing documentation (table

10). The cumulative effects of these recorded epidemics among the Texas Caddoan groups were a known 94 percent population reduction between 1690 and 1890 (Ewers 1973:table 1). Taking into consideration, therefore, the possibility of even more virulent and devastating epidemics between 1520 and 1680, the combined effect on aboriginal populations was unparalleled (Thornton 1987).

One of the more important aspects of the demographic issue which has been recently raised is that of disease diffusion (see Dobyns 1983; Ramenofsky 1987). Essentially disease diffusion concerns (1) the potential of introduced diseases to diffuse through native populations in advance of direct transmission from European settlers and explorers, and (2) the means of transmission and diffusion beyond points of initial introduction.

Henry Dobyns (1983:337) has pointed out that diseases such as smallpox, measles, and bubonic plague may spread widely and rapidly on a continental level (pandemics), and that the earliest virgin soil episodes of disease transmission caused the greatest mortality. He identified major epidemics, namely "decisive demographic events of the first magnitude in terms of their influence on Native American settlement and population" (Dobyns 1983: 337), in 1519–24, 1564–70, 1613–19, and 1633–39. The diffusion of disease pathogens from Cuba and Mexico is assumed to have had an effect over a large section of North America, in this case from Florida north to New England.

Kathleen Deagan (1985) and Anne Ramenofsky (1985, 1987a) list only a few suspected epidemics in Florida, the Lower Mississippi Valley, and Texas (table 11). The divergences in illustration 32 point out quite clearly different perspectives on what constitutes disease contact, as much as they do the occurrence of epidemics at those times. Direct references to epidemic episodes typify the lists provided by Deagan, Ramenofsky, and Ewers. The others are those disease outbreaks which Dobyns (1983:8–32) speculated diffused from Mexico and Cuba.

TABLE 10. Known Epidemics in the Caddoan Area of Texas (after Ewers 1973).

| Date | Type of Disease |
|---|---|
| 1691 | ? (Unidentified) |
| 1718 | ? (Unidentified) |
| 1731 | Smallpox |
| 1759 | Measles |
| 1777–1778 | Cholera or Bubonic Plague |
| | Smallpox |
| 1801–1802 | Smallpox |
| 1803 | Measles |
| 1816 | Smallpox |
| 1864* | Smallpox |
| 1867* | Cholera |
| 1892* | Measles, Influenza, Whooping Cough |

* Recorded among the Caddoan peoples living in Indian Territory, within the present boundaries of Oklahoma.

TABLE 11. Known or Suspected Sixteenth-Century Epidemics in Florida, the Lower Mississippi Valley, and Texas.

| FLORIDA (Deagan 1985) | FLORIDA (Dobyns 1983) | LOWER MISSISSIPPI (Ramenofsky 1985a, 1987b) | TEXAS (Ewers 1973) |
|---|---|---|---|
| | 1513 | | |
| | 1519 | | |
| | | | 1528 |
| | 1535 | | |
| | 1545-8 | | |
| | 1545-8 | | |
| | 1549 | | |
| | 1550 | | |
| | 1559 | | |
| 1570 | 1564-1570 | | |
| 1586 | 1585-6 | | |
| 1591 | | | |
| | 1596 | | |
| 1613 | 1613-7 | | |
| 1617 | | | |
| 1649 | 1649 | | |
| | 1653 | | |
| 1659 | 1659 | | |
| 1670 | | | |
| 1672-4 | 1672 | | |
| | 1675 | | 1674-5 |
| 1686 | | | 1686 |
| | | | 1691 |
| | | 1698 | |

The means of transmission was examined in Ramenofsky's (1987, 1987a) analyses of the diffusion potential of the different reported (or inferred) sixteenth- or seventeenth-century diseases to estimate the probability by which certain diseases could have diffused to North America, and what type of spatial pattern they might take. She distinguished between pathogens directly transmitted between humans such as measles, influenza, viruses, and smallpox, and those transmitted through an intermediate host or vector, the zoonoses (typhus, plague, and malaria). Human populations are not essential for the zoonotic pathogen to survive. The spread of the infection to humans usually occurs through accidents of proximity (Ramenofsky 1987a), and these infections have a higher diffusion potential than most of the directly transmitted diseases.

It was unlikely that the period of communicability of the directly communicated pathogens would have persisted long enough to survive European voyages across the Atlantic Ocean. Smallpox, however, was an exception because it could remain viable in a dried state for more than a year (Ramenofsky 1987a). That being the case, it could have been transmitted from Mexico or Cuba to North America during the pandemic of 1520–24, and then diffused widely across the continent, certainly into the Caddoan

Area. If the introduction of the smallpox epidemic caused at least a 50 to 75 percent reduction in population (Dobyns 1983:14; Upham 1986), the effects would have been disastrous.

That a major demographic decline probably occurred among Caddoan populations prior to a documented and sustained European presence in the area has major implications for interpreting the nature of the archeological record during the Protohistoric period, as well as for the periods following the first detailed European accounts of Caddoan peoples. Fundamental changes in aboriginal lifeways during these periods need to be evaluated in respect to new and more reliable information on the composition and formation of socio-political entities described in the written documents, and in interpreting possible systemic continuity between the archeological and historical cultures during a period of rapidly changing conditions (e.g., Trigger 1986; Ramenofsky 1987a).

## DISEASE DURING THE PERIOD OF DIRECT CONTACT

European contact in the Caddoan Area from an aboriginal perspective has two important but related components:

(1) The relative intensity of face-to-face contact; and

(2) The types of products associated with particular phases of face-to-face contact.

The most virulent effects of disease introduced in the New World probably took place during early epidemics rather than after repeated direct contact had been established between Europeans and Native Americans (Crosby 1967; Dobyns 1983). Each episode brought a lower rate of mortality than previous episodes (Robinson, Kelly, and Rubertone 1985), but populations declined as a consequence of the epidemics coming at regular intervals (ten to twenty years) after direct contact had been established (e.g., Dobyns 1988:69).

## RESEARCH QUESTIONS

Relevant questions which relate to the effects of European contact, particularly the role of diseases, on Caddoan groups include the following:

1. What is the historical significance of European-introduced diseases in the region? When did diseases have a significant effect on population reduction or social structure (Trubowitz 1984)?

2. Can demographic decline, stress, and health status among Caddoan groups be identified in the paleodemographic and bioarcheological records and what are the consequences?

3. Are there changes in settlement density, location, and the tempo of abandonment which relate to episodes of epidemics? If so, how does the process of regional abandonment relate to the development of Caddoan confederacies?

4. Do the effects of European contact and the spread of European diseases engen-

der the same types of responses by Caddoan groups living along major rivers as they do among those Caddoan groups inhabiting upland and hinterland areas?

5. Are there changes in mortuary practices, socio-political complexity, and mound building following the introduction of diseases which indicate significant changes in hierarchical ranking?

## When Did Diseases Have a Significant Effect on Caddoan Population?

No overall estimates of aboriginal population for the Caddoan area during the Indirect and Intermittent Contact Period have been made. Archeological data suggest that Caddoan settlements were arranged in dispersed settlement patterns characterized by a relatively low regional population density when compared to the denser nucleated populations in the Mississippi Valley and parts of the interior Southeast (cf. Steponaitis 1986; B. Smith 1986; M. T. Smith 1987). Relatively higher densities may have been found near the Caddoan civic-ceremonial mound centers, but in general the civic-ceremonial centers were separated from domestic habitations (Schambach 1982; Story 1990).

Henry Dobyns' (1983:42) estimate of 2.53 persons per square kilometer for horticultural peoples living along the Mississippi River Valley and its tributaries, including the Red and Arkansas rivers in the Caddoan area, would indicate, very generally, 200,000 to 250,000 people living in the Caddoan area in 1520. This figure would be higher were it not for the fact that there was only a minimal Late Caddoan permanent utilization of sections of the Ouachita Mountains and Ozark Highlands (Sabo et al. 1988). Although there is no way at present to evaluate the accuracy of this population estimate, it is well to keep in mind that Mooney's (1928) estimate of populations for all Caddoan groups at sustained European contact (1690) was only 8,500 persons.

Russell Thornton (1987:30) proposed a method of population estimation based on multiplying the population of an aboriginal group at its nadir, or lowest point in the historical record, by a constant of 20 or 25 (see also Dobyns 1966). The two constants express varying estimates of the rate of population decline in the contact era. The nadir in Caddoan population was reached around 1890 to 1900 when 507 Caddo were enumerated on their Oklahoma reservation (Thornton 1986:Appendix E). Using this method, the total Caddoan population can be estimated to have ranged between 10,140 and 12,675 at the time of sustained contact.

Differences in the approaches to estimates of Native American population sizes depend primarily upon consideration of the impact of European diseases (Ramenofsky 1987a:6–21). Lower population estimates, such as Mooney's, are based on a disregard of acute infectious diseases as a factor in population estimation prior to sustained European contact. That epidemics after 1690 in the Caddoan area severely reduced population sizes (illustration 31) is acknowledged (e.g., Swanton 1942:17). But when European acute diseases are considered as a major factor affecting the population during the Indirect and Intermittent Contact period, assumptions of population size changes are less predictable. For example, the population size in 1690 in the Caddoan area would show little correlation with populations in 1520. Projecting backwards in time from 1690, population sizes would be inappropriate because of the different effects of each epidemic on population loss.

## Two Views of Caddoan Demographic Change

Thus, two opposing views of demographic change in the Caddoan area may be proposed based upon presumptions concerning when the introduction of European diseases affected Caddoan populations. Assuming that the population estimate of 8,500 Caddoan peoples at 1690 is fairly realistic (cf. Ubelaker 1976), the basic difference between the two demographic models is in their assumptions about when depopulation began.

In the first view, no epidemics would have taken place among any Caddoan groups until 1691, based upon when the first historically recorded epidemic was described by the Spanish. The period between 1520 and 1690, therefore, would be one of continual Caddoan population growth (perhaps on the order of 1 percent annually [cf. Dobyns 1988]), and the population maximum would have been reached about 1690 (Mooney 1928; Swanton 1942). Based on historical records, population sizes then decreased approximately 80 percent between 1700 and 1780 (from 7,000 to 1,400 individuals), and continued to decrease until around 1900 (Thornton 1986, 1987:127–31; Swanton 1942:24). The overall depopulation trend resembles the line to the right in illustration 32. Although the trend is portrayed as a smooth monotonic decrease, in fact it would probably have taken a stair-step form; that is, one reflecting some population recovery or rise between epidemics and then further population decline.

The depopulation trend depicted in the line to the left in illustration 32, conversely, assumes that the aboriginal population maximum for Caddoan peoples occurred around the time of initial European contact in the Southeast (1520). Because of the possibility that a series of epidemics was transmitted along aboriginal trading routes, populations would have declined precipitously between 1520 and 1690. Based on Dobyns' (1983:Table 1, 2, and 4) arguments about disease diffusion, the Caddoan area pandemics of 1519–24, 1531–33, and 1545–48 could have caused the greatest relative depopulation.

A total population on the order of 200,000 at around 1520 and 8,500 at around 1690 would mean an estimated 96 percent decline in population over that time. This is congruent with overall demographic losses elsewhere in the Southeast among populations which were probably episodically exposed to the same types of epidemic diseases (Dobyns 1983:288). Using population figures presented above for the 1690–1880 period, a 95 percent decline during that time can be predicted. The earlier and steeper depopulation trend (see illustration 32), therefore, takes into account the likely possibility that the initial epidemics of the sixteenth century were actually responsible for the greatest absolute declines in population.

## Can Health Status Be Identified in the Caddoan Bioarcheological Record?

Caddoan area skeletal data for the historical period (see Harmon and Rose 1989:348–49; Burnett 1990b:399–400, 408, 410; Rose and Burnett 1990:147) remain inadequate for a consideration of issues of depopulation or demographic stress. This is because of unsystematic excavations and collection procedures, poor preservation, and a paucity of available information concerning possible intra-community or regional variations in horizontal or vertical differentiation (see O'Shea 1984). Thus, a study of the parameters of cultural change in the contact era dealing with Caddoan skeletal remains must await a more comprehensive areal and/or research effort.

## What Is the Process of Regional Abandonment?

John C. Ewers (1973:109) has suggested that only rarely did Caddoan group size fall below about 150 people before the group merged with another. This minimum group size was probably an attempt to maintain stable population levels and population fertility within the group. Amalgamation would have occurred following the effects of European diseases as the labor and defense forces were diminished. The coalescence of formerly discrete entities was necessary in order for the new unit to remain a viable social and economic system (see Milner 1980). As a result of this amalgamation of population groups, original settlement areas may have been abandoned and the areas where population remnants amalgamated actually may have been represented in early historical phases as a local population increase at that time.

## Are There Differential Responses Related to Settlement Pattern?

Within the Caddoan area, there are settlement system differences that have implications for differential population densities at initial contact. The contrast is between major riverine "town" communities (in the sense described by Schambach, this volume) that had denser populations than rural communities located away from major streams (cf. Dobyns 1983; Morey and Morey 1973). Therefore, while the estimates of total numbers of people living in the Caddoan area from 1520 to 1690 are unverifiable, it is possible to suggest relationships between Late Caddoan phases in potential population density differences that would have their basis in community/settlement differences.

The de Soto narratives note variations in populations between major riverine and hinterland provinces that seemingly are reflected in the current initial contact period Caddoan archeological record (Perttula 1989a:68–70). The province of *Naguatex* on Red River is illustrative of a "town" community. It was described by one of the chroniclers as "the most populous of all the provinces through which the army passed during this expedition" (Swanton 1942:32). Archeologically, the Belcher phase (illustration 33) is the most appropriate candidate for identification as *Naguatex* (see Webb and Gregory 1978; Schambach this volume).

Rural community phases include the Frankston, Titus, Fort Coffee, Angelina, and Neosho phases (see illustration 33). Absolute differences in population between the rural community phases cannot be estimated even roughly. However, the de Soto narratives do provide some discussion of recognizable differences in populations between the *Guasco* and *Hais* provinces in East Texas that refer basically to population rank differences between the Frankston and Late Angelina phases (Elvas in Robertson 1933). Of course, these differences may have stemmed from the Caddoan efforts to make their communities look less attractive to the Spaniards because they had advance notice of de Soto's history of depredation.

Differential population densities within the Caddoan area have direct implications for the study of contact and the consequences of European epidemic diseases. Smaller, dispersed rural communities had an adaptive advantage over denser populated town communities in minimizing direct contact with Europeans and thereby lessening the impact of the spread of epidemic diseases (Trubowitz 1984:36). Therefore, while Caddoan area population densities were probably not as high as those in nucleated settlements in the Mississippi Valley and major eastern tributaries, there still existed patterns of differential population density (attested to in the archeological and ethnohistorical records) that formed the demographic constraints within which the effects of European-introduced diseases need to be viewed.

The dispersed nature of Caddoan settlement systems, the *rancherias* of the Spanish documents, also precludes the type of basic demographic analyses employed in other parts of North America which rely upon quantitative differences in settlement frequencies through time (e.g., Ramenofsky 1987a; M. T. Smith 1987). A count of the number of sites in a dispersed settlement system cannot be readily compared with the count of sites in a nucleated or consolidated settlement system. This is due to the differences in occupation span and the necessity to have appropriate regional settlement data for demographic inferences. Thus, in the archeological record for the Caddoan area, inferences about population or settlement change are made most appropriately at the regional scale. In this way, one can circumvent nondirectional variations caused by the sampling problems mentioned above. Also, one can avoid differences based on probable shifts in settlement size, movements, and amalgamation of different groups in the historic period that affect the changing character of the record.

## Are There Changes in Social Complexity?

In a situation in which population size was declining significantly and/or continuously due to the effects of disease, population loss can be expected to have exerted a considerable influence on the existing scale of supra-community organization. For instance, the loss of the support population for elite ranked individuals in Caddoan society should be evidenced by a general decline or collapse of the civic-ceremonial system and of those facilities that constitute integrative mechanisms (Knight 1986).

To focus on elements of the archeological record that are informative about processes of integration in past societies is to be concerned with evidence of social differentiation and complexity, i.e., the existence of social ranking in economic, socio-political, and ceremonial spheres of different communities. As O'Shea (1984:4) pointed out, ranking and differentiation are key aspects of complexity in social relationships. Egalitarian societies are simple societies; ranked or stratified societies are complex in organization. A ranked society is one "regulated by mechanisms (i.e., inheritance) that fix the potential number of statuses an individual may aspire to beyond those dictated by personal characteristics" (Rogers 1983:22). This means that there is limited access to positions of prestige, and that holding a position of rank confers privilege in different spheres of society. Rank distinctions are those which tend to elevate certain individuals above others in the social system and may be referred to as *vertical differentiation. Horizontal differentiation* includes those social differences which generally cross-cut age and sex categories or rank distinctions (see O'Shea 1984:Table 4.3).

In the archeological record, there are two primary means by which matters of social organization and complexity may be inferred: (1) the study of mortuary practices, and (2) the study of hierarchical organization, specifically the hierarchy of settlements or site types.

Burial assemblages from the Caddoan area dating to the period between 1520 and 1800 may be examined for systemic changes in social differentiation, especially vertical differentiation (Perttula 1989:152–64, 260–84). Key criteria include the diversity of grave offerings, the spatial segregation of the individuals, the inclusion of valued symbols and trappings of authority (Rogers 1983:67), and the differences in treatment of the burial (i.e., complexity of the burial ritual).

In the Caddoan area, hierarchical systems are identified in the archeological record by the presence of civic-ceremonial centers and supralocal or multi-community cemeteries. Both elements occur in the Caddoan area beginning around 900 (see Sabo et al. 1988; Jeter et al. 1989; Story 1990), but later manifestations are important in the present context. Civic-ceremonial centers are manifestations of a highly developed system of ceremonial activity. The construction of specialized facilities such as platform mounds, public buildings, plazas, and charnel houses are assumed to represent expressions of a regional and centralized socio-political structure, one maintained by an elite group of individuals to sanctify chiefly authority, political power, ritual, and supernatural prerogatives of the community (Knight 1986:681). Traditions of ceremonial activity in a mortuary context include the processing and interment of individuals in specialized mound contexts that can be interpreted as the result of hierarchic differences in rank or status which exist within the larger society as a whole.

Supralocal cemeteries are a related manifestation of the presence of a specialized structural context based upon social differences within a population. They are recognized by type of burial interment, cemetery size, grave good association, and isolation from habitation sites, characteristics that can be duplicated in a civic-ceremonial context. Both the civic-ceremonial centers and supralocal cemeteries exhibit a pattern of spacing and isolation from habitation sites that is probably dictated in part by the relative densities of the surrounding support populations. In a situation where population size is declining significantly and/or continuously due to the effects of disease, population loss can be expected to exert a considerable influence on the scale of supracommunity organization and the number of functions able to be performed. In addition, the loss of the support population of the elite ranked individuals in Caddoan society should be evidenced in a general decline in complexity, or even abandonment, of the civic-ceremonial system during the phase of European contact and a replacement by newer and more viable forms of political integration such as confederation and annexation (Knight 1986:683).

# AN ANALYSIS OF THE ARCHEOLOGICAL RECORD

The archeological record of the Caddoan area during the period between 1520 and 1680 was examined critically to study Caddoan-European interaction and Caddoan cultural changes following European contact (Perttula 1989:126–210) by comparing the archeological record of the historic period within each of the three subareas of the Caddoan area: the Western Caddo, Central Caddo, and Arkansas Basin Caddo (Schambach 1983). The archeological record for this period of time was analyzed to detect systemic cultural change from pre-contact to early historic times among Caddoan peoples and to determine how such change might be the manifestation of a comprehensive reorientation in Caddoan life arising from the interaction with Europeans.

The lack of regionally based representative samples of settlements in the Caddoan area prohibited accurate archeological estimates of population changes during the early historic period. Instead, qualitative differences in socio-political and community-wide aspects of Caddoan lifeways were reviewed (Perttula 1989) as a means of characterizing Caddoan cultures and of examining apparent group or phase differences as they relate to inferred population loss from disease, settlement movements, and changes in social and political organization.

By the time of sustained European contact beginning in 1680, large portions of the Caddoan area had been abandoned. Spatial continuity between late prehistoric (1400–1520), early historic phases, and historical groups is variable within each recognizable region, producing a fragmentary and disjunctive historic record (illustration 34).

Particularly along the major streams such as the Arkansas, Red, and Ouachita rivers, abandonment seems to have occurred between 1600 and the first substantial face-to-face European contact. This abandonment was not a unitary process, but involved common features of: (1) substantial movement of groups in the late sixteenth and seventeenth centuries, and (2) coalescence with other groups only in major riverine settlements on the Red River or on the lower Arkansas River.

## The Arkansas River Basin Caddo

In the Arkansas River Basin of Eastern Oklahoma, Caddoan settlement ended around 1550 to 1600. Indications of more mobile settlement systems becoming successful about this time on the Southern Plains are accompanied not only by a reorientation of regional subsistence exploitation patterns, but by differences in socio-political complexity congruent with a non-hierarchical or egalitarian system of political organization. The archeological record suggests a rapid movement out of the Arkansas River basin by the remaining population during the seventeenth century. That movement towards the Red River, or west up the Arkansas River, was accompanied by the intensification of a plains-oriented subsistence system based on seasonal bison hunting using the horse (Bell 1984).

In the Ouachita River valley, Caddoan groups may have moved downriver through the sixteenth and seventeenth centuries into areas that had been vacant since about 1400 (Gibson 1985:328–31). These Caddoan groups appear to have been made up of formerly separate socio-political entities. Discontinuation of mound construction and shaft burials in the Caddoan part of the Ouachita River valley took place in the late sixteenth century. Mounds and shaft burials were apparently replaced by community cemeteries since these are limited to the location of intrusive burial plots on the tops of mounds.

## The Central Caddo

The Red River Valley in the Central Caddo subarea is one of the better-known regions for the early historic period. Excavations at the Belcher and Cedar Grove sites (C. H. Webb 1959; Trubowitz 1984; Jeter et al. 1989) have provided substantial evidence on diachronic patterns of mound use, mortuary practices, and community complexity between 1500 and 1740. Periods of mound use and mound pit burials on the Red River for the McCurtain and Belcher phase areas predate 1650, and their discontinuation coincides with patterns of decreased social differentiation and/or complexity, as well as less extensive settlement within the Red River valley (table 12). Settlements are widely separated even in the early historic period, and they appear to be made up of clusters of farmsteads and family communities. These localities are maintained throughout the early historic period, and up to about 1730 or later, and were the focus of whatever regional processes of population amalgamation and settlement that took place. This kind of regional settlement density is consistent with local population amalgamation and regional population decline. The amalgamation, however, did not bring populations within these locales up to the densities probably characteristic of the area at precontact times.

## The Western Caddo

In the Western Caddo subareas of East Texas and the Ouachita Mountains, the historic archeology of Caddoan rural communities is indicative of changes in socio-political complexity, accompanied by a localization of community systems, similar to the record in the Red River Valley. In the Ouachita Mountains, moreover, it is possible that much of the region was not permanently inhabited after 1600. Relatively specific changes in the nature of Caddoan community organization during the early historic period were noted in the Cypress Creek/Upper Sabine archeological records. Examples of nonmound shaft burials and isolated community cemeteries associated with distinct spatial groups (referred to as clusters or subclusters in Thurmond 1985) were readily identified as manifestations of socio-political integration which replaced mound centers. Mound centers were replaced by the formation of community-wide cemeteries around 1550 to 1600. However, both the community cemeteries and the nonmound shaft burials are considered short-lived phenomena, lasting in the archeological record until 1650–70.

Therefore, while processes of regional abandonment and possible depopulation affected East Texas and Western Caddoan populations in the early historical period, the fact that community reintegration did occur may mean that depopulation was not initially as severe among rural communities as it was along the major river valleys.

TABLE 12. Temporal Trends in the Archeological Record. Courtesy of Timothy K. Perttula.

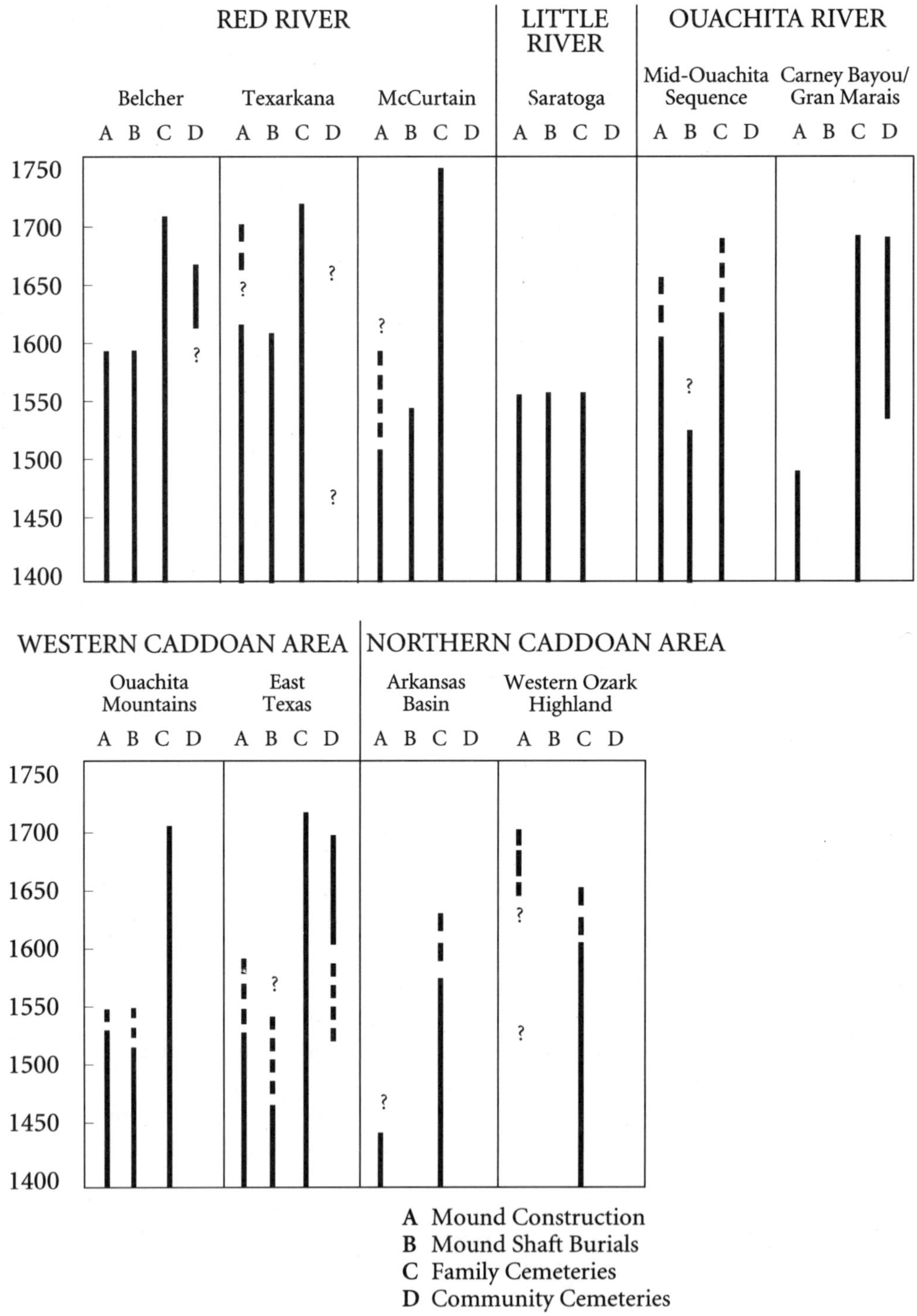

That the Sabine, Neches, and Angelina River basins in East Texas appear to have had a higher density of early historic and post-1680 settlements than is the case on major rivers within the Caddoan area also suggests a greater depopulation in town communities on major rivers than in rural communities following European contact and interaction. Even in these areas the occupations are more scattered than they were around 1520, with many of the minor river valleys unoccupied or with a smaller overall population. Even in 1700, the Caddoan populations in East Texas were larger than the Kadohadacho and the Natchitoches on Red River, and they maintained that numerical superiority throughout the eighteenth century while the total Caddoan population decreased from about 7,000 to 1,400 individuals (Swanton 1942).

At one time all Caddoan-speaking groups in the Caddoan area appear to have spoken separate dialects (Lesser and Weltfish 1932), but the linguistic evidence parallels the socio-political changes noted above in its progressive between-group homogeneity, and the subsequent disappearance of most dialects. The confederacies existed at the time of sustained European contact, and while still referred to as confederacies throughout the eighteenth century, the overall control of Caddoan society was apparently based more on the individual kin group by around the middle of the eighteenth century (e.g., Wyckoff and Baugh 1980; Gregory 1973). The confederacies are best considered short-lived products of intra-group fragmentation and inter-group agglomeration in a few select locales. Groups changed alliances and relationships from generation to generation and were often divided between the confederacies. They were probably also a response to regional depopulation, but ensuing local settlement aggregation had an important effect on how diverse kin/dialect groups could be integrated into a newly created functioning society.

# Notes

1. Further discussions on the demographic issue and the consequences of disease introduction on Native-American populations may be found in Thomas (1990, 1990a).

# Appendix I: Reply to Henige

Charles Hudson, Chester B. DePratter, and Marvin T. Smith

Our reconstruction of the route of the Hernando de Soto expedition has stimulated a number of challenges from both laymen and scholars in the last ten years, most of which have taken exception to particular portions of our route. Did the expedition land at Tampa Bay or Charlotte Harbor? Was Guasili near Murphy, North Carolina, or Asheville? Was Mabila near the junction of the Alabama and Tombigbee rivers or near the lower Cahaba River? Was the crossing of the Mississippi River near Memphis, Tennessee, or near Clarksdale, Mississippi? By and large these criticisms and alternate solutions have come from individuals who are knowledgeable about the archeology of the southeastern United States.

David Henige's criticism of our work proceeds from a different basis. He betrays no knowledge of Southeastern archeology, and in fact argues that the archeological site preservation is so imperfect that archeology can have no bearing on reconstructing de Soto's route. And from his final gibe—"there is no good reason to say that 'de Soto slept here'" (Henige this volume)—we can only conclude that he is contemptuous of all attempts to reconstruct the de Soto route, implying that the effort is prompted by no more than an antiquarian and provincial fascination with small particulars.

We have quite a different assessment of the value of reconstructing the de Soto route. Our assertion when we began this research in 1980 was that if the route can be laid on a map with reasonable accuracy, it would become possible to link the historical information from the era of Spanish exploration and colonization together with the very considerable body of archeological information which has been amassed in the Southeast over the past century and a half. As we have said repeatedly, linking these two bodies of information together will make it possible to begin reconstructing the social geography of the sixteenth-century Southeast, and it will become possible to say at least something about a period of more than a century of the history of the Southeast. To be able to say anything at all about the social and cultural world that existed from the sixteenth-century entradas until the late seventeenth century, when Europeans next visited the interior of the Southeast (an area comprising about one-fourth of the United States), would not, in our opinion, constitute a small achievement.

Henige's principal criticisms are as follows:

*I.* Not all of the four chronicles of the de Soto expedition are firsthand; some of the chroniclers may have borrowed from others; none have to date been subjected to detailed critical scrutiny, and until this is done no headway can be made in reconstructing de Soto's route.

*II.* The destruction of archeological sites has been so extensive that it is impossible to identify the locations of sixteenth-century native polities or to identify areas where Indians were not living, and the discovery of sixteenth-century European artifacts in Indian archeological sites can tell us nothing about the activities of the Spanish explorers.

*III.* We rely excessively upon Garcilaso de la Vega's *La Florida del Ynca,* which Henige has argued elsewhere is a work of fictional history. (He also criticizes us for *not* citing Garcilaso in a number of instances.)

*IV.* The four chronicles taken together do not provide enough detailed and corroborated information to support our reconstruction of the route.

*V.* We assume that all of the chroniclers computed distances in terms of the *legua común* (3.46 miles to the league), and using this measure we hypothesize that Juan Pardo and Hernando de Soto averaged 17.5 miles per day, every day.

*VI.* Our claim that the documents of Juan Pardo's second expedition confirm the location of Chiaha is without foundation.

*VII.* Using proper historical methods it is impossible to reconstruct de Soto's route.

This is a rough bill of particulars. Let us examine these criticisms case by case and determine whether we are guilty as charged.

We wish to make plain from the outset that we have never been under the illusion that reconstructing the de Soto route is anything but a precarious enterprise. We knew from the start that it was risky and we knew that a solution satisfying the highest standards of historical evidence was out of the question. If the historical evidence for the expedition had been ample, allowing the luxury of conclusive results, someone would have achieved a usable reconstruction long ago. This is why we have spoken of achieving a "best fit"—a reconstruction of where de Soto and his army went that is consistent (i.e., having very few contradictions) with the documentary data, archeological data, and geographical information. We have not proceeded by simply linking archeological sites together by a connect-the-dot approach, but rather by trying many alternative routes and by selecting the one that best fits the total body of information. We have never promised finality, and neither did the United States De Soto Expedition Commission (Swanton 1939:1), even though Henige implies that such was their intention.

I. Henige's statement that the de Soto expedition seems to be documented by four firsthand accounts is an extraordinary claim. We know of no modern scholar who has thought that Garcilaso de la Vega's 1605 *La Florida del Ynca* was based on a firsthand account. Perhaps Henige makes this exaggerated statement to heighten his own claim in his 1986 article that not only is *La Florida del Ynca* a secondary work, it is a work of fictional history or pseudohistory. It has, he says, "no demonstrable historical worth."

According to Garcilaso, he based *La Florida del Ynca* upon his conversations or interviews with several who participated in the expedition, and with one in particular, who from internal evidence appears to have been Gonzalo Silvestre. He also used two written accounts, which are not known to have survived, by Alonso de Carmona and Juan Coles. But Henige argues that there was a source in the woodpile. The *Relaçam* by the Gentleman of Elvas was published in 1557, almost fifty years prior to the publication of *La Florida del Ynca,* and while Henige has no evidence that Garcilaso owned or read the book, he argues that he *could* have done so. But if Garcilaso used information from the *Relaçam* in this way, it is curious that when his narrative is compared with that of the Gentleman of Elvas (whose narrative is consistent with those of Ranjel and Biedma) there are such notable lacunae, scrambled itineraries, and instances of out-of-place information (Hudson, Smith, and DePratter 1984:65). Perhaps to explain this awkward inconsistency, Henige (1986a) proposes an even more insidious possibility: It may have been Silvestre who read the *Relaçam* of the Gentleman of Elvas. Henige (1986a:6) even speculates that reading the *Relaçam* and finding himself not mentioned prompted Silvestre to collaborate with Garcilaso in telling his story "in order to 'balance' the historical record." Finally, Henige (1986a:19) states that because of Silvestre's advanced age we cannot be sure that he was not senile. There is more: Silvestre may have been a notorious liar (Henige 1986a:20), and we cannot even be sure that Garcilaso collaborated with Silvestre (Henige 1986a:12). If a dubiety prize in history were to be awarded, Henige should be the first recipient. In fact, Henige is here piling doubt upon doubt, which is the obverse of pyramiding hypotheses, a practice which he deplores.

Our reading of *La Florida del Ynca* persuades us that it is to be taken as primarily a work of oral history, and it is rife with the problems inherent in this genre. In addition, we see no reason to doubt that Garcilaso had access to the two brief written accounts which he appears to use more as verification than as information to fill in gaps in Silvestre's oral narratives. But Garcilaso did not write an oral history in the modern sense. Rather, it was one which would appeal to the literary tastes of Spaniards in the latter half of the sixteenth century. Hence, it is full of high-blown rhetoric and exaggeration and employs devices from myths and legends which were familiar to Garcilaso's intended audience (Lankford this volume). But this is no justification for consigning *La Florida del Ynca* to the same shelf with Geoffrey of Monmouth's *Legendary History* and James Macpherson's Ossian poems.

The exaggerated numbers in *La Florida del Ynca* are well known (see Henige 1986a:14–16). To this we can add that *La Florida del Ynca* cannot be used to establish the dates on which events occurred, and it is dubious that it will ever be useful in establishing the locations of any Indian towns. We did try to use *La Florida del Ynca* for this purpose on several occasions, before learning better, and it has misled us in every case. But we think it imprudent to say that it could *never* be used to help establish the location of a town.

*La Florida del Ynca* contains information about incidents not contained in the other de Soto chronicles and in some cases information which appears to be more plausible than information in the other accounts. Only *La Florida del Ynca* tells how a contingent of men under Baltasar de Gallegos at Ilapi followed a trail to rendezvous with de Soto as he marched northward from Cofitachequi to Xuala (Hudson, Smith, and DePratter 1984:74). Both the *Relaçam* of the Gentleman of Elvas and *La Florida del Ynca* recount the journey of the contingent of cavalry which de Soto sent from Apalachee back to the camp at Tampa Bay. But the *Relaçam* (B. Smith 1866:47–48) states that they captured twenty female slaves at Ytara and Potano, about half way along their journey, and that they took these slaves with them even though they were traveling on their horses as rapidly as they could. It is not believable that these enslaved women could have kept up. Garcilaso, on the other hand, recorded that they enslaved some Indians whom they found fishing in Tampa Bay the night before they arrived at the camp (Garcilaso 1951:220–21). This is plausible. Silvestre was probably a participant in this action; the Gentleman of Elvas apparently was not.

What of the incidents described in *La Florida del Ynca* which are not mentioned in the other three accounts? Some of them partake of the legendary (Lankford this volume), as at the battle of Mabila, when the shaft of Nuo Tovar's lance was pierced by an Indian arrow as if it had been drilled through (Garcilaso 1951:368). Did this really occur? Perhaps. But even if it did not occur precisely as stated in *La Florida del Ynca,* this incident makes vivid the nature of this battle (arrows vs. lances), and it reveals something about the mentality of the Spanish soldiers who fought on that day.

Henige cites with favor Patricia Galloway's claim that the *Relaçam* of the Gentleman of Elvas is partly based on a manuscript by Rodrigo Ranjel. In our judgment Galloway's argument is flimsy at best. But even if it can be proven that the author of the *Relaçam* actually used Ranjel's account, Galloway does not claim that the *Relaçam* is wholly derived from it. Hence, the independent status of the *Relaçam* may be diminished but not completely undermined.

Why is it that the *Relaçam* is many pages longer than Ranjel's account, from which it is supposedly derived? Henige says it is padded with irrelevant details and speechifying. But some of these details of native life are consistent with other information established on the basis of documents and archeological information. If the author of the *Relaçam* invented this detail, he was either prescient or clairvoyant (e.g., in B. Smith 1866:52–53). Even the speeches, which are literary devices, contain elements of information that are consistent with features of Southeastern Indian social organization. For example, the chief of Chiaha's reference to avuncular succession to office is consistent with the matrilineal descent that predominated in the Southeast (Elvas 1866:71). Hence, even the speeches may not be completely fabricated.

II. Henige apparently believes that we think that the presence of a sixteenth-century European artifact on an archeological site "must represent evidence that events related to them occurred at that very spot" (Henige this volume). Nothing can be further from the truth. Marvin T. Smith (1987:25–27) discussed many potential mechanisms by means of which European artifacts reached the interior. They could have entered native exchange systems and have moved inland from areas of coastal contact with Europeans; they could have been given out by Spanish explorers in the interior; or they could have been distributed by Europeans in the interior but subsequently moved about, as was material given by Juan Pardo to an Indian who was visiting from several days' travel away (Hudson 1990:96). What we have firmly argued, based on both historical and archeological evidence, is that the material did not stay in circulation very long, and it is thus useful in determining which Indian towns were occupied in the mid sixteenth century. Historical information from the de Soto narratives suggests that European items the Spaniards themselves attributed to the Ayllón colony less than fifteen years previously were already found in the mortuary temple at Talomeco.

Were these European materials used for long periods? It is clear that the earliest, most diagnostic artifacts (especially Nueva Cadíz beads) are virtually never found in direct association (for example, in the same grave pit) with later types of artifacts. We must look at the total assemblage of European artifacts from a site before assigning a date (usually based on comparison with documented Spanish settlements in the New World). The mid sixteenth century assemblage is quite distinctive, and we know of no archeological evidence that this material was passed on to future generations (M. T. Smith 1987). Thus we have argued that sites producing such artifacts date to the mid sixteenth century. Most European artifacts from this period are not diagnostic enough for us to say which expedition may have brought them into the interior, although there are many useful clues. Pardo did not have any horses, so horseshoes found near the proposed route probably came from de Soto or Luna, and probably did not come from coastal contacts. Neither de Soto nor Pardo was planning to found an agricultural colony, so sickles found in the interior probably originated with the Luna colonizing venture. When these sites with European artifacts are consistent with estimates of distances traveled, with geographical parameters mentioned in the documents (islands, stream confluences, mountains, relationships to other towns, etc.), and the sites fit into the overall shape of the route, then we feel rather confident in suggesting that we have located specific towns.

Henige questions our use of the King site sword as evidence that de Soto passed through the area of the King site. Perhaps we were remiss in not citing work in progress, but we were privileged to share in the early results of research by David Mathews and Robert Blakely of Georgia State University. Mathews and Blakely presented evidence that many of the occupants of the King site had been killed or wounded in a conflict with a European military force. By comparing the distribution of wounds on the King site with the distribution of wounds on European battle victims, an identical pattern emerged. This suggests that the King site victims were attacked by Europeans, fighting in a European manner, not by native Americans fighting with European weapons (Blakely 1988; Blakely and Mathews 1990). The only logical perpetrator of this "massacre" was the force under de Soto (see also Hudson, DePratter, and Smith 1988). Thus there was far more evidence than a single European artifact, the sword, to suggest the presence of de Soto in the vicinity of the King site.

One of the principal objectives of our research has been to identify archeological sites and clusters of sites which were probably occupied in the sixteenth century. This is the real benefit to be derived from the discovery and identification of sixteenth-century European artifacts. Hence, we are more concerned with where de Soto might have slept than with where he did sleep. This is reflected in Hudson's (1990a) attempt to assess the probability (in most cases low) of linkages between places named in the narratives and specific archeological sites. We hope that this will stimulate additional archeological research at these sites in the future.

Henige fails to understand the nature of the archeological record. While it is true that not all archeological sites survive in the strict sense, the truth is that usually it is only the small campsites of nomadic foragers that are likely to disappear from the archeological record. The native people of the de Soto era in the Southeast lived in villages, some of which were quite large. These villages consisted of numerous houses (for example, there were about forty at the King site, a medium-sized village) constructed of poles set in the ground with mud-plastered walls and thatched roofs. Given the nature of their combustible superstructure and the apparent frequency of native warfare in the sixteenth century, it should come as no surprise that a very large proportion of these houses burned, leaving readily recognizable areas of burned, brick-like clay and charcoal. But there is much more. In many areas of Georgia, Tennessee, and Alabama (where we have archeological documentation), these houses were constructed with sunken floors, often a foot or even two feet below the surface of the ground. After abandonment, these house pits filled with refuse, washed-in soils, etc., and are readily recognizable in the archeological record *even when they did not burn.* Include with this evidence the numerous other pits, postholes, burial pits, fortification walls and ditches, broken pottery, animal bones, stone tools and debris from their manufacture, etc., and it becomes very hard to argue that such a town could disappear without a trace. Any town occupied more than one year would possess these characteristics, and these people were not known for frequent movements of their villages until after they were impacted by Europeans.

What about modern urban construction? It is conceivable that modern construction could erase traces of sixteenth-century Indian towns, but in fact this rarely occurs. Most Indian towns of this period in the Southeast were located immediately adjacent to rivers, areas which were avoided by more flood-conscious Euroamericans. While one might expect that large cities, such as Atlanta, destroyed evidence of large Indian towns, in actuality most of these archeological sites are still present in the floodplains—areas not developed by Euroamericans.

Indian towns are known to have been lost to urban expansion, but local historians or early archeologists often provide some information. For example, we believe that the Indian town of Ulibahali was located near the junction of the Etowah and Oostanaula Rivers in the area now occupied by Rome, Georgia. While no trace of Ulibahali now exists (i.e., that can be seen on the surface), its former presence was recorded by Charles C. Jones in his *Antiquities of the Southern Indians* (1873:253). Even earlier, in 1820, Blanding (1848) mapped mounds on the Wateree River, and William Bartram (1791) described mounds in the second half of the eighteenth century. Early records often provide much information on sites in developed areas, and we have frequently utilized this information.

The one problem that we see as seriously limiting the archeological record is the large reservoirs that were constructed prior to any archeological research. In our area, the middle reaches of the Little Tennessee River in western North Carolina constitutes such an area. Early in our researches, we considered this avenue as a possible route of the expedition but simply had little real data to help affirm or refute the hypothesis. We cannot and do not claim to know what was here. Luckily, such areas are few.

On the other hand, many of the areas where we are most confident in our identifications of specific archeological sites with towns named in the chronicles of the sixteenth-century Spaniards are among the most thoroughly investigated of any place in the world. Work dating back to the late nineteenth century and continuing with modern research by many professional archeologists, interested amateurs, and even avaricious collectors have located the majority of the large town sites. We have tested our hypotheses by further survey in areas between documented sites to see if they were indeed vacant at the time and to help us better define site clusters.

While we cannot claim that we know the location of every Indian town contemporary with the de Soto expedition, this may not be relevant. In the sixteenth century, the Indians of the Southeast were organized in a series of chiefdoms, that is, multiple town political entities. These chiefdoms are observable in the archeological record as discrete clusters of towns separated by uninhabited zones (Hally, Smith, and Langford 1990), and this organization is implicit in the de Soto narratives. Some of these chiefdoms had many outlying hamlets and farmsteads, making the presence of such polities especially visible in the archeological record. The location of these clusters of towns is well documented in many portions of the Southeast. De Soto went from chiefdom to chiefdom searching for wealth. When a cluster of sites produces artifacts which date to the sixteenth century, matches details of terrain given in the narratives, and fits the overall route, we feel justified in arguing that we have located specific towns in the narratives.

The debate about the occupation or lack of it in the Savannah River valley at the de Soto dateline will no doubt continue. It is clear to us that the river was not occupied (except for its headwaters) at this time. This statement is based on the accumulation of over a hundred years of archeological observation, recently compiled by David G. Anderson (1990a) in his doctoral dissertation. It is possible that a site or two dating to the sixteenth century may yet be discovered in the Savannah River valley, but we argue that at the present level of survey and analysis, there could not be a cluster of sixteenth-century sites in the area. A cluster is necessary because the documents mention multiple towns on either side of the wilderness of Ocute. The middle Savannah valley matches what the documents describe about the wilderness of Ocute, and we are confident that it always will match them, even after another century of research. All known sites in the valley are either earlier or later than the mid sixteenth century by at least a hundred years.

In regard to this controversy, we find it interesting that Henige, who champions the strictest of standards concerning the use of scholarly evidence, would accept the unsupported argument of W. S. Eubanks (1989), who is not an archeologist, over the scholarly findings of several full-time professional archeologists possessing a cumulative total of more than fifty years of experience working in the Savannah River valley and adjacent areas.

Henige notes that archeologists must do research on an unknown portion of a once extant data base, and on this basis he dismisses conclusions by archeologists, saying that they require a "suspension of disbelief." He hazards no examples. But later he admits that all students of the past (both archeologists and historians) hope "that they will be able, on the basis of whatever evidence has happened to survive and come into their hands, to reconstruct a picture that faithfully reflects past general patterns, or at least to escape being shown not to." Does this mean that like archeologists, historians must also work with only a part of the data that once existed about the past, and using this must construct their interpretations of events and conditions in the past?

III. Henige criticizes us for relying overmuch on Garcilaso in our reconstruction of de Soto's route. In view of his argument that *La Florida del Ynca* is pseudohistory, any use of it would be excessive. In part, Henige bases this criticism on his count of the number of times we cite *La Florida del Ynca* in our route from Apalachee to the Mississippi River. It would have been much more to the point to criticize *how* we cite *La Florida del Ynca.* We invite anyone who is interested to go through our three papers on the route from Apalachee to the Mississippi River and to strip out all of the information from *La Florida del Ynca* to see whether it makes any difference in de Soto's movements on a day-by-day basis. Anyone who does so will see that we do not use *La Florida del Ynca* to establish the chronology or the itinerary of the expedition, nor the locations of places visited, but rather we cite Garcilaso's descriptions of incidents and places (several of which we note are inconsistent with other information or are suspicious on other grounds).

Amazingly, in several instances Henige takes us to task for *not* citing Garcilaso or for citing him but not taking him seriously. For example, he upbraids us for not taking Garcilaso seriously when he attempts to fault our location for Chiaha. In view of his argument that *La Florida del Ynca* contains nothing of historical value, surely this is a case of "damned if you do, damned if you don't."

IV. Henige goes on to state that all of the chronicles taken together lack the kind of precise information and the corroboration of data necessary to support our reconstruction of the route from Apalachee to the Mississippi River. We obviously do not agree.

There are two types of information contained in the de Soto expedition chronicles. The first type consists of observations made by the Spaniards themselves. They were certainly capable of observing the direction in which they traveled each day, and certainly the distance covered would have been a topic for discussion around campfires each evening. By the same token, each of the chroniclers traveled across the same southeastern landscape, and they could certainly distinguish between flat pine woods and mountain ridges. The Southeast contains numerous rivers, and de Soto's army crossed most of them, and some of them were crossed more than once. The accounts are filled with descriptions of difficult and sometimes hazardous crossings.

Because these geographic observations were made directly by the chroniclers, we put a great deal of stock in them. For instance, when all four of the chronicles say that the army nearly perished in an uninhabited wilderness ten to twelve days' travel across between Ocute and Cofitachequi, we accept the fact that this uninhabited wilderness existed. Moreover, the accounts make repeated reference to the rivers encountered in crossing this wilderness. Ranjel (Bourne 1904, 2:93–94), Elvas (Bourne 1904, 1:60), and

Garcilaso (Garcilaso 1951:283) each describe three very large rivers and the great difficulties involved in crossing them. We believe that the accounts provide accurate descriptions of these rivers.

In reference to these types of geographic evidence, Henige (this volume) states that "it is clearly necessary to have virtually complete data on both distances and directions" to reconstruct an expedition itinerary. He goes on to say that for the Apalachee-to-Chiaha segment of the route that he chooses as his example, there are few indications of direction traveled. According to Henige's count, the Elvas narrative provides no directional indicators for this part of the route, while Biedma and Ranjel's chronicles "provide at most two or three indications of directions traveled." He concludes that in the absence of specific directional indicators, we turn to "marching de Soto from modern archeological site unerringly to the next" in our reconstruction of the route. Henige is incorrect here on all counts. First, the accounts provide numerous references to direction of travel for this portion of the route. Second, Henige is incorrect concerning the number of directional references that the accounts provide (table 13). He states that the Elvas chronicle gives no directional references, but in reality it provides an abundance of information relating to the route taken by de Soto. Henige says that the Ranjel and Biedma accounts each provide only two or three pieces of directional information, but our reading of Ranjel's account indicates that there are no directional references in Ranjel for this portion of the expedition. The Biedma account provides only a few directional indicators, but in each case they agree with the directions given by Elvas. Even directions provided by Garcilaso agree totally with those of Elvas and Biedma.

An outline map of this portion of our route shows how we have fitted this directional information onto the southeastern landscape (see illustration 35; table 13). Within the framework provided by these directional referents, we used rates of travel, river crossings, and other geographic information to plot day by day movements of the army. We have already cited the evidence for the vast wilderness, with its three major rivers, between Ocute and Cofitachequi. Our reconstruction places this wilderness between the Oconee River in Georgia and the Wateree River in South Carolina. As discussed above, there is no archeological evidence for occupation of the Savannah River Valley or the Broad River Valley between approximately A.D. 1450 and 1650. Too little work has been conducted along the Ogeechee River to allow any definitive statements, but certainly no major sites are known from this river valley. There is no other place where this huge uninhabited wilderness could fit on the Georgia/South Carolina landscape. By the same token, it is clear that the expedition passed through the southern edge of the Appalachian Mountains. Ranjel (Bourne 1904, 2:104) indicated that the day after departing from Xuala, the army entered a very high mountain range. Beyond Xuala, Elvas (Bourne 1904, 1:71) described the expedition encountering rough and lofty ridges. Garcilaso de la Vega (1951:331–33) noted that Xuala was located at the foot of a mountain, and upon leaving there the army spent several days passing through a mountain range. Clearly there was a mountain range beyond Xuala, and our reconstruction places a major ridge of the Appalachians between Xuala and Chiaha. We remain confident in our reconstruction of this portion of the route.

TABLE 13. Directional References in de Soto Accounts for Terrain between Apalachee and Mabila.

| Location | Direction | Reference |
|---|---|---|
| Departure from Apalachee | To north | Biedma (1904:2,9) |
| Departure from Apalachee | To north | Garsilaso (1951:263) |
| Apalachee to Cofitachequi | Northeast | Elvas (1904:1, 89) |
| Apalachee to Xuala | Northeast . . . and north | Garcilaso (1951:329) |
| Ocute/Patofa to Cofitachequi | Toward sunrise | Elvas (1904:1, 59-60) |
| Ocute/Patofa to Cofitachequi | Directly east | Biedma (1904:2, 11) |
| Ocute/Patofa to Coosa | To northwest | Elvas (1904:1, 60) |
| Departure from Cofitachequi | To north | Biedma (1904:2, 15) |
| Cofitachequi to Xuala | North | Elvas (1904:1, 89, 221) |
| Xuala to Coosa | West | Elvas (1904:1, 89) |
| Xuala to Coosa | Westwardly | Elvas (1904:1, 221) |
| Coosa to Tuscaloosa | Southwardly | Elvas (1904:1, 89) |
| Coosa to Talisi | West and southwest | Biedma (1904:2, 16) |
| Talisi to Tuscaloosa | South | Biedma (1904:2, 16) |

On the other hand, the accounts contain a second kind of information. As the Spaniards traveled across the Southeast, they encountered populations who spoke a number of distinct languages and dialects. De Soto was dependent on translators in his communication with chiefs and other individuals at each stop, and the farther he traveled, the more translators he required. Garcilaso's (1951:422) *La Florida del Ynca,* for instance, provides a description of de Soto being forced to employ twelve to fourteen translators by the time he reached Chicasa in northern Mississippi. The information obtained by de Soto from these translated conversations must be highly suspect both because of the translation problem and the strong possibility that on occasion the Indians may have intentionally provided the Spaniards with incorrect information (DePratter 1989:146).

As an example of problems relating to translations, we can look at an example cited by Henige. Henige (this volume) refers to a possible epidemic at Cofitachequi in the years just prior to de Soto's arrival there. Information relating to this epidemic could only have come from translated conversations between Spaniards and Indians. Elvas (Bourne 1904, 1:66) reported that there were abandoned villages surrounding Cofitachequi, and he attributed their abandonment to "a pest in the land" two years earlier. Garcilaso de la Vega (1951:298) also mentioned a recent "pestilence" and the related abandonment of several towns. Neither Ranjel nor Biedma mentioned the "epidemic." This secondhand information can be interpreted in several ways, and we have individually interpreted it in divergent ways (Hudson 1990a; M. T. Smith 1987; DePratter 1989:146–47).

Perhaps an epidemic occurred at Cofitachequi. Perhaps not. But whatever the case may have been, semantic problems such as those based on translated information have little to do with our ability to trace exploration routes based on directions, distances, and firsthand observations of the landscape as provided by the chronicles.

V. There has been much confusion over our use of the league as a unit of measure in our research. The following points are essential:

1. In our reconstruction of the Juan Pardo expedition we found that Juan de la Bandera, the scribe of the expedition, specifies on many days the number of leagues they traveled. We at first tried to convert these to mile distances by using the *legua legal* (2.63 miles per league). We were unable to achieve a good fit with archeological sites and geographical conditions using these measurements, and so we were delighted when we learned of Roland Chardon's (1980) research which showed that there was a second Spanish linear league, the *legua común* of 3.46 miles. Using the *legua común* we were able to fit Pardo's route to a map, and in doing so established that Pardo and his men regularly traveled five leagues per day, about 17.5 miles. We do not know how Bandera measured or estimated this distance.

2. In our reconstruction of de Soto's route from Apalachee to Chiaha we used this 17.5-mile distance as a rough guide in plotting de Soto's route, feeling it reasonable to assume that they traveled at comparable speeds, since both were sixteenth-century Spanish armies in the Southeast. And we noted that in some places, as in their travel from Cofitachequi to Xuala, de Soto does indeed seem to have traveled at the same rate Pardo did.

3. When we went on to reconstruct the route from Chiaha to Mabila we began to see that de Soto traveled a bit slower than Pardo did, which was not surprising, given the much larger size of his expedition. We began using an estimated travel distance for de Soto of about 15 miles per day. This estimate of travel speed is the same as that used by the U. S. De Soto Commission (Swanton 1939:104–06). It should be noted that it has nothing to do with any league measures employed by any of the de Soto chronicles.

4. We also wanted a distance to serve as the upper limit of daily travel for a plausible reconstruction of de Soto's route. For this we thought it reasonable to use 17.5 miles per day. We felt that we had good evidence that de Soto could travel at this rate, as when he went from Cofitachequi to Xuala. We are suspicious of route reconstructions which require the entire expedition to travel faster than this, and particularly so if the distance greatly exceeds this.

On rare occasions this rule must be relaxed. The most notable exception is for March 23, 1540, when de Soto led a party of 40 horsemen from the Flint River to the Ocmulgee River, traveling rapidly for about eighteen hours straight and covering about 12 leagues, 30 to 40 miles (Hudson, Smith, and DePratter 1984:68). There may have been a few other instances when the expedition (or contingents thereof) traveled faster than 17.5 miles per day.

5. None of the de Soto chronicles consistently notes how far the expedition traveled on particular days. For this reason, the question of which league (or leagues) was used by the de Soto chroniclers is largely irrelevant for reconstructing the route.

6. Several of the chronicles give occasional estimates of distance, but these are difficult to interpret. Exactitude should not be expected. It was not a scientific mapping expedition. The Gentleman of Elvas is the chronicler who most frequently gave these estimates, but the Elvas estimates are so inconsistent with other information that it has so far proven impossible to figure out what league he was using, or whether he was using different leagues on different occasions (Swanton 1939:302–04).

In several instances we have used, perhaps too optimistically, the *legua común* to interpret distances cited in the de Soto chronicles. Garcilaso wrote that from Apalachee to Xuala they traveled 4 1/2 leagues, more or less, per day, or about 15.5 miles (Garcilaso 1951:329). And he noted that between Coste and Coosa they traveled about 4 leagues per day, or about 13.8 miles per day (Garcilaso 1951:342). These are believable distances, but we have little confidence in these figures because of the uncertainty over which league the de Soto chroniclers were using, and this is quite apart from the general unreliability of Garcilaso's figures.

7. From the above it should be clear that we do not, as Henige says, hypothesize that de Soto traveled at a rate of 17.5 miles per day, every day, rain or shine, over mountain and plain. And there is no need to hypothesize about Pardo's travel distances. Bandera recorded them.

Apparently, Henige imagines de Soto and his men hacking their way through jungles. In fact, they almost always traveled on distinct trails, as a casual reading of the documents shows.

VI. A cornerstone of our reconstruction of de Soto's route is our earlier reconstruction of the route of Juan Pardo's two expeditions. After penetrating the interior of South Carolina, Pardo and his men visited five or six of the same towns visited twenty-six years earlier by de Soto. Pardo and his men came upon these towns in the same order as did de Soto while spending about the same number of days crossing the same kinds of terrain.

But Henige (this volume) undertakes to prove that our location for one of these towns—Chiaha—is unsound. From this attempted proof the reader may judge whether Henige is the exemplar of strict historical method he pretends to be.

All of the de Soto sources describe the town of Chiaha as being situated on an island in a river. The most detailed description of this island is in the *Relaçam* of the Gentleman of Elvas. But Henige sees an inconsistency because the *Relaçam* says the island was a league in length, whereas its actual length was about 2.5 miles, or about a mile less than the *legua común.* Regardless of our prematurely optimistic use of the *legua común* in our "Chiaha to Mabila" paper (not for establishing the route, but for other ruminations), for all we know the Gentleman of Elvas used the *legua legal*—very close to the length of the island. Henige notes that the Gentleman of Elvas was at Chiaha for three weeks and therefore had plenty of time to accurately measure the length of the island. Time enough, that is, if the members of the expedition were interested in such exactitude.

As previously mentioned, Henige cites here as part of his argument Garcilaso's muddled description of Chiaha, and he takes seriously Garcilaso's estimate that the island was five leagues long.

Was Chiaha on an island at all? Not so, says Henige, who notes that Francisco Martinez, who went with Pardo on his first expedition, wrote that Chiaha was situated not on an island, but on a "mountain ridge" (*cabo de la sierra*). But this is based on a slipshod reading of the Martinez document. There are problems with this document. It reports information, but it never describes Martinez's role in the expedition. It reports that a letter from Sergeant Moyano arrived in Santa Elena a month after Pardo returned there from his first expedition, i.e., the letter arrived in early April 1567. This implies that Martinez was in Santa Elena when the letter arrived. Then the document recounts activities by Sergeant Moyano which Martinez could only have known by hearsay. It is possible that Pardo ordered Martinez to go into the interior carrying a letter replying to Moyano and that he did so, continuing on to Chiaha with Moyano. Then he returned to Santa Elena to make his deposition on July 11, 1567.

If all this came to pass, it is possible that Martinez actually saw Chiaha. But Henige misconstrues the passage in question. According to Martinez, Moyano traveled to "the great chief that was in that head of the mountain range, who is called Chiaha, [and] he arrived at one of his towns, having traveled four days. . . . This town was between two heavily flowing rivers [or streams]" (Hudson 1990:320).

In the first instance, Martinez was referring to the location of Chiaha the chief, not Chiaha the town. The description of one of Chiaha's towns as being between two rivers (or streams) is consistent with an island in a large river. Unlike an island in a lake or an ocean, an island in a river does have streams flowing on both sides.

Henige thinks it anomalous that Bandera described Chiaha as a large village "surrounded by rivers" and that one had to cross "three copious rivers to reach it." This language of Bandera is not at all troublesome if one bothers to look at a map of the upper Tennessee Valley. The Spaniards had to wade through three large rivers in their approach to Chiaha (Hudson 1990:268). In the space of a day or so they had to ford the French Broad River, the Pigeon River, and again an arm of the French Broad River in which Zimmerman's Island was located.

We invite Henige to name an island in the Tennessee River system other than Zimmerman's that is consistent with the total body of information in the Pardo and de Soto documents.

Henige uses the seeming confusion in the documents caused by the naming customs of the Indians to argue that Chiaha migrated from one place to another between 1540 and 1567. He cites no evidence for this assertion. The naming customs of the Indians at Chiaha and elsewhere in the Southeast are complex:

1. In several locations along de Soto's route the chronicles use a single name to both refer to the chief of a polity and to the principal town of the polity. In addition, in several instances the de Soto chronicles refer to rivers with names that refer, in turn, to the polity through which they flowed, e.g., *rio de Capachequi* (Ranjel in Bourne 1904, 2:82). This naming pattern is our basis for interpreting the referent(s) of the name *Apafalaya.*

2. In several instances the de Soto chronicles extend the name of the principal town to refer to the polity at large. They use *Chiaha* to refer to both a capital town and a polity (B. Smith 1866:68–69). The Indians may have also used these names in this way, though it is difficult or impossible to prove it.

3. This was complicated at Chiaha by the fact that the main town (on the island) was also called *Olameco* (also erroneously called *Lameco*). Bandera wrote—whether rightly or wrongly—that both *Chiaha* and *Olameco* were alternative names for the town on the island. The word *Olameco* is the Koasati word for "chief town" or "town of

the chief," and hence it may be a word which is not so much a name as a description of the position of the town in the larger polity (Booker, Hudson, and Rankin 1992).

De Soto and his army encountered a similar custom at Cofitachequi, where they came to a town called *Talomeco,* which in Creek means "town of the chief" (Booker et al. in press).

4. The terminology becomes even more confusing when Pardo returned from his foray to Chalahume and Satapo, and on his approach came to a town named Chiaha, which was about a day's travel from the town on the island, and which was therefore different from it. For whatever reason, Bandera used *Chiaha* to refer to two different towns.

5. We do not know why the Indians named their towns in this way, or even if Bandera was getting it all straight. Perhaps this is a further example of confusion caused by difficulties in translation and cultural understanding, as mentioned earlier. But these were chiefdoms, not states, and we have no reason to expect that their naming customs should parallel European naming customs.

6. We agree that Henige's translation of *varzea* as "a stretch of flat land suitable for cultivation" is marginally preferable to Buckingham Smith's (1866:70) "vale." This fits Zimmerman's Island even better, since neither it nor any other island in the French Broad or Tennessee River is large enough to contain hills and "vales." At the same time, we can see how one would see Zimmerman's Island and other islands in the French Broad and Tennessee rivers as simply parts of the Tennessee Valley. And standing near Zimmerman's Island, with mountains visible in the distance we can see how "vale" would be an appropriate translation.

VII. Henige (1986a:5) asserts that "unless and until it can be determined that a given source is uninfluenced by other sources, it cannot be used to *confirm* their testimony." But how on earth could anyone prove that Garcilaso de la Vega (or Gonzalo Silvestre) *did not* read the *Relaçam* of the Gentleman of Elvas? It is a requirement that is so difficult to meet it is unrealistic. It would seem to be far more reasonable to require that if a source can be proven to have been influenced by another source, then it cannot be used as confirmation.

Henige notes how little confirmation we can marshall in reconstructing the route from Mabila to the Mississippi River. But this is not to say that we have neglected evidence. We have used all the evidence that is available.

The basic question we would raise in our reply to Henige is this: in the era in which the historical record begins, to what degree can one insist on methods that can be applied to eras documented by an ample written record? In such an era, must one not be prepared to consider solutions and formulations that are, for want of corroboration, contestable? Must one not be willing to use kinds of evidence that are of less value in eras which are amply documented, as for example, archeological information? We and others think that this is the case. The problem has been aptly described by Inga Clendennin (1989:xi) in her book *Ambivalent Conquests: Maya and Spaniard in Yucatan, 1517-1570*:

It takes patience and perseverance to hear those faint long-ago Indian voices at all, speaking as they do from an unfamiliar world and an unfamiliar experience. The attempt also requires from both reader and author a tolerance of ambiguities, and of inherently contestable judgements. But to offer interpretations without acknowledging their uncertain ground would be less than candid, while to state only what is certainly known would be to leave unexplored what matters most.

# Appendix II: The University of Arkansas Museum de Soto Symposia

## FIRST SYMPOSIUM, OCTOBER 3, 1988

8:30 A.M.–12:00 noon The De Soto Route in Arkansas

Jeffrey Brain, Harvard University. "Historical Perspectives on the Route of De Soto in Arkansas."

Richard Weinstein, Coastal Environments, Inc., and Jim Atkinson, Natchez Trace Parkway. "Archeological Evidence for the Town of Chicasa and Implication for Selecting a Southern Route."

Sam Dickinson, Prescott, Arkansas. "De Soto Narratives and Spain's Historians."

Charles Hudson, University of Georgia, and Dan Morse, Arkansas State University. "Evidence for a New Route of the De Soto Expedition."

Bob Lancaster, *Arkansas Times* magazine. Discussant.

1:00 P.M.–3:30 P.M. Perspectives on the Native People of the Era

Robert Rankin, University of Kansas. "Language Affiliations of the Native People from Archival Narrative Evidence."

Michael Hoffman, University of Arkansas. "The Ethnic Identities of the De Soto Era Peoples."

Phyllis Morse, Arkansas Archeological Survey. "People of the Parkin Site."

George Sabo, University of Arkansas. "Perceptions of 16th Century Native Americans Toward Europeans."

Marvin Jeter, Arkansas Archeological Survey. Discussant.

7:30 P.M. Evening Lecture

J. T. Milanich, Florida State Museum. "Hernando De Soto and Spain's Effort to Settle North America."

## SECOND SYMPOSIUM, MARCH 28–MARCH 30, 1990

Wednesday, March 28

9:00 A.M.–10:30 A.M.

Dr. Gloria A. Young, The University of Arkansas Museum. "How Do We Know Anthing about the De Soto Expedition of A.D. 1541–43 in Arkansas?"

Dr. Charles M. Hudson, University of Georgia. "What Was the Expedition Like and What Was Its Route across *La Florida*?"

10:30 A.M.–11:00 A.M.

Map Activities for Classrooms and Workshops.

Dr. W. Fredrick Limp, Arkansas Archeological Survey. "What Can Computerized Maps Tell Us about the De Soto Expedition Route?"

1:00 P.M.–2:30 P.M.

Dr. Michael P. Hoffman, University of Arkansas Anthropology Department. "Lifestyles of the Mississippian People of Eastern Arkansas."

Dr. Ann Early, Arkansas Archeological Survey, Arkadelphia. "The Caddoan People and Their Descendants."

Richard A. Young, Harrison High School. "Native Tales of Arkansas: A Monologue."

Evening Lecture 7:30 P.M.

Dr. Charles Ewen, Arkansas Archeological Survey (formerly of Florida Department of State, Division of Historical Resources). "The De Soto Winter Camp Site in Tallahassee."

Thursday, March 29

8:00 A.M.–12:00 noon

Dr. Frank Schambach, Southern Arkansas University and the Arkansas Archeological Survey. "A.D. 1541–43: Hypothesis for the Route of the Expedition in the Caddo Area."

Dr. James E. Bruseth and Nancy Kenmotsu, Texas Historical Commission. "Moscoso and the Expedition in Texas."

Dr. David Dye, Memphis State University. "The De Soto River Crossing: A Geomorphological Reconstruction."

Dr. W. Fredrick Limp, Arkansas Archeological Survey. "Computer Analysis of the Hypothesized Routes of the Expedition in Arkansas, Louisiana, and Texas."

Dr. Michael Hoffman, University of Arkansas; Dr. James Corbin, Stephen F. Austin State Unversity; Dr. Skip Stewart-Abernathy, Arkansas Tech University and Arkansas Archeological Survey; Charles Hudson, University of Georgia. Round Table Discussion.

1:30 P.M.–4:30 P.M.

David Henige, Memorial Library, University of Wisconsin, Madison. "Written Sources, Archeology and the De Soto Expedition."

George E. Lankford, Arkansas College, Batesville. “Legends of the Adelantado.”

Samuel D. Dickinson, Prescott, Arkansas. “De Soto and the Law.”

Dr. George Sabo, University of Arkansas and Arkansas Archeological Survey; Dr. Paul Hoffman, Louisiana State Unversity; Dr. Tom Greer, Ouachita Baptist University; Dr. Charles Hudson, University of Georgia. Round Table Discussion.

Friday, March 30

8:30 A.M.–12:00 noon

Dr. Joseph Sanchez, University of New Mexico and the National Park Service. “Archival Resources and the De Soto Expedition.”

Dr. Wallace Chafe, University of Santa Barbara. “The Caddo and Their Language.”

Dr. Timothy Perttula, Advisory Council on Historic Preservation. “Effects of the *Entrada* into East Texas on the Aboriginal Caddoan Population.”

Barbara Burnett and Katherine Murray, University of Arkansas. “Biological Effects of the *Entrada* of the De Soto Expedition in Arkansas.”

Dr. Clark Larsen, Purdue University; Dr. Ann Early, Henderson State University and Arkansas Archeological Survey; Dr. Helen Tanner, The Newberry Library; Dr. Marvin Smith, University of Georgia. Round Table Discussion.

# Bibliography


Agassi, Joseph

1973 When Should We Ignore Evidence in Favour of a Hypothesis? *Ratio* 15:183–205.

Ahern, Maureen

1989 The Certification of Cíbola: Discursive Strategies in *La relación del descubrimiento de las siete ciudades* by Fray Marcos de Niza (1539). *Disposito* 36–38:303–13.

Akridge, Scott

1986 De Soto's Route in North Central Arkansas. *Fieldnotes: Newsletter of the Arkansas Archeological Society* 211 (July/August):3–7.

Albornoz, Miguel

1971 Hernando de Soto. El Amadís de la Florida. Madrid: Ediciones de la Revista de Occidente.

———

1986 Hernando de Soto: Knight of the Americas. New York: F. Watts.

Allen, Barbara, and Lynwood Montell

1981 From Memory to History. Nashville: AASLH.

Añasco, Pedro de

1939 Carta al Rey de Espana, diciendo que por falta de armas y otras cosa necesarias habian desamparado la tierra volviendo al rio del Espiritu Santo. Pp. 98–99 in Epistolario de Nueva Espana, 1505–1818, *Bibliographia Historica Mexicana Segunda Serie* 4, Francisco del Paso y Troncoso, ed. Mexico, D.F.: Jose Porrua y hijos.

Anderson, David G.

1990 The Mississippian Occupation and Abandonment of the Savannah Valley. *The Florida Anthropologist* 43(1):13–35.

———

1990a Political Change in Chiefdom Societies. Cycling in the Late Prehistoric Southeastern United States. Ann Arbor: University Microfilms.

Anderson, David G., David J. Hally, and James L. Rudolph

1986 The Mississippian Occupation of the Savannah River Valley. *Southeastern Archeology* 5:42.

Andrews, Anthony P.

1983 Maya Salt Production and Trade. Tucson: University of Arizona Press.

Arkansas Archeological Survey

1989 Arkansas Archeological Survey, Geographic Information Systems Activities, December 12, 1989. (Ms., Arkansas Archeological Survey, Fayetteville.)

Arkansas Department of Planning

1974 Arkansas Natural Area Plan. Little Rock.

Aten, L. E.

1984 Woodland Cultures of the Texas Coast. Pp. 72-93 in Perspectives on Gulf Coast Prehistory. D. D. Davis, ed. *The Florida State Museum Ripley P. Bullen Monographs in Anthropology and History* 5. Gainesville.

Atkinson, James R.
1987 The De Soto Expedition Through North Mississippi in 1540–41. *Mississippi Archaeology* 22(1):61–73.
Auerbach, Eric
1957 Mimesis: The Representation of Reality in Western Literature. New York: Doubleday (Anchor Books).
Avellaneda, Ignacio
1990 Los Sobreviventes de la Florida: The Survivors of the de Soto Expedition. Bruce Chappell, ed. *Research Publications of the P. K. Yonge Library of Florida History* 2. Gainesville.
Axtell, James
1982 Bronze Men and Golden Ages: The Intellectual History of Indian-White Relations in Colonial America. *Journal of Interdisciplinary History* 12(4):663–75.
———
1985 The Invasion Within: The Contest of Cultures in Colonial North America. New York: Oxford University Press.
Baber, Adin
1942 Food Plants of the DeSoto Expedition 1539-1543. *Tequesta* 1:34–40.
Baird, W. David.
1980 The Quapaw Indians. Norman: University of Oklahoma Press.
Bandelier, Ad. F., ed.
1905 The Journey of Alvar Nuñez Cabeza de Vaca and his Companions from Florida to the Pacific, 1528–1536. Fanny Bandelier, trans. New York: A. S. Barnes and Co.
Barthes, Roland
1977 Image, Music, Text. S. Heath, trans. New York: Hill and Wang.
Barton, Charles A.
1927 Where Did De Soto Discover the Mississippi River? Pp. 52–96 in A Symposium on the Place of Discovery of the Mississippi River by Hernando de Soto, D. Rowland, ed. *Mississippi Historical Society Special Publication* 1. Jackson.
Bartram, William
1791 Travels. Philadelphia: James and Johnson.
Bauxar, J. Joseph
1978 History of the Illinois Area. Pp. 594–601 in Handbook of North American Indians. Vol. 15: Northeast. Bruce G. Trigger, ed. Washington, D.C.: Smithsonian Institution Press.
Bell, R. E.
1984 Protohistoric Wichita. Pp. 363–78 in Prehistory of Oklahoma. R. E. Bell, ed. New York: Academic Press.
Biedma, Luýs Hernández de
1865 Relacion de la Isla de la Florida. Pp. 437–39 in Colección de Documentos ineditor Relatives al Descubrimiento, Conquista y Colonización de las Posesiones Españolas en América y Oceania, collectado por Munoz. Vol. 3. Madrid: Manuel B. de Quiros.
———
1971 Relación del suceso dela Jornada del Capitán Soto. Pp. 211-61 in Vol. 14 of Colección de documentos y manuscriptos compilados por Fernandez de Navarrete. 31 vols. Nendeln: Museo Naval Madrid.
Bizzell, David W., ed.
1981 A Report on the Quapaw: Letters of Governor George Izard to the American Philosophical Society, 1982–1827. *Pulaski County Historical Review* 29:66–79.

Blake, Alan

1988 Legua Legal or Legua Comun: A Discussion. *Alabama de Soto Commission de Soto Working Paper* 5. Tuscaloosa.

Blake, R. B.

1936 Early Spanish Missions Built in Nacogdoches County, 1716. (Ms., Special Collections, Steen Library, Stephen F. Austin State University, Nacogdoches, Texas.)

Blakely, Robert L., ed.

1977 Introduction: Changing Strategies for the Biological Anthropologist. Pp. 1–9 in Biocultural Adaptation in Prehistoric America. Robert L. Blakely ed. *Southern Anthropology Society Proceedings* 11.

———

1988 The King Site: Continuity and Contact in Sixteenth-Century Georgia. Athens: University of Georgia Press.

Blakely, Robert L., and David S. Mathews

1990 Bioarcheological Evidence for a Spanish-Native Conflict in the Sixteenth-Century Southeast. *American Antiquity* 55:718–44.

Blanding, William

1848 Remains on the Wateree River, Kenshaw District, South Carolina. Pp. 105-08 in Ancient Monuments of the Mississippi Valley, E. G. Squier and E. H. Davis, eds. *Smithsonian Contributions to Knowledge* 1. Washington, D.C.

Bolton, Herbert Eugene

1908 The Native Tribes about the East Texas Missions. *Quarterly of the Texas State Historical Association* 11:249–76.

———

1952 Spanish Explorations in the Southwest 1542–1706. New York: Barnes & Noble Inc.

———

1987 The Hasinais: Southern Caddoans as Seen by the Earliest Europeans. R. M. Magnaghi, ed. Norman: University of Oklahoma Press.

Bomar, George W.

1983 Texas Weather. Austin: University of Texas Press.

Bongaarts, John

1976 Intermediate Fertility Variables and Marital Fertility Rates. *Population Studies* 30(2):227–41.

Booker, Karen, Charles Hudson, and Robert Rankin

1992. Place Name Identification and Multilingualism in the Sixteenth-Century Southeast. *Ethnohistory.*

Boon, James A.

1982 Other Tribes, Other Scribes: Symbolic Anthropology in the Comparative Study of Cultures, Histories, Religions, and Texts. Cambridge: Cambridge University Press.

Boruchoff, David A.

1991 Beyond Utopia and Paradise: Cortés, Bernal Días, and the Rhetoric of Consecration. *Modern Language Notes* 106:330–69.

Bost, David Herbert

1983 The *Naufragios* of Alvar Núñez Cabeza de Vaca: A Case of Historical Romance. *Southeastern Latin Americanist* 27:3–12.

Boston, Barbara

1939 The Route of de Soto: Delisle's Interpretation. *Mid-America* 10:277–97.

Bourne, Edward Gaylord, ed.

1904 Narratives of the Career of Hernando de Soto in the Conquest of Florida, as Told by a Knight of Elvas and in a Relation by Luýs Hernández de Biedma, Factor of the Expedition, . . . together with an Account of de Soto's Expedition Based on a Diary of Rodrigo Ranjel . . . Buckingham Smith, trans. 2 vols. New York: A. S. Barnes and Co. (Reprinted: Allerton, New York, 1922, 1973.)

Bowman, Isaiah

1911 Forest Physiography: Physiography of the United States and Principles of Soils in Relation to Forestry. London: John Wiley and Sons.

Boyd, C. Clifford, Jr., and Gerald F. Schroedl

1987 In Search of Coosa. *American Antiquity* 52:84–44.

Brain, Jeffrey P.

1975 Artefacts of the Adelantado. *Conference on Historic Site Archaeology Papers* 8:129–38.

———

1978 The Archaeological Phase: Ethnographic Fact or Fancy? Pp. 311–18 in Archaeological Essays in Honor of Irving B. Rouse, R. C. Dunnell and E. S. Hall, eds. New York: Mouton.

———

1979 Tunica Treasure. *Peabody Museum of Archaeology and Ethnology Papers* 71. Cambridge.

———

1981 Tunica Archaeology. Pp. 43-50 in Traces of Prehistory: Papers in Honor of William G. Haag, F.H. West and R.W. Neuman, eds. Louisiana State University. School of Geoscience. *Geoscience and Man* 22. Baton Rouge.

———

1984 The De Soto Entrada into the Lower Mississippi Valley. *Mississippi Archaeology* 19(2):48–58.

———

1985 Introduction: Update of De Soto Studies Since the United States De Soto Expedition Commission Report. Pp. xi–xxxii in Final Report of the United States De Soto Expedition Commission by J. R. Swanton. (Reprinted: *Classics of Smithsonian Institution.* Washington, D.C. Originally published 1939.)

———

1985a The Archaeology of the Hernando de Soto Expedition. Pp. 96–107, 205–07 in Alabama and the Borderlands: From Prehistory to Statehood, R. R. Badger and L. A. Clayton, eds. University, Ala.: University of Alabama Press.

———

1988 Tunica Archaeology. *Peabody Museum of Archaeology and Ethnology Papers* 78. Cambridge.

1988a Historical Perspectives on the Route of De Soto in Arkansas. (Paper presented at The De Soto Era in Arkansas Symposium, Fayetteville, Oct. 3, 1988.)

Brain, Jeffrey P., Alan Toth, and Antonio Rodriguez-Buckingham

1974 Ethnohistoric Archaeology and the De Soto Entrada into the Lower Mississippi Valley. *Conference on Historic Site Archaeology Papers (1972)* 7:232–89.

Brandon, William

1986 New Worlds for Old: Reports from the New World and Their Effect on the Development of Social Thought in Europe, 1500–1800. Athens, Ohio, and London: Ohio University Press.

Braun, Lucy
1950 Deciduous Forests of Eastern North America. New York: Hafner Press.
Brody, Robert
1987 Bernal's Strategies. *Hispanic Review* 55:323-336.
Brown, Calvin S.
1926 Archeology of Mississippi. University, Miss.: Mississippi Geological Survey.
Brown, Ian W.
1980 Salt and the Eastern North American Indian, an Archeological Study. *Lower Mississippi Survey Bulletin* 6. Cambridge, Massachusetts.
Brown, James A., Robert E. Bell, and Don G. Wycoff
1978 Caddoan Settlement Patterns in the Arkansas River Drainage. Pp. 169–200 in Mississippian Settlement Patterns, B. D. Smith, ed. New York: Academic Press.
Bruseth, James E., Daniel E. McGregor, and William A. Martin
1987 Hunter-Gatherers of the Prairie Margin: Summary of the Prehistoric Archaeological Record. In Hunter-Gatherer Adaptations along the Prairie Margin, Site Excavations and Synthesis of Prehistoric Archaeology, D. E. McGregor and J. E. Bruseth, eds. *Southern Methodist University. Institute for the Study of Earth and Man. Archaeology Research Program. Richland Creek Technical Series* 3. Dallas.
Bruseth, James E., and Nancy A. K. Kenmotsu
1991 Soldiers of Misfortunes: The de Soto Expedition Through Texas. *Heritage* 9:12–18.
Bruseth, James E., and Timothy K. Perttula
1981 Prehistoric Settlement Patterns at Lake Fork Reservoir. *Southern Methodist University and Texas Antiquities Committee. Texas Antiquities Permit Series Report* 2. Austin and Dallas.
Bruseth, James E., L. Mark Raab, and Daniel E. McGregor
1987 Late Holocene Paleoecology of the Prairie Margin of Texas. Pp. 29–48 in Introduction to the Richland Creek Archaeological Project: Environmental Background and Cultural Setting, J. E. Bruseth and Randall W. Moir, eds. *Southern Methodist University. Institute for the Study of Earth and Man. Archaeology Research Program. Richland Creek Technical Series* 1. Dallas.
Bueno Silveira, Francisco da
1963–1967 Grande dicionário etimológico-prosódico da língua Portuguêsa. 8 vols. São Paulo: Edição Saraiva.
Burnett, Barbara
1988 The Bioarchaeological Synthesis. Pp. 193–220 in Human Adaptation in the Ozark and Ouachita Mountains, George Sabo, et al. Final Report submitted by the Arkansas Archeological Survey to the U.S. Army Corps of Engineers, Southwestern Division. Study Unit 1 of the Southwestern Division Archeological Overview, Fayetteville, Arkansas.

———
1990 The Bioarcheology of Goldsmith Oliver 2 (3PU306). Pp. 146–216 in Goldsmith Oliver 2 (3PU306): A Protohistoric Archeological Site Near Little Rock Arkansas. M. D. Jeter, K. H. Cande, and J. J. Mintz, eds. Final report submitted to Federal Aviation Administration, Southwest Region, Fort Worth, Texas.

———
1990a The Bioarcheology of the Hardman Site (3CL418): Prehistoric and Protohistoric Caddoan Sample. Pp. 11-1 through 11-147 in Hardman (3CL418) A Prehistoric Salt

Processing Site, Ishmael Williams and A. M. Early, eds. Final report submitted to Arkansas Highway and Transportation Department, Little Rock, Arkansas.

———

1990b The Bioarcheological Synthesis of the Eastern Portion of the Gulf Coastal Plain. Pp. 385–418 in The Archeology and Bioarcheology of the Gulf Coastal Plain by D. A. Story, et al. *Arkansas Archeological Survey, Research Series* 38, Fayetteville, Arkansas.

Byington, Cyrus

1915 A Dictionary of the Choctaw Language. *Bureau of American Ethnology Bulletin* 46. Washington, D.C.: Smithsonian Institution Press.

Callender, Charles

1978 Illinois. Pp. 673–80 in Handbook of North American Indians. Vol. 15: Northeast. Washington, D.C.: Smithsonian Institution Press.

Cassen, R.

1978 Current Trends in Population Change and Their Causes. *Population and Development Review* 4: 331.

Casteñeda, Paulino, Mariano Cuesta, and Pilar Hernández

1983 Transcripción, Estudio y Notas del "Espejo de Navegantes" de Alonso Chaves. Madrid: Instituto de Historia y Cultura Naval.

Cavelier, Jean.

1938 The Journal of Jean Cavelier, J. Delanglez, ed. and trans. The Account of a Survivor of La Salle's Texas Expedition, 1684–1688. Chicago: Institute of Jesuit History.

Chafe, Wallace

1976 A Brief Look at the Caddo Language. Pp. 55–82 in The Caddoan, Iroquoian, and Siouan Languages. *Trends in Linguistics, State-of-the-Art Reports* 3. The Hague: Mouton.

———, ed.

1976a The Caddoan, Iroquoian, and Siouan Languages. *Trends in Linguistics, State-of-the-Art Reports* 3. The Hague: Mouton.

Chamberlain, Robert S.

1948 The Conquest and Colonization of Yucatan, 1517–1550. *Carnegie Institution of Washington Publication* 582. Washington, D.C.

Chamberlin, T. C.

1890 The Method of Multiple Working Hypotheses. *Science* 15:92–96.

Chapman, Carl H.

1959 The Origin of the Osage Indian Tribe: An Ethnographical, Historical and Archaeological Study. (Unpublished Ph.D. dissertation in Anthropology, University of Michigan, Ann Arbor.)

Chapman, Carl H., and Leo O. Anderson

1955 The Campbell Site: A Late Mississippi Town Site and Cemetery in Southeast Missouri. *The Missouri Archaeologist* 17(2/3):45–140.

Chardon, Roland

1980 The Elusive Spanish League: A Problem of Measurement in Sixteenth-Century New Spain. *Hispanic American Historical Review* 60(2):294–302.

Chaussegros de Léry, Gaspard-Joseph

1923 Journal de la Campagne Faite par le Détachement du Canada sur les Chicachas en Février 1740 au Nombre de 201 Français, et 337 Sauvages de Canada, Illinois, Missouris et 58 Chactas Faisant en Tout 596 Hommes. *Rapport de L'Archiviste de la Province de Quebec pour 1922-23*:157–65.

Chesnut, Mary Boykin
1981 Mary Chesnut's Civil War, C. Vann Woodward. New Haven: Yale University Press

Clancy, Phyllis M.
1985 The Carden's Bottom Puzzle Elucidated. (Unpublished Master's Thesis in Anthropology, University of Arkansas, Fayetteville.)

———
1985 Laboratory Notes for the Gordon Site (3AS152). (Ms., Osteology Laboratory, University of Arkansas, Fayetteville.)

Clark, G. A., M. A. Kelly, J. M. Grange, and M. C. Hill
1987 The Evolution of Mycobacterial Disease in Human Populations. *Current Anthropology* 28:45–62.

Clark, John W., Jr., and James E. Ivey
1972 Archeological and Historical Investigations at Martin Lake, Rusk and Panola Counties, Texas. *The University of Texas at Austin. Texas Archeological Survey Research Report* 32. Austin.

Clendinnen, Inga
1989 Ambivalent Conquests: Maya and Spaniard in Yucatan, 1517–1570. Cambridge: Cambridge University Press.

Cliff, Maynard B., and Duane A. Peter
1990 Cultural Resources Input to BRACO EIS Red River Depot, Bowie County, Texas. *Geo-Marine, Inc. Miscellaneous Reports of Investigations* 14. Plano, Texas.

Collins, Michael B., and C. Britt Bousman
1992 Cultural Implications of Quaternary Environmental Change in Northeastern Texas. (Ms., Texas Historical Commission, Austin.)

Cook, Robert L.
1984 Texas. In White-Tailed Deer, Ecology and Management, L. K. Halls and Cindy House, eds. Harrisburg, Pennsylvania: Stackpole Books.

Corbin, James E.
1986 Nacogdoches Historic Site Survey: Archaeological Survey and Assessment of Nacogdoches, Nacogdoches County, Texas. Vol. 1: The Survey. (Ms., Texas Historical Commission, Austin.)

Corbin, James E., Heather A. Brown, Mary G. Canavan, and Sharon Toups
1990 Mission Dolores de los Ais (41SA25): San Augustine County, Texas, Archaeological Investigation, 1984. *Stephen F. Austin State University. Papers in Anthropology* 5. Nacogdoches.

Corbin, James E., Arlan Kalina, and Thomas C. Alex
1980 Mission Dolores de los Ais, Archaeological Investigations of an Early Spanish Colonial Mission, San Augustine County, Texas. *Stephen F. Austin Papers in Anthropology* 2 and *Texas Antiquities Permit Series Report* 3. Austin.

Cordell, Linda
1989 Durango to Durango: An Overview of the Southwest Heartland. Pp. 17–40 in Columbian Consequences. Vol. 1. Perspectives on the Spanish Borderlands West. David Hurst Thomas, ed. Washington D.C.: Smithsonian Institution Press.

Costa, Agenor
1958 Dicionário de sinônimos e locuções da língua portuguêsa. 2 vols. Rio de Janeiro: Departemento de Impr. Nacional.

Cottier, John W., and Gregory A. Waselkov
1977 Environmental Parameters of Mississippian Settlement Strategy. *The Missouri Archeologist* 38:13–48.

Crane, Cathy J.
1992 Archaeobotanical Remains. Appendix G (pp. 1–14) in Archaeological Investigations at Copper Lake: 1987 Season Report by R. W.Moir, Daniel E. McGregor, and David H. Jurney. Dallas: Southern Methodist University.

Crawford, James M.
1975 Southeastern Indian Languages. James M. Crawford, ed. Pp.1–120 in Studies in Southeastern Indian Languages. Athens: University of Georgia Press.

Crook, Wilson W., Jr.
1988 Did Moscoso (Latter Part of the de Soto Expedition) Reach the Trinity River in the Dallas Region? *The Record* 42:109–10.

Crosby, Alfred W.
1967 Conquistador y Pestiléncia: The First New World Pandemic and the Fall of the Great Indian Empires. *Hispanic American Historical Review* 47:321–37.

———
1986 Ecological Imperialism: The Biological Expansion of Europe, 900-1900. Cambridge: Cambridge University Press.

———
1987 The Columbian Voyages, the Columbian Exchange, and Their Historians. Essays on Global and Comparative History, American Historical Association.

Cumming, W. P., R. A. Skelton, and D. B. Quinn
1972 The Discovery of North America. New York: American Heritage Press.

Curren, Caleb
1987 The Route of the Soto Army Through Alabama. *Alabama De Soto Commission Working Paper* 3. Tuscaloosa.

Davis, E. Mott
1961 The Caddoan Area. *Bulletin of the Texas Archeological Society* 31(1960):3–10.

———
1970 Archeological and Historical Assessment of the Red River Basin in Texas. Pp. 27–65 in Archeological and Historical Resources in the Red River Basin, H. A. Davis, ed, *Arkansas Archeological Survey Research Series* 1. Fayetteville, Arkansas.

Davis, Hester A.
1966 An Introduction to Parkin Prehistory. *The Arkansas Archeologist* 7(1–2):1–40.

Davis, T. Frederick
1935 Juan Ponce de Leon's Voyages to Florida. *Florida Historical Quarterly* 14:5–70.

Deagan, Kathleen A.
1985 Spanish-Indian Interaction in Sixteenth-Century Florida and Hispaniola. Pp. 281–318 in Cultures in Contact, W. W. Fitzhugh, ed. Washington, D.C.: Smithsonian Institution Press.

———
1987 Artifacts of the Spanish Colonies of Florida and the Caribbean, 1500-1800. Vol. I: Ceramics, Glassware, and Beads. Washington, D.C.: Smithsonian Institution Press.

Deliette, Louis
1934 Memoir of De Gannes Concerning the Illinois Country [1702], T. C. Pease and R. C. Werner, eds. *Collections of the Illinois State Historical Library* 23:302–95. Springfield.

DePratter, Chester B.

1989 Cofitachequi: Ethnohistorical and Archeological Evidence. Pp. 133–36. In Studies in South Carolina Archeology: Essays in Robert L. Stevenson, A. C. Goodyear III and G. T. Hanson, eds. *Anthropological Studies* 9. Columbus, S. C.: South Carolina Institute of Archeology and Anthropology.

———

1991 Late Prehistoric and Early Historic Chiefdoms in the Southeastern United States. New York: Garland Publishing, Inc.

DePratter, Chester B., Charles M. Hudson, and Marvin T. Smith

1983 The Route of Juan Pardo's Explorations in the Interior Southeast 1566–1568. *Florida Historical Quarterly* 62:125–58.

———

1985 The Hernando de Soto Expedition: From Chiaha to Mabila. Pp. 108–26 in Alabama and the Borderlands, from Prehistory to Statehood, R. R. Badger and L. A. Clayton, eds. University, Ala.: The University of Alabama Press.

DePuy, Henry F.

1920 An Early Account of the Establishment of Jesuit Missions in America. *American Antiquarian Society* n.s. 30:68.

Diaz del Castillo

1982 Historia verdadera de la conquista de la Nueva España. C. Sáenz de Santa María, ed. Madrid: Instituto Gonzalo Fernández de Oviedo.

Dickinson, Samuel D.

1980 Historic Tribes in the Ouachita Drainage System in Arkansas. *The Arkansas Archeologist* 21:1–11.

———

1986 The River Cayas, the Ouachita or the Arkansas River? *Field Notes: Newsletter of the Arkansas Archeological Society* 209:5–11.

———

1987 Arkansas's Spanish Halberds. *The Arkansas Archeologist* 25/26:53–62.

Dickinson, Samuel D., and Samuel C. Dellinger

1940 A Survey of the Prehistoric Earthenware of the Lower Arkansas Valley. *Texas Archeological and Paleontological Society, Bulletin* 12:76–96.

Dobyns, Henry F.

1966 An Appraisal of Techniques for Estimating Aboriginal American Population with a New Hemispheric Estimate. *Current Anthropology* 7:395–441.

———

1983 Their Number Become Thinned: Native American Population Dynamics in Eastern North America. Knoxville: The University of Tennessee Press.

———

1988 Indians in the Colonial Spanish Borderlands. Pp. 67–93 in Indians in American History, F. E. Hoxie, ed. Arlington Heights: Harlan Davidson, Inc.

Dorsey, James Owen

1895 Quapaw Folk-Lore. *Journal of American Folk-Lore* 8:130–31.

———

[1895] [Quapaw dictionary file.] (Ms., National Anthropological Archives, Smithsonian Institution, Washington, D.C.)

Dorsey, James Owen, and John R. Swanton

1912 A Dictionary of the Biloxi and Ofo Languages. *Bureau of American Ethnology Bulletin* 47. Washington.

Dorson, Richard M.

1971 American Folklore and the Historian. Chicago: University of Chicago Press.

Dye, David H.

1986 Introduction. Pp. xi–xiv in The Protohistoric Period in the Mid-South: 1500–1700. D. H. Dye and R. C. Brister, eds. *Mississippi Department of Archives and History. Archeological Reports* 18. Jackson.

———

1989 Death March of Hernando de Soto. *Archaeology* 42(3):26–31.

———

[1990] The Hernando de Soto Expedition and the Mississippi River Crossing: A Geomorphological Reconstruction. (Ms., Anthropology Department, Memphis State University, Memphis.)

Early, Ann M.

1981 Summary. Pp. 51–62 in The Pope Site by Raymond W. Wood. The Arkansas Archeologist 22.

———

1982 Caddoan Settlement Systems in the Ouachita River Basin. Pp. 198–233 in Arkansas Archeology in Review, N. L. Trubowitz and M. D. Jeter, eds. *Arkansas Archeological Survey Research Series* 15.

———

1988 Standridge: Caddoan Settlement in a Mountain Environment. *Arkansas Archeological Survey Research Series* 29. Fayetteville.

———

1990 History of Archeological Research in the Ouachita River Valley. Chapter 2 in Hardman (3CL418) A Prehistoric Salt Processing Site, Ishmael Williams and A. M. Early, eds. Final report submitted to Arkansas Highway and Transportation Department, Little Rock, Arkansas.

———

1990a The Central Arkansas Route. (Paper presented at the de Soto Colloquium, Arkansas Archeological Society Annual Meeting, Jonesboro, October 3.)

———

1990b Look to the Southern Hills: Late Prehistoric Relationships Between the Arkansas River Valley and Ouachita Mountains of Arkansas. (Paper presented at the 55th Annual Meeting of the Society For American Archaeology, Las Vegas, Nevada.)

———

1991 Prehistoric Caddoan Saltmaking in Arkansas. (Paper presented at the Southeastern Archeological Conference, Jackson, Mississippi.)

Elliott, J. H.

1970 The Old World and the New, 1492–1650. Cambridge: Cambridge University Press.

———

1973 The Discovery of America and the Discovery of Man. *Proceedings of the British Academy* 58. London.

Elvas See Relaçam verdadeira, Bourne 1904, Lewis 1907, Smith 1857, Smith 1866, Robertson 1933, Rye 1851.

Eubanks, W. S.

1989 Studying de Soto's Route: A Georgian House of Cards. *The Florida Anthropologist* 42:374–76.

———

1991 More Than A Footnote: Is Cofatachequi Really Cofetazque? Pp. 110–25 in *Soto States Anthropologist* 91:110–25.

Ewen, Charles E.

1988 The Discovery of de Soto's First Winter Encampment in Florida. *Alabama De Soto Commission, De Soto Working Paper* 7. Tuscaloosa.

———

1989 Apalachee Winter. *Archaeology* 42(3):37–39.

———

1989a Anhaica: Discovery of Hernando de Soto's 1539–1540 Winter Camp. Pp. 110–18 in First Encounters, Spanish Explorations in the Caribbean and the United States, 1492–1570. J. T. Milanich and Susan Milbraith, eds. Gainesville: University of Florida Press.

———

1990 Soldier of Fortune: Hernando de Soto in the Territory of the Apalachee, 1539-1540. Pp. 83–91 in Vol 2. of Columbian Consequences. D. H. Thomas, ed. Washington: Smithsonian Institution Press.

Ewers, J. C.

1973 The Influence of Epidemics on the Indian Populations and Cultures of Texas. *Plains Anthropologist* 18:104–15.

Fagan, Brian

1990 A Clash of Cultures. *Archaeology* 43(1):32–37.

Fahnestock, Jeanne

1989 Arguing in Different Forms: The Bering Crossover Controversy. *Science, Technology, and Human Values* 14:26–42.

Fairbanks, Charles H.

1968 Early Spanish Colonial Beads. *Conference on Historic Site Archaeology* 2:3–21.

———

1985 From Exploration to Settlement: Spanish Strategies for Colonization. Pp. 128–39 in Alabama and the Borderlands from Prehistory to Statehood. R. R. Badger and L. A. Clayton, eds. University, Ala.: University of Alabama Press.

Farley, James A., W. Fredrick Limp, and Jami Lockhart

1990 The Archeologist Workbench: Integrating GIS, Remote Sensing, EDA, and Database Management. (Invited paper presented at 53rd Annual Society for American Archeology Meetings, Phoenix, Arizona.)

Fehling, Detlev

1989 Herodotus and His 'Sources': Citation, Invention, and Narrative Art. Liverpool: Francis Cairns.

Fish, S. K., and S. A. Kowalewski, eds.

1990 The Archaeology of Regions: A Case for Full-Coverage Survey. Washington, D.C.: Smithsonian Institution Press.

Fisk, Harold N.

1944 Geological Investigation of the Alluvial Valley of the Lower Mississippi River. Vicksburg: U.S. Army Corps of Engineers.

Fletcher, Alice, and Francis La Flesche
1911 The Omaha Tribe. Vol. 1. *Bureau of American Ethnology Annual Report* 27. (Reprinted: University of Nebraska Press, Lincoln, 1972.)
Flores, Dan
1985 Journal of an Indian Trader, Anthony Glass and the Texas Trading Frontier, 1790–1810. College Station: Texas A & M University Press.
Fogelson, Raymond D.
1989 The Ethnohistory of Events and Nonevents. *Ethnohistory* 36(2):133–47.
Ford, James A.
1961 Menard Site: The Quapaw Village of Osotouy on the Arkansas River. *Anthropological Papers of the American Museum of Natural History* 48:133–91.
Fowells, H. A., comp.
1965 Silvics of Forest Trees of the United States. *U.S. Department of Agriculture. Agriculture Handbook* 271. Washington, D.C.
Freeman, Thomas, and Peter Custis
1806 An Account of the Red River in Louisiana. Washington, D.C.: U.S. War Office.
Fuller, Myron L.
1912 The New Madrid Earthquake. *U.S. Geological Survey Bulletin* 494. Washington, D.C.
Galloway, Patricia K.
1986 The Direct Historical Approach and Early Historical Documents: The Ethnohistorian's View. Pp. 14–23 in The Protohistoric Period in the Mid-South: 1500–1700. D. H. Dye and R. C. Brister, eds. *Mississippi Department of Archives and History Archaeological Report* 18. Jackson.

———
1993 The Historiography of the de Soto Expedition. Lincoln: University of Nebraska Press.

———
[Forthcoming] Sources for the Hernando de Soto Expedition: Intertextuality and the Elusiveness of Truth.
Garcilaso de la Vega
1605 La Florida del Ynca. Lisbon: Pedro Crasbeeck.

———
1609 Comentarios reales de los Incas. Lisbon: Pedro Crasbeek.

———
1616 Historia general del Peru. Cordoba: Por la viuda de Andre de Barrera.

———
1951 The Florida of the Inca. J. G. Varner and J. J. Varner, trans. and eds. Austin: University of Texas Press.
Gibson, J. L.
1985 Ouachita Prehistory. *Louisiana Archaeology* 10:319–35.
Gilmore, Kathleen
1980 Mission Dolores de los Ais: Historical Background and Field Investigations, 1972–73. Pp. 223–76 in Mission Dolores de los Ais, Archaeological Investigations of an Early Spanish Colonial Mission, San Augustine County, Texas, by James E. Corbin, Arlan Kalina, and Thomas C. Alex. *Stephen F. Austin, Papers in Anthropology* 2 and *Texas Antiquities Permit Series, Report* 3. Austin.
Goggin, John M., and William C. Sturtevant
1964 The Calusa: A Stratified Nonagricultural Society (with Notes on Sibling Marriage).

Pp. 179–219 in Explorations in Cultural Anthropology: Essays in Honor of George Peter Murdock. W. H. Goodenough, ed. New York: McGraw-Hill.

Gómara, Francisco López de

1943 Historia de la conquista de México, J. R. Cabañas, ed. Mexico City: Editorial Pedro Robredo.

Gore-Browne, Robert

1953 Chancellor Thurlow: The Life and Times of an XVIIIth Century Lawyer. London: Hamilton.

Gregory, Hiram Ford, Jr.

1973 Eighteenth Century Caddoan Archaeology: A Study in Models and Interpretation. (Unpublished Ph.D. Dissertation in Anthropology, Southern Methodist University, Dallas.)

———

1980 A Continuity Model for Caddoan Adaptation on the Red River in Louisiana. Pp. 347–60 in The Hanna Site, An Alto Village in Red River Parish by Prentice M. Thomas, Jr., L. J. Campbell, and S. R. Ahler. *Louisiana Archaeology* 5. Lafayette.

Griffith, William J.

1954 The Hasinai Indians of East Texas as Seen by Europeans, 1687–1772. *Middle American Research Institute,Philological and Documentary Studies* 2(3). New Orleans.

Guzmán, Eulalia

1958 Relaciones de Hernan Córtes a Carlos V sobre las invasión de Anáhuac. Aclaraciones y rectificaciones. Mexico City: Libros Anáhuac.

———

1989 Una visión crítica de la historia de la conquista de México-Tenochtitlán. Mexico City: Universidad National Autónoma de México.

Haas, Mary R.

1940 Tunica. In Handbook of American Indian Languages. Vol. 4. New York: J. J. Augustin.

———

1950 Tunica Texts. *University of California Publications in Linguistics* 6(1):1–174. Berkeley.

———

1953 Tunica Dictionary. *University of California Publications in Linguistics* 6(2):175–332. Berkeley.

Hakluyt, Richard, trans. see Rye 1851.

Hally, David, Marvin T. Smith, and James B. Langford, Jr.

1990 The Archeological Reality of de Soto's Coosa. Pp. 121–138 in Columbian Consequences, Vol. 2, David Hurst Thomas, ed. Washington, D.C.: Smithsonian Institution Press.

Hann, John H.

1990 Summary Guide to Spanish Florida Missions and Visitas with Churches in the Sixteenth and Seventeenth Centuries. *The Americas* 46:417–513.

Hanna, Henry, Jr.

1940 Most Interesting Dallas County Indian Campsite. *The Record* 2:8–11.

Harmon, A. M., and J. C. Rose

1989 Bioarcheology of the Louisiana and Arkansas Study Area. Pp. 323–54 in Archeology and Bioarcheology of the Lower Mississippi Valley and Trans-Mississippi South in Arkansas and Louisiana. M. D. Jeter, J. C. Rose, G. I. Williams, Jr., and A. M. Harmon, eds. *Arkansas Archeological Survey, Research Series* 37. Fayetteville.

Harrington, Mark R.
1920 Certain Caddo Site in Arkansas. *Museum of the American Indian, Heye Foundation Indian Notes and Monographs (Misc.)* 10. New York.
Harris, R. K.
1951 French or Spanish or What Is It? *The Record* 10:2–3.
Harrisse, Henry
1892 The Discovery of North America: A Critical, Documentary and Historical investigation. London. (Reprinted: N. Israel, Amsterdam, 1961.)
Hathcock, Roy
1983 The Quapaw and Their Pottery. Camden, Arkansas: Hurley Press.
Helms, Mary W.
1987 Ulysses' Sail: An Ethnographic Odyssey of Power, Knowledge, and Geographical Distance. Princeton: Princeton University Press.
Hemmings, E. Thomas
1982 Spirit Lake (3LA83): Test Excavations in a Late Caddo Site on the Red River, Southwest Arkansas. Pp. 55-89 in Contributions to the Archeology of the Great Bend Region, Frank F. Schambach and F. Rackerby, eds. *Arkansas Archeological Survey, Research Series* 22. Fayetteville.

———
1982a Human Adaptation in the Grand Marais Lowland. *Arkansas Archeological Survey Research Series No. 17.* Fayetteville.
Hendershot, B., W. Mosher, and W. Pratt
1982 Infertility and Age: An Unresolved Issue. *Family Planning Perspectives* 14:287.
Henige, David
1986 Primary Source by Primary Source? On the Role of Epidemics in New World Depopulation. *Ethnohistory* 33:293–312.

———
1986a The Context, Content, and Credibility of *La Florida del Ynca. The Americas* 43(1):1–24.

———
1991a A Mismatched Pair: Hudson at the Feast of Hoffman. *Documentary Editing* 13(2):30–34.

———
1991 In Search of Columbus: the Sources for the First Voyage. Tucson: University of Arizona Press.
Hilliard, Jerry E., and John Riggs
1986 AMASDA Site Encoding Manual, Version 2.0. *Arkansas Archeological Survey Technical Paper* 1. Fayetteville.
Hockensmith, Charles
1977 The Steck Site: A Titus Focus Midden, Wood County, Texas. (Paper presented at the 1977 Caddo Conference, Natchitoches, Louisiana.)
Hodge, Frederick W.
1910 Handbook of American Indians North of Mexico. *Bureau of American Ethnology Bulletin* 30. Washington, D.C.
Hodges, T. L., and Mrs. T. L. Hodges
1944 Suggestions for Identification of Certain Mid-Ouachita Pottery as Cahinnio Caddo. *Bulletin of the Texas Archeological and Paleontological Society* 16:98–116. Abilene.
Hoffman, Michael P.
1971 A Partial Archeological Sequence for the Little River Region, Arkansas. (Unpublished Ph. D. Dissertation in Anthropology, Harvard University, Cambridge.)

———
1977 The Kinkead-Mainard Site, 3PU2: A Late Prehistoric Quapaw Phase Site Near Little Rock, AR. *The Arkansas Archeologist* 16–18:1–41.

———
1977a An Archeological Survey of the Ozark Reservoir in West-Central Arkansas. Pp. 1–43 in Ozark Reservoir Papers: Archeology in West-Central Arkansas 1965–1970. *Arkansas Archeological Survey Research Series* 10. Fayetteville.

———
1983 Protohistory of the Lower and Central Arkansas River Valley in Arkansas. (Paper presented at the Mid-South Archeological Conference, Memphis, Tennessee.)

———
1986 Protohistory of the Lower and Central Arkansas River Valley in Arkansas. Pp. 24–37 in The Protohistoric Period in the Mid-South: 1500-1700, Proceedings of the 1983 Mid-South Archaeological Conference, D. H. Dye and R. C. Brister, eds. *Mississippi Department of Archives and History, Archaeological Report* 18. Jackson.

———
1987 Who's Wearing the White Hats? The Arkansas Act to Prohibit Burial Desecration and its Implications for Caddoan Archaeology. *Newsletter of the Southeastern Archaeological Conference* 29(2):22–28.

———
1987a An Examination of the Evidence for the Tunica People on the Arkansas River. (Paper presented at the Conference on Native American Traditions in the South, Mid-South Folklore Association, Clarksville, Ark.)

———
1988 A Comparison of Terminal Mississippian Period Ceramics of the Lower Arkansas River Valley With Those of Northeastern Arkansas. (Paper presented at the 1988 Mid-South Archeological Conference, Paducah, Ky.)

———
1990 The Terminal Mississippian Period in the Arkansas River Valley and Quapaw Ethnogenesis. Pp. 208–26 in Towns and Temples Along the Mississippi. D. H. Dye and C. A. Cox, eds. *Mississippi Department of Archives and History Archeological Report* 18. Jackson.

Hoffman, Paul E.
1984 The Chicora Legend and Franco-Spanish Rivalry. *Florida Historical Quarterly* 62:419–38.

Hopkins, Donald R.
1983 Princes and Peasants. Chicago: University of Chicago Press.

House, John H.
1975 Summary of Archeological Knowledge Updated with Newly Gathered Survey Data. Pp. 153–62 in The Cache River Archeological Project. Michael B. Schiffer and J. H. House, comps. *Arkansas Archeological Survey, Research Series* 8. Fayetteville.

———
1987 Kent Phase Excavations in Eastern Arkansas, 1978-1984. *Mississippi Archaeology* 22(1):46–60.

Hrdlicka, A.
1908 Report on a Collection of Crania from Arkansas. *Journal of the Academy of Natural Sciences of Philadelphia* 13:558–63.

Hudson, Charles M.
1976 The Southeastern Indians. Knoxville: University of Tennessee Press.

———

1985 De Soto in Arkansas: A Brief Synopsis. *Field Notes: Newsletter of the Arkansas Archeological Society* 205 (July/August):3–12.

———

1987 An Unknown South: Spanish Explorers and Southeastern Chiefdoms. Pp. 6-24 in Visions and Revisions: Ethnohistoric Perspectives on Southern Cultures. George Sabo III and M. Schneider, eds. *Southern Anthropological Society Proceedings* 20. Athens, Ga.

———

1987a The Uses of Evidence in Reconstructing the Route of the Hernando de Soto Expedition. *Alabama de Soto Commission, Working Paper* 1. Tuscaloosa.

———

1988 A Spanish-Coosa Alliance in Sixteenth-Century North Georgia. *The Georgia Historical Quarterly* 72:599–626.

———

1989a A Synopsis of the Hernando de Soto Expedition, 1539–1543. In Appendix B, Feasibility Study, de Soto National Historic Trail, Atlanta: National Park Service, Southeast Regional Office.

———

1990 The Juan Pardo Expeditions: Spanish Explorers and the Indians of the Carolinas and Tennessee, 1566–1568. Washington, D.C.: Smithsonian Institution Press.

———

1990a A Synopsis of the Hernando de Soto Expedition, 1539–1543. Pp. 75–109 in De Soto Trail, National Historic Trail Study, Final Report. Atlanta: National Park Service.

Hudson, Charles, and Joyce R. Hudson

1989 Tracking the Elusive De Soto. *Archaeology* 42(3):32–36.

Hudson, Charles M., C. B. DePratter, and M. T. Smith

1988 The Victims of the King Site Massacre: A Historical Detective's Report. Pp. 117-34 in *The King Site: Continuity and Contact in Sixteenth-Century Georgia.* Athens: University of Georgia Press.

———

1989 Hernando de Soto's Expedition through the Southern United States. Pp. 77–98 in First Encounters: Spanish Explorations in the Caribbean and the United States, 1492–1570. J. T. Milanich and S. Milbrath, eds. *Ripley F. Bullen Monographs in Anthropology and History* 9, Gainesville.

Hudson, Charles M., and Jerald T. Milanich

Hudson Charles M., and Marvin T. Smith

1990 Reply to Eubanks. *The Florida Anthropologist* 43:37–38.

Hudson, Charles M., Marvin T. Smith, and C. B. DePratter

1984 The Hernando De Soto Expedition: From Apalachee to Chiaha. *Southeastern Archaeology* 3:65–77.

———

1990 The Hernando de Soto Expedition: From Mabila to the Mississippi Rover. Pp. 181-207 in Towns and Temples Along the Mississippi. D. H. Dye and C. A. Cox, eds. Tuscaloosa: University of Alabama Press.

Hudson, Charles M., Marvin T. Smith, C. B. DePratter, and Emilia Kelley

1989 The Tristan de Luna Expedition, 1559–1561. Pp. 119–34 in First Encounters, Spanish Explorations in the Caribbean and the United States, 1492–1570. Jerald T. Milanich and Susan Milbrath, eds. *Ripley F. Bullen Monographs in Anthropology and History* 9. Gainesville.

Hudson, Charles M., Marvin T. Smith, D. Hally, R. Polhemus, and C. B. DePratter
1985 Coosa: A Chiefdom in the Sixteenth-Century Southeastern United States. *American Antiquity* 50:723–37.

———
1987 Reply to Boyd and Schroedl. *American Antiquity* 52:852.

Humes, Jesse, and Vinnie May James Humes, comp.
1973 A Chickasaw Dictionary. Durant, Oklahoma: Creative Informatics.

Iglesia, Ramón
1980 Cronistas y historiadores de la conquista de México: el cíclo de Hernan Cortés. Mexico City: El Colegio de México.

Izard, General George
1827 [Quapaw vocabulary] (Ms. sent to the American Philosophical Society in Philadelphia. Smithsonian Institution, Washington, D.C.).

Jackson, A. T.
1932 Excavations at the Hunt Brothers Farm, Cass County, Texas. (Ms., Texas Archeological Research Laboratory, The University of Texas at Austin.)

———
1932a Excavations of a Prehistoric Site at the Clements Place, Cass County, Texas. (Ms., Texas Archeological Research Laboratory, The University of Texas at Austin.)

Jelks, Edward B.
1961 Excavations at Texarkana Reservoir, Sulphur River, Texas. *Bureau of American Ethnology Bulletin* 179:1–78. Washington, D.C.

———
1965 The Archeology of McGee Bend Reservoir, Texas. (Unpublished Ph.D. Dissertation in Anthropology, The University of Texas at Austin.)

———
1988 Historical Dictionary of North American Archeology. Westport, Conn.: Greenwood Press.

Jeter, Marvin D.
1986 Tunicans West of the Mississippi: A Summary of Early Historic and Archeological Evidence. Pp. 324–37 in The Protohistoric Period in the Mid-South: 1500–1700. D. H. Dye and R. C. Brister, eds. Proceedings of the 1983 Mid-South Archaeological Conference. *Mississippi Department of Archives and History, Archaeological Report* 18. Jackson.

———
1989 Protohistoric and Historic Native Americans. Pp 221–48 in Archeology and Bioarcheology of the Lower Mississippi Valley and Trans-Mississippi South in Arkansas and Louisiana. M. D. Jeter, J. C. Rose, G. I. Williams, Jr., and A. M. Harmon eds. *Arkansas Archeological Survey Research Series* 37. Fayetteville.

Jeter, Marvin D., Kathleen H. Cande, and John J. Mintz
1990 Goldsmith Oliver 2 (3PU306): A Protohistoric Archeological Site Near Little Rock Arkansas. Final report submitted to Federal Aviation Administration, Southwest Region, Fort Worth, Texas.

Jeter, Marvin D., J. C. Rose, G. I. Williams, Jr., and A. M. Harmon
1989 Archeology and Bioarcheology of the Lower Mississippi Valley and Trans-Mississippi South in Arkansas and Louisiana. *Arkansas Archeological Survey, Research Series* 37. Fayetteville.

Johnson, J. G.

1924 Myths, Legends, Miracles, and Mysteries, Related by the First Historians of Florida. *Georgia Historical Quarterly* 8:293.

Johnson, Samuel

1825 The Works of Samuel Johnson, LL.D. 11 vols. Oxford: Pickering.

Jones, Buddy Calvin

1968 The Kinsloe Focus: A Study of Seven Historic Caddoan Sites in Northeast Texas. (Unpublished M.A. Thesis in Anthropology, The University of Oklahoma, Norman.)

Jones, Charles C.

1873 Antiquities of the Southern Indians, Particularly of the Georgia Tribes. New York: Appleton and Co.

Jordan, Terry J., with John L. Bean, Jr., and William M. Holmes

1984 Texas, A Geography. Boulder: Westview Press.

Jorde, L. B., K. J. Pitkanen, and J. H. Mielke

1989 Predicting Smallpox Epidemics: A Statistician Analysis of Two Finnish Populations. *American Journal of Human Biology* 1:621–29.

de Josselin de Jong, J. P. B.

1930 The Natchez Social System. Pp. 553–62 in *Proceedings of the 23rd International Congress of Americanists.*

Kelley, Jane H., and Marsha P. Hanen

1988 Archeology and the Methodology of Science. Albuquerque: University of New Mexico Press.

Kellogg, Louis Phelps, ed.

1917 Early Narratives of the Northwest, 1634–1699. New York: Charles Scribner's Sons.

Kimball, Geoffrey

1985 A Descriptive Grammar of Koasati. (Unpublished Ph.D. dissertation in linguistics, Tulane University, New Orleans.)

Kirkpatrick, A. Y.

1963 The Early Settler's Life in Texas and the Organization of Hill County. (Ms., Hillsboro Public Library, Hillsboro, Texas.)

Klinger, Timothy

1977 Parkin Archeology: A Report on the 1966 Field School Test Excavation at the Parkin Site. *The Arkansas Archeologist* 16–18:45–80.

Kniffen, Fred B.

1968 Louisiana: Its Land and People. Baton Rouge: Louisiana State University Press.

Knight, Vernon J., Jr.

1986 The Institutional Organization of Mississippian Religion. *American Antiquity* 51:675–87.

Kolb, C. R., W. B. Steinriede, Jr., E. L. Krinitzsky, R. T. Saucier, F. R. Mabrey, F. L. Smith, and A. R. Fleetwood

1968 Geological Investigation of the Yazoo Basin, Lower Mississippi Valley. *Waterways Experiment Station Technical Report* 3–480. Vicksburg.

Kuchler, A. W.

1964 Potential Natural Vegetation of the Coterminous United States. *American Geographical Society, Special Publication* 36.

Larsen, Clark S.

1987 Stress and Adaptation at Santa Catalina de Guale: Analysis of Human Remains. (Paper presented at the Society for Historical Archaeology Symposium "Missions of Spanish Florida: New Perspectives from Guale, Timucua, and Apalachee," Savannah.)

———
1987a Bioarchaeological Interpretation and Early Contact Populations on St. Catherines Island, Georgia. (Paper presented at the Annual Meeting of the American Association of Physical Anthropologists, New York.)

Leader, Jonathan M.
1989 Technological Analysis of Metal Ornaments from the Goldsmith Oliver 2 Site. In A Protohistoric Archeological Site near Little Rock, Arkansas. M. D. Jeter, ed. (Report submitted by Sponsored Research Program, Arkansas Archeological Survey to Federal Aviation Administration, Southwest Region, Fort Worth.)

Lenzer, John
1980 Geology and Geomorphology. Pp. 45–70 in The Hanna Site: An Alto Village in Red River Parish, by Prentice M. Thomas, Jr., L. J. Campbell, and S. R. Ahler. *Louisiana Archaeology* 5. Lafayette.

Le Page du Pratz, Antoine Simon
1774 Histoire de la Louisiane. Facsimile edition of Joseph G. Tregle, Jr. Baton Rouge: Louisiana State University Press. (Original, Paris: DeBure, 1758.)

Lesser, Alexander and Gene Weltfish
1932 Composition of the Caddoan Linguistic Stock. *Smithsonian Miscellaneous Collections*, 87(6). Washington, D.C.

Lewis, Robert E.
1982 *Los Naufragios* de Alvar Núñez: Historia y Ficcion. *Revista Iberoamericana* 48(121):681–94.

Lewis, Theodore H.
1900 The De Soto Expedition through Florida. *American Antiquarian* 22(6):351–57.

———
1901 The De Soto Expedition through Florida. *American Antiquarian* 23(2):107–11.

———
1901a The De Soto Expedition through Florida. *American Antiquarian* 23(4):242–47.

———
1902 Route of De Soto's Expedition from Taliepacana to Huhasene. *Mississippi Historical Society Publication* 6:449–67.

———, ed.
1907 The Narrative of the Expedition of Hernando de Soto by the Gentlemen of Elvas. Buckingham Smith, trans. Pp. 127–272 in Spanish Explorers in the Southern United States, 1528-1543. New York: Charles Scribners' Sons. (Reprinted 1984 Texas State Historical Association and the University of Texas, Austin.)

———
1927 Route of de Soto's Expedition from Taliepacana to Huhasene. *Publications of the Mississippi Historical Society, Special Bulletin* 1. Jackson.

Liette, Pierre-Charles de
1934 Memoir of De Gannes Concerning the Illinois Country. T. C. Pease and R. C. Werner, eds. *Collections of the Illinois State Historical Library* 23:302–95.

Littlefield, Daniel F.
1973 The Salt Industry in Arkansas Territory, 1819–1836. *Arkansas Historical Quarterly* 32(4):312–36.

Lockhart, James M.
1972 The Men of Cajamarca: A Social and Biographical Study of the First Conquerers of Peru. *Institute of Latin American Studies, University of Texas, Latin American Monograph* 27. Austin.

Lorrain, D.
1969 Archaeological Excavations in the Fish Creek Reservoir. *Southern Methodist University, Contributions in Anthropology* 4. Dallas.
Lynott, Mark J.
1979 Prehistoric Bison Populations of North Central Texas. *Bulletin of the Texas Archeological Society* 50:89–101.
Lyon, Eugene
1976 The Enterprise of Florida. Gainesville: University Presses of Florida.
———
1982 The Cañete Fragment: Another Narrative of Hernando de Soto. (Ms., St. Augustine Foundation, St. Augustine, Fla.)
———
1988 Pedro Menéndez's Strategic Plan for the Florida Peninsula. *Florida Historical Quarterly* 67:1–14.
Malone, James R.
1922 The Chickasaw Nation: A Short Version of a Noble People. Louisville: John F. Morton.
Marquardt, William H.
1987 The Calusa Social Formation in Protohistoric South Florida. Pp. 98–116 in Power Relations and State Formations. Thomas C. Patterson and C. W. Gailey, eds. Washington, D.C.: Archaeology Section, American Anthropological Association.
———
1988 Politics and Production among the Calusa of South Florida. Pp. 161–88 in Hunters and Gatherers. Vol. I: History, Environment, and Social Change among Hunting and Gathering Societies. David Richies, T. Ingold, and J. Woodburn, eds. London: Berg Publishers.
Martin, Ernest R.
1990 The Dillard Site, A Late Prehistoric Plains Village Site in Cooke County, Texas. (Manuscript in possession of the author, Gainesville, Texas.)
Martin, Robert Sidney, and James C. Martin
1982 Contours of Discovery. Austin: Texas State Historical Association.
Martin, William A., Bonnie C. Yates, and Gayle J. Fritz
1988 Exploitation of Subsistence Resources within the Mountain Creek Drainage. In Late Holocene Prehistory of the Mountain Creek Drainage, Duane E. Peter and Daniel E. McGregor, eds. *Archaeology Research Program, Southern Methodist University, Joe Pool Lake Archeological Project* I. Dallas.
Mason, C. I.
1976 Historic Identification and Lake Winnebago Focus Oneoto. Pp. 335–48 in Cultural Change and Continuity. C. E. Cleland, ed. New York: Academic Press.
McCall, Edith
1983 The Attack on the Great Raft. *American Heritage of Invention and Technology* 3(3):10–16.
McEwan, B. G., and J. M. Mitchem
1984 Indian and European Acculturation in the Eastern United States as a Result of Trade. *North American Archaeologist* 5:271–85.
McFalls, Joseph A., and Marguerite Harvey McFalls
1984 Disease and Fertility. New York: Academic Press, Inc.
McQuick, W. P.
1986 Proceedings: Conference on Reburial Issues. Chicago: Newberry Library, Society for American Archaeology and Society of Professional Archeologists. Chicago.

Merbs, C. F.

1989 Patterns of Health and Sickness in the Precontact Southwest. Pp. 41–55 in Columbian Consequences. Vol. I. D. H. Thomas, ed. Washington, D.C.: Smithsonian Institution Press.

Milanich, Jerald T.

1987 Corn and Calusa: De Soto and Demography. Pp. 173–84 in Coasts, Plains and Deserts, Essays in Honor of Reynold J. Ruppe. S. W. Gaines, ed. *Arizona State University, Anthropological Research Papers* 38. Tempe.

———

1989 Where Did de Soto Land? Identifying Bahia Honda. *Florida Anthropologist* 42:295–302.

———

1989a Hernando de Soto and the Expedition in La Florida: An Overview. *The Florida Anthropologist* 42:303–16.

Milanich, Jerald T., and Charles Hudson

1993 Hernando de Soto and the Indians of Florida. Gainesville: University Press of Florida.

Milanich, Jerald T., and Susan Milbrath, eds.

1989 First Encounters: Spanish Explorations in the Caribbean and the United States, 1492–1570. *Ripley F. Bullen Monographs in Anthropology and History* 9. Gainesville.

Miller, Elizabeth

1988 Health and Disease among Contact Populations in Texas. (Paper presented at the 59th Texas Archeological Society Meeting, Houston.)

Milner, George R.

1980 Epidemic Disease in the Postcontact Southeast: A Reappraisal. *Mid-Continental Journal of Archaeology* 5:39–56.

Mitchem, Jeffrey M.

1989 Artifacts of Exploration: Archaeological Evidence from Florida. Pp. 99–109 in First Encounters: Spanish Explorations in the Caribbean and the United States, 1492-1570, J. T. Milanich and S. Milbrath, eds. *Ripley F. Bullen Monographs in Anthropology and History* 9. Gainesville.

———

1989a Redefining Safety Harbor: Late Prehistoric/Protohistoric Archaeology in West Peninsular Florida. (Unpublished Ph.D. Dissertation in Anthropology, University of Florida, Gainesville.)

———

1990 Initial Spanish-Indian Contact in West Peninsular Florida: The Archaeological Evidence. Pp. 49-59 in Columbian Consequences. Vol 2. D. H. Thomas, ed. Washington: Smithsonian Institution Press.

Moir, Randall W., Daniel E. McGregor, and David H. Jurney

1992 Archaeological Investigations at Copper Lake: 1987 Season Report. Dallas: Southern Methodist University.

Montell, William Lynwood

1970 The Saga of Coe Ridge. New York: Harper.

Mooney, James

1928 The Aboriginal Population of America North of Mexico. J. R. Swanton, ed. *Smithsonian Miscellaneous Collections* 80(7). Washington, D.C.

Moore, Clarence B.

1900 Certain Mounds of Arkansas and Mississippi, Part 1. Mounds and Cemeteries of the Lower Arkansas River. *Academy of Natural Sciences of Philadelphia Journal* 13:448–557.

———
1908 Certain Mounds of Arkansas and of Mississippi. Part I. Mounds and Cemeteries of the Lower Arkansas River. *Journal of the Academy of Natural Sciences of Philadelphia* 13:481–563.

———
1910 Antiquities of the St. Francis, White and Black Rivers, Arkansas. *Journal of the Academy of Natural Sciences of Philadelphia* 14:255–364.

———
1911 Some Aboriginal Sites on the Mississippi River. *Journal of the Academy of Natural Sciences of Philadelphia* 14:364–480.

———
1912 Some Aboriginal Sites on the Red River. *Journal of the Academy of Natural Sciences of Philadelphia* 14(4):481–644.

Morey, N. C., and R. V. Morey
1973 Foragers and Farmers: Differential Consequences of Spanish Contact. *Ethnohistory* 20:229–46.

Morse, Dan F.
1986 On the Possible Origin of the Quapaw in Northeast Arkansas. (Paper presented at the Arkansas Post Tricentennial Symposium.)

———
1986a Protohistoric Hunting Sites in Northeastern Arkansas. Pp. 89–94 in The Protohistoric Period in the Mid-South: 1500–1700. D. H. Dye and R. C. Brister, eds. *Mississippi Department of Archives and History, Archaeological Report* 18. Jackson.

———
1989 The Nodena Phase. Pp. 97–113 in Nodena: An Account of 90 Years of Archeological Investigation in Southeast Mississippi County, Arkansas. Dan F. Morse, ed. *Arkansas Archeological Survey Research Series* 30. Fayetteville.

———
1989b ASU Spring Break Archeology Project. *Field Notes: Newsletter of the Arkansas Archeological Society* 228:3–6.

———
1990a The Nodena Phase. Pp. 69–97 in Towns and Temples Along the Mississippi. D. H. Dye and C. A. Cox, eds. Tuscaloosa: University of Alabama Press.

Morse, Dan F., and Scott Akridge
1988 Salt Procurement in Arkansas. *Field Notes: Newsletter of the Arkansas Archeological Society* 224:3-4.

Morse, Dan F., and Phyllis A. Morse
1983 Archaeology of the Central Mississippi Valley. New York: Academic Press.

———
1983a Recent Findings in the Mississippi Valley. New York: Academic Press.

———
1990 The Spanish Exploration of Arkansas. Pp. 197–210 in Columbian Consequences. Vol. 2. Archeological and Historical Perspective on the Spanish Borderlands East. D. H. Thomas, ed. Washington D.C.: Smithsonian Institution Press.

Morse, Phyllis A.
1981 Parkin: The 1978–1979 Archeological Investigations of a Cross County, Arkansas Site. *Arkansas Archeological Survey, Research Papers* 13. Fayetteville.

———
1990 The Parkin Site and the Parkin Phase. Pp. 118–34 in Towns and Temples Along the Mississippi. D. H. Dye and C. A. Cox, eds. Tuscaloosa: University of Alabama Press.

Murray, Katherine A.
1985 Bioarcheology of the Parkin Site. (Unpublished Honors Thesis in Anthropology, University of Arkansas, Fayetteville.)

———
1989 Bioarchaeology of the Post Contact Mississippi and Arkansas River Valleys 1500–1700 A.D. (Unpublished M.A. thesis in Anthropology, University of Arkansas, Fayetteville.)

National Park Service
1990 De Soto Trail. National Historic Trail Study Final Report. Atlanta: National Park Service.

Neuman, Robert W.
1989 Review of Morse and Morse, Findings. *Review of Archaeology* 10(2):9–18.

Newkumet, Vynola Beaver, and Howard L. Meredith
1988 Hasinai, A Traditional History of the Caddo Confederacy. College Station: Texas A & M University Press.

Niza, Marcos de
1539 Descubrimiento de las siete ciudades, por el P. Fr. Niza. Pp. 325-350 in Colección de documentos ineditos relativos al descubrimiento, conquista y organización de las antiguas posesiones españoles de América y Oceania, Vol. 3, Madrid: Manual B. de Quiros.

Núñez, Cabesa de Vaca, Alvar
1962 Adventures in the Unknown Wilds of North America. C. Covey, trans. and ed. New York: Macmillan.

———
1972 The Narrative of Alvar Núñez Cabeza de Vaca. Fanny Bandelier, trans. Barre, Massachusettes: The Imprint Society.

Nuttall, Thomas
1821 Journal of Travels into the Arkansas Territory, During the Year 1819, with Observations on the Manners of the Aborigines. Philadelphia: T. M. Palmer.

Omernik, James W.
1987 Ecoregions of the Southeast States. Map. Corvallis: U.S. Environmental Protection Agency, Environmental Research Laboratory.

O'Shea, J. M.
1984 Mortuary Variability: An Archaeological Investigation. New York: Academic Press.

Oviedo y Valdés, Gonzalo Fernández de
1851–1855 Historia General y Natural de las Indias. José Amador de los Ríos, ed. 4 vols. Madrid: Impr. de la Real Académia de la Historia. (Reprinted: Editorial Guarania, Ascunción del Páraguay, 1944.)

Palkovich, A. M.
1981 Demography and Disease Patterns in a Protohistoric Plains Group: A Study of the Mobridge Site (39WW1). *Plains Anthropologist, Memoir* 17:71–84.

Pearson, Charles E.
1982 Geomorphology and Prehistoric Settlement Patterns in the Great Basin Region. Pp. 12–29 in Contributions to the Archeology of the Great Bend Region. F. F. Schambach and F. Rackerby, eds. *Arkansas Archeological Survey, Research Series* 22. Fayetteville.

Pell, William F.
1983 The Natural Divisions of Arkansas: A Revised Classification and Description. *Natural Areas Journal* 3(2):12–23.
Perino, Gregory
1966 The Banks Village Site, Crittenden County, Arkansas. *Missouri Archaeological Society, Memoir* 4. Columbia.
Perttula, Timothy K.
1989 Contact and Interaction between Caddoan and European Peoples: The Historic Archaeological and Ethnohistorical Records. (Unpublished Ph.D. Dissertation in Anthropology, University of Washington, Seattle.)
———
1989a The Looting and Vandalism of Archaeological Sites in East Texas: A Status report. (Unpublished Manuscript, Project conducted for Archeological Planning and Review and Office of the State Archeologist, Texas Historical Commission, Austin.)
———
[1990] The Hurricane Hill Site (41HP106), Cooper Lake, Hopkins County, Texas. Review Draft. *Institute of Applied Sciences, Contributions in Archaeology* 9. Denton.
Perttula, Timothy K., and James E. Bruseth
1983 Early Caddoan Subsistence Strategies Sabine River Basin, East Texas. *Plains Anthropologist* 28(99):9–22.
Perttula, Timothy K., C. J. Crane, and J. E. Bruseth
1983 A Consideration of Caddoan Subsistence. *Southeastern Archeology* 1(2):89–102.
Perttula, Timothy K., and K. K. Gilmore
1988 Archaeological Survey along Mill Race Creek and Tributaries, Wood County, Texas: 1987-1988. *Institute of Applied Sciences, University of North Texas, Contributions in Archaeology* 6. Denton.
Perttula, Timothy K., B. D. Skiles, M. B. Collins, M. C. Trachte, and F. Valdez, Jr.
1986 "This Everlasting Sand Bed": Cultural Resources Investigations at the Texas Big Sandy Project, Wood and Upshur Counties, Texas. *Reports of Investigations* 52. Austin: Prewitt and Associates, Inc.
Peter, Duane E., and Daniel E. McGregor
1988 Understanding the Dynamics of Hunter/Gatherer Settlement—Subsistence Patterns: A Regional Perspective. Pp. 114–31 in Late Holocene Prehistory of the Mountain Creek Drainage, D. E. Peter and D. E. McGregor, eds. *Joe Pool Lake Archeological Project* 1. Dallas: Southern Methodist University.
Phillips, Philip
1970 Archeological Survey in the Lower Yazoo Basin, Mississippi, 1949–1955. *Papers of the Peabody Museum of Archeology and Ethnology* 60. Cambridge.
Phillips, Philip, James Ford, and James B. Griffin
1951 Archaeological Survey in the Lower Mississippi Alluvial Valley, 1940-1947. *Papers of the Peabody Museum of Archaeology and Ethnology* 25. Cambridge.
Pirandello
1954 Right You Are. New York: Columbia University Press.
Population Reports
1979 Age at Marriage and Fertility. *Series M* 4 (November).
Powell, Mary L.
1989 The People of Nodena. Pp. 65–95 in Nodena: An Account of 90 Years of Archeological Investigation in Southeast Mississippi County, Arkansas. D. F. Morse ed. *Arkansas Archeological Survey, Research Series* 30.

Prewitt, Elton R., John W. Clark, Jr., and David S. Dibble
1972 An Assessment of the Archeological and Historical Resources of the Bayou Loco Reservoir Area, Nacogdoches County, Texas. *University of Texas, Texas Archeological Salvage Project, Research Report* 11. Austin.

Price, James E., and Cynthia R. Price
1990 Protohistoric/Early Historic Manifestations in Southeastern Missouri. Pp. 59–68 in Towns and Temples Along the Mississippi. D. H. Dye and C. A. Cox, eds. Tuscaloosa: University of Alabama Press.

Price, James E., Cynthia R. Price, and Suzanne E. Harris
1976 An Assessment of the Cultural Resources of the Fourche Creek Watershed. (Report submitted to the USDA-SCS by American Archaeology Division, University of Missouri, Columbia.)

Priestley Herbert I., ed. and Trans.
1928 The Luna Papers, Documents Relating to the Expedition of Don Tristán de Luna y Arellano for the Conquest of La Florida in 1559–1561. 2 vols. *Florida State Historical Society Publication* 8. DeLand.

Prikryl, Daniel
1987 A Synthesis of the Prehistory of the Lower Elm Fork of the Trinity River. (Unpublished M.A. Thesis in Anthropology, The University of Texas at Austin.)

______
1990 Lower Elm Fork Prehistory, a Redefinition of Cultural Concepts and Chronologies along the Trinity River, North-Central Texas. *Texas Historical Commission, Office of the State Archeologist Report* 37. Austin.

Putnam, J. A., and Henry Bull
1932 The Trees of the Bottomlands of the Mississippi River Delta Region. *Southern Forest Experiment Station, Occasional Paper* 27:1–207. (mimeographed)

Quinn, David B.
1979 New American World: A Documentary History of North America to 1612. Volume II: Major Spanish Searches in Eastern North America. Franco-Spanish Clash in Florida. The Beginnings of Spanish Florida. Volume V: The Extension of Settlement in Florida, Virginia, and the Spanish Southwest. New York: Arno Press.

______, ed.
1979a The Expedition of Hernando de Soto and His Successor, Luís de Moscoso, 1539–1543. Pp. 90–188 in New American World: Major Spanish Searches in Eastern North America. Vol. 2. New York: Arno Press.

______, ed.
1979b Major Spanish Searches in Eastern North America. Franco-Spanish clash in Florida. The Beginnings of Spanish Florida. Pp. 127–83 in New American World: A Documentary History of North American to 1612. Vol. 2. New York: Arno Press.

Raiz, Erwin T.
1957 Landforms of the United States. Map. In The Physiographic Provinces of North America by Wallace W. Atwood. New York: Ginn.

______
1986 Physiography. Pp. 80–81 in Goode's World Atlas. E. B. Espenshade, ed. New York: Rand McNally.

Ramenofsky, Anne F.
1982 The Archaeology of Population Collapse: Native American Response to the Introduction of Infectious Disease. (Unpublished Ph.D. Dissertation in Anthropology, University of Washington, Seattle.)

———
1985 The Introduction of European Disease and the Aboriginal Population Collapse. *Mississippi Archaeologist* 20:2–18.

———
1987 Diffusion of Disease at European Contact. (Paper presented at the 52nd Annual Meeting of the Society for American Archaeology, Toronto.)

———
1987a Vectors of Death: The Archaeology of European Contact. Albuquerque: The University of New Mexico Press.

Rankin, Robert L.
[1985] Quapaw as a Historically Dhegiha Language: Grammar. (Manuscript in author's possession.)

———
1986 Quapaw Lexicon. (Unpublished data base printout, Lawrence, Kansas.)

———
1988 Quapaw: Genetic and Areal Affiliations. Pp. 629–650 in In Honor of Mary Haas. From the Haas Festival Conference on Native American Linguistics, W. Shipley, ed. Berlin: Mouton de Gruyter.

Redford, Donald B.
1981 The Acquisition of Foreign Goods and Services in the Old Kingdom. *Scripta Mediterrenea* 2:5–16.

Relaçam verdeira
1557 Relaçam verdadeira dos trabalhos que o gournador dõ Fernão de Souto e certos fidalgos portueses passarom eno desubrim~eto da provincia da Frolida [sic]. Evora: A. de Burgos.

———
1686 A relation of the invasion and conquest of Florida by the Spaniards, under the command of Fernando de Soto/Written in Portuguese by a gentleman of the town of Elvas; now Englished; To which is subjoyned To [two] journeys of the present emperor of China into Tartary in the years 1682 and 1683; with some discoveries made by the Spaniards in the island of California, in the year 1683. London: Printed for J. Lawrence.

Ricoeur, Paul
1971 The Model of the Text: Meaningful Action Considered as a Text. *Social Research* 38:529–62.

Robertson, James A., trans. and ed.
1933 True Relation of the Hardships Suffered by Governor Fernando de Soto and Certain Portuguese Gentlemen During the Discovery of the Province of Florida, Now Newly Set Forth by the Gentleman of Elvas. 2 vols. *Publications of the Florida State Historical Society* 11. DeLand.

Robinson, P. A., M. A. Kelley, and P. E. Rubertone
1985 Preliminary Biocultural Interpretations from a Seventeenth Century Narragansett Indian Cemetery in Rhode Island. Pp. 107–30 in Cultures in Contact: The Impact of European Contacts on Native American Cultural Institutions A.D. 1000–1800. W. W. Fitzhugh, ed. Washington, D.C.: Smithsonian Institution Press.

Rogers, J. D.
1983 Social Ranking and Change in the Harlan and Spiro Phases of Eastern Oklahoma. Pp. 17–128 in Southeastern Natives and Their Pasts. D. G. Wyckoff and J. L. Hofman, eds. *Studies in Oklahoma's Past* 11. Norman: Oklahoma Archeological Survey.

Rohrbaugh, Charles L.

1982 Spiro and Fort Coffee Phases: Changing Cultural Complexes of the Caddoan Area. (Unpublished Ph. D. dissertation in Anthropology, University of Wisconsin-Madison.)

——

1984 Arkansas Valley Caddoan: Fort Coffee Focus and Neosho Focus. Pp. 265–85 in Prehistory of Oklahoma. R. E. Bell, ed. New York: Academic Press.

Rolingson, Martha Ann

1976 The Bartholemew Phase: A Plaquemine Adaptation in the Mississippi Valley. Pp. 99–119 in Cultural Change and Continuity: Essays in Honor of James Bennett Griffin. C. E. Cleland, ed. New York: Academic Press.

Rolingson, Martha Ann, and Frank F. Schambach

1981 The Shallow Lake Site (3UN9/52) and Its Place in Regional Prehistory. *Arkansas Archeological Survey Research Series* 12. Fayetteville.

Rose, Jerome C.

1984 Bioarcheology of the Cedar Grove Site. Pp. 227–56 in Cedar Grove: The Red River Valley. N. L. Trubowitz ed. *Arkansas Archeological Survey Research Series* 23.

Rose, Jerome C., and B. A. Burnett

1990 Bioarcheology of the Eastern Portion of the Gulf Coastal Plain. Pp. 132-48 in The Archeology and Bioarcheology of the Gulf Coastal Plain. D. A. Story, et al., eds. *Arkansas Archeological Survey Research Series* 38. Fayetteville.

Rose, Jerome C., J. P. Harcourt, and B. A. Burnett

1988 Bioarcheology of the OAO Study Area. Pp. 171–92 in Human Adaptation in the Ozark and Ouachita Mountains. G. Sabo, et al., eds. (Final Report submitted by the Arkansas Archeological Survey to the U.S. Army Corps of Engineers, Southwestern Division. Study Unit 1 of the Southwestern Division Archeological Overview. Fayetteville.)

Ross, Jonathan

1989 A Time For Dying. London: Constable.

Rowland, Dunbar

1927 Did De Soto Discover the Mississippi River in Tunica County, Mississippi? Pp. 31–35 in A Symposium on the Place of Discovery of the Mississippi River by Hernando De Soto. D. Rowland, ed. *Mississippi Historical Society Special Publication* 1. Jackson.

——

1927a A Second Chapter Concerning the Discovery of the Mississippi River by De Soto, in Tunica County, Mississippi. Pp. 45–51 in A Symposium on the Place of Discovery of the Mississippi River by Hernando De Soto. D. Rowland, ed. *Mississippi Historical Society Special Publication* 1. Jackson.

Ruidíaz y Caravia, Eugenio

1893 La Florida, su conquista y colonizacion por Pedro Menéndez de Aviles. 2 vols. Madrid: Imprenta de los hijos de J. A. Garcia.

Russell, Richard J.

1967 River and Delta Morphology. *Coastal Studies Series* 20. Baton Rouge: Louisiana State University Press.

Rye, William B., ed.

1851 The Discovery and Conquest of Terra Florida by Don Fernando De Soto. R. Hakluyt, trans. (Facsimile, New York: Burt Franklin, Publisher, 1966.)

Sabo, George III, A. M. Early, J. C. Rose, B. A. Burnett, L. Vogele, and J. P. Harcourt

1988 Human Adaptation in the Ozark-Ouachita Mountains. *Arkansas Archeological Survey Research Series* 31. Fayetteville.

Sahlins, Marshall
1983 Other Times, Other Customs: The Anthropology of History. *American Anthropologist* 85(3):517–44.

———

1985 Islands of History. Chicago and London: The University of Chicago Press.

Salmon, Merrilee H.
1982 Philosophy and Archaeology. New York: Academic Press

Santos, Richard G.
1981 Aguayo Expedition into Texas, 1721. An Annotated Translation of the Five Versions of the Diary Kept by Fr. Juan Antonio de la Peña. Austin: Jenkins Publishing Company.

Saucier, Roger
1964 Geological Investigation of the St. Francis Basin, Lower Mississippi Valley. *U.S. Army Engineer Waterways Experiment Station, Corps of Engineers, Technical Report* 3–659. Vicksburg.

———

1970 Origin of the St. Francis Sunk Lands, Arkansas and Missouri. *Geological Society of America Bulletin* 81:2847-54.

———

1974 Quaternary Geology of the Lower Mississippi Valley. *Arkansas Archeological Survey Research Series* 6. Fayetteville.

———

1981 Current Thinking on Riverine Processes and Geologic History as Related to Human Settlements in the Southeast. *Geoscience and Man* 22:7–18.

Schambach, Frank F.
1982 The Archeology of the Great Bend Region in Arkansas. Pp. 1–11 in Contributions to the Archeology of the Great Bend Region. F. F. Schambach and F. Rackerby, eds. *Arkansas Archeological Survey Research Series* 22. Fayetteville.

———

1988 [The Archeology of Oklahoma.] *The Quarterly Review of Archeology* 9(4):5–9.

———

1989 The End of the Trail: The Route of Hernando De Soto's Army through Southwest Arkansas and East Texas. *The Arkansas Archeologist* 27/28:9–33.

———

1990 The Place of Spiro in Southeastern Prehistory: Is it Caddoan or Mississippian? *Southern Archaeology* 9:67–69.

———

1990a Coles Creek and Mississippian Period Foragers in the Felsenthal Region of the Lower Mississippi Valley. *Arkansas Archeological Survey Research Series* 39.

Schambach, Frank F., and A. M. Early
1982 Southwest Arkansas. Pp. SW1–SW149 in A State Plan for the Conservation of Archeological Resources in Arkansas. H. A. Davis ed. *Arkansas Archeological Survey Research Series* 21. Fayetteville.

Schambach, Frank F., and John E. Miller
1984 A Description and Analysis of the Ceramics. Pp. 109–70 in Cedar Grove: An Interdisciplinary Investigation of a Late Caddo Farmstead in the Red River Valley. N. L. Trubowitz, ed. *Arkansas Archeological Survey Research Series* 23. Fayetteville.

Schambach, Frank F., and Frank Rackerby, eds.
1982 Contributions to the Archeology of the Great Bend Region. *Arkansas Archeological Survey Research Series* 22. Fayetteville.

Schell, Rolfe F.
1966 De Soto Didn't Land at Tampa. Ft. Myers Beach: Island Press.
Schilz, T. F., and D. E. Worcester
1987 The Spread of Firearms among the Indian Tribes on the Northern Frontier of New Spain. *The American Indian Quarterly* 11(1):1–10.
Schneider, David M.
1972 What is Kinship All About? Pp. 32–63 in *Kinship Studies in the Morgan Centennial Year.* P. Reining, ed. Washington, D.C.: Anthropological Society of Washington.
Schwartz, D., and M. Mayaux
1982 Female Fecundity as a Function of Age. *New England Journal of Medicine* 307:4
Scurlock, J. Dan
1962 The Culpepper Site, A Late Fulton Aspect Site in Northeastern Texas. *Bulletin of the Texas Archeological Society* 32:285–316.
Shea, J. G.
1852 Discovery and Exploration of the Mississippi Valley with the Original Narratives of Marquette, Allouez, Memabre Hennepin, and Anastase Douay. New York: Redfield, Clinton Hall.
Shelford, Victor E.
1963 The Ecology of North America. Urbana: University of Illinois Press.
Smith, Bruce D.
1986 The Archaeology of the Southeastern United States: From Dalton to De Soto, 10,500 B.P.–500 B.P. Pp. 1–92 in Advances in World Archaeology. F. Wendorf and A. E. Close, eds. New York: Academic Press.
Smith, Buckingham, ed.
1857 Coleccion de varios documentos para la historia de la Florida y tierras adyacentes. Tomo I. London: Trübner & Co.
_____, trans.
1866 Narratives of the Career of Hernando de Soto in the Conquest of Florida as Told by a Knight of Elvas and in a Relation by Luýs Hernández de Biedma, Factor of the Expedition. New York: The Bradford Club. (Reprinted: Palmetto Books, Gainesville, Florida, 1968.)
Smith, Fred, and Roger T. Saucier
1971 Geological Investigations of the Western Lowlands Area, Lower Mississippi Valley. *Waterways Experiment Station Technical Report* S-715. Vicksburg.
Smith, Gerald P.
1990 The Walls Phase and Its Neighbors. Pp. 129-163 in Towns and Temples Along the Mississippi. D. H. Dye and C. A. Cox, eds. Tuscaloosa: University of Alabama Press.
Smith, Marvin T.
1977 The Chevron Trade Bead in North America. *The Bead Journal* 3: 15–17.
_____
1987 Archaeology of Aboriginal Culture Change in the Interior Southeast: Depopulation During the Early Historic Period. *The Florida State Museum, Ripley P. Bullen Monographs in Anthropology and History* 6. Gainesville.
_____
1989 Indian Responses to European Contact: The Coosa Example. Pp. 135–49 in First Encounters: Spanish Exploration in the Caribbean and the United States, 1492-1570, J. T. Milanich and S. Milbreath, eds. *Ripley F. Bullen Monographs in Anthropology and History* 9. Gainesville.

———
1989a Glass Beads from the Goldsmith Oliver 2 Site. In Goldsmith Oliver 2 (3PU396): A Protohistoric Archeological Site Near Little Rock, Arkansas. M. D. Jeter, ed. (Report submitted to Federal Aviation Administration, Fort Worth, Texas, by Sponsored Research Program, Arkansas Archeological Survey. Fayetteville.)

Smith, Marvin T., and Mary Elizabeth Good
1982 Early Sixteenth Century Glass Beads in the Spanish Colonial Trade. Greenwood, Mississippi: Cottonlandia Museum.

Smith, Michael M.
1974 The "Real Expedicion Maritima de la Vacuna" in New Spain and Guatemala. *Transactions of the American Philosophical Society* 64(Part 1):5–74.

Snow, Dean R., and Kim M. Lanphear
1988 European Contact and Indian Depopulation in the Northeast: The Timing of the First Epidemics. *Ethnohistory* 35:15–33.

Stahle, David W., M. K. Cleveland, and J. G. Hehr
1985 A 450-year Drought Reconstruction for Arkansas, United States. *Nature* 316:530-32.

Steponaitis, V. P.
1986 Prehistoric Archaeology in the Southeastern United States, 1970–1985. *Annual Reviews in Anthropology* 15:363–404.

Stevenson, Robert Louis
1925 Virginibus Puerisque. London: T. Nelson.

Steward, Julian H.
1954 Theory and Application in a Social Science. *Ethnohistory* 1:292-302.

Story, Dee Ann
1981 An Overview of the Archaeology of East Texas. *Plains Anthropologist* 26(92):139–56.

———
1982 Introduction. Pp. 1–12 in The Deshazo Site, Nacogdoches County, Texas, Volume 1. *Texas Antiquities Committee, Texas Antiquities Permit Series* 7. Austin.

———
1990 Culture History of the Native Americans. Pp. 163–366 in The Archeology and Bioarcheology of the Gulf Coastal Plain. D. A. Story, et al., eds. *Arkansas Archeological Survey Research Series* 38. Fayetteville.

Story, Dee Ann, Janice A. Guy, Barbara A. Burnett, Martha Doty Freeman, Jerome C. Rose, D. Gentry Steele, Ben W. Olive, and Karl J. Reinhard
1990 The Archeology and Bioarcheology of the Gulf Coastal Plain. Vol. 1. Fayetteville: Arkansas Archeological Survey.

Story, Dee Ann, and Darrell G. Creel
1982 The Cultural Setting. Pp. 20–34 in The Deshazo Site, Nacogdoches County, Texas. Vol. 1. *Texas Antiquities Committee, Texas Antiquities Permit Series* 7. Austin.

Stubbs, John
1982 The Chickasaw Contact with the La Salle Expedition in 1682. Pp. 41–48 in La Salle and His Legacy: Frenchmen and Indians in the Lower Mississippi Valley. P. K. Galloway, ed. Jackson: University of Mississippi Press.

Stuiver, M., and G. W. Pearson
1986 High-precision Calibration of the Radiocarbon Time Scale, A.D. 1950–500 B.C. *Radiocarbon* 28:805–38.

Swanton, John R.
1911 Indian Tribes of the Lower Mississippi Valley and Adjacent Coast of the Gulf of Mexico. *Bureau of American Ethnology Bulletin* 43. Washington, D.C.

———
1932 Ethnological Value of the De Soto Narratives. *American Anthropologist* 34(4):570–90.
1939 Final Report of the United States De Soto Expedition Commission. United States House of Representatives Document 71, 76th Congress, 1st Session. Washington, D.C. (Reprinted: Smithsonian Institution Press, Washington, D.C., 1985.)

———
1942 Source Material on the History and Ethnology of the Caddo Indians. *Bureau of American Ethnology Bulletin* 132. Washington, D.C.

———
1952 Hernando De Soto's Route Through Arkansas. *American Antiquity* 18:156–62.

Terán de los Ríos, Domingo
1690–1692 Diario del general Domingo Terán de los Ríos en su Expedición a Texas (1691–1692). Pp 167–223 in Primeras Exploraciones Poblamiento de Texas (1686–1694), Lino Gómez, ed. *Serie: Historia* 6. Monterrey: Publicaciones del Instituto Superiores de Monterrey.

Texas Archeological Research Laboratory
[1989] [Site files.] Austin: The University of Texas at Austin.

Thomas, D. H., ed.
1989 Columbian Consequences, vol. 1: Archaeological and Historical Perspectives on the Spanish Borderlands West. Washington, D.C.: Smithsonian Institution Press.

———
1990 Columbian Consequences, Vol. 2: Archeological and Historical Perspectives on the Spanish Borderlands East. Washington, D.C.: Smithsonian Institution.

———
1990a Columbian Consequences, Vol. 3: The Spanish Borderlands in Pan-American Perspective. Washington, D.C.: Smithsonian Institution.

Thomas, Henry
1920 Spanish and Portuguese Romances of Chivalry. Cambridge: Cambridge University Press.

Thornton, Russell
1986 We Shall Live Again: The 1870 and 1890 Ghost Dance Movements as Demographic Revitalization. New York: Cambridge University Press.

———
1987 American Indian Holocaust and Survival: A Population History Since 1492. Norman: University of Oklahoma Press.

Thurmond, John Peter
1981 Archeology of the Cypress Creek Drainage Basin, Northeastern Texas and Northwestern Louisiana. (Unpublished M.A. Thesis in Anthropology, The University of Texas at Austin.)

———
1985 Late Caddoan Social Group Identifications and Sociopolitical Organization in the Upper Cypress Basin and Its Vicinity, Northeastern Texas. *Bulletin of the Texas Archeological Society* 54:185–200.

———
1990 Was the Cypress Cluster One of the (Many) Victims of the 1539–1543 De Soto Expedition? *Caddo Archaeology Newsletter* I(3):5–9.

Thwaites, R. G. ed.
1900 The Jesuit Relations and Allied Documents, Travels and Explorations of the Jesuit Missionaries in New France 1610–1791. Cleveland: The Burrows Brothers.

Transeau, Edgar M.
1935 The Prairie Peninsula. *Ecology* 16(3):423–37.
Trigger, Bruce G.
1983 American Archaeology as Native History: A Review Essay. *The William and Mary Quarterly* 40:413–52.
———
1985 Natives and Newcomers: Canada's 'Heroic Age' Reconsidered. Montreal: McGill-Queen's University Press.
———
1986 Ethnohistory: The Unfinished Edifice. *Ethnohistory* 33: 253–67.
Trimble, M. K.
1985 Epidemiology on the Northern Plains: A Cultural Perspective. (Unpublished Ph.D. Dissertation in Anthropology, University of Missouri, Columbia.)
Trubowitz, Neal L.
1984 Aboriginal Settlement. Pp. 83–96 in Cedar Grove: An Interdisciplinary Investigation of a Late Caddo Farmstead in the Red River Valley. N. L. Trubowitz, ed. *Arkansas Archeological Survey Research Series* 23. Fayetteville.
———, ed.
1984a Cedar Grove: An Interdisciplinary Investigation of a Late Caddo Farmstead in the Red River Valley. *Arkansas Archeological Survey Research Series* 23. Fayetteville.
Tucker, Sarah Jones
1974 [1942]. Indian Villages of the Illinois Country. Vol. 2, Part I, Atlas. *Illinois State Museum, Scientific Papers.* Springfield.
Turner, Robert L.
1978 The Tuck Carpenter Site and Its Relation to Other Sites within the Titus Focus. *Bulletin of the Texas Archeological Society* 49:1–109.
Ubelaker, D. H.
1976 The Sources and Methodology for Mooney's Estimates of North American Indian Populations. Pp. 243–88 in The Native Populations of the Americas in 1492. W. M. Denevan, ed. Madison: University of Wisconsin Press.
Ubelaker, D. H., and R. L. Jantz
1986 Biological History of the Aboriginal Population of North America. *Rassengeschichte der Menschheit* 2:7–79.
Upham, S.
1986 Smallpox and Climate in the American Southwest. *American Anthropologist* 88:115–28.
Valcárel Martínez, Simón
1989 Una aproximación a Francisco López de Gómara. *Caravelle* 53:7–24.
Van Tuyl, Charles D.
1979 The Natchez: Annotated Translations from Antoine Simon le Page du Pratz's Histoire de la Louisiane and A Short English-Natchez Dictionary. *Oklahoma Historical Society Series in Anthropology* 4. Oklahoma City.
Varner, John Grier
1968 El Inca, The Life and Times of Garcilaso de la Vega. Austin: University of Texas Press.
Vega, Garcilaso de la, *El Inca.* See Garcilaso de la Vega
Veldink, Connie
1989 The Honey-Bee Controversy. *Interdisciplinary Science Reviews* 14:166–75.
Walker, P. L., P. Lambert, and M. J. DeNiro
1989 The Effects of European Contact on the Health of Alta California Indians. Pp. 349–64

in Columbian Consequences. Vol. I. D. H. Thomas, ed. Washington, D.C.: Smithsonian Institution Press.

Webb, Clarence H.

1959 The Belcher Mound: a Stratified Caddoan Site in Caddo Parish, Louisiana. *Society for American Archeology Memoir* 16. Salt Lake City.

Webb, Clarence H., and H. F. Gregory

1978 The Caddo Indians of Louisiana. *Louisiana Archaeological Survey and Antiquities Commission, Anthropological Study* 2. Baton Rouge.

Webb, Clarence B., Forrest E. Murphey, Wesley G. Ellis, and H. Roland Green

1969 The Resch Site, 41HS16, Harrison County, Texas. *Bulletin of the Texas Archeological Society* 40:3–106.

Weber, David J.

1988 Myth and the History of the Hispanic Southwest. Albuquerque: University of New Mexico Press.

Weddle, Robert S.

1985 Spanish Sea, the Gulf of Mexico in North American Discovery, 1500-1685. College Station: Texas A & M University Press.

Wedel, Mildred Mott

1978 La Harpe's 1719 Post on Red River and Nearby Caddo Settlements. *The Texas Memorial Museum Bulletin* 30. Austin.

———

1981 The Deer Creek Site, Oklahoma: A Wichita Village Sometimes Called Ferdinandina, An Ethnohistorian's View. *Oklahoma Historical Society, Series in Anthropology* 5. Oklahoma City.

Weinstein, Richard A.

1985 Some New Thoughts on the De Soto Expedition Through Western Mississippi. *Mississippi Archaeology*, 20(2):2–25.

———

[ ] The De Soto Expedition and its Route Through Western Mississippi. *American Archeology*

Westervelt, James

1988 An Introduction to GRASS. (Manuscript, U.S. Army Construction Engineering Research Laboratory.)

White, Hayden

1988 Metahistory. Baltimore: Johns Hopkins University Press.

Widmer, Randolph

1988 The Evolution of the Calusa, a Nonagricultural Chiefdom on the Southwest Florida Coast. Tuscaloosa: University of Alabama Press.

Wilkinson, Warren H.

1954 Opening the Case against the U.S. de Soto Commission's Report and Other de Soto Papers. Jacksonville Beach: Alliance for the Preservation of Florida Antiquities.

Williams, Ishmael, and Ann M. Early

1990 Hardman: A Prehistoric Salt Processing Site. Report to the Arkansas Highway and Transportation Department. (Arkansas Archeological Survey Project 642.)

Williams, Lindsey W.

1986 Boldly Onward. Charlotte Harbor, Fla.: Precision Publishing Co.

———

1989 A Charlotte Harbor Perspective on de Soto's Landing Site. *The Florida Anthropologist* 42:280-94.

Williams, Norman F.
1959 Mineral Resources of Arkansas. Little Rock: Arkansas Geological and Conservation Commission.

Williams, Stephen
1964 The Aboriginal Location of the Kadohadacho and Related Tribes. Pp. 545–70 in Explorations in Cultural Anthropology. W. Goodenough, ed. New York: McGraw-Hill.

——— 1980 Armorel: A Very Late Phase in the Lower Mississippi Valley. *Southeastern Archaeological Conference Bulletin* 22:105-10.

——— 1983 Some Ruminations on the Current Strategy of Archaeology in the Southeast. *Southeastern Archaeological Conference Bulletin* 21:72–81.

——— 1990 The Vacant Quarter and Other Late Events in the Lower Valley. Pp. 164–74 in Towns and Temples Along the Mississippi. D. H. Dye and C. A. Cox, eds. Tuscaloosa: University of Alabama Press.

Woodall, Joe Ned
1969 Cultural Ecology of the Caddo. (Unpublished Ph.D. Dissertation in Anthropology, Southern Methodist University, Dallas.)

Wright, Muriel H.
1951 A Guide to the Indian Tribes of Oklahoma. Norman: University of Oklahoma Press.

Wyckoff, Don G.
1964 The Jug Hill Site, My-18, Mayes County, Oklahoma. *Bulletin of the Oklahoma Anthropological Society* 12:1–53.

——— 1980 Caddoan Adaptive Strategies in the Arkansas Basin, Eastern Oklahoma. (Unpublished Ph.D. Dissertation in Anthropology, Washington State University.)

Wyckoff, Don G., and T. G. Baugh
1980 Early Historic Hasinai Elites: A Model for the Material Culture of Governing Elites. *Midcontinental Journal of Archaeology* 5:225–83.

Young, John P.
1927 De Soto at Chickasaw Bluffs: A Review of the Works of Various Historians of the Great Spaniards Life. Pp. 36-44 in A Symposium on the Place of Discovery of the Mississippi River by Hernando De Soto. D. Rowland, ed. *Mississippi Historical Society Special Publication* 1. Jackson.

Zamora, Margarita
1988 Language, Authority, and Indigenous History in the Comentarios Reales de los Incas. Cambridge: Cambridge University Press.

# Index